The Destiny Series Volume II

WORLD RELIGIONS & ATHEISM: A CHRISTIAN PERSPECTIVE

Dr. Ron Woodworth

Copyright © 2013 by Dr. Ron Woodworth

WORLD RELIGIONS & ATHEISM: A CHRISTIAN PERSPECTIVE
The Destiny Series Volume II
by Dr. Ron Woodworth

Printed in the United States of America

ISBN 9781625097552

All rights reserved solely by the author. The author guarantees all contents are original and do not infringe upon the legal rights of any other person or work. No part of this book may be reproduced in any form without the permission of the author. The views expressed in this book are not necessarily those of the publisher.

Unless otherwise indicated, Bible quotations are taken from The New International Version (NIV); THE HOLY BIBLE, NEW INTERNATIONAL VERSION®, NIV®. Copyright © 1973, 1978, 1984, 2011 by Biblica, Inc.™ Used by permission. (See http://www.biblegateway.com/versions/New-International-Version-NIV-Bible/)

www.xulonpress.com

Table of Contents

Prologue .....Background, Objectives & Einstein xi

Introduction......................Showdown at ASU &
    Transcendence vs. Relativism.......................xv

Chapter One ...... Definition, Facts, and Theories
    of Religion 19

Chapter Two .The Nature of a Christian Critique 25

Chapter Three................................Christianity 35

Chapter Four ....Judaism 49

Chapter Five ....Islam 70

Chapter Six.............................Hinduism 92

Chapter Seven .... Buddhism 106

Chapter Eight .... Chinese Religions 116

Chapter Nine .... Atheism 134

Addendum Articles:

1. Oprah Winfrey: New Age Spirituality 195
2. Lady Gaga: A Christian Moral Response
   to Homosexuality 218
3. Twenty-Seven of the Most Important People and
   Events in Christian History 223
4. Top Ten Things No One, In The Know, Believes
   Any More About Evolution 255
5. Secularism and the Misinterpretation of the First
   Amendment 268
6. Faith and Education: How to Get a Higher Education
   Without Losing Your Faith 276
7. Ghosts and Other Occult Phenomena 286
8. How to Become an Authentic Follower of Jesus:
   Tips for Beginners 294
9. Twelve Reasons I Believe 301

Acknowledgements...

I want to gratefully and humbly acknowledge the following people for helping to make this book become a reality. First and foremost is the inspiring guidance and presence of the Lord Jesus Christ, to whom I have pledged my life's devotion since 1972. Next is my editorial consultant, and beloved wife, Patricia Ann Woodworth, whose encouragement is a constant source of strength and perseverance. Highly commendable also is my co-writer and colleague, Stan Reynolds; who is a brilliant source of scientific knowledge, as well as one of my life-long best friends. I further want to thank the Board Members of GKM/RWM Inc., including Bill Duncan, Jim & Lynn McHood, and Steve & Gail Weber, whose encouraging friendship and business insight have provided excellent personal and practical advice for more than a decade. In addition to the publisher's editorial review board, I would also like to recognize a few other manuscript editors, including my Executive Publishing Assistant, Steve Pugh, Willie Hintze, and Virginia Eckel. Finally, a noteable thanks to my special media/technical assistants, Randy Rohde and Free Beck.

Dedication...

This book is affectionately dedicated to our third grandchild: Elle Sienna Shober. *Elle* means "the shining light of God's promise." Biblical verse: "The Lord is my light and my salvation—whom shall I fear? The Lord is the stronghold of my life—of whom shall be afraid?" (Psalm 27:1). *Sienna* means "colorful one," indicating an attractive personality with a depth of understanding beyond her years. May the Lord Jesus cause his promises to give you courage as you allow the light of his truth and grace to shine forth from your life and your acts of kindness toward others.

Prologue

Background

The original impetus to write this book came from my doctoral dissertation project called *Toward a Christian Critique of the Major World Religions* (Woodworth, 2007). Additionally, my collegiate and university teaching resume includes instructing courses on World Religions, Critical Thinking and Christian Worldview—all of which have extensively contributed to the content of this text.

Furthermore, my background in full time pastoral ministry—having spanned 25 years[1] has provided me with personal insight regarding the challenges Christians are facing in a modern/post-modern world. On another personal note, I was also appreciatively raised in a religious family (Woodworth, 2009, p. 224), which has enabled me to transition from a sincere religiously-based home to a dynamically empowered relationship with Jesus Christ.

As a result of this background, in this series of articles, I will review the definition and theories of the origin of religion itself, the various founders of the major religions, their distinctive beliefs, their respective sacred texts, and historical developments, in the following sequence: Christianity, Judaism, Islam, Hinduism, Buddhism, Chinese religions, and Atheism. Throughout all of the articles to follow, I will make special note of comparisons and contrasts between the world religions in general, and to Christianity in particular.

The objectives of this series will be as follows:

1. To accurately inform all readers (Christian or otherwise) regarding the essential historical background of the major world religions of our era.
2. To provide a rational defense (apologetic) of the Christian faith when engaging others who are either honest in their inquiry or debating with those who may be critical of Christianity itself.
3. To strengthen the personal faith of Christian believers who, perhaps for the first time, will be able to see how favorably Christianity compares with the other major religions of the world.
4. To equip Christians with a genuine love for differing others, which may also be expressed in a desire to share their faith in as winsome a way as possible. (Pr.11:30; 1 Pet. 3:15; James 3:17-18)

> "They drew a circle to shut me out;
> A heretic, a thing to flout.
> But love and I had the wit to win;
> We drew a circle and took them in."
> (Edwin Markham)

From the theocratic ideals of Islam; to the highly adaptable polytheism of India; to the sacrificial atonement of Jesus Christ; to the Buddhist concept of suffering and enlightenment; to the Jewish historic struggle with persecution; to the communist religious repression of China; to the atheism of leading evolutionary biologists, such as Richard Dawkins... join us as we briefly tour the landscape of religion (and *religious* thought) throughout the various cultures of the world today.

Selected Religious Quotes by Albert Einstein
(Physicist and professor, 1879-1955)

[Note: Though various quotes from Einstein are used by both religious proponents and religious detractors, the following religiously *favorable* quotes of Einstein have been selected to demonstrate at least his thoughtfulness regarding the compatibility between religious contemplation and scientific inquiry.]

- "All religions, arts and sciences are branches of the same tree."
- "God does not play dice."
- "Humanity has every reason to place the proclaimers of high moral standards and values above the discoverers of objective truth. What humanity owes to personalities like Buddha, Moses, and Jesus ranks for me higher than all the achievements of the inquiring constructive mind."
- "God is subtle...but he is not malicious."
- "Relativity is for physics—not ethics."
- "I assert that the cosmic religious experience is the strongest and the noblest driving force behind scientific research."
- "I want to know God's thoughts...all the rest are just details."
- "My religion consists of a humble admiration of the illimitable superior spirit who reveals himself in the slight details we are able to perceive with our frail and feeble mind."
- "True religion is real living; living with all one's soul, with all one's goodness and righteousness."
- "Science without religion is lame; religion without science is blind."
- "As a child I received instruction both in the Bible and in the Talmud. I am a Jew, but I am enthralled by the luminous figure of the Nazarene...No one can read the Gospels without feeling

the actual presence of Jesus. His personality pulsates in every word. No myth is filled with such life."
- "You may call me an agnostic, but I do not share the crusading spirit of the professional atheist whose fervor is mostly due to a painful act of liberation from the fetters of religious indoctrination received in youth. I prefer an attitude of humility corresponding to the weakness of our intellectual understanding of nature and of our own being."[2]

Introduction

Showdown at Arizona State University

> "There is no such thing as Christianity;
> There are no universal truth claims;
> Everything is relative to the cultural context."
> (ASU Professor of World Religions)

I was shocked when I personally heard these words on the very first day of class while a graduate student in World Religions at Arizona State University. I was equally stunned when the same professor, some two months later, asked me to substitute for him because of an illness. Barely had I begun the class when another student raised his hand and asked, "Is it true that there are no universal truth claims in Christianity?" I thought to myself: Is this a trap, or a set up from God?! Well, with a little trepidation, regarding the potential consequences of telling the truth, I nevertheless rather boldly, and yet academically asserted that there were indeed at least five universal truth claims in Christianity (See 1 Cor. 15:1-8, New International Version, NIV)[3]:

1. Jesus Christ was sent from God to accomplish the redemption of the human race.
2. Jesus was crucified for sin and buried.
3. Jesus was bodily raised from the dead.
4. Jesus ascended to heaven where he is now reigning as Lord of all.
5. Jesus is returning in the future to render judgment and make visible his everlasting kingdom of which all the redeemed are heirs.

"That's very interesting," was the student's reply. Well, when the professor returned after the weekend of convalescing, his first words were, "I'm feeling a little 'out-of-the-loop.' What did you discuss when I was gone?" You guessed it! That same student raised his hand again and reported about how "Ron had told the class about the five universal truth claims of Christianity." Let's just say that after that exchange my substituting days were over. However, I did get an *A* for the course! The moral of the story is that we need to know what we believe and be prepared to give an account-defense (without being defensive) of our faith—because you never know when, or where, God may open a door!

The reason I began with this introduction is because Christianity is all about Jesus Christ. Furthermore, it is not about a religion, but a relationship with Jesus. As I often like to say, Jesus did not come to establish the Christian religion, but rather to restore man's relationship with God—by grace through faith in Jesus Christ—the Son of God (John 3:16; Eph. 2:8-9, NIV). When/if we lose sight of this relational emphasis with Jesus, Christianity just becomes another irrelevant and legalistic religion. So even though we can, and should study the history of Christianity, we must never surrender the personal dynamic of faith in Christ as foundational to the historical facts of the Christian tradition.[4]

Transcendence vs. Relativism

> "Though there may be some truth in all religions;
> this does not make all religions equally true."
> (Mesa Community College[5])

Many people cite relativism as a major philosophical objection to religious truth-claims. For instance, in the modern secular education enterprise, truth is often described as being relative to any number of situations. For truth to be relative implies that the context is perhaps the most important criteria in assessing the claim of truth. In other words, depending on the circumstances, a truth-claim might be either true or false. Consider the statement: there are no adverse consequences to jumping off of a bridge. This is true if the bridge is just three feet above water, but false if the bridge is sixty feet above concrete. Therefore, the immediate circumstance (or historical context) is the main factor in determining the accuracy of a claim to truth. As a result, the relativist adamantly asserts that there is absolutely no such thing as an absolute truth-claim![6] This very assertion is humorously self-contradicting by insisting that the only absolutes are what a relativist absolutely believes or denies. This is similar to the college student who was informed by his professor that "Anyone who is absolutely certain about anything is a fool!" to which the student's response was, "Are you absolutely certain?!" Such claims are not only laughable, but also show a complete lack of appreciation for the reality of transcendent claims to truth.

Indeed, transcendent truth-claims are those assertions that point toward a reality that is above and beyond the world as we know it.[7] As a result, what is true can and must be redefined in an absolute or transcendent sense, where situational relativism holds no sway. This is the realm of the eternal in which time and circumstance are nullified by that which is of *infinite duration,* without beginning or end. Such is the religious contemplation of God. It is not that the eternal never transacts with the temporal, as was most certainly the case in the incarnation of Christ. But rather, that in the final analysis, the eternal is not subject to the empirical laws of physics. In this sense, eternal or transcendent claims to truth are not scientifically falsifiable.[8]

As a result, this non-falsifiability of transcendent truths renders the scientific irrelevant in the argument over determining what is ultimately true. However, even after addressing the popular objection of relativism by an appeal to an absolute transcendent reality, one is still left with the question as to how to address the obvious contradictions that exist between the various transcendent-religious truth-claims themselves. Are some religious truth-claims less truthful than others? If so, how do we compare and contrast them so as to determine the most credible claimant among them?

There are many ways to address the issue of contradictions such as, logical fallacies, internal inconsistencies, historic-scientific contradictions, deception, superstition, and violations of truth theories (correspondence, coherence, and pragmatic)[9], etc.

However, in the text that follows, the author will not focus on attempts to *absolutely prove* the superiority of any religious claim to truth over another. Rather, what will be offered is a Christian perspective /critique of the major world religions (Christianity, Judaism, Islam, Hinduism, Buddhism, Chinese Religions, and Atheism) by way of comparison and contrast. In other words, presupposing the truthfulness of Christianity[10], the author will observe how other religious truth-claims measure up to this *Christian standard* for truth. Though this approach will be most appreciated by Christians, the academic-historical-theological analysis offered here will provide any inquirer an informed scholarly assessment.

Furthermore, it is hoped that the result of this work will be a promotion of a conversation that is wise and winsome rather than combative and bigoted. After all, the ultimate objective of Christianity should be to win people—not just arguments. Such a conversation should fulfill the biblical mandate to:

> "Establish Jesus Christ as Lord in our hearts. Always being ready to give an answer to everyone who asks us to give the reason for the hope that we have. But do this with gentleness and respect..." (1 Pet. 3:15-16).

Chapter I

Definition, Facts, and Theories of Religion

Religion is a very broad field of human experience that can, in general terms, be academically defined as:

> A personal and/or communal conviction concerning the nature of ultimate reality (such as a Supreme Being or controlling principle of some sort) who or which has the power to influence human behavior and destiny.[11]

This academic definition of religion includes a number of interesting components. First is the personal and/or communal aspect of religion whereby a conviction can be as small as one or as large as billions of people. Next is the direction of that conviction—the nature of ultimate reality. The ultimate reality could be a supreme being as in Christianity or Islam; a divine principle as in Hinduism; or an ultimate reality void of divinity, as in Buddhism. Whatever the ultimate source of religious truth is—he, she, or it has the power to influence human behavior either by grace or karmic consequence. Finally, the reality behind religious devotion also has the power to influence human destiny, either by reward/penalty (Islam or Christianity), or by becoming released from the endless cycle(s) of life and united with the divine (Hinduism) or the ultimate reality behind all of perceived existence (Buddhism).

Religion: Facts and Figures

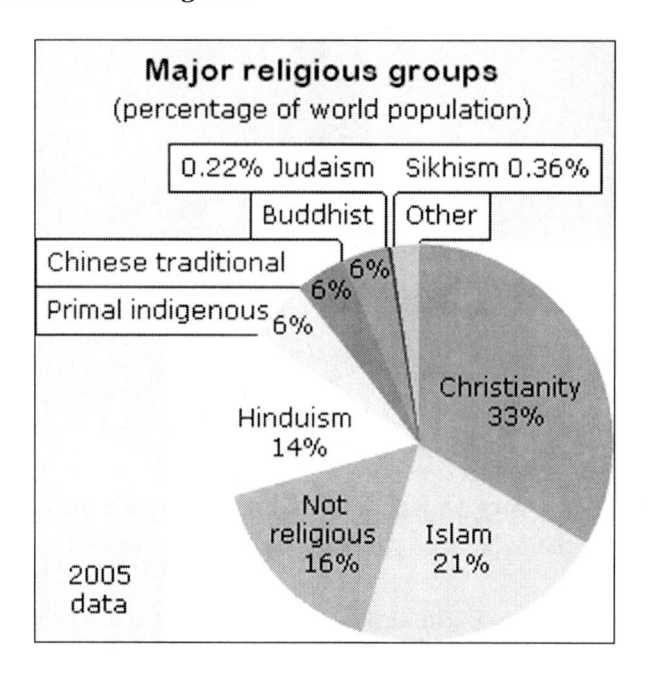

Major religious groups (percentage of world population), 2005 data:
- Christianity 33%
- Islam 21%
- Not religious 16%
- Hinduism 14%
- Chinese traditional 6%
- Primal indigenous 6%
- Buddhist 6%
- Other 6%
- Sikhism 0.36%
- Judaism 0.22%

Note: The total percentages add up to 102.58% due to rounding and upper bound estimates being used for each group. Also, the "Other" category would roughly contain around 200 million adherents from other religions or about 2%.[12]

This would approximately equate to the following[13]:

- 2.4 billion: Christianity (Roman Catholic-1.2 billion, Eastern Orthodox-300 million, Protestants-850 million)
- 1.5 billion: Islam/Muslim (Sunni-80%, Shiite-20%)
- 1 billion: Hinduism
- 1 billion: non-religious (secular 75%, agnostic 15%, atheist 10%,)
- 450 million: Chinese Folk (Confucian, ancestor veneration, Taoism, etc.)
- 375 million: Buddhist (Mahayana, Theravada, etc.)
- 350 million: Primal indigenous "pagan" (animistic, polytheistic, spiritualism, African Voodoo, Native Americans, Wicca/neo-pagan, etc.)

- 14.1 million: Judaism
- 13.8 million: Latter Day Saints (Mormonism)

Religious Chronology: Dating the origins of the world religions

2,500(?)-1600 BC—Shang dynasty/primitive Chinese religion
2,500BC—Aryan migration to India/Hinduism emerges
2,000BC—Abraham/Judaism
563 BC—Siddhartha/Buddhism
4BC—Jesus/Christianity
AD 570—Muhammad/Islam

History of Civilizations

3100 BC...Mesopotamia and Egypt or the Sumerians and Egyptians (See Genesis 2:10-14 for reference to Eden, the birthplace of Adam and Eve. Note that from Eden flowed four rivers, including the Tigris and Euphrates, which are still in existence)
2500 BC...The Indus/First civilization of India
2000 BC...The Aegean/Sea-based Culture
1600 BC...China/Longest consistent civilization in human history, but without identifiable precedents before the Shang dynasty
1200 BC...America/Olmecs (Central America) and Andes (Chavin) are earliest American Civilizations
1000 BC...The Mediterranean/Aegeans and Phoenicians
AD 400-1500...Regional civilizations/Greece and Rome in the west/central and south America/China in the east/Islam from north Africa to north India
16th -21st century AD...Global civilizations/Spanish, European, America, Russian, Chinese, Asian, etc.[14b]

Theories of the Origin of Religion

In every course on religion there is always the question of where religion originated. Over the years I have collected the multiple options of religious origination into the following six main categories:

1. No Origination

2. Alien Manipulation
3. Human Imagination
4. Intelligent Manifestation
5. Divine Revelation
6. Demonic Impersonation

First, *no origination* implies that religion had no beginning—it has always been. This is the perspective of Hinduism with its insistence that time is cyclical, comprising creation, destruction, suspension, and recreation. In direct contrast to this is the biblical concept of time having a beginning—in creation (Gen. 1:1), and an end when the *day of the Lord* comes and the heavens and earth will be destroyed by fire (2 Pet. 3:10, 12). In other words, time, as we know it in this age, will cease and a new heaven and earth will replace the old creation order and be without restriction by the space-time continuum (Rev. 21:23, 25) in which we presently live our lives.

Second, *alien manipulation* is the belief that religion is a product of extraterrestrial beings who have periodically visited the earth for either benign or cruel intentions. Such visitations, though generally clothed in secrecy, have not been without notice. As a result, human beings have developed a cult around the worship of such advanced space civilizations, which have been dramatized in movies (Star Trek, the X-Files, Alien, ET, etc.). Incredibly, even Sir Francis Crick, the co-discoverer of the DNA molecule, has suggested that evolution has been assisted by the intentional deposit of alien genetic material into the primordial soup phase of our galaxy's formation.[14]

Third, *human imagination* would include the ideas of religion emerging from the projection of human needs such as: "Religion is a form of [human] wishing" (L. Feuerbach); to a tool for suppressing the underclass: "[Religion] is the opium of the people/masses" (K. Marx); to a need for the security of a father-figure or a guilt-inducing illusion to be cast off as one matures. (S. Freud). In essence, all the notions of religion as emerging from a projection of human needs or greeds are asserting that humanity is not created in the image of God, but rather that God is created in the image of humanity—the exact opposite of the Genesis account, which states that "...God created mankind in his own image, in the image of God he created them; male and female he created them" (Gen. 1:27).

Human imagination can also contain theories of the origin of religion stemming from animism (spirits are in everything), veneration of ancestors (dreaming of the dead), nature worship (seasonal phenomenon), explanation of life's mysteries (birth, death, earthquakes, etc), the perceived evolution or devolution of religion (from simple-animism to complex-monotheism and/or vice versa), the employment of magic in an attempt to control nature, events, or other people, etc. Finally, human imagination as a religion can also consist of the modern preoccupation with science as a truth claim rather than simply a method of inquiry into empirical knowledge. More on this later, but suffice it to say here that when science becomes a substitute for religion by asserting that it is the ultimate truth (as in macro-Darwinism) it has ceased to be a guide to objective reality and instead becomes a stumbling block to the spiritually/religiously gullible among us.

Fourth, *intelligent manifestation* is the idea that the complexity of the world around us indicates that there must be some kind of intentional design emanating from some form of intelligence that is superior to our own. It should be noted that such an intelligent design proposition does not assert that the intelligent designer is God, but rather that Intelligent Design (ID) is a "scientific theory that stands on equal footing with, or is superior to, current scientific theories regarding the evolution and origin of life."[15] Opponents of this view accuse ID as being a thinly disguised version of scientific creationism.[16]

Fifth, *divine revelation* represents the perspective of the monotheistic religions of Judaism, Christianity, and Islam, where they each claim that God supernaturally, and yet historically, revealed himself to Abraham (Genesis 12), in Jesus Christ, or to Muhammad respectively. Man did not create God, but the one and only living God created man—"in his image" according to the Old Testament (Gen. 1:27). There is controversy however, regarding whether or not this one and only God is the same God in Christianity and Judaism as he is in Islam. This, as we will cover later, is due to the contradictions between the Koran and the Bible vis-à-vis the primacy of Ishmael over Isaac and the denial of Jesus' divine son-ship.

Sixth, *demonic impersonation* has to do with the reality of satan[17], fallen angels, demonic spirits, and the entire realm of occult phenomenon. The Old and New Testaments make it clear that God's people have an archenemy, satan (the devil), who disguises himself as an angel of light in order to deceive unsuspecting humanity (2 Cor. 11:14).

Furthermore at satan's command are a host of fallen angels and demonic spirits who are similarly opposed to God's kingdom of truth and light (Matt. 25:42; 1 Tim. 4:1). Finally, and in league with this demonic enterprise,[18] there is the entire realm of the occult[19] with its magical incantations, spiritualists, sorcerers, necromancers, satanists, neo-pagans, witches, astrologers, etc. which are specifically condemned in Deuteronomy 18:9-13.

> Moses said to Israel: Soon you will go into the land that the LORD your God is giving you. The nations that live there do things that are disgusting to the LORD, and you must not follow their example. Don't sacrifice your son or daughter. And don't try to use any kind of magic or witchcraft to tell fortunes or to cast spells or to talk with spirits of the dead. The LORD is disgusted with anyone who does these things, and that's why he will help you destroy the nations that are in the land. Never be guilty of doing any of these disgusting things (Deut. 18:9-13).

All of these influences seek to lure humanity's attention away from the truth of God's grace in Christ Jesus to the preoccupation of the demonic, the worship of the self, or the intrigue with magical-spiritual phenomenon.

Chapter 1: Review Questions

1. What was the most interesting thing that you learned from Chapter 1 and why?
2. How does the academic definition of religion relate to our own view of religion?
3. Explain why secularists could actually be either religious or non-religious
4. Which two rivers in Genesis 2 directly coincide with the Mesopotamian civilization?
5. What is the difference between Intelligent Manifestation and Divine Revelation regarding the theories of the origin of religions?

Chapter II

The Nature of a Christian Perspective/Critique

A critique is the "art, skill or profession of making discriminating judgments and evaluations."[20] The word "critique" comes from the original Greek word "*krinos*" which means to discern, to judge, to decide or to choose. Additionally, from "critique" we derive the word "criterion" from which we infer the word "critic." A critic can be a judge, a review writer, or a fault-finder. It is this negative connotation of fault-finding that generally hinders people from appreciating the importance of the art of criticism and critical thinking. While there are undoubtedly many fault-finding and negative people among us, there is another much more noble definition regarding a critique.[21] To offer a critique actually implies that one has considered the merits and demerits of a given subject and then judges (or renders an assessment) accordingly. A critique is therefore synonymous with the term "evaluation," which is a determination of the significance, worth, or condition of something—usually by careful appraisal and study. For instance, an appraisal of a home is a way to fix a valuation rather than simply a predisposition to critical judgment and negativity. Essentially then, a critique is a formal and yet fair-minded analysis of an idea, statement or text that includes an explanation of our approach and conclusions. Note that the terms "fair and reflective judgment" and "discerning analysis" have also been proffered over the more negative designations for a critique.

A Critique and the Process of Critical Thinking

In the professional-academic literature writing a critique is the result of the artful process of using critical thinking. Critical thinking by definition is a pervasive human process that employs the reflective mechanisms of discernment, analysis, and evaluation in order to form a solid judgment regarding scientific evidence, common sense, or transcendent truth-claims. The Northeast Texas Consortium and the Center for Educational Technologies insightfully defines critical thinking as an "essential tool of inquiry; purposeful, self-regulatory judgment that results in interpretation, analysis, evaluation, and inference, as well as explanation of the evidential, conceptual, methodological, criteriological, or contextual considerations upon which that judgment is based."[22]

Additionally, critical thinking, though rooted in these intellectual criteria, nevertheless goes far beyond mere subject-matter considerations to also include the importance of "clarity, credibility, accuracy, precision, relevance, depth, breadth, logic, significance, and fairness."[23] As such, critical thinking involves at least two things: a) a set of cognitive skills, intellectual standards and traits of mind (humility, empathy, integrity and fair-mindedness and b) the disposition to use those skills to improve thinking and guide behavior (Paul and Elders, 2006).

Finally, it is important to guard against the greatest challenges that affect the outcome of an exercise of critical thinking, namely, prejudice, propaganda, socio-centricity, intellectual arrogance and hypocrisy. Interestingly, the emerging value of critical thinking is being acknowledged by modern educators to such an extent that many are proposing that the teaching of children focus on the mastery of critical thinking in place of memorizing facts by rote learning.

The Christian Criteria of a Critique/Perspective

A key synonym for the word *criteria* is the word *standard*. A standard is any definite rule, principle, or measure established as authoritative. For instance, the word *canon* as in the *Canon of Scripture* also literally means the standard, measure, or rule by which Scripture is judged as legitimate (Grudem, 1994, p. 54-72). Such a scriptural standard is, for Christians, found in the biblical record of the Old and New Testaments. Hence, when determining the criteria for measuring the truthfulness of the major world religions, we need only to enumerate those essential truths of the Bible as foundational to any discussion of the Christian faith. However, since not all Christians interpret the Bible in the same way, it is necessary to describe those perspectives that inform the author's personal assumptions be they philosophical and/or theological.

Briefly stated, the author's epistemological paradigm encompasses the binary propositions of *foundational eclecticism* and *integrated dualism*. (Woodworth, 2009, p. 313-21). This essentially implies that upon the foundation of a belief in God there is any number of reasonable options in describing how knowledge can be acquired and utilized. Furthermore, such knowledge, though embracing the dualism between spiritual and material realities, nevertheless argues that such realms can and must be interwoven in the process of living one's life as a disciple of Jesus Christ.

Similarly, the author's ontological perspective has been described as that of a post-modern neo-Protestant relative-absolutist. This essentially implies that modernism has significant cultural limitations, demonstrated its limitations, evangelicalism must be wedded to a dynamic encounter with the Holy Spirit, and that absolute truth, though foundational and inviolable, can be moderated in its application to the given situations of daily reality. As a result, these designations signify a western (American) evangelical Protestant rather than a Roman Catholic or Eastern Orthodox theological predilection.

Furthermore, the author has identified himself with a new strain of evangelicalism that is traceable from the 1990's onward. Such evangelicalism is characterized by the empowering Holy Spirit, Kingdom-centeredness, flexible church structures, contemporary apostolic and prophetic ministries, higher education and cultural engagement, world evangelization, and theological balance.[24] Upon the basis of these philosophical and theological assumptions we can now more readily list the criteria for this research project. There are essentially four categories of criteria.

1. The Bible (its authority, inspiration, and interpretation)
2. Jesus Christ (his birth, ministry, death and resurrection)
3. The Kingdom of God (its reality and relation to the world and state)
4. The Christian Church (its identity, history, and mission)

What follows is a brief list and description of several items under each category. Further elaboration of these categories and items will be undertaken as warranted depending upon the particular critique of a given world religion. In other words, the task at this point in our research is simply to sketch the main categories of criteria while at the same time indicating a number of descriptive elements that are deemed fundamentally essential to the Christian faith.

1. The Bible

Both Old and New Testaments comprise what is definitively called the sacred Scriptures of Christianity. The Bible is the record of God's redemptive history among the Old Testament Jewish followers of the Law of Moses and among the New Testament believer-disciples of the Lord Jesus Christ. As John observes, "For the law was given through Moses; grace and truth came through Jesus Christ" (John 1:17).

Inspiration and interpretation

The Bible is spoken of as being inspired by God[25] in that it is a product of God's superintending grace with the cooperation of willing human vessels. Indeed, the biblical documents bear the mark of each writer's personality and his linguistic habits. As such, inspiration does not block the author's individuality, rather, the doctrine of inspiration affirms that the words the writers chose were used by God to accurately convey his message to humanity (Richards, 1990, p 155).

Furthermore, the doctrine of inspiration does not mean that God dictated or recited his revelation, as is the claim in Islam regarding the Quran (Hopfe and Woodward, 2007, p. 326). Nor does the doctrine of inspiration necessarily imply that every letter, word and phrase that we have in our modern translations is without the possibility of a minor change from the original.[26] Rather, what we currently have is the most accurately translated and transmitted piece of ancient documentation in the history of the world. And though there is some debate about whether the Bible is the Word of God or contains the Word of God (or both)—there is no doubt that even from the standpoint of literature, the Bible is far and away the most credible literary witness to the ultimate revelation of God in Christ.

Beyond the question concerning the nature of inspiration there is the all important task of interpretation that also needs some clarification. Again, unlike the Quran, (lit. "to recite") whose adherents claim is beyond rational dispute, the Bible must be carefully, prayerfully and arduously interpreted with accuracy (2 Tim. 2:15). Accurate interpretation, among other things, implies that recognition of the different kinds of biblical literature is essential in the hermeneutical task. Various kinds of literature include historical, legal, wisdom, poetic, prophecy, narrative, parables, doctrinal, and apocalyptic. In addition to these differing kinds of literature there are also figures of speech, symbols, types, allegories, idioms, grammatical meanings usage of words, etc.[27] Finally, a discerning Bible student must be aware of the author and his intention, the audience addressed and the cultural-historical context—not to mention the recurring use of words, ideas, and themes through the biblical text as a whole that often help to shed light on the meaning of Scripture.

When these interpretive items are not comprehensively considered, they can have a profound effect on the meaning of the biblical text. For instance, when interpreting Genesis chapter one, several literalistic Bible commentators have insisted that the earth was created in six literal 24 hour days.[28] That would make the creation events of Genesis chapter one span a time of exactly 144 hours. Needless to say, the sciences of geology and astrophysics, which date the universe at around 14.5 billion years and the earth at about 4.5 billion years, would object vehemently. As a result, hermeneutical literalism must always begin with an attack on conventional scientific research in order to justify its *scientific contradictions* to biblical interpretation.

Another example of this same tendency to be overly literal also relates to the interpretation of Bible prophecy. By way of example, Biblical literalism argues that the millennium mentioned in Revelation 20, whereby Satan is bound for 1,000 years (verse 2-3), coinciding with the 1,000 year rule of resurrected martyrs with Christ must also be a literal 1,000 year period. The problem with this interpretation is that Revelation is apocalyptic and hence highly symbolic literature. After all, do three frogs literally come out of the mouth of the antichrist and false prophet (Rev. 16:3), or could the frogs be types of uncleanness (Lev. 11:10) suggesting the "deceptive propaganda that will, in the last days, lead people to accept and support the cause of evil."[29] Indeed, many biblical scholars now maintain that the millennium can be interpreted metaphorically as an indefinite period of time as reflected in both the a-millennial and post-millennial eschatological perspectives (Erickson, 1985, p. 55-106).

2. Jesus Christ

The Bible definitively teaches that Jesus Christ is the incarnate (lit. *in flesh*) Son and Servant of God and that he was born of the virgin Mary through the impregnation of the power of the Holy Spirit (Rom 1:1-4; Matt. 1:18). By way of brief review, Jesus labored in the trade of a carpenter until he was about 30 years of age. At this time he was baptized by John the Baptist and the Holy Spirit descended upon him in great power. (Matt. 3:13-17) Being led by the Holy Spirit, Jesus spent the next 40 days in the wilderness being tempted by his chief rival, the devil. (Luke 4:1-13) When he had overcome various satanic temptations he then returned to Galilee in the power of the Holy Spirit and began his preaching and healing ministry (Luke 4:13; Matt. 4:23).

During Jesus' ministry he prophesied that he was to die for the sin of humanity (McGrath, 2001, 326-380), be raised from the dead, and return to judge the earth on the last day (John 14:2-4). Jesus was crucified on a cross and laid in a borrowed tomb. The third day after his crucifixion, Jesus rose from the dead and appeared to the apostles and more than 500 other disciples over the period of 40 days prior to his bodily ascension into heaven where he is now reigning as Lord of all (1 Cor. 15:1-6; Phil. 2:6-11). It was by virtue of Jesus' life, death, and resurrection that a New Covenant, or *relational arrangement,* with the people of God has been inaugurated. No longer is obedience to the Law of Moses to be the means of righteousness, but the gift of God in Christ has now brought a right relation with God by faith in Jesus (Phil. 3: 9). Based on this new relationship with God in Christ we have a guarantee of our own future resurrection and the promise of an eternal home in heaven, where we will live in the presence of God forever (1 Thess. 4:13-18). For the believer, this hope of the resurrection (McDowell, 1972, p. 273) from the dead is the "anchor of the soul" moderating all of life's trials in this age (Heb. 6:19-20).

3. The Kingdom of God

The main subject of Jesus' message was the Gospel of the Kingdom of God, which required repentance, faith and water baptism on the part of those who received his ministry (Mark 15:15-16; Matt. 28:19). This Kingdom was to be the central pursuit and proclamation of all disciple-citizens who believed in the divine mission of Jesus (Luke 9:60). God's Kingdom was often juxtaposed with the *world*. "For he has delivered us from the dominion of darkness [the world, Eph. 6:12] and transferred us to the Kingdom of his beloved Son" (Col. 1:3). Christians are instructed to resist loving the world, while at the same time making the pursuit of the kingdom their first priority. "Love not the world, nor the things in the world..." (1 John 2:15). "But seek first the Kingdom of God..." (Matt. 6:33).

Jesus often elaborated about the mysteries and reality of the Kingdom in the form of some 40 parables, which referenced natural objects to teach spiritual truths (Matt. 13:24, 31, 44; See also Wayne, 1981, p. 109-11). An important mystery regarding the Kingdom of God was that it was both present (Mark 1:15; Rom. 14:17) and yet future (Rev. 11:15). Indeed, the present-ness of God's Kingdom was limited in that it would not be propagated nor defended by the use of force—military or otherwise. "Jesus said, 'My Kingdom is not of this world. If it were, my servants would fight to prevent my arrest by the Jews. But now my Kingdom is from another place'" (John 18:36).

In this temporal age of human history, the transcendent nature of the Kingdom of God would require no theocratic construct (as in Islam[30]) to realize its global commission and intentions (Matt. 24:14). Rather, by the proclamation of the divinely revealed truth in Christ, the government of God would be enthroned in the hearts of believers until the entire world would be reached with a proclamation of the Gospel of God's Kingdom—thereby triggering the *eschaton*, or the visible manifestation of God's kingdom rule on earth. "And this Gospel of the Kingdom will be preached in the whole world as a testimony to all nations, and then the end will come" (Matt. 24:14).

It should also be noted that this non-violent feature of God's present Kingdom, as articulated by Jesus, has historically contributed to the idea of the American doctrine of the "separation of church and state,"[31] as well as to the Hindu spiritual leader, Mohandas Gandhi's application of

Satyagraha—the resistance to evil through active, non-violent means. By such means, Gandhi not only managed to secure India's independence from Great Britain, but has also inspired various movements for civil rights as championed by Martin Luther King Jr., et al, in the United States during the 1950's and 1960's (Hopfe and Woodward, 2007, p. 100).

4. The Christian Church

Most biblical scholars trace the birth of the Christian church to the outpouring of the Holy Spirit on the feast of Pentecost, some 50 days after the crucifixion and resurrection of Jesus (Acts 2:1-4). Earlier, Jesus had promised that he would build his church (lit. *"called out ones,"* Matt. 16:18). The church that Jesus promised to build is, according to Paul, dynamically related to Jesus and the apostles and prophets whom Jesus appointed before and after his resurrection and ascension.

Consequently, you are no longer foreigners and aliens, but fellow citizens with God's people and members of God's household, built on the foundation of the apostles and prophets, with Christ Jesus himself as the chief cornerstone." (Eph. 2:19-20)

It was he [the ascended Christ] who gave some to be apostles, some to be prophets, some to be evangelists, and some to be pastors and teachers, to equip God's people for the work of ministry, so that the body of Christ may be built up until we all reach unity in the faith and become mature (Eph. 4:11-13).

Furthermore, relationship with Christ through the indwelling Holy Spirit was the experience of all believers (Acts 2:4; Rom. 8:9-11). Such a relationship served as the foundational reality upon which these five leadership gifts (apostles, prophets, evangelists, pastors, and teachers) labored in establishing, maintaining, and extending the reality of the Body of Christ, the church (Eph. 1:22-23), and the message of God's kingdom throughout the earth (Conner, n.d., p. 133-38). Life in the early apostolic church was characterized by four things: the apostles teaching (regarding what Jesus had taught them), fellowship (sharing life together), breaking of bread (eating meals and taking the Lord's supper together), and prayer (public and private; Acts 2:42).

They devoted themselves to the apostles' teaching and to the fellowship, to the breaking of bread and to prayer. Everyone was filled with awe, and many wonders and miraculous signs were done by the apostles. All the believers were together and had everything in common. Selling their possessions...as anyone had need. Every day they continued to meet together with glad and sincere hearts, praising God and having favor with all the people. And the Lord added to their number daily those who were being saved (Acts 2:42-47).

Historically speaking, after the early apostles came the bishops, who were/are believed to be the spiritual successors of the apostles. For two centuries following the early apostles, the church entered into a period of intense although intermittent persecution from the Roman Emperors. Finally, Emperor Constantine I in 313 AD issued the Edict of Milan (Cairns, 1967, p. 134), which served as a catalyst for the eventual establishment of Christianity as the official religion of the Roman Empire in AD 380. The Fourth Century century also saw the convening of a number of church councils to address issues regarding the nature of Christ and various heresies (Gnosticism, Arianism, Marcionism) resulting in the construction and affirmation of early creedal statements (Apostles, Nicaea, Nicene) and the final determination of the canon of Scripture (Carthage, 397AD).

By the fifth century the highest ranking bishops became recognized as a Pentarchy overseeing five leading patriarchal spheres of authority, or "Sees" (Rome, Alexandria, Antioch, Jerusalem, and Constantinople) among whom the bishop of Rome was regard as *first among equals*. However, although the Roman See was granted primacy this did not mean supremacy nor unilateral authority over all others patriarchal sees, especially the jurisdiction of the eastern Bishop of Constantinople. Gradually things began to worsen between the East and West until finally, in AD 1054, came the Great Schism (Shelley, 1995, p. 98), which created independent eastern (Orthodox) and western (Catholic) churches. In the 16th century, the Western church again was split, this time by the Protestant Reformation. Today, these three branches of Christianity (Roman Catholicism, Eastern Orthodoxy, and Protestantism) comprise the largest of all the major world religions with a collective constituency of approximately 2.4 billion people.

Chapter 2: Review Questions

1. What was the most interesting thing that you learned from Chapter 2 and why?
2. What is the difference (if there is one) between a critique and being critical?
3. What are some evidences of people who do not know how to employ the process of critical thinking?
4. Please explain the four criteria for a specifically Christian Critique?
5. What is the Pentarchy?

Chapter III

-Christianity-

The primary criticisms of Christianity are its internal divisions among fellow Christians and its external objections by non-Christians to its fundamental truth claims.

Internal Divisions

Internal divisions have always afflicted Christianity from its very beginning. In fact, the apostle Paul argued that divisions were actually an unfortunate necessity in order to distinguish between those who had God's approval from those in error. "But, of course, there must be divisions among you so that you who have God's approval will be distinguished from those who are in the wrong" (1 Cor. 11:17-19, New Living Translation & New Life Version). Indeed, Jesus warned that there would be false prophets who would infiltrate the Christian ranks as "sheep in wolves clothing" (Matt. 7:15). Both the apostles Paul and Peter insisted that false shepherds-elders, and false teachers were already wrecking havoc in the early church (Acts 20:29-31; 1 Tim. 6:3-5; 2 Pet. 2:1-3). Indeed, the New Testament is replete with internal criticism against Gnostics (Col. 2:18), Judaizers (Gal. 6:12), hypocrites (Gal. 2:11), Balaamites and Nicolaitans (Rev. 2:14-15; and Baker, 1994, p. 1144-45) to name a few.

However, the most significant internal divisions within Christianity, which even today are a continual cause of reproach to the Christian message, are the Great Schism of 1054 AD and the Protestant Reformation of 1517 (D'Aubigne, 1980, p. 109-99).

The Great Schism of 1054

The split, or Great Schism between the Western (Latin) and Eastern (Greek) segments of the Church was primarily over the issue of papal authority. At the time, Pope Leo IX (1049-1054) claimed that he held authority over the other four leading Eastern patriarchs of Constantinople, Alexandria, Antioch, and Jerusalem. Additionally, the Roman Bishop authorized the insertion of the filioque clause* into the Nicene Creed—which was seen as another attempt of the unwarranted extension of his presumed authority. The Orthodox argument was that the "primacy" of the Patriarch of Rome was only honorary (primacy vs. supremacy)—which did not include a right to unilaterally change the decisions of the Ecumenical Councils like Nicaea.

As a result, mutual excommunications were exchanged in 1054 and the Great Schism began—which still persists today. However, in 1965, during Vatican II, both sides issued a joint expression of regret for past actions that led to the Great Schism. Such a joint expression, which is called the *Catholic-Orthodox Joint Declaration of 1965*, also resulted in lifting the mutual excommunications of 1054. Nevertheless, there remain far too many major doctrinal differences for the complete cessation of the Great Schism to be completely effected.

* The *filioque clause* was added to the Nicene Creed which indicated that the Holy Spirit proceeded from both the Father and the Son, rather than from the Father alone.

The Protestant Reformation (1517-1648)

On October 31, 1517, Martin Luther nailed his Ninety-Five Theses On the Power and Efficacy of Indulgences to the door of the Wittenberg Castle Church. This action, combined with his public denial to recant before the Diet of Worms in 1521 served to symbolically initiate the Protestant Reformation.[32]

> Unless I am convicted by Scripture and plain reason—I do not accept the authority of popes and councils, for they have contradicted each other— my conscience is captive to the Word of God. I cannot and will not recant anything, for to go against conscience is neither right nor safe... Here I stand. I can do no other. God help me. Amen. (Martin Luther, Diet of Worms, 1521)

The main Protestant criticisms of the Roman Catholic Church during the Reformation and beyond were regarding indulgences (paying for release from purgatory suffering and/or paying for the construction costs of St. Peter's Basilica in Rome[33]); simony (paying for church offices); clergy corruption (materialism; sexual immorality, lust for secular power); forced clergy celibacy; Marianism (excessive devotion to Mary/immaculate conception and bodily assumption); the intercession of deceased saints; purgatory; the inspiration of the Apocrypha; sacramentalism—especially as mediated by the Catholic hierarchy; papal infallibility; contraceptive denial; the merits of pilgrimages to holy sites; the authority of church tradition over biblical revelation; the primacy of Peter; apostolic succession; transubstantiation (the physical transformation of the bread and wine into the literal body and blood of Jesus; and the universal authority of the Pope in all matters of faith.[34]

Other historic factors in the origin and rise of the Protestant Reformation include the rise of nationalism, the breakdown of the monastic institution and Scholasticism, peasant uprisings (poverty and disease), Papal scandals (Avignon Papacy, 1308-1378 and the papal schism, 1378-1416), Renaissance humanism, moveable type, etc.

Results of the Protestant Reformation include:

- The Peace of Westphalia (1648) bringing the end of the ecclesiastical supremacy of the Pope in Western Christendom by the legal establishment of Protestant churches.
- The end of the political dominance of the Pope[35] by the redistribution of power and wealth previously held by the feudal nobility and the Roman Catholic hierarchy—now passed to the middle classes and to monarchial rulers of nation states.[36]
- The emergence of the ideal of democratic governments based on the notion of the *consent of the governed* and of the future doctrine of the *separation of church and state*.

Criticisms of the Reformation:

- The Reformation is criticized for the effects of its *reactionary theology*. For instance, the Five Sola's of the Reformation are solus Christus (Christ alone), sola scriptura (scripture alone), sola fide (faith alone), sola gratia (grace alone), and Soli Deo gloria (glory to God alone).[37] However, postulated as reactions to Catholicism, Protestants are often seen as radically individualistic and independent[38]; as against tradition and hence historically impoverished; as so fearful of works that grace and faith are often hollow and unconfirmed by actions[39]; and as emphasizing God's sovereignty to such a degree that it excuses man from any responsibility to align his will with the purpose of God on earth.
- The Roman Catholic Church still criticizes Protestants for a heretical *subjective arbitrariness* as evidenced by its rampant denominationalism[40] which can only be remedied by the "return of all dissenters to the Catholic Church".[41]
- On the other hand, Protestants still criticize the Roman Catholic Church by refusing to embrace their Protestant brethren as a legitimate part of the larger Body of Christ and relinquish their exclusive claim to be the only legitimate church on earth.[42] After all, church-divisions, according to the apostle Paul, can serve a necessary purpose when they expose and correct error (1 Cor. 10:19)—leading to repentance (Rev. 3:19).

The fact is, however, that both Protestant and Roman Catholics are so intransigent that they seem deaf to the Lord's call to mutual repentance and restoration (Acts 3:19-21). One wonders how Christians will ever be able to make peace among the nations if they cannot make peace within their own household (Matt. 5:9; James 3:17-18). May the Lord lift off this reproach of perpetual division from the Body of Christ by giving us a heart of humility and a vision to "rebuild the ancient ruins and restore the places long devastated" (Isaiah 61:4; 58:9-12).

Be completely humble and gentle; be patient, bearing with one another in love. Make every effort to keep the unity of the Spirit in the bond of peace. There is only one body and one Spirit—just as you were called to one hope when you were called—one Lord, one faith, one baptism; one God and Father of all, who is over all and through all and in all (Eph. 4:2-6).

Part of the reason why these divisions exist in Christianity is a failure to recognize the legitimacy of diversity. In essence, some Christian groups have mistaken unity for uniformity where differences are suspect rather than valued. The apostle Paul sought to correct this misperception by demonstrating the value of diversity among Christians through utilizing the metaphor of the Church as the "Body of Christ." In both 1 Corinthians 12 and Romans 12 Paul argues that the various parts of a physical body with different functions can be directly compared to the spiritual reality of the Body of Christ with different gifts and performance capabilities. However, in the midst of such necessary diversity the essential unity in the Christian Church is based on the recognition that we are all a part of the same body: "The body is a unit, though it is made up of many parts; and though all its parts are many, they form one body. So it is with Christ" (1 Cor. 12:12-13).

Furthermore, this unity is spiritual, relational, and organic rather than organizational. Indeed, failure to understand the spiritual nature of Christian unity is the fundamental reason for division regarding the rejection of Protestantism by the Roman Catholic Church. For it is by an unflinching embrace of the Catholic doctrines of the "primacy of Peter" and "apostolic succession"[43] that Catholics are unable to accept any ecclesiastical legitimacy beyond the bounds of their own organizational structure.

> ### What is the Apocrypha and why do Protestants deny its inspiration?
>
> The Apocrypha are some 14 books in the Old Testament, which the Roman Catholic Church regards as Deutero-canonical, or the second canon of Scripture. Protestants regard them as historically interesting, but not inspired. A few of the reasons for such Protestant resistance include the following:
>
> - The basis of prayer for the dead and the doctrine of purgatory. 2 Maccabees 12:43-45, "2,000 pieces of silver were sent to Jerusalem for a sin-offering...Whereupon he made reconciliation for the dead, that they might be delivered from sin."
> - Salvation by works:
>
>   o Ecclesiasticus 3:30, "Water will quench a flaming fire, and alms maketh atonement for sin."
>   o Tobit 12:8-9, "It is better to give alms than to lay up gold; for alms doth deliver from death, and shall purge away all sin."
>
> - Endorsement of magic: Tobit 6:7, "If the Devil, or an evil spirit troubles anyone, they can be driven away by making a smoke of the heart, liver, and gall of a fish...and the Devil will smell it, and flee away, and never come again anymore."
> - Mary was born sinless (immaculate conception): Wisdom 8:19-20, "And I was a witty child and had received a good soul. And whereas I was more good, I came to a body undefiled."

Rise of the Roman Catholic Papacy (Third-Sixth centuries)

The Roman Catholic Church claims that based on their interpretation of Matthew 16:18, the first *Pope* was Simon Peter[44] — who was later Bishop of the church in Rome prior to his death. Protestant theologians dispute the claim of Catholic supremacy and of the apostle Peter being the *rock* upon which Jesus would build his church by, among other arguments, the following:

- *Christianity* -

1. Peter (lit. *petros*) means a small/detached stone whereas the bedrock (lit. *petra*) of the Body of Christ (the Universal Church) is Jesus alone—the head of the body (Eph. 1:22-23). Hence, the *rock* is the revelation given to Peter by God the Father regarding Jesus' identity as the Christ/Messiah. In fact, both Peter and Paul subsequently agreed that the only sufficient foundational cornerstone was/is none other than Jesus Christ (1 Cor. 3:11; Eph. 2:20; 1 Pet. 2:4-7).
2. Peter never accepted or argued for any title of preeminence over the other apostles. Indeed, the words of the Lord Jesus undermine any such notion that one of the 12 should ever desire to rule or exercise authority over the others:

> Jesus called them together and said, 'You know that those who are regarded as rulers of the Gentiles lord it over them, and their high officials exercise authority over them. Not so with you. Instead, whoever wants to become great among you must be your servant, and whoever wants to be first must be slave of all. For even the Son of Man did not come to be served, but to serve, and to give his life as a ransom for many' (Mark 10:42-45).

> For who is the greater, one who reclines at table or one who serves? Is it not the one who reclines at table? But I am among you as the one who serves (Luke 22:27).

3. Just five verses later (Matt. 16:23), Jesus sternly rebukes Peter for his spiritual ignorance in seeking to hinder Christ from his work of atonement.

The Roman Catholic Church also claims that based on the doctrine of *apostolic succession* they alone are the legitimate heirs of Peter's throne and therefore all universal spiritual authority, except perhaps the Eastern Orthodox Church[45] earth resides with the Roman See. In fact, the Pope is himself now called the Vicar, or chief representative of Christ on earth.

The Protestant and Eastern Orthodox problem with this claim of exclusivity is that the New Testament contradicts it with the apostle

Paul unequivocally indicating that his call and authority were from God and not man (Gal. 1:1, 12, 2:6-10) — especially implying Peter, whom he publicly rebuked for hypocrisy (Gal. 2:11-14). In fact, even Peter warmly commends Paul's writings to be on the same level of authority as the scriptures themselvs[46] (2 Pet. 3:15-16). It is also clear that both Paul and Peter regarded each other as no more or less than fellow apostolic bond-servants of Jesus Christ (Rom. 1:1; 2 Pet. 1:1) — neither deriving their authority from the other, but from Christ Jesus alone.

As a result, the rise of the Roman papacy, as we know it today, was the result of a process that took literally hundreds of years to develop. At every turn there was opposition to this universal imposition by the bishop of Rome — undergirded by the force of the Roman Emperors, which eventually lead to the Great Schism of 1054 and the Protestant Reformation in 1517.

External Objections

External objections to Christianity include the early Roman accusations, Christian brutality and war, and various modern criticisms including liberal Christianity, the science vs. religion debate, the prosperity gospel and the clergy sex scandals.

Early Roman Accusations

The earliest external criticisms of Christians were the Roman accusations of atheism, insurrection, cannibalism, and sex orgies.[47]

Early Christian accusations: atheism, cannibalism, and sex orgies

The Romans accused early Christians of being atheists because they refused to worship the pantheon of the Greek and Roman gods. Christians were also accused of insurrection because of their insistence that they were citizens of a heavenly kingdom under the Lordship of Jesus Christ. Cannibalism was the accusation regarding the misconception over the Lord's Supper that was spoken of as being the body and blood of Jesus. Finally, the accusation of sex-orgies grew out of the Christian designation of having Love Feasts — where they would greet one another with a holy kiss.

To these accusations apologists, including such Church Fathers as Ignatius, Justin Martyr, Irenaeus, and Tertullian arouse to articulate a rational defense of the Christian faith to critics and Emperor alike.

Christianity Brutality and War

Christian brutality and war have often been cited as reasons for criticism including the political hegemony and moral corruption of the Church throughout the Middle-Ages, the Crusades, Inquisition, and the 123 years of religious wars in Europe (Peasants' War in 1525 to the Peace of Westphalia in 1648). In response, Christian brutality and war are direct contradictions to the life and teachings of Jesus Christ, who said that his Kingdom was not of this world as evidenced by the fact that his disciple-servants would not fight to prevent his arrest (John 18:36). Essentially, the Church is the vehicle God uses to reveal the kingdom—not to enforce it (Woodworth, 2002, p. 3-4). However, this is not to say that as citizens of a secular nation that Christians cannot help defend their nation in time of war.

Furthermore, Paul asserted that Christians (citizens of the kingdom of God) were not to battle (struggle or fight) against people but rather against spiritual forces of evil in heavenly realms (Eph. 6:11-12). Finally, Peter's instruction to submit to the governing authorities (1 Pet. 2:13-14), including the then reigning Emperor Nero, makes it very clear that the early church of the New Testament was forbidden to engage in war as a tactic of defending themselves or extending the Kingdom of God on earth.

Unfortunately, the Church of the Middle-Ages exchanged its call to *servanthood* for political power thereby losing its moral authority and redemptive mission. Indeed it took over a thousand years for the Church to finally divest itself of the trappings of secular power. What emerged in its place were the modern nation-states of Europe free from Papal control and the understanding of the "freedom of conscience" leading to the doctrine of the separation of church and state as enshrined in the American Constitution. And although democracy is certainly not without its failings,[48] such a political structure has thus far proven to be the best that can be crafted in a fallen world that is awaiting the ultimate realization of the Kingdom of God on earth at the end of this age (Rev. 11:15).

Various Modern Criticisms

A significant form of modern criticism of Christianity that has emerged since the Enlightenment is called biblical criticism, which is the foundational hermeneutic of what is often called "liberal Christianity." Biblical criticism (Geilser, 2000, 86-91), with its anti-supernatural bias, can be broadly divided between Higher Criticism, which is the study of biblical texts to discover their composition, history, and meaning, and Lower Criticism (textual criticism), which is the close examination of the text to establish variant and original readings. The problem with Higher Criticism is that it redefines the biblical text as non-propositional and historically contextualized, meaning that the Bible is not a source of statements of truths, but rather a collection of narratives that should be understood to merely "explain, epitomize, or symbolize the essence and significance of Christianity."[49]

As a result, such terms and doctrines like sin, salvation, repentance, atonement, incarnation, Trinity, resurrection, the Second Coming of Christ, and eternal judgment all need to be redefined in modern terms without their ancient limitations in order to grasp their essential contemporary meaning and application (Borg, 2003, p. 167, 171). As such, Christianity should no longer make an exclusive claim to salvation in Christ alone (Acts 4:12) lest it be accused of producing a feeling of alienation. Indeed, all religion must now be a tool for affirming the goodness of humanity rather than criticizing man's innate evilness and requiring a radical repentance from sin and wholehearted pursuit of righteousness and truth in Christ Jesus (Eph. 4:20-24). From the perspective of the author, liberal Christianity should be vigorously disputed and exposed as a dangerous non-Christian form of Christianity (Woodworth, 2000, p. 247-55).

Another modern criticism has to do with what is called the science vs. religion debate. Essentially, the debate revolves around scientific disconfirmations of supposedly biblical revelations. This debate began with the 16th century heliocentric assertions of Copernicus that was later elaborated by Kepler and defended by Galileo becoming the center of a major religious dispute.[50] Allegedly, Galileo was threatened with death if he did not recant for the notion that the earth revolved around a stationary sun instead of the reverse as was referenced in the biblical text.

The actual verses in question were Psalm 93:1; 96:10, and 1 Chronicles 16:30, which state that "the world is firmly established, it cannot be moved." Additionally, Ecclesiastes 1:5 says that "the sun rises and the sun sets and hurries back to where it rises." Though apparently stating that the sun, not the earth, is in motion, Galileo took Augustine's position that Scripture was not to be taken literally in every passage—especially in a book of poetry and songs. Rather, the writers of the Old Testament (OT) wrote from the perspective of the terrestrial world—where the sun does appear to rise and set, whereas in fact, it is the earth's rotation which gives the impression of the sun in motion across the sky. Galileo suggested that perhaps the interpretation of the Bible was the issue rather than a scientific contradiction of the text itself.

This same issue of biblical interpretation also applies to the science vs. religion debate regarding evolution and creationism, which will be covered in depth in the final chapter of this text. Essentially, the argument centers on the meaning of Genesis One where *young earth theorists* insist that the six days of creation are literal 24 hour days. The problem is that modern geologists date the earth to around 4.5 billion years (and the universe at 14.5 billion years) based on various radiometric dating techniques, which compare the observed abundance of a naturally occurring radioactive isotope with its decay products using *known decay rates*.[51] By using such dating techniques geological timescales have been established providing a significant source of information about the ages of fossils and the deduced rates of evolutionary change.[52]

The apparent contradiction between the text of Genesis One and the geological date of the earth has been theologically resolved, at least for some, by what is called the *old earth theory*. Such a theory postulates that the creation days of Genesis One can be understood as *day-ages* consisting of an indeterminate amount of time, perhaps thousands, millions or billions of years each. Note that although the old earth theory accepts the geological time periods and the idea of a God-caused big-bang, it is still challenging the Darwinian claims of macro-evolution in favor of the special creation of man in the image of God.[53]

The Prosperity Gospel and Clergy Sex Scandals

The final two criticisms of Christianity have to do with the recent clergy sex scandals and what is being called the *prosperity Gospel* whereby certain Charismatic Protestant ministers are indulging in extravagantly lavish lifestyles in the name of biblical prosperity.

The 2008 senatorial review of six marquee prosperity preachers[54] by Republican Sen. Charles Grassley of Iowa, a member of the Senate Finance Committee, has many from inside and outside of the Christian church agreeing with the investigation into possible violations of federal tax-exemption policies.[55] Theologically, the criticism is that too many charismatic charlatans are masquerading as legitimate ministers, whose ministries have ostensibly become little more than a front for financially fleecing the flock of God with a distorted version of the "seed faith money doctrine"—promising financial gain, marriage partners, obedient children, salvation of family members, supernatural healing from disease, new cars and new clothes, free airplanes, in return for obedience to the "command of God" requiring them to "get off the sofa now and go to your phones to make a financial 'faith-pledge.'" "In their greed these teachers will exploit you with stories they have made up"(2 Pet. 2:3).

What is confusing is that the *falsity* of these false teachers and prophets is not that what they are preaching is blatantly unbiblical, but rather that their motives and methods are skewed resulting in a "prosperity gospel" that creates an anxiousness about one's material means rather than a trusting submission to pursue faithful service to Christ—regardless of the status of one's earthly bank accounts. (Matt. 6:19-21) It is not that prosperity is not taught in Scripture; rather, these ministers are making money (and material possessions) the primary objective and measure of faith.[56]

> If anyone teaches false doctrines and does not agree to the sound instruction of our Lord Jesus Christ and to godly teaching, he is conceited and understands nothing. He has an unhealthy interest in controversies and quarrels about words that result in envy, strife, malicious talk, evil suspicions and constant friction between men of corrupt mind, who have been robbed of the truth and who think that godliness is a means to financial gain.

But godliness with contentment is great gain. For we brought nothing into the world, and we can take nothing out of it [either]. But if we have food and clothing, we will be content with that. People who want to get rich fall into temptation and a trap and into many foolish and harmful desires that plunge men into ruin and destruction. For the love of money is a root of all kinds of evil. Some people, eager for money, have wandered from the faith and pierced themselves with many grief's (1 Tim. 6:3-10).

The response to the clergy sex scandal, be it Catholic or Protestant, should be one of sorrow and repentance. However, since the Catholic church continues to require celibacy of its priests; many critics objectionably point to the apostle Paul's specific recommendation of marriage as a protection against sexual immorality:

But because of the temptation to sexual immorality, each man should have his own wife and each woman her own husband...[For those who are married] Do not deprive one another, except perhaps by agreement for a limited time, that you may devote yourselves to prayer; but then come together again, so that Satan may not tempt you because of your lack of self-control. Now as a concession, not a command, I say this. I wish that all were as I myself am. But each has his own gift from God, one of one kind and one of another (1 Cor. 7:2-7).

In response, Catholic leadership points to a lack of scholarly/scientific evidence (which is rejected by non-Catholic scholars on the basis of Catholic bias) that there is any connection between the compulsion to celibacy and sexual temptation to fornication—and/or homosexuality. Critics further cite that Paul's teaching on the subject is based on human nature and common sense rather than questionable scientific studies. Furthermore, even though Paul admittedly encourages celibacy, he ultimately gives freedom to all believers to follow their own personal conviction regarding marriage. After all, even the apostle Peter, the Vicar of Christ himself, was married (Matt. 8:14).

Finally, most non-Catholic scholars and conservative theologians observe that Paul's prophetic warning regarding the prohibition of anyone to marry, including spiritual leadership, could be indirectly indicative of those who, in the last days, would "abandon the faith following deceiving spirits and doctrines of demons," including the act of "forbidding of marriage" (1 Tim. 4:1-3). Nevertheless, Catholics continue to insist that no priest is actually *forced* to become celibate; even though if they chose to be married their priesthood training would be immediately terminated. Furthermore, if a priest were to marry after his vows, he would be officially "defrocked," or suffer the humiliation of *laicization* in which he becomes a layman again.[57]

Even though Paul's instruction to Timothy directly applies to Gnostic asceticism, it nevertheless could also indirectly relate to the Roman Catholic practice of disallowing priests to claim their biblical freedom to marry. Consider the following biblical examples: "...the overseer (bishop, shepherd, elder, pastor) must be above reproach, the husband of one wife..." (1 Tim. 3:1-2) "Marriage should be honored by all..." (Heb. 13:4). And while it may be highly advisable for pastors in local church ministry to be married; we simply cannot go so far as to require all pastors to be married—any more than we should allow a doctrine mandating that all pastors should be celibate. However, whether a pastoral minister is married or single the prohibition against adultery or sexual immorality (fornication and/or immorality) applies to both equally (Heb. 13:4b).

Chapter 3: Review Questions

1. What was the most interesting thing that you learned from Chapter 3 and why?
2. What was the main issue of the Great Schism of 1054?
3. Who was Martin Luther? (a) an American civil rights leader, (b) the instigator of the Protestant Reformation, (c) a popular movie starring Arnold Schwarzenagger.
4. Name one key problematic result of the Protestant Reformation for the Roman Catholic Church.
5. Name one of the key criticisms of the Protestant Reformation from the perspective of the Roman Catholic Church.

Chapter IV
-Judaism-

"As a child I received instruction in the Bible and in the Talmud. I am a Jew, but I am enthralled by the luminous figure of [Jesus] the Nazarene." (Albert Einstein)

Introduction: Judaism's Turning Point

Many modern scholars divide the history of Judaism into two major eras with the turning point being the destruction of the second temple in 70 A.D.[58] This key historic *transitional event* signifies the demarcation between *biblical* Judaism and *rabbinic* Judaism. On the one hand, biblical Judaism was centralized (in Jerusalem) and temple-based, with priests performing a key ministerial role. Rabbinic Judaism, on the other hand, is decentralized by virtue of the Diaspora (dispersion of the Jews beyond Israel) and focusing on the role of Scripture and its interpretation with rabbis (teachers) being the primary ministerial figures. To put it succinctly, with the cessation of the temple sacrifice in Jerusalem and the wholesale ejection of the Jews from their homeland, Judaism, as we now speak of it, has undergone a profound change.[59] Within this framework, and prior to a specific Christian critique, we will now to turn our attention to a brief historic overview of Judaism itself.

Historical Overview of Judaism

Biblical Judaism: Beginnings to 70 A.D.

Judaism began around 2000 B.C. when Yahweh[60] appeared to Abram (later Abraham) and first established the following covenant-promise with him:

> The Lord [YHWH] said to Abram, "Leave your country, your people and your father's household and go to the land I will show you. I will make you into a great nation and I will bless you; I will make your name great, and you will be a blessing. I will bless those who bless you, and whoever curses you I will curse; and all peoples of the earth will be blessed through you (Gen. 12:1-3).

Abraham had two sons: Ishmael and Isaac. From Ishmael descended all of the Arabs including Muhammad, who became the founder of Islam (the Muslims) in the 6th century A.D.[61] From Isaac descended all of the Hebrews or Israelites, later called the Jews after the giving of the Law of Moses at Mt. Sinai. In fact, Moses is known for both the Exodus and the receiving/giving of the Law at Mt. Sinai. Under Moses' leadership the Israelites were led through the wilderness to the edge of the *Promised Land*. However, it was Moses' understudy Joshua who successfully subdued the land of promise thus partially fulfilling the Covenant, which Yahweh had made with Abraham nearly 700 years earlier.[62]

After the period of the Judges[63] came the monarchy, during which time King David was prophetically promised by God that the Messiah would descend through his lineage—the tribe of Judah.[64] Nevertheless, it was David's son Solomon who built the first temple which was destroyed by the Babylonians in 586 B.C. The exiled Jews later returned to Jerusalem where they rebuilt the 2nd Temple nearly 70 years after the destruction of the first temple.[65] Another significant figure of history is the Seleucid King Antiochus IV Epiphanies who, by murderous blasphemy[66], provoked the Maccabean revolt leading to Jewish independence. Such a qualified independence was carried over from the Greek to the Roman Empire and was the rule of the land under King Herod the Great[67] at the time of Jesus Christ. Even so, the Jews continued to struggle with the Romans for more complete independence—to such a degree that their rebellion was finally and decisively ended in 70 A.D. with the capturing of Jerusalem and the destruction of second Temple.[68]

Rabbinical Judaism: 70 A.D. to the Present

As we have previously noted, the destruction of Jerusalem and its temple, along with the dispersion of the Jewish population, signified the transition from biblical to rabbinical Judaism. The emphasis was now on Jewish scripture and its interpretation in a post-temple era. The following, according to the author, is a brief chronological overview of some of the more significant developments affecting Judaism during this period of time.

The first notable event was the official canonization of the Hebrew Scriptures[69] around 90 A.D. Within a hundred years of the completion of the canon, another principally theological development was the production of the Talmud, which is the authoritative body of Jewish tradition comprising the Mishnah[70] and Gemara or rabbinic commentaries on the Mishnah, which both date between AD 200 to AD 600.

The interval spanning the years between 622 and 1258 A.D. witnessed the birth and rise of the *Golden Age of Islam* where Jews participated and contributed to public and economic life through art, literature, science, and philosophy.[71] Seminal figures during the Golden Age of Islam were Saadia ben Joseph (Said al-Fayyumi, 882-942) who translated the Hebrew Scriptures into Arabic and attempted to synthesize Jewish and Greek thought.

Moses Maimonides (1135-1204), was one of the most renowned Jewish philosophers of all time. Maimonides was also a profound theological thinker and Talmudist, as well as the court physician to Saladin (Sultan of Egypt).[72] Maimonides went on to pen, in Arabic, *The Guide to the Perplexed,* in which he argued that Judaism was a rational religion and that faith and reason were complementary.[73] From the 11th through the 13th centuries, the Christian Crusades (1095-1291) combined their mission to free Jerusalem from Muslim control with an equal commitment to "rid the world of as many non-Christians as possible including both Muslims and Jews." This misguided zeal resulted in the extermination of tens of thousands of Jews in the Rhine

Valley (Germany)—an event that is characterized by some Jewish writers as the *first holocaust* in Germany.[74] Also during the 13th century Kabbalahism rose to become a very popular form of Jewish mysticism combining a belief in the descending stages of creation[75] with the development of a numerological Bible Code.[76] Jewish exiles of the late middle ages (14th -17th centuries) witnessed the killing and expulsion of their Jewish countrymen from England, France, Spain,[77] Portugal, and ultimately Russia.

The Renaissance (14th – 17th centuries) and subsequent Protestant Reformation (16th century) challenged and fundamentally changed both Judaism as well as Christianity. As a reaction to cultural syncretism, the mystic faith-healer ben Eliezer (1700-1760), who was affectionately called Baal Shem Tov (the *good master of the Holy Name*), helped launch a traditional *Hasidic* revival in Eastern Europe and insisted that Judaism remain pure to its own traditions rather than assimilating with the larger Christian society. On the other hand, the modernist Moses Mendelssohn (1729-1786)[78] advocated an accommodation of Judaism (in Western Europe) with the culture at large. It was this call to modernize Judaism that was later termed the Reform movement—officially beginning in the late 18th century. By the mid 19th century (1843), the Reform movement in Germany postulated the following three declarations that have become the basis for Reform (or secular) Judaism today:

1. There is a continuation of the development of Judaism. In other words, Judaism should expand and adapt as society changes with the increase of scientific knowledge.
2. The Talmud has no authority for the modern Jew. In other words, Jewish people should no longer look to ancient rabbinic teachings as a guide to modern living.
3. We seek no Messiah, and we know no homeland but the land of our birth. In other words, we will no longer look to ancient Israel and its Messianic hope of deliverance as our defining focus for identity and life today.

Ultimately, the debate between traditionalists and modernists resulted in the following three main branches of Judaism as they exist today.[79]

```
                    Judaism
                       ▼
  ──────────────────────────────────────
  |              |                |
Orthodox       Reform         Conservative
```

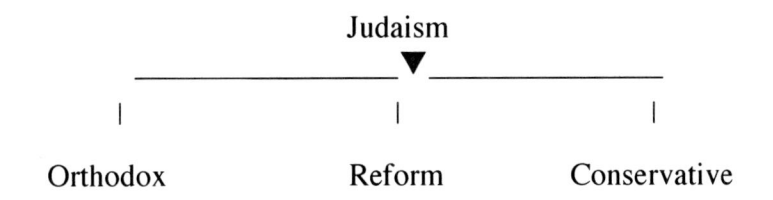

Orthodox Judaism is strict in its adherence to the Torah and Talmud — and in its ancient ritual observance in the modern world. *Reform Judaism* is marked by a liberal approach in non-observance of much legal tradition regarded as irrelevant to the present and in shortening and simplification of traditional ritual. *Conservative Judaism* as practiced especially among some United States Jews maintains a belief in the Torah and Talmud but makes allowance for some departures in keeping with differing times and circumstances.

One of the most horrific atrocities ever perpetrated against the Jewish people was undoubtedly the Holocaust (1933-1945) of German chancellor, Adolf Hitler where an estimated 6 million Jews (one-third of the world's Jewish population at the time), including 1.5 million children died in the Nazi concentration camps (Molly, 2008, p. 325-27).

From the ashes of the Holocaust came the creation of the State of Israel (1948). There are at least three main factors that have historically contributed to the creation of the State of Israel including, *Zionism*. As popularized by Theodor Herzl in his book *The Jewish State* (1896), Zionism was the call for the creation of a separate Jewish nation in Jerusalem. The word *Zionism* actually comes from the word *Zion* (Hebrew: ציון, *Tzi-yon*), one of the names of Jerusalem and the Land of Israel, as mentioned in the Hebrew Scriptures: "And the ransomed of the LORD will return. They will enter Zion with singing; everlasting joy will crown their heads. Gladness and joy will overtake them, and sorrow and sighing will flee away." (Isaiah 35:10)

A second impetus for the creation of the State of Israel was the Balfour Declaration (1917) in which Britain endorsed the notion of a Jewish homeland and allowed a limited immigration of the Jews to Palestine. The third historic motivation for a Jewish national identity was the 1948 decision by the United Nations to divide the old British Mandate of Palestine thus creating the modern Jewish state of Israel.

The creation of the modern Jewish State in the middle-east has been a source of continual conflict between the Israeli's and their Arab neighbors to such a degree that the United States has been requested by both the Palestinians and the Israeli's to try to broker a plan for peace. The resultant *Roadmap for Peace* (2002) was crafted by the George W. Bush administration and calls for an independent Palestinian state living side by side with Israel in peace. "The Roadmap represents a starting point toward achieving the vision of two states, a secure State of Israel and a viable, peaceful, democratic Palestine. It is the framework for progress towards lasting peace and security in the Middle East..."[80]

It is worth noting that the majority of Jews living in Israel today accept the prospect of peace that a two-state solution portends. Indeed the only people against it are fundamentalist Jews and Muslims— including dispensational[81] Christian theologians.

The Four Criteria

The four criteria of a Christian critique have already been established namely, the Bible, Jesus Christ, the Kingdom of God, and the Christian Church. A systematic comparison and contrast of each of these four criteria between Judaism and Christianity is now the task at hand.

Judaism and the Bible

The sacred scriptures of Judaism, called the Tanakh, are virtually identical with what Protestant Christians refer to as the Old Testament. The Tanakh consists of three main sections: a). the Torah (Law), b). the Nevi'im (Prophets), and c.) the Kethuvim (Writings)—from which the acronym TaNaKh is formed.[82] Roman Catholics and Eastern Orthodox Old Testament versions include additional books called the *Apocrypha* and/or the *Deuterocanonical* books.[83] Hence, not only are the Old Testament Hebrew Scriptures compatible with Christianity, but they are also actually foundational to the biblical revelation of the New Testament itself as reflected in these verses:

"A record of the genealogy of Jesus Christ the son of David [Messianic lineage], the son of Abraham [covenant originator]" (Matt. 1:1).

"...for salvation is from the Jews" (John 4:22)

And he [Abraham] received the sign of [Jewish] circumcision, a seal of the righteousness that he had by faith while he was still uncircumcised [Gentile]. So then, he is the father of all who believe but have not been circumcised, in order that righteousness might be credited to them (Rom. 4:11).

Given the mutual agreement between Jews and Christians with the Old Testament, the primary contradictions with Judaism and the Christian Bible revolve around the theological implications of the New Testament documents, which a many Jews generally reject as an affront to their religious heritage.

Judaism and Jesus

The greatest objection between Judaism and Christianity is unquestionably over the person of Jesus. Whereas the New Testament document clearly reveals Jesus as the Son of God and the Messiah-Christ (lit. *anointed one*),[84] Judaism's stance, since the New Testament times, has been one of utter denial in Jesus as either God's Son or the coming Jewish Messiah.

Jewish arguments against Jesus' divinity

The Jewish rejection of Jesus being the Son of God is nearly exclusively based on their understanding of monotheism, which they claim would be violated if God were to have a Son, unless such a *Son* was perhaps a Gnostic emanation from God rather than one who shared in the divine essence. Indeed, the most popular Jewish statements on monotheism occur in the *Shema* prayer of Deuteronomy 6:4: "Hear, O Israel: the LORD our God, the LORD is one," the first of the Ten Commandments in Exodus 20:2:

"...Thou shalt have no other gods before Me," and the second of the Thirteen Principles of Faith of Moses Mainmonides: "I believe with perfect faith that the Creator, blessed be His Name, is One, and that there is no unity in any manner like His, and that He alone is our God, who was, and is, and will be."

Even the carefully reasoned doctrine of the Trinity,[85] which is argued to have been implied in both the Old and New Testaments,[86] has not been sufficient enough justification to countervail Jewish (or Islamic) monotheistic convictions. The best answer to the arguments *against* Jesus' Trinitarian divinity is the argument from the Bible itself. The following are a number of Scriptural texts that are the most definitive *proofs*, at least for conservative scholars, regarding the divine nature of Jesus Christ:[87]

"For to us a child is born, to us a son is given; and the government shall be upon his shoulders and his name shall be called Wonderful Counselor, Mighty God, Everlasting Father, Prince of Peace." (Isaiah 9:6, ESV)

"In the beginning was the Word, and the Word was with God and the Word was God. He was in the beginning with God." (John 1:1-3, ESV)

"And the Word became flesh and dwelt among us, and we have seen his glory, glory as of the only Son from the Father, full of grace and truth." (John 1:14, ESV)

"I and the Father are one. Again the Jews picked up stones to stone him, but Jesus said to them, '...For which of these [miracles] do you stone me? [And the Jews answered] We are not stoning you for any of these [miracles]...but for blasphemy, because you, a mere man, claim to be God.'" (John 10:30, 33, ESV)

"Christ is God over all, blessed forever." (Romans 9:5, ESV)

"[We are] waiting for our blessed hope, the appearing of the glory of our great God and Savior Jesus Christ." (Titus 2:13, ESV)

"[Jesus] is the image of the invisible God, the firstborn of all creation. For by him all things were created...for God was pleased to have all his fullness dwells in him..." (Colossians 1:15-17, 19, ESV & NIV)

"The Son is the radiance of God's glory and the exact representation of his being/image, sustaining all things by his powerful word." (Hebrews 1:3)

"For in Christ all the fullness of the Deity lives in bodily form..." (Colossians 2:9)

Jewish arguments against Jesus' Messiahship

Regarding to Jesus' Messiahship, Jewish scholars argue from carefully selected list of *sanctioned Messianic texts* and argue that Jesus, if he ever existed, could not be the Messiah because he did not fulfill all of the criteria.[88] The Christian response should be to argue (without being argumentative) from the texts they provide as well as to show them additional Messianic texts from the Tanakh itself.

A number of the preferred list of the Messianic texts of Judaism are the following:

"...you may appoint a king over you, whom the Lord your God shall choose: one from among your brethren shall you set as king over you." (Deut. 17:15)

Jewish argument: The Messiah must be a Jew. Christian Response: Jesus was a Jew (Matt.1:1-16)

"The staff shall not depart from Judah, nor the sceptre from between his feet..." (Gen. 49:10)

Jewish Argument: The Messiah must be a member of the tribe of Judah. Christian Response: Jesus was from the tribe of Judah (Matt. 1:2-3) "And when your days (David) are fulfilled, and you shall sleep with your fathers, I will set up your seed after you, who shall issue from your own body, and I will establish his kingdom. He shall build a house for my name, and I will make firm the throne of his kingdom forever..." (2 Sam. 7:12 - 13)

Jewish Argument: The Messiah must descend from King David. Christian Response: Jesus was directly descended through David's lineage (Matt. 1:1, 6; Luke 3:31). [Note: Though there are many answers to the differences in these genealogical lists (Joseph vs. Mary genealogies, legal vs. direct bloodline descent, mnemonic considerations, gematria symbolism, modern vs. ancestral records, evidence of numerical symmetry,[89] etc) one fact in which there is no disagreement is that Jesus is listed in both as having descended from King David.] "And he shall set up a banner for the nations, and shall assemble the outcasts of Israel, and gather together the dispersed of Judah from the four corners of the earth." (Isaiah 11:12)

Jewish Argument: The Messiah must re-gather the Jewish people from exile and return them to the land of Israel. Christian Response: Many dispensational Christian theologians see a fulfillment of this in the 1948 UN declaration of Israel as a nation-state and the subsequent invitation to the Jews from all nations to re-gather in Israel. Others see the message of the Gospel being heralded throughout the world to Jew and Gentile alike as fulfillment to this universal call to co-inheritance with the seed of Abraham in the spiritual Kingdom of God (Rom. 14:17).

"...and I will set my sanctuary in their midst forever and my tabernacle shall be with them..." (Ezek. 37:26 - 27) Jewish Argument: The Messiah will rebuild the Jewish temple. Christian Response: Dispensationalists say a third Jewish temple will be physically rebuilt during the millennial reign of Christ, whereas others see this temple as the Body of Christ which is even now being built up for a dwelling of God in the Spirit (Eph. 2:21-22).

"...they shall beat their swords into plowshares, and their spears into pruning hooks; nation shall not lift up sword against nation, neither shall they learn war anymore." (Micah 4:3-4). Jewish Argument: The reign of the Messiah will be marked by a time of world-wide peace and prosperity. Christian Response: Dispensationalists say this will happen during the millennium, whereas others believe this fulfillment will be at the regeneration of the cosmos at the commencement of the next age.

Additional Messianic texts from the Tanakh

In addition to the preceding texts about the Messiah there are also many other Messianic texts from the Tanakh that can be cited as evidence for Jesus' Messiahship.[90]

First is the famous quote from the major prophet Isaiah who declared: "Therefore the LORD himself will give you a sign: The virgin will be with child and will give birth to a son, and will call him Immanuel." (Isaiah 7:14) The New Testament corollary is found in the book of Matthew and show a direct fulfillment in the birth of Jesus:

> But...an angel of the Lord appeared to him in a dream and said, "Joseph son of David, do not be afraid to take Mary home as your wife, because what is conceived in her is from the Holy Spirit. She will give birth to a son, and you are to give him the name Jesus, because he will save his people from their sins." All this took place to fulfill what the Lord has said through the prophet [Isaiah]: "The virgin will be with child and will give birth to a son, and they will call him Immanuel'—which means, 'God with us'(Matt. 1:20-23).

Some would argue that the Hebrew word for *virgin* could also be *young maiden or woman*. However, notice that the context of the virgin-birth promise (Is. 7:10-16) indicates that such a birth would be a supernatural sign from God. The fact that young maidens/women have children is no sign at all, but a virgin giving birth would indeed qualify as a miraculous sign from God identifying the Messiah with certainty. Such is the New Testament case for Jesus' birth.

According to the prophet Micah, the Messiah will also be born in Bethlehem: "But you, Bethlehem Ephrathah though you are small among the clans of Judah, out of you will come for me one who will be ruler over Israel, whose origins are from of old, from ancient times." (Micah 5:2) Luke locates Bethlehem as the exact place of Jesus' Birth:

> So Joseph also went up from the town of Nazareth in Galilee of Judea, to Bethlehem the town of David, because he belonged to the house and line of David. He went there to register with Mary, who was pledged to be married to him and was expecting a child. While they were there, the time came for the baby to be born, and she gave birth to her firstborn, a son (Matt. 2:4-7).

Overlooked also by many Jewish scholars is the famous reference to the Messiah being called the Son of God: "I will proclaim the decree of the LORD; He said to me, "You are my Son; today I have become your Father...Kiss the Son lest he be angry and you be destroyed in your way, for his wrath can flare up in a moment. Blessed are all who take refuge in him." (Psalm 2:7) In the New Testament, the apostle Peter makes a direct connection to the resurrection of Jesus with the decree of Sonship: "We tell you the good news: What God promised our fathers he has fulfilled for us, their children, by raising up Jesus. As it is written in the second Psalm: 'You are my Son; today I have become your Father'" (Acts 13:32-33).

Also regarding the divine Sonship of Jesus, in Hosea, God declares that he will call from Egypt his son, *Israel*. "When Israel was a child, I loved him, and out of Egypt I called my son." Matthew identifies in Jesus' return from Egypt a typological prophetic fulfillment of the nation of Israel's deliverance from Egypt also. "So he [Joseph] got up, took the child and his mother during the night and left for Egypt, where he stayed until the death of Herod. And so was fulfilled what the Lord had said through the prophet: 'Out of Egypt I called my son'" (Matt. 2:14).

The coming salvation of the Messiah is also linked to supernatural healing: "Be strong, do not fear; your God will come...to save you. Then will the eyes of the blind be opened and the ears of the deaf unstopped. Then will the lame leap like deer, and the mute tongue shout for joy." (Isaiah 35:4-6) The physician Luke specifically records the supernatural signs that Jesus performed among the people:

> At that very time Jesus cured many who had diseases, sickness, and evil spirits, and gave sight to many who were blind. So he replied to the messengers, 'Go back and report to John what you have seen and heard: The blind receive sight, the lame walk, those who have leprosy are cured, the deaf hear, the dead are raised, and the good news is preached to the poor' (Luke 7:21-22).

Furthermore, Jesus declared that his mission was to specifically fulfill the mandate of the Messiah when he took the scroll of the prophet Isaiah and read: "The Spirit of the Lord is on me, because he has anointed me to preach good news to the poor. He has sent me to proclaim freedom for prisoners and recovery of sight for the blind, to release the oppressed, to proclaim the year of the Lord's favor." (Luke 4:18-19 c. f. Isaiah 61:1-2a).

The Messiah was also to minister in Galilee—exactly where Jesus' ministry was often concentrated:

Leaving Nazareth, he went and lived in Capernaum, which was by the lake in the area of Zebulun and Naphtali—to fulfill what was said through the prophet Isaiah: 'Land of Zebulun and land of Naphtali, the way to the sea, along the Jordan, Galilee of the Gentiles—the people living in darkness have seen a great light; on those living in the land of the shadow of death a light has dawned' (Matt. 4:13-16 c. f. Isaiah 9:1-2).

And from one of the most often neglected Messianic texts of the Tanakh, Psalm 22 is replete with prophetic promises regarding the Messiah that were precisely fulfilled in Jesus' crucifixion:

My God, my God, why have you forsaken me...I am poured out like water, and all of my bones are out of joint...Dogs have surrounded me; a band of evil men has encircled me, they have pierced my hands and my feet...people stare and gloat over me. They divide my garments among them and cast lots for my clothing (Psalm 22:1, 14-16, 18 c. f. Matt. 27:46, 27-31, 35).

Seminal also among the Messianic promises is Isaiah 53:

He was despised and rejected by men...Surely he took up our infirmities and carried away our sorrows, yet we considered him stricken by God...but he was pierced for our transgressions, he was crushed for our iniquities; the punishment that brought us peace was upon him, and by his wounds we are healed...He was oppressed and afflicted, yet he did not open his mouth; he was led like a lamb to the slaughter, and as a sheep before her shearers is silent, so he did not open his mouth...For he was cut off from the land of the living; for the transgression of my people he was stricken...After the suffering of his soul, he will see the light of life...by his knowledge my righteous servant will justify many, and he will bear their iniquities. Therefore I will give him a portion among the great...because he poured out his life unto death, and was numbered with the transgressors.

For he bore the sin of many...(Isaiah 53 c.f. 1 Pet. 2:21-25; John 1:29).

Finally, Peter locates the fulfillment of the resurrection of Jesus in Psalm 16:10 where David prophesies: "Therefore my heart is glad and my tongue rejoices; my body also will rest secure, because you will not abandon me to the grave, nor will you let your Holy One see decay" (Psalm 16:10 c.f. Acts 2:26-31).

There are many more Messianic references in the Tanakh that were literally fulfilled in Jesus Christ.[91] However, this sampling should suffice to at least indicate the prophetic significance and foundation of Jesus' birth, ministry, death, and resurrection—especially as it relates to the Hebrew Scriptures themselves. And though Jews may continue to vociferously deny any relation with Jesus to the Messiah, the evidence herein referenced has proven sufficient for hundreds of millions of people who see a complimentary and compelling narrative emerge from a comparison between the Old/Hebrew and New/Greek Testament documents.

Judaism and the Kingdom of God

Theologically Understanding the Kingdom of God

The Kingdom of God is to be understood, not so much as a geographical location, but rather as the "realm or sphere of God's authority" (Richards, 1985, p. 372-82). Other synonyms for the word "kingdom" would include rule, dominion, throne, authority, power, sovereignty or government (Richards, 1990, p. 605-07).

When reviewing the theological implications of the Kingdom of God one can identify at least four distinct aspects that are progressively unfolded throughout both Old and New Testaments.

1. The first foundational aspect of the Kingdom is "providential sovereignty," which means the overarching authority and power of God's Kingdom in regard to his entire creation. Yahweh is Lord of all and over all!
   "The Lord [Yahweh] has established his throne in heaven, and his Kingdom rules over all" (Psalm 103:19; Psalm 24:1; 145:11-13).

2. Second, the kingdom refers to "prophetic nationalism" which specifically implied the appearance of God's rule on earth through his old covenant people Israel (Cox, 1966, p. 34-45).

> Yet the Lord, the God of Israel, chose me from my whole family to be king over Israel forever. He chose Judah as leader, and from the house of Judah he chose my family, and from my father's sons he was pleased to make me king over all Israel. Of all my sons—and the Lord has given me many—he has chosen my son Solomon to sit on the throne of the kingdom of the Lord over Israel (1 Chronicles 28:4-5).

3. Third, the kingdom can be understood as "present spiritual reality." (Rom. 14:17). This signifies that aspect of the kingdom representing the "now-ness" of God's rule through Christ over the hearts of his willing subjects. The Kingdom is present in both the hearts of individuals in whom Christ resides, as well as in the corporate body of Christ over which He presides.[92]

> Consequently, you are no longer foreigners and aliens, but fellow citizens with God's people and members of God's household, built on the foundation of the apostles and prophets, with Christ Jesus himself as the chief cornerstone. In him the whole building is joined together and rises to become a holy temple in the Lord. And in him you too are being built together to become a dwelling in which God lives by his Spirit (Ephesians 2:19-22).

4. Finally, the Kingdom pertains to a time of "future visible manifestation" which denotes a time in future world history when the kingdoms of this world will be cataclysmically confronted with the return of the Messiah (Jesus Christ) in triumphal judgment. "In the time of those kings, the God of heaven will set up a Kingdom that will never be destroyed, nor will it be left to another people. It will crush all those kingdoms and bring them to an end, but it will itself endure forever." (Daniel 2:44; Luke 1:32-33; Revelation 11:15; Matthew 25:31-32). "The seventh angel sounded his trumpet, and there were loud voices in heaven, which said: 'The kingdom of the world has become the

kingdom of our Lord and of his Christ, and he will reign forever and ever'" (Rev. 11:15).

Eschatological Meanings and Options

When one compares the preceding four aspects of God's governance with Jewish beliefs regarding the Kingdom of God/Heaven[93], a number of similarities and differences are immediately apparent. Both the Mishnah and Haggadah (liturgy of the Passover Seder), identify the Kingdom of Heaven as the reign or sovereignty of God as contrasted with the kingdom of worldly powers, which must be cleansed of all idolatry in order for God's kingdom to be realized on the earth.[94] Specifically, the Midrash (Cant. R. ii.12) prophesies, "when the Kingdom of Rome [with all of its many abominable idolatries] has ripened enough to be destroyed, the Kingdom of God will appear." However, the problem is that with the traditional fall of Rome date in the fifth century (AD 476) there has yet to be a universal appearance of God's Kingdom on earth. Indeed, dating the revelation of God's kingdom has led to a number of eschatological options that are virtually identical to Christianity.

For instance, Jewish scholars critique Christian eschatology by blaming the spiritualization of God's Kingdom on Roman antagonism. Christians, they criticize, introduced a prophetic dualism when it was not politically expedient to believe in the imminent return of Christ in the face of Roman persecution. As evidence, they cite the Apostle Paul's spiritual description of the Kingdom as "righteousness, peace, and joy in the Holy Spirit" (Rom. 14:17). However, even Jewish theology has a spiritualized view of the Kingdom of God as evidenced by a nearly identical comment by Rav in the Babylonian Talmud: "In the world to come, there will be neither eating nor drinking nor procreation nor business dealings nor jealousy nor hate nor competition [strife]. But righteous men will sit with crowns on their heads and they will enjoy the splendor of the Divine Presence [Shekinah]."[95]

Similar also to Christian eschatological options is the tethering of the expectation of God's Kingdom to the promised restoration of the nation of Israel (implying the themes of regathering and purification) and its concomitant rulership of the Moshiach/Messiah from the tribe of David (1 Sam. 13:14; 1 Kings 9:5).

Judaism and the Christian Church

"...I will build my church, and the gates of Hades will not overcome it" (Matt. 16:18).

"Consequently, you are no longer foreigners and aliens, but fellow citizens with God's people and members of God's household, built on the foundation of the apostles and prophets, with Christ Jesus himself as the chief cornerstone. In him the whole building is joined together... being built together to become a dwelling in which God lives by his Spirit" (Eph. 2:20).

Historians have long asserted that Christianity was considered a sect within Judaism, at least by the Romans, until the destruction of the second temple in Jerusalem and the ejection of the Jews in AD 70. However, long before this event, when Jesus first declared that he would build his church, the seeds of separation between Judaism and Christianity were already sown. Not that Jesus was inciting separation, but perhaps because he could prophetically discern that Jews would ultimately reject him, his message, and his disciples. Therefore, the church, as a necessarily separate institution from "historic Judaism" would need to be built in order for Jesus' global mission to be fulfilled (Matt. 28:18-20) and his disciples to be nurtured (Eph. 4:15-16).

First mentioned by Jesus, and then elaborated by the apostles after him, the Lord was building a new structure in the earth (called the Church) that will unite all open-hearted Jews and Gentiles under a New Covenant of grace rather than under the Old Covenant of Torah-righteousness (Phil. 3: 8-9). The Law of Moses was not going to be destroyed, but rather fulfilled in Christ's atoning sacrifice for sin and the gift of the indwelling Holy Spirit to empower believers to keep the Law-word of God from their heart. This New Covenant was already indicated throughout many places in the Tanakh including especially Jeremiah 31:31-34:

> The time is coming," declares the LORD, "when I will make a new covenant with the house of Israel and with the house of Judah. It will not be like the covenant I made with their forefathers when I took them by the hand to lead them out of Egypt

[under Moses' leadership], because they broke my covenant, though I was a husband to them," declares the LORD. "This is the covenant I will make with the house of Israel after that time," declares the LORD, "I will put my law in their minds and write it on their hearts...No longer will a man teach...his brother, saying, 'Know the LORD,' because they will all know me, from the least of them to the greatest," declares the LORD. "For I will forgive their wickedness and will remember their sins no more (Jer. 31:31-34).

Jesus definitively indicated that such a New Covenant was being inaugurated through his death on the cross. To that end he declared at the Last Supper, "This cup is the new covenant in my blood" (Luke 22:20). From now on, salvation was a communal act of sharing through ingesting the body and blood of Christ in symbolic form.[96] However, beyond the symbolism of the elements is the reality that believers have now been united with Christ and sustained in that unity by daily feeding on the living Word of God (Matt. 4:4). As a result, relationship with Christ would replace religious formalism as promoted by the externalistic interpretation of rabbinic traditions. Such a new covenant proposition was destined to jeopardize the status quo of the religious power brokers of Jesus' day. Predictably, Jesus encountered continual opposition from the Sadducees and Pharisees culminating in the Sanhedrin's (Jewish Supreme Court) decision to demand the death penalty for the apparent *seditious behavior* that Jesus was recommending against Rome (Mark 14:55-64; 15:1-15).

After Jesus' resurrection and the outpouring of the Holy Spirit on the Day of Pentecost (Act 2), one could reasonably estimate the growth of the early church into the tens of thousands within 10-15 years.[97] However, parallel to this explosive growth was the incessant opposition of the "Jewish leadership in Jerusalem"—comprised of the Sanhedrin and other "rulers, elders, and teachers of the law."[98] The crucifixion of Jesus was one thing, but now they had to deal with his disciples who were boldly declaring the bodily resurrection of Jesus from the dead (Acts 2:32). Furthermore, the preaching of these disciples-apostles was now very popular, especially since it was accompanied by similar miraculous signs and wonders that were characteristic of the ministry of Jesus himself.[99] The antagonism between the Jewish leadership and the Christian church in Jerusalem finally erupted with the martyrdom of Stephen (Acts 7) and the subsequent persecution and dispersion of Christians throughout Judea and Samaria (Acts 8:1). As a result, in addition to the crucifixion of Jesus, initial Jewish hostility, whether directly or indirectly, helped contribute to the Roman execution of two of the most seminal apostolic founders of the early church, Peter and Paul (Acts 12:3; 21:1-27:1).

Deicide or the *killing of god* has been the Christian accusation toward the Jews who have been collectively *held responsible for the death of Jesus*. It should be specially noted that after a long history of Jewish persecution by the Roman Catholic Church,[100] this charge of deicide as well as all direct and indirect anti-Semitism was decreed as unacceptable by Vatican II (1962):

> True, the Jewish authorities and those who followed their lead pressed for the death of Christ; still, what happened in His passion cannot be charged against all the Jews, without distinction, then alive, nor against the Jews of today. Although the Church is the new people of God, the Jews should not be presented as rejected or accursed by God, as if this followed from the Holy Scriptures...Furthermore, in her rejection of every persecution against any man, the Church, mindful of the patrimony she shares with the Jews and moved not by political reasons but by the Gospel's spiritual love, decries hatred, persecutions, displays of anti-Semitism, directed against Jews at any time and by anyone.[101]

Similar to Roman Catholics, Protestants have also been culpable for their own share of anti-Semitic bias, persecutions and injustices perpetrated against the Jewish people. In perhaps the most infamous book ever written by a Protestant reformer, Martin Luther wrote that the Jews were a "base, whoring people, that is, no people of God, and their boast of lineage, circumcision, and law must be accounted as filth."[102] They are full of the "devil's feces ... which they wallow in like swine," and the synagogue is an "incorrigible whore and an evil slut ..." He recommends that "their synagogues and schools be set on fire, their prayer books destroyed, rabbis forbidden to preach, homes razed, and property and money confiscated."[103] They should be shown "no mercy or kindness, afforded no legal protection, and these 'poisonous envenomed worms' should be drafted into forced labor or expelled for all time."[104] Many Lutheran church bodies, since the 1980's, have formally rejected Luther's writings on the Jews. For instance, in November 1998, the Lutheran Church of Bavaria issued the following statement:

> It is imperative for the Lutheran Church, which knows itself to be indebted to the work and tradition of Martin Luther, to take seriously also his anti-Jewish utterances, to acknowledge their theological function, and to reflect on their consequences. It has to distance itself from every [expression of] anti-Judaism in Lutheran theology."[105]

Unlike the acrimony within many Islamic countries against their Jewish neighbors,[106] within Christendom itself there has long been favorable relations—as evidenced by the pro-Israeli policies of the United States in which the vast majority of its citizenry are Christians (78.5%). This is undoubtedly why beyond Israel; the majority of Jews live in the U.S.[107]

- *Judaism* -

Pew Global Attitudes Project[108]

	Christians Fav %	Christians Unfav %	Jews Fav %	Jews Unfav %	Muslims Fav %	Muslims Unfav %
United States	87	6	77	7	57	22
Canada	83	9	78	11	60	26
Great Britain	85	6	78	6	72	14
France	84	15	82	16	64	34
Germany	83	13	67	21	40	47
Spain	80	10	58	20	46	37
Netherlands	83	15	85	11	45	51
Russia	92	3	63	26	55	36
Poland	86	5	54	27	46	30
Turkey	21	63	18	60	83	11
Pakistan	22	58	5	74	94	2
Indonesia	58	38	13	76	99	1
Lebanon	91	7	0	99	92	7
Jordan	58	41	0	100	99	1
Morocco	33	61	8	88	97	3
China	26	47	28	49	20	50
India	61	19	28	17	46	43

Chapter 4: Review Questions

1. What was the most interesting thing that you learned from Chapter 4 and why?
2. Why is AD 70 called the turning point in Jewish history?
3. What was a key component in God's promise to Abraham in Genesis 12?
4. What was the reason for and the result of the Maccabean revolt?
5. Define the three branches of Judaism in the 21st Century?

Chapter V

-Islam-

Introduction: Facts of Interest

Islam is the youngest and yet second largest religion in the world today with approximately 1.5 billion adherents.[109] The other major world religions, according to size and including date of origin, are Christianity (2.4 billion, First-Century A.D.), Islam (1.5 billion, Sixth Century A.D.), Hinduism (1 billion, 3,000 B.C.), Buddhism (375 million, Sixth Century B.C.), and Judaism (14.1 million, 3,000 B.C.).[110] Islam was formed in the historical context of, and with religious reference to, Judaism and Christianity. However, Islam considers both of these religions as distorted and in need of restoration and realignment with the religion of Islam.

Islam claims that it is a divinely revealed religion when, at the age of 40, Muhammad began to receive encounters with the angel Gabriel beginning in AD 610 "...This day have I perfected your religion for you, completed My favor upon you, and have chosen for you Islam as your religion."[111] Islam literally means *submission* or the total surrender of one's self to the will of *Allah*—which is the Arabic word of *God*. A Muslim is a follower of the Islamic faith and, by extension, means one who is submitted to the will of Allah. The two major sects within Islam are the Sunni (75%) and the Shiite (20%). For the first time in world history, there are now more Sunni Muslims than there are Roman Catholics.[112] However, unlike Roman Catholicism, there is no central teaching authority (Magisterium) or Vatican-like entity within Islam.

In 2007 there were an estimated 2.5 million Muslims living in the United States. The first U.S. Mosque was built in Cedar Rapids, Iowa in 1934. Fifty percent of all Muslims are African Americans. More than one million Muslims join in the annual Hajj pilgrimage to Mecca, Saudi Arabia. The Quran is four-fifths the size of the New Testament.

From here on, this chapter on Islam will be different from the last chapter on Judaism. The difference will be that the four criteria of a Christian critique (the Bible, Jesus Christ, the Kingdom of God, and the Christian Church) will be enjoined in the context of the proceeding historical and theological overview rather than waiting afterwards to engage such criteria.

Pre-Islamic Arab Religion

Islam began in the Arabian Desert in the cultural-historical context of Jewish, Christian, and Zoroastrian influences (Hopfe and Woodward, 2007, p. 320). In other words, these three religions pre-dated Islam by hundreds to thousands of years in the Arabian Peninsula—even though they were ostensibly on the periphery of social consciousness and conduct. The peripheral marginalization of these three monotheistic religions was because the Arabs, who preceded Muhammad and Islam, were polytheistic and animistic in their religious predilections. For instance, Allah, was the supreme High God (or moon god) surrounded by a lesser pantheon of gods, spirits, and demons (Hopfe and Woodward, 2007, p. 321). Furthermore the Kaaba Stone in Mecca, which also pre-dated Muhammad, was already an object of veneration and a center of idol worship. Indeed, the cultural significance of the Kaaba Shrine became a major source of pre-Islamic conflict among warring tribes who were eager to secure such a symbol of prominence in the region.

According to Muhammad, this polytheistic background into which he was born was virtually identical to the challenge of his patriarchal ancestor Abraham, who was personally called by God to renounce polytheism nearly 2,000 years before Muhammad's birth. In this way, Muhammad and all of Islam consider themselves the rightful heir of the covenant that God originally made with Abraham—especially since Ishmael (father of the Arabs) was the firstborn and hence the direct legal heir of Abraham. Indeed, the Old Testament promises that indicate that Abraham's second son, Isaac, who was 13 years younger, would be the principal heir of the covenant is offensive and blatantly denied as a Jewish redaction of the original story and text.[113]

> Then God said, "Yes, but your wife Sarah will bear you a son, and you will call him Isaac. I will establish my covenant with him as an everlasting covenant for his descendants after him. And as for Ishmael, I have heard you: I will surely bless him; I will make him fruitful and will greatly increase his numbers. He will be the father of twelve rulers, and I will make him into a great nation. But my covenant I will establish with Isaac, whom Sarah will bear to you by this time next year" (Genesis 17:19-21).

Muslims especially cry foul with the story recorded in Genesis 22 where God calls Abraham to sacrifice his son Isaac on Mt. Moriah. Rather than Isaac, the Quran insists, that Abraham took Ishmael to Mt. Marwah in Saudi Arabia, where Allah/God substituted a sheep or ram in place of Abraham's first born son Ishmael.[114] This story is central to the celebration of the annual Muslim holiday called the Feast of Sacrifice (Id al-Adha) and is held during the most holy month of Ramadan.

The Life of Muhammad (570-632)

The Prophet of Islam, Muhammad, was born in AD 570 and died in AD 632. The Islamic calendar however, does not follow the Gregorian calendar. Rather the Islamic calendar began on July 16, AD 622, which was the date of Muhammad's emigration to Medina called the Hijra. Accordingly, Muslims use the term A.H. meaning *Anno Hegirae*, or the year of the Hijra rather than A.D. or *Anno Domini*, which is the Christian designation for "in the year of our Lord."[115] Furthermore, since the Islamic calendar is a purely lunar calendar, it is shorter than the Gregorian calendar by about eleven days per year. As a result, the

Islamic Calendar will actually catch up with the Gregorian calendar on the first day of the fifth month of 20,874 A.D./A.H.[116]

This idea of a special religious calendar was undoubtedly borrowed from the Jewish Torah. For according to the book of Exodus, God/Yahweh commanded that the Jews keep a special religious calendar that began during the first Passover in Egypt just prior to Israel's exodus from 400 years of bondage: "The Lord said to Moses and Aaron in Egypt, 'This month is to be for you the first month, the first month of your year'" (Exodus 12:1-2).

Muhammad was an orphan whose father died before he was born. His mother also passed away when he was just six years of age. He was then raised by his grandfather, who died two years later, leaving the eight year old boy to the nurture of his uncle, Abu Talib.[117] Abu Talib was a merchant who was part of the Quarish clan, who were also responsible for the care, maintenance, and protection of the Kaaba Shrine in Mecca. Muhammad traveled extensively with his uncle in trading caravans throughout the Middle East becoming familiar with the cultures, religions and economy of the Arab peoples of the region.

At the age of 25, Muhammad married a wealthy 40 year old widow named Khadija, who financed and encouraged Muhammad's spiritual contemplations in the hillside of Mecca. Tradition even suggests that Khadija comforted and convinced a frightened Muhammad to continue his religious quest during his early days of intense uncertainty.[118] Indeed, Khadija was defended by Muhammad to his other future wives as the "only person who believed in him when all people disbelieved... and the only one to bear him children when all his [other] wives did not bear him children."[119] Khadija bore Muhammad two sons (who died in infancy) and four daughters. Muhammad also persuaded Khadija to purchase a slave named Zaid bin Haritha, whom he later adopted as his only legal son. Only after Khadija's death (after 25 years of marriage) did Muhammad begin to practice polygamy—marrying at least eleven other wives, including a nine year old girl (when he was 53) named Aisha.[120] Aisha was the daughter of Abu Bakr—a close confidant and advisor who later became the first successor-Caliph after Muhammad's death.

Muslim scholars defend Muhammad's polygamy on the grounds that it was often practiced in cultures of the Prophet's time and generally for inter-tribal political alliances, compassion toward widows of fallen comrades, and *affairs of the heart*—all of which were undoubtedly Muhammad's varied motivations.[121] In the New Testament, some 550 years earlier, the prohibition against polygamy was already established as the Christian norm—first hinted by Jesus and then affirmed by the Apostle Paul: "Haven't you read...that at the beginning the Creator made them male and female...and the two will be one flesh. So they are no longer two, but one. Therefore what God has joined together, let men not separate" (Matt. 19:4-6). "Now the overseer must be above reproach, the husband of but one wife..." (1 Tim. 3:2). The Islamic practices of polygamy and theocracy (covered later) are primary evidences that Muhammad drew more from the Old Testament model of Judaism than from the New Testament example of the Christian church.

Muhammad's Prophetic Ministry

Muhammad's prophetic ministry allegedly began in the hillside of the outskirts of Mecca, when in AD 610 the angel Gabriel appeared to him with divine revelations later to be coalesced into the Koran/Quran (lit. "recite").[122] Many Muslim scholars believe that the Quran was actually miraculously revealed to Muhammad chapter by chapter and letter by letter from a "mother book" in heaven to the Prophet on earth. Such revelations, be they angelically instigated, trance-induced, or signaled by the ringing of a bell, continued throughout the rest of Muhammad's life for more than 20 years.

Since many Islamic scholars claim that Muhammad was illiterate[123], the Quranic revelations were allegedly and eventually written down by his trusted confidants. However, others assert that more than a dozen individuals, including Muhammad himself—who must have been able to write as part of his career as a merchant[124], were involved in the authorship of the Quran. Specific individuals suggested are: Imrul Oays—and ancient poet of Arabia who died a few decades before Muhammad's birth, Salman—Muhammad's advisor, Bahira—a Nestorian monk of the Syrian church, Ibn Qumta—a Christian slave, Khadija—Muhammad's first wife, Jabr Qumta—a Christian slave, Murkhyariqu—a Rabbi and convert to Islam, etc.[125] Muhammad, say the secular skeptics, crafted the Quranic text for purely political reasons in order to build an Arabic empire on Islamic values.

Other biblical scholars point out that, similar to Mormonism, there might indeed be an angelic component to Islam, though such a angelic revelation would be part of a satanic deception intended to obfuscate the truth (2 Cor. 11:14; Gal. 1:8). Furthermore, since both Mormonism and Islam claim angelic revelation, there is an intrinsic prohibition against rational dispute of the Quran or of the Book of Mormon. After all, if an angel said it was from God, then it must be from God.

> The Qur'an is a Message from Allah to humanity. It was transmitted to us in a chain starting from the Almighty Himself to the angel Gabriel to the Prophet Muhammad... the Qur'an is quite literally the Word of Allah...The Qur'an has not been expressed using any human's words. Its wording is letter for letter fixed by no one but Allah.[126]

> I told the brethren that the Book of Mormon was the most correct of any book on earth...and a man would get nearer to God by abiding by its precepts, than by any other book...The ancient record...translated into modern speech by the gift and power of God as attested by Divine affirmation... (Joseph Smith Jr.)[127]

Therefore, all empirical questioning and disputations lead only to doubt and apostasy which must be resisted by the faithful. Contrary to these biases, the Bible engages the rational component of the believer by permitting and encouraging critical inquiry, empirical analysis, and ardent study in search and confirmation of the truth (Luke 1:1-4; Acts 17:11; 2 Tim. 2:15).

Rejection of Muhammad's Message

At the first preaching of Muhammad (AD 613), the Meccans were offended by his insistence that there was only one God and that idol worship was a grievous, though forgivable sin against the one true God— Allah. Gradually, Muhammad's message was received by a growing number of converts, which drew the consternation of the Meccan authorities, who viewed such preaching as an economic and religious affront to their cultural sensitivities and stability. Finally, when a plot to assassinate Muhammad was discovered, he escaped to Yathrib, which was about 300 kilometers (200+ miles) to the north of Mecca.[128]

This escape or emigration from Mecca to the oasis of Yathrib was called the Hijra and, as previously stated, marks the beginning (year 1) of the Muslim holy calendar. Rivalry between Yathrib and Mecca helped to garner Muhammad a warm reception by the people of Yathrib—who eventually renamed the city Madinat al Nabi (Medina), the "city of the Prophet." Indeed, in Medina, Muhammad was awarded positions as a political arbitrator, chief legislator, military leader, and finally head of state. At Medina, Muhammad even established the first theocratic state that was based on Islamic, or Sharia Law. Unfortunately, tensions between the wealthy Jewish population of Yathrib and Muhammad resulted in the annihilation/decapitation of some 600-900 men at the direct behest of Muhammad who had just then received "permission from the angel Gabriel" to violate two previous treaties and to slaughter the Jews as Allah's enemies.[129]

Indeed, the military battles and bloodshed of Muhammad mark the most obvious differences between him and Jesus. For Muhammad, similar to the Old Testament battles of Joshua to subdue the Promise Land, insisted that he was being directed by the angel of Allah to undertake military campaigns against the enemies of Allah. Jesus, on the other hand, advocated against all violence in his ministry and life style to establish God's kingdom on earth. And whereas Muhammad fought under a black banner of vengeance, Jesus left all vengeance to the Father in his mission to redeem humanity by his substitutionary death for sin and victorious resurrection life.

With Muhammad's increasing military authority in Medina, he amassed an army of more than 10,000 soldiers in order to especially address the deteriorating relationship with the neighboring Meccans. Finally, in 630 Muhammad marched on Mecca, wherein the majority of the city was willing to surrender to both the ominous Muslim force and political negotiation skill of Muhammad—who promised not to destroy the Kaaba stone, but instead to thereafter promote Kaaba pilgrimages as a central feature of the new Islamic religion.[130] The political negotiations effectively resulted in the conversion of the vast majority of the Meccan population who were also willing to witness a destruction of all idols sparing only the sacred Black Stone of the Kaaba Shrine. The celebration of the near bloodless conquest of Mecca is contained in the Quran: "When comes the Help of Allah, and Victory, and thou dost see the People enter Allah's Religion in crowds" (Quran 110:1-2).

For the next two years Muhammad was engaged in a number of strategic military campaigns whereby he succeeded in conquering (by force and/or negotiation) virtually all of the remaining tribes—including the Bedouins of Arabia. Thus, by the end of Muhammad's life he had effectively established a singular monolithic Muslim religious theocracy throughout the Arabian Peninsula.

Farewell Pilgrimage of Muhammad

Muhammad's first official Islamic pilgrimage to Mecca was to be his last. During this inaugural pilgrimage he delivered what was to become his farewell speech (Khutbat al-Wadaa') in which he solemnized Islam as the true global religion of Allah, upheld the sacredness of four lunar months of each year, encouraged vigilance against Satan (Iblis), abolished old blood feuds between former tribal systems, mandated keeping the Five Pillars of Islam (creed recital, daily prayers, fasting, almsgiving, and Hajj), encouraged men to treat their wives fairly, forbade false claims to paternity, etc.[131] Shortly after this speech Muhammad became ill from being poisoned by his Jewish chef, following his attack upon and conquest of the Jewish settlement of Khaibar. At 63 Muhammad died on June 8, 632 in Medina in the arms of his favorite child-bride wife, Aisha, who was then 18 years old.

The Rise of the Caliphate Empires (632-1918)

The Four Rightly-Guided Caliphs (632-661)

After the death of Muhammad, a dispute of historic proportions arose as to who should succeed "the Prophet." The next four successors became known as the four "rightly guided" Caliph's and include, Abu Bakr, Umar, Uthman, and then Ali. It should be noted that the Shia (lit. "party of Ali") sect rejects the first three caliphs in favor of Ali, whom they insist was the rightful designated heir of Muhammad from the beginning, especially since Ali was Muhammad's cousin and son-in-law (McDowell and Stewart, 1983, p. 381-382). The Sunni (lit. "way of the Prophet") sect prefers communal elections over the notion of genealogical inheritance and accepts Ali as the fourth Caliph. These four initial Caliphs expanded the territories under Muslim rule into much of Persia and Byzantine, thus creating one of the most powerful states of the Middle East at the time.

The Umayyad Caliphate-Dynasty (661-750)

After the assassination of Ali, Mu'awiyah (d. 680) forcefully assumed power and initiated the Umayyad Empire (661-750). From their capital city of Damascus, the Umayyad Caliphate expanded the borders of the Muslim world to North Africa, Spain and France in the West and to Central Asia and the western border of China in the East. The Umayyads are credited for having established the basic social and legal institutions of the Islamic world. However, they were greatly criticized for turning the Caliphate away from its origin as a religious institution and into a dynastic kingship where upper class elitists marginalized the lower class and religious scholars.[132] The Umayyads also constructed famous buildings such as the Dome of the Rock at Jerusalem, and the Umayyad Mosque at Damascus.[133]

The Abbasid Caliphate Empire (750-1258)

After the Umayyad Dynasty the Abbasid Empire arose on a wave of idealism fostered by the popular revolutionary, Abu Muslim. The Abbasid Empire ushered in what has been called the Islamic Golden Age or Islamic Renaissance, with Baghdad as its cosmopolitan capital. This new age of Islamic learning resulted in many new legal, philosophical, and religious developments. Of major theological significance were the codification and standardization of the Hadith, the recognition of the four major schools of Sunni thought, development of mystical Sufism, scholastic confrontation with western philosophical thought, and Shia divisions over the succession of Imams.[134] Tangential to religious-theological developments, the Islamic Golden Age also made significant contributions to art, agriculture, mathematics (specifically the invention of algebra), economics, industry, law, literature, navigation, etc.

However, winds of demise for the Abbasid Empire began to blow in the 9th century—lasting nearly 750 years, when the Reconquista (reconquering) occurred. The Reconquista was a military campaign whereby the Christian kingdoms in the region of the Iberian Peninsula (modern Spain) systematically subdued the lands that were previously lost to the conquering Muslims.[135] In the 11th century another alliance between the European Christian kingdoms was formed to launch a series of military campaigns called the Crusades against the Muslim occupation of the Holy Land. Finally, in the East, the Mongol Empire, led by Genghis Khan's grandson, destroyed the remaining stronghold of the Abbasid dynasty at the Battle of Baghdad in 1258, a battle in which over a million Muslims were killed, bringing to an end a remarkable Era in Islamic history.

The Ottoman Empire: The Final Caliphate

For over six centuries (1299 to 1923) the Ottoman-Turkish Empire was the dominant Islamic dynasty between the Eastern and Western world (Swartley, 2005, p. 49). With its capital at Constantinople, the Ottoman Empire occupied the territories around both the Mediterranean and Black seas. Deemed the last Islamic Caliphate, the Ottoman Empire was, in many ways, the successor to the earlier Roman and Byzantine empires. The demise of the Ottoman Empire (1828-1908) was the result of many things including, a failure in its economic structure, poor communication technologies, tensions among the different ethnic groups, slowness of reform, the emerging nationalistic and secessionist sentiments, and the rise of Western colonialism. The final dissolution (1908-1922) of the Ottoman Empire came as a direct result of its siding with the Central Powers of Germany, Austria-Hungary, and Italy against the "Allied Powers" (Triple Entente) in World War I. The dissolution of the Ottoman Empire brought about the creation of the modern Arab world (Saudi Arabia, Iraq, Iran, Egypt, Lebanon, Palestine, Jordan, Sudan, Syria, etc.) and the Republic of Turkey.[136]

Islam: 1920's to the Present

East vs. West: A Clash of Cultures

A number of the main factors that have influenced Islamic history since the 1920's are the identification of the Ottoman successor states, the adoption of various models of European nationalism (Egypt and Syria), the attempt to introduce the secular notion of the separation of church-Islam and state (Turkey), and the embrace of radical strains of anti-west propaganda in the form of Wahhabism (Saudi Arabia), which has led to jihadist terrorism against the United States (killing 3,000 on 9/11/2001) and other western nations and their allies.[137] This Wahhabi radicalism,[138] at the behest of Osama bin Laden (the founder of the jihadist group called Al-Qaeda), resulted in fifteen of the nineteen hijackers on 9/11 coming from Saudi Arabia, even though the Saudi rulers insist they reject this heretical form of Islamic extremism. Still such phobia and hatred of the west runs deep within the psyche of fundamentalist Islamic people and some countries—who still blame the west for the Crusades, colonialism, and the fracturing of the Islamic Empire (Ottoman) leading to the massive poverty and disorientation of the modern Islamic world (Swartley, 2005, p. 49).

For instance, this clash of cultures was clearly represented in 2005 when a Danish newspaper published cartoons of the prophet Muhammad, including one with a bomb on his head, drawn by Jullands-Posten. Part of the purpose for printing potentially inflammatory pictures was to critique Islamic censorship in Denmark. Predictably, much of the Islamic world erupted with public riots (killings over 100 people), burning of embassies, storming European buildings, desecrating flags and death threats from Hamas and others calling for the blasphemers of the Prophet to have their "hands and heads cut off."[139]

Further inflaming the situation, a liberal news commentator rather arrogantly declared to the effect that *"Muslims will just have to learn that democracy means that we have the right to blaspheme."* But, is this really what freedom of speech means in a democratic society? Does freedom actually give us the right to purposefully offend and even blaspheme the religious sentiments of others?[140] And though no one is ever justified in killing others over a religious icon, it does seem incredibly obnoxious to incite the deepest passions in differing others in the name of freedom. Freedom, after all, is not the right to do what we want, but the power to do what we ought or that which we should.

Wisely did Viktor Frankl[141] call for a cultural iconic balance to the Statue of Liberty on the east coast with a Statue of Responsibility on the west coast of the United States. Indeed, with every right comes a responsibility to freely use that right for the good of others rather than rudely abuse our rights in order to purposefully and offensively mock and insult others. This issue is addressed in principle in the New Testament by the Apostle Paul in 1 Corinthians chapter eight: "Be careful, however, that the exercise of your freedom does not become a stumbling block to the weak" (1 Cor. 8:5; see also Rom. 14). Suffice it to say that there are extremely radical elements in Islam that must be resisted. However, there are also radical freedoms in the West that must be exercised in wisdom, grace, and love for the good of one's fellow-man. To not understand both sides of the issue is to continually court conflict and hinder the larger purpose of promoting the Constitutional objective of the *common good* by the "consent of the governed."[142]

Arab-Israeli Conflict

Another historic development in Islam is the current Arab-Israeli conflict in the Middle East. The more immediate circumstance behind the conflict was when in 1947, the United Nations approved the partition of the British Mandate of Palestine into two states, one Jewish and one Arab.[143] The Arab League protested the plan, which meant certain displacement of the Arabs living on the land partitioned for the Jewish state of Israel. Nevertheless, Israel declared itself an independent nation on May 14, 1948, one day before the expiration of the British Mandate of Palestine, thus resulting in the Arab-Israeli War.

Other Developments: India, OPEC, Iran and Iraq

Four other historic developments that have direct bearing on Islam in the world today are the partition of India, the oil wealth of OPEC member nations, the Iranian revolution, and western allied wars with Iraq. First, the partitioning of India in 1947 has resulted in three of the largest Muslim nations in the world outside of Indonesia (India, Pakistan, and Bangladesh) with Pakistan being the sole Muslim nation with nuclear weaponry. The concern here is that radical Muslims will succeed in their repeated attempts to assassinate the former pro-west President, Pervez Musharraf, and seize control of the nation's nuclear weapons.

Second, the oil wealthy countries of Islam have dominated OPEC[144] from the beginning and have used their collective power to manipulate oil prices and embargos against any nations with whom they have political disagreements—as demonstrated in the 1973 embargos against nations in support of Israel including the US. Third, the Iranian revolution of 1979 saw the rise of a new Islamic republic under the "supreme leadership" of the radical Shia cleric Ayatollah Khomeini. Such a Shia revolution was considered a threat to the region as well as to the West, as evidenced by the Iran Hostage Crisis. As a result, regional Arab and global powers (US and USSR) united to oppose Iran, by among other ways, in their support of the President of Iraq, Saddam Hussein, in his war with Iran. Even today, Iran's President (Mahmoud Ahmadinejad) and its "Supreme Leader" (Grand Ayatollah Ali Khamenei) continue their anti-west propaganda and their call to destroy the nation of Israel and anyone else who supports the "Zionist pigs."[145] The concern here is that Iran will continue to seek to develop nuclear technology/weaponry thus destabilizing the region again with its anti-west rhetoric and acquired capability.

Finally, the wars with Iraq specifically imply the Persian Gulf War (1990-1991) to liberate oil-rich Kuwait from Iraqi invasion and the Iraq war (2003 to 2011) to capture and/or destroy Osama Bin Laden and his Al-Qaeda network for their terrorist attacks on the United States, September 11, 2001. The concern here is that since the US has not been able to decisively win the war against Al Qaeda in Iraq that this could suggest an attempt to broaden the conflict with Islamic terrorists on the back of the general anti-west sentiments throughout the Islamic world. However, the killing of Osama Bin Laden by the United States on May 2, 2011 signaled the end of the Iraq War and the splintering of Al Qaeda.

Islamic Theology: The Five Pillars of Islam

"The Messenger of Allah (may the blessings and peace of Allah be upon him) said: Islam is to testify that there is no god but Allah and Muhammad is the Messenger of Allah, to perform the prayers, to pay the Zakat, to fast in Ramadan, and to make the pilgrimage to the House if you are able to do so."[146] The primary obligation of every Muslim is to practice the Five Pillars of Islam. The Five Pillars are the Shahada (creed), the Salat (prayers), the Zakat (almsgiving), Sawn (fasting), and Hajj (pilgrimage). To these Five Pillars the Shia have added a sixth pillar called Jihad (struggle or holy war).

Shahada: The Islamic Creed

As referenced above, the creed of Islam is: *"Ilaha illa Allah. Muhammad rasul Allah"* — "There is no god but Allah, and Muhammad is his messenger" (Quran 3:18 & 33:40). Wholehearted declaration of this creed automatically makes one a Muslim thereby qualifying such a confessor the right to membership in the community (umma) of the faithful.[147] This creed is also recited fourteen times in the daily prayers. It is whispered into the ear of every newborn Muslim child and also at the time of one's death. Muslims find in this creed a "road map for life" by their declared submission to Allah and devotion to following the example of their final prophet, Muhammad.

This radical submission to Allah is one of the central most articles of Islam. "It is not piety that you turn your faces towards East or West — but truly pious is he who believes in Allah and the Last Day, and the Angels, and the Book of the Messengers" (Quran 2:177). In Islam, belief in Allah (the Arabic word for "God") is one of the six articles of faith. Judaism also has a creed called the Shema with a similar commitment to the monotheistic nature of the one true God, "Hear oh Israel: the Lord our God, the Lord is one" (Deut. 6:5).

Historians are quick to point out that Allah (whose symbol was the crescent moon) was originally the pre-Islamic name for the pagan moon-god. For instance, in ancient Syria and Canaan the moon-god "Sin" was often symbolically represented by the crescent moon. Furthermore, sacrifices to the moon-god are described in many ancient pre-Islamic texts including the Pas Shamra texts and the Ugaritic texts." In Egypt and Persia, the moon-god was also engraved on murals and the heads of statues.[148] Even throughout the Old Testament the worship of the moon was a pagan cult that was strictly forbidden in the Torah as idolatry.[149]

A survey of the Quran reveals that there are 99 different names for Allah/God including Creator, Just, Absolute, Beneficent, Eternal, etc. One name however that is conspicuously absent from the Quran is "Father." Many scholars believe this is direct contradiction to Jesus' teaching in the Sermon on the Mount, where Jesus refers to God as "Father" some seventeen times. Indeed, in the Quran itself, Allah directly contradicts the "Trinitarian" concept of God: "They surely disbelieve who say: Lo! Allah is the third of three: when there is no

God save the One God. If they desist not from so saying a painful doom will fall on those of them who disbelieve." (Quran 5:73-74)

Christian theologians counter this text by pointing out the Muslim misunderstanding of the Trinity, or the three-fold unity of the one God, rather than tri-theism, or there being three separate gods. Classical Islamic theology also emphasizes the radical transcendence of God to such a degree that, similar to Hinduism, God (Brahman/Allah) is impersonal and unknowable. This doctrinal approach to the knowledge of God was countered by Sufism (7th century), which is a mystical tradition within Islam (both Shia and Sunni) whose objective is the personal and spiritual unity of the worshipper with Allah through contemplation and ecstatic heart devotion.[150]

Salat: The Daily Prayers

Sunni Muslims pray five times a day: at dawn, noon, mid-afternoon, sunset, and bedtime.[151] As a Muslim enters into prayer they must be mindful of a number of things including, the necessary cleanness of body, clothes, and place of prayer. This is why carpets are often placed on the ground upon which to kneel in prayer. This requirement of prayerful purity also explains why ritual ablutions (washings) must be performed if unclean.[152] From a Christian perspective, this detail to physical purity in prayer can place too much emphasis on the external body rather than the internal condition of the heart. Furthermore, such customs can pose a legalistic imposition upon the individual rather than a grace-based motivation from within the heart of the worshipper. This can result in a self-righteousness that is more earned by performance than faith-righteousness, which is received by grace.

Jesus and the Apostle Paul give the New Testament critique of such religious practices that have the appearance of religious efficacy but render little to no true value to one's relationship with the Lord:

> Woe to you teachers of the law and Pharisees, you hypocrites! You clean the outside of the cup and dish, but inside they are full of greed and self-indulgence. Blind Pharisee! First clean the inside of the cup and dish, and then the outside also will be clean (Matt. 23: 25-26).

These are matters which have, to be sure, the appearance of wisdom in self-made religion and self-abasement and severe treatment of the body, but are of no value against fleshly indulgence (Col. 2:20-23).

...that I may gain Christ, and may be found in Him, not having a righteousness of my own derived from the Law, but that which is through faith in Christ, the righteousness which comes from God on the basis of faith (Phil. 3: 8-9).

In Islamic prayer, women are required to cover their hair and bodies as a sign of modesty and dignity—as well as to protect them from the lustful gaze of men.[153] Christianity also teaches that women should "dress modesty, with decency and propriety" (1 Tim. 2:9), which are all virtually disregarded in western cultures. However, the requirement to wear *head covering* as well as the Islamic requirement that women must be completely covered from head to foot "showing only the hands and face" is more a cultural custom than continual biblical command.[154]

Finally, all Islamic prayer should be performed facing Mecca, which is the birth place of Muhammad and the location of the Kaaba Shrine—the central feature of the annual pilgrimage of Islam. The directionality of Christian prayer is from the heart of a spiritually empowered worshipper and toward a loving heavenly father, who in Christ, has determined to glorify himself by establishing his kingdom (will, purpose, sovereign destiny) in the lives of all who unreservedly trust him. And because God's kingdom is ubiquitous, there is no need to direct our prayers in the direction of any particular human location.

Zakat: Almsgiving

Zakat means *purification* and *growth*.[155] Muslims regard their income as an entrustment from Allah and are therefore obligated to purify their income (if they have earned any and generally after bills are paid) by returning to Allah a portion (one fortieth, or 2.5%) annually. Specifically, this alms tax is used for proselytizing, to free Islamic slaves, to relieve the debt of the poor, support needy travelers, given to Islamic clerics, etc. Shia Muslims pay two different kinds of alms:

Kohms (*the fifth*) and Zakat, which are alms due on certain goods like gold, silver, camels, cows, etc. The *growth* meaning of Zakat is associated with the principle of pruning, whereby the cutting back of plants causes balance and growth—so too does the giving of one's alms facilitate economic growth through the reward of Allah toward faithful Muslims.

The giving of the Zakat is similar to the commandment of tithing (a tenth, or 10%) in Judaism.[156] However, whereas both the Old Testament law of tithing and the Islamic law of Zakat is a legal and/or religious obligation, the New Testament argues more from the conscience-based principle of voluntary generosity in one's faithful giving rather than a religious requirement for righteousness with God. "Remember this: Whoever sows sparingly will also reap sparingly, and whoever sows generously will also reap generously. Each man should give what he has decided in his heart to give, not reluctantly or under compulsion, for God loves a cheerful giver" (2 Cor. 9:6-7).

It is true that some fundamentalist Christian churches still teach tithing as a pre-Mosaic rule/law that must be specifically obeyed today. Still, other evangelicals interpret the rather conspicuous absence of a lawful requirement to tithe in the epistles as an invitation to cultivate a New Covenant grace-based conviction. Such a conviction will seek to lovingly honor God from the first-fruits of all that one earns (Prov. 3:9-10) and to cheerfully contribute one's means as an act of worship to a God who rewards faith and faithfulness (2 Cor. 9:5-8).

Sawn: Fasting

Each year all able adult Muslims, except children, the sick, the elderly, those traveling, or pregnant or nursing mothers, are enjoined to fast the entire month of Ramadan.[157]

> The month of Ramadan in which was revealed the Qur'an, a guidance for mankind, and clear proofs of the guidance, and the Criterion (of right and wrong). And whosoever of you is present, let him fast the month, and whosoever of you is sick or on a journey, (let him fast the same) number of other days. Allah desireth for you ease; He desireth not hardship for you; and (He

desireth) that ye should complete the period, and that ye should magnify Allah for having guided you, and that peradventure ye may be thankful (Quran 2:185).

Any of those who are not able to fast during the ninth month are required to make up an equal numbers of days later that year. If for some reason the person is still unable to physically abstain from food, they can still fulfill the required fast by feeding a needy person for each day that was missed. From puberty, all children are required to observe the fast of Ramadan, though many begin much earlier. During the fast, there must be complete abstention from food, drink, smoking and sexual relations from sunrise to sunset. Concomitant to the physical requirement of the fast there is also a moral-behavioral responsibility on the worshipper to intentionally abstain from lying, malicious gossip, quarreling, and trivial nonsense.[158]

The primary purpose of fasting is for *self-purification*. In the denial of worldly comforts the participating Muslim thereby gains greater empathy for the poor and needy, as well as learning self-discipline, patience, and flexibility. Indeed, a primary focus of the Sawn is to enhance one's spiritual life. This is done through the encouragement to personally read the entire Quran during the month and to participate in special prayers held each night. The nightly prayer services in the mosque include recitation of large sections of the Quran so that by the end of Ramadan the entire Quran is heard quoted. These special prayer services are in commemoration of Muhammad receiving the very first Quranic revelations in AD 610.

Sometime during the last ten days of Ramadan is held the Night of Power (Laylatul-Qadr).[159] By attending this all night worship service Muslims believe they can "gain extra credit of righteousness" by earning one thousand months of credit and that special future blessings for the coming year will be sovereignly decreed upon those attending.

Lo! We revealed it on the Night of Predestination. Ah, what will convey unto thee what the Night of Power is! The Night of Power is better than a thousand months. The angels and the Spirit descend therein, by the permission of their Lord, with all decrees. (The night is) Peace until the rising of the dawn (Quran 97:1-5).

The fast is broken the first day of the tenth month (Shawwal), at which time the feast of Eid ul-Fitr is celebrated. The feast consists of a donation of food to the poor, communal prayer in the morning, and the rest of the day of visiting with family, relatives, and friends. And though Muslims are encouraged to fast throughout the year on Mondays and Thursdays, there is strict condemnation toward excessive withdrawal from the world, which Islam sees prevalent in Roman Catholicism, including excessive fasting, monasticism, and celibacy. This Islamic criticism of Roman Catholicism is echoed in Scripture where Paul argues against both harsh treatment of the body in the name of spirituality (Gnosticism) and any religious requirement of enforced celibacy (Col. 2:23; 1 Tim.4:3).

Hajj: The Pilgrimage

Once in the life time of every able bodied Muslim who can afford to do so is the obligation to attend the Hajj—thereupon earning the title Hajji. The Hajj occurs on every 12th month (Dhu' al-Hijjah) of the Islamic lunar calendar. Though the Hajj predates Islam, Muhammad promised the Meccan people that he would continue to make the Hajj, minus its former polytheistic components, a central feature of Islam by ordaining the Kaaba Shrine as the House of God from then on. All male pilgrims on the Hajj are required to dress in two white sheets and sandals. The white dress (Ihram clothing) is intended to symbolize purity from sins and equality of all men before Allah. While wearing the Ihram clothing on the Hajj, no one can shave, clip their nails, wear deodorant or perfume, quarrel, kill any living thing, or engage in sexual intercourse.

The pilgrimage around Mecca involves ritual symbolic re-enactments of the lives of Abraham (Ibrahim) and his concubine-wife Hagar (Hajar). Such rituals include, among other things, circumambulating the Kaaba Stone seven times, offering prayers in the "Place of Abraham" (Muqaam E Ibrahim), and running or walking seven times back and forth between the hills of Safa and Marwah (*sa`i*). Legend suggests that it was here that Hagar was frantically looking for water for Ishmael when an angel spared their lives by revealing to them the Zamzam Well. The pilgrims must also visit Mount Arafat near a hill from which Muhammad gave his farewell sermon shortly before he died. Here pilgrims spend the day in contemplative vigil. Afterwards the pilgrims collect 49 stones each as they journey to Mina where they will perform the "Stoning of the Devil" ritual thus ending the Hajj proper, which has lasted for three days. This stoning signifies Abraham's trial regarding God's command to sacrifice of his son Ishmael.

> And when (his son) was old enough to walk with him, (Abraham) said: O my dear son, I have seen in a dream that I must sacrifice thee. So look, what thinkest thou? He said: O my father! Do that which thou art commanded. Allah willing, thou shalt find me of the steadfast. Then, when they had both surrendered (to Allah), and he had flung him down upon his face, We called unto him: O Abraham! Thou hast already fulfilled the vision. Lo! thus do We reward the good. Lo! that verily was a clear test. Then We ransomed him with a tremendous victim. And We left for him among the later folk (the salutation): Peace be unto Abraham! (Quran 37:102-109)[160]

Though repeatedly tempted by satan, Abraham resists each time. As a reward for Abraham's faithfulness, his son is not sacrificed but spared by God providing a ram in Ishmael's stead. Though not an official part of the pilgrimage, many Muslims also visit the city of Medina in order to see the Mosque of the Prophet in which Muhammad's tomb is contained.

Though the Hajj is in principle similar to kinds of pilgrimages made by Christians to Jerusalem to revisit the stages of the life of Jesus Christ, it nevertheless contradicts the biblical story of Genesis 22. For in this story Abraham does not take Ishmael to Mount Marwah near Mecca but rather Isaac to Mount Moriah near Jerusalem. As referenced earlier in this chapter, Muslims insist that the Jews have corrupted the biblical text in violation of Middle East custom to always honor the firstborn son above the others.

Jihad: The Sixth Pillar of Shia Islam

Jihad literally means struggle, striving, or *Holy War*. Over 160 times throughout the Quran,[161] Muhammad encouraged his followers to undertake holy war on behalf of Allah.

They ask thee (O Muhammad) of the spoils of war. Say: The spoils of war belong to Allah and the messenger, so keep your duty to Allah, and adjust the matter of your difference, and obey Allah and His messenger, if ye are (true) believers." (Quran 8:1) "Let those fight in the way of Allah who sell the life of this world for the other. Whoso fighteth in the way of Allah, be he slain or be he victorious, on him We shall bestow a vast reward (Quran 4:74).

There are however, many definitions and denials regarding the term "jihad." Some definitions include a "greater and lesser jihad," which are described as the striving against sin (in order to be a more moral person) and/or an armed military conflict, respectively. Most Shia Muslims argue that the prevalence of the call to jihad throughout the Quran ostensibly makes it the Sixth Pillar of Islam. On the other hand, most Sunni Muslims insist that there are only Five Pillars and that to argue otherwise is heretical and that it tends to cast doubt on the "peaceful" nature of Islam. Comprehensively speaking, there are at least four major categories of jihad that are now generally agreed upon including: Jihad against one's own self *(Jihad al-Nafs)*—in moral self-perfection against evil; Jihad of the tongue *(Jihad al-lisan)*—rhetorical defense of Islam; Jihad of the hand/pen *(Jihad al-yad)*; Jihad of the sword *(Jihad as-sayf)*—a state sanctioned offensive or defensive military campaign.[162]

Of these four categories, the Jihad of the sword is the most problematic. The problem is that Islam is founded upon the right and responsibility to wage war on behalf of Allah. In other words, Islam is a non-negotiable theocratic[163] state, where "separation of church and state" are blasphemous western innovations against the rule of God/Allah. Needless to say, this is in direct opposition to the words of Jesus Christ, who specifically disallows any and all of his followers to mount military campaigns (offensively or defensively) in behalf of the Kingdom of God: "Jesus said, 'My kingdom is not of this world. If it were, my servants would fight to prevent my arrest by the Jews. But now my Kingdom is from another place.'" (John 18:36)

This prohibition is one of the great motivations for the modern idea of the separation of church and state. For it is by the creation of the "separate state" that the governmental necessity of laws against crimes, the punishment of willful criminals (including capital punishment), and even the concept of just war[164] can be rightly effected by the "consent of the governed"—be they Christian and/or non-Christians. In this way, Christians have been able to reconcile the just requirement of the defense of the innocent, while at the same time assuring that their more purely religious concerns (kingdom and church) could thereby be shielded from the mundane though necessary lawful issues of the state.

In other words, Christians have dual citizenship (heavenly and earthly) with rights and responsibilities in both realms. And though both realms should, from a Christian perspective, seek a mutually agreeable integration, the victory of the heavenly battle is already assured—without the resort to physical violence, by virtue of Christ's triumph over sin and death.[165] As a result, there is no need to utilize earthly weapons of war because the battle (jihad) in which Christians are engaged is fundamentally spiritual in nature:

> For though we live in the world, we do not wage war as the world does. The weapons we fight with are not the weapons of the world. On the contrary, they have divine power to demolish [spiritual] strongholds..." (2 Cor. 10:3-4).

> For our struggle is not against flesh and blood, but against the rulers, against the authorities, against the power of this dark world and against the spiritual forces of evil in the heavenly realms (Eph. 6:12).

Chapter 5: Review Questions

1. What was the most interesting thing that you learned from Chapter 5 and why?
2. Who was/is the founder of Islam, and how was Islam established?
3. From whom were the Arabs descended? How does this help to explain the Arab and Israeli conflict today?
4. In addition to Zoroastrianism, what were the other two religions that influenced Muhammad the most? Hint: These two are called the people of the Book in the Quran.
5. How are the Book of Mormon and the Quran similar?

Chapter VI

-Hinduism-

Hinduism is one of the oldest[166] and also the third largest (1 billion) of the major world religions today. Hindu was an ancient Sanskrit name for the Indus (or Sindhu) river, which was one of the most important rivers in the Indian subcontinent. Previously occupied by an advanced civilization[167] for over 1,000 years, around 1750 BCE to 1200 BCE, the Indus Valley became home to the Aryans, who either co-opted this region that was now in decline and/or conquered it by force. The Aryans were a nomadic-migrant people from Iran. The non-migrating ancestors of the Aryans founded the religion of Zoroastrianism in the 9th and 10th centuries BCE, as well as the Persian Empire in the Sixth through the Fourth centuries BCE. In fact, the modern name *Iran* means "land of the Aryans." Even though Hinduism claims to be an eternal religion (without beginning or end), most scholars agree that it was the result of the cultural combination of the pre-Aryan natives and the Aryan nomads that formed much of the foundation of classical Hinduism. As a result, it is very difficult to discern the demarcation between the pre-Aryans and Aryans, especially since much of the Aryan literature refuses to acknowledge the pre-Aryan cultural contributions that archeologists and historians insist was prevalent.

The Aryans were led by tribal chieftains called *rajas* who began to develop minor kingdoms in the Sixth century BCE. Early Aryan society consisted of three basic "classes of people" called *varnas* (lit. "Colors") that later became the basis of the Indian caste system.[168] These ancient classes of people were the traveling cult priests called *Brahmins*, the rulers (chieftains and warriors) called *Kshatriyas*, and the craftsmen and merchants called *Vaishyas*. The pre-Aryans also had a sub-class called the *Shudra* indicating the non-citizens and slaves.

The earliest record of the Aryan religion[169] is contained in the Vedic literature. Similar to the Quran, which Muslims maintain as divinely revealed, so too does Hindu tradition insist that the Vedas are *apauruseya* or "not of human agency." Rather, the Vedas are knowledge that has been directly revealed from the divine to human. This belief is the basis of eastern mantraism or chanting, whereby repeating the exact wording (sound vibrations) of a sacredly revealed text is alleged to have the power to deliver the mind from illusion and material inclinations. As a result, the mantra sounds themselves are manifestations of ultimate reality and have inherent meaning independent of the understanding of the person uttering them.[170]

This eastern non-cognitive muttering of sounds, such as the syllable "Aum" in the quest of spiritual enlightenment, was similar in principle to what Jesus had in mind when he prohibited such "vain repetitions and babbling" in prayer (Matt. 6:7). Indeed, Christianity is not to be a preoccupation with superstition as is often evoked in repetitive prayers as in the *Our Father* and the *Hail Mary*. This does not mean that Christians cannot earnestly repeat a prayer or even pray for an extended period of time. However, all prayer must be moderated by a purity of motive (before God vs. man), sincerity of heart (genuine expression of faith), and a trust in God—who is much more responsive to relationship than to mystical repetition. And while it is true that the nature of Christian reality is beyond the mere rational comprehension of humanity, this does not imply that our rationality should be necessarily denied in our quest for relationship with God. Quite the contrary, the Bible often exhorts believers to engage their minds in pursuit of godliness. "Jesus replied: 'Love the Lord your God with all your heart, and with all your soul, and with all your mind'" (Matt. 22:37). "Be renewed in the spirit of your mind" (Eph. 4:23). "The mind set on the flesh is death, but the mind set on the spirit is life and peace" (Rom. 8:6).

It should be here noted that there is a biblical phenomenon called "speaking in tongues" (lit. *glossolalia*, in Greek)[171] in which nonsensical ecstatic utterances (1 Cor. 14:14-16), prompted by the Spirit of God, are expressed by Christians in prayer and praise to God.[172] Such utterances, though they are clearly spiritual in nature, can however be interpreted in the language of the speaker[173] so as to reveal the mind and heart of God in a given situation and/or to a particular person.[174] As a result, beyond the personal edification of the speaker (1 Cor. 14:4; Jude 20), the interpretation of such an utterance has the ability to encourage other believers present and to convince even non-believers of the reality of God's immediate presence and loving regard for them as well (1 Cor. 14:24-25).

In other words, for Christians, "utterances in tongues" have a discernable objective—they are a means to an end, not an end in themselves. Rather than the mesmerizing effect of mantra repetition, *glossolalia* is a spiritual gift intended to reveal/affirm the mysteries of Christ and his resurrection thereby empowering/embolding the testimony of Christian believers worldwide.[175]

The Vedas

The Vedas (lit. *knowledge* or *wisdom*) are purported to be the source books of all universal truth. Christian apologetics critique such a claim in light of the fact that the Vedas are rooted in polytheism,[176] philosophical monism (universal unity with the divine), superstition (false concept of causation), eastern mysticism (subjective intuition as the primary means of spiritual knowledge), the denial of sin, and salvation/ *moksha* by human achievement, to name a few. Originally written in the Vedic language,[177] there are four basic early Vedic books: the *Rigveda* containing hymns to be recited by the chief priest, *Yajurveda* containing formulas to be recited by the officiating priest, *Samaveda* containing formulas to be sung by the chanting priest, and *Atharvaveda* containing magical spells for healing, charms against evil spirits, sorcery, and witchcraft—including power to do harm to one's enemies and exercise control over nature. In modern Hinduism the Vedic literature is highly regarded but its texts are only known by a few scholars. The primary function of the ancient Vedas is that they serve as background for other developments in Hinduism—in much the same way as the Hebrew Scriptures are foundational to Christianity and to a lesser degree, Islam.

Written after the four basic Vedic Books, the Upanishads are known as *Vedanta* ("the end/culmination of the Vedas") and are therefore regarded as part of the Vedic Hindu Scriptures—and the basis for later Hindu philosophy. The Upanishads argue for a monistic rather than a dualistic reality. In dualism there is a distinction between matter and spirit. For instance, in radical dualism, such as Gnosticism, these two realms are irreconcilable with matter being evil and spirit being good. This is why Gnosticism found the idea of the incarnation of Jesus Christ so problematic (Woodworth, 2009, p, 206-07). After all, how could God, who is pure spirit ever occupy a physical body, which was "fundamentally evil"? Rather than embracing the God-man duality of Jesus Christ, the solution for the Gnostics was to separate the man Jesus from the spirit of Christ. The spirit of Christ, according to Gnosticism, came upon Jesus at his baptism and left just prior to the crucifixion. The resurrection of Jesus was not physical but spiritual in nature. This is the same argument that is made today by liberal theologians who prefer the "Christ event" of God's universal show of love for humanity rather than the Gospel's call for repentance from sin, a new life in Christ Jesus, the churches mission to disciple the nations, and the certainty of the resurrection from the dead (Woodworth, 2009, p, 247-55).

Monism, on the other hand, suggests that there is one unitary organic whole (ultimate reality) with no independent parts. In essence, there is no duality to either the nature of human beings or the universe itself. All is one and only one. Any perceived distinction is an illusion/delusion of the mind that must be liberated with spiritual knowledge available by meditating on the truth contained in the Vedic literature and especially that of the Upanishads. This single ultimate reality is called the Brahman.[178] The Brahman is the impersonal divine-being that is sexless, eternal, infinite, unknowable, and without past, present, or future. All that is not Brahman is not real, but only an illusion seeking to blind us to the reality of our essential connectedness with the ultimate reality of the Brahman. All living souls (*atman*) are part of the Braham and must find their way back to Brahman in order to be released from *samsara*—the "endless cycle of life" consisting of birth, life, death, and rebirth. This reincarnation or "transmigration of the soul" can occur countless lifetimes in order for the soul to be sufficiently enlightened so as to attain *moksha* or release from the endless cycle of life. And since we are all deceived by what we see, the task of religion is to reveal the Brahman or divine spirit within us all so that we can live from a new sense of universal oneness and peace. As a result, the problem with humanity is not sin but ignorance (*avidya*). We do not need to be reconciled to God by the sacrifice of his Son, but simply to realize that we are already at one with the Brahman. The truth is already within us. There is no need to speak of redemption, because the soul was never separated from divinity in the first place, and therefore is in no need of reconciliation.

From a Christian perspective, these ideas of the nature of God (Brahman), human life (reincarnation), spiritual liberation (salvation) and the mission of the church/religion (fellowship and evangelization),[179] are a serious contradiction to the Gospel of Jesus Christ.

The Triune God vs. Human Deification

In the first place, though God is eternal, infinite, and spiritual, in the New Testament we are told that God is also a loving heavenly Father who can be personally known in Christ. "Now this is eternal life: that they may know you, the only true God, and Jesus Christ whom you have sent" (John 17:3). And since Christ Jesus is fully reflective of the character of God, to know Jesus Christ is to know the Father. "The Son is the radiance of God's glory and the exact representation of his being, sustaining all things by his powerful word. After he had provided purification for sins, he sat down at the right hand of the Majesty in heaven" (Heb. 1:3).

"Anyone who has seen me has seen the Father...the words I say to you are not just my own. Rather, it is the Father, living in me, who is doing his work. Believe me when I say that I am in the Father and the Father is in me" (John 14:9-11).

Indeed, the mystery of the triune nature of God is completely lacking in Vedanta philosophy, which argues for self-realization, cosmic consciousness or achieving the *state of transcendence*. In essence, it is the proposition that humans can achieve divinity or *godhood* by becoming one with the Brahman. According to the *advaita* sub-schools of Vedanta philosophy, just like a drop of water in the ocean, the "soul and God are equal in every respect [atman is Brahman], and liberation entails realization of one's Godhood. Thus, one's mistaken sense of individuality is dissolved, and one merges into the all-pervading Supreme."[180]

This is similar to the Mormon doctrine of *eternal progression* whereby man can become a god by virtue of their "pre-existent spirit through incarnation on earth, then on to godhood."[181] "God himself was once as we are now, and is an exalted man, and sits enthroned in yonder heavens." (Joseph Smith Jr.)[182] "As man is, God once was, and as God is, man may become." (Lorenzo Snow)[183] Christian theologians have also noted how satan maligned God in the Garden of Eden by tempting Eve with, "You will not surely die, the serpent said to the woman. For God knows that when you eat of it your eyes will be opened, and you will be like God, knowing good from evil." (Gen. 3:4)

In Christian theology, there is eternally only one triune God who will ever be exalted and served in the heavenly state of the resurrection. "The throne of God and of the Lamb will be in the city, and his servants will serve him" (Rev. 22:3). It is a biblical truth that we do now "share the divine nature" whereby we can escape the lustful corruption of the world (2 Pet. 1:4), are members of the one spiritual body of Christ (See 1 Cor. 6:15-17 and Eph. 2:22), and are called children of God by virtue of our rebirth (John 1:12-13). However, such a relationship with God, rather than transcending our humanness, actually empowers our humanity with divine life now and will ultimately clothe our mortality with immortality in the resurrection.

> So will it be with the resurrection of the dead. The body that is sown is perishable, it is raised imperishable; it is sown in weakness, it is raised in power; it is sown a natural body, it is raised a spiritual body...For the perishable must clothe itself with the imperishable and the mortal with immortality.(1 Cor. 15:42-44, 53)

In other words, we will not become self-existent gods nor equally divine with the Lord God in the next life. Rather, we will remain distinct creations who have been transformed in our being and bodies into a similar glorified body that the Lord Jesus himself now possesses.

> But our citizenship is in heaven. And we eagerly await a Savior from there, the Lord Jesus Christ, who, by the power

that enables him to bring everything under his control, will transform our lowly bodies so that they will be like his glorious body (Phil. 3:20-21).

Notice the distinction that Paul here conveys between "our bodies" and the "Lords' body." Both are similarly glorified and yet they/we remain physically separate in the resurrected state. In the final analysis, our relationship with God is certain: God is not simply a kind of unknowable and impersonal divine principle, but a compassionate creator who, in Christ, has revealed himself to humanity bringing life and immortality to light through the Gospel (2 Tim. 1:9-10).

Reincarnation vs. Eternal Judgment

Regarding the second issue of reincarnation, Hinduism claims that humans must go through countless transmigrations[184] of the soul in order to ultimately achieve release from the endless cycle of life as a result of burning out all of our negative karmic consequences. The most definitive biblical contradiction to this notion of repeated incarnations is the text in (Heb. 9:27), which says, "For it is appointed for man to die once and after that to face judgment." In other words, after death we are not reincarnated to face another lifetime, but rather to face a judgment that will result in an eternal state that is biblically characterized by either the joy of life or the condemnation of death "Multitudes who sleep in the dust of the earth will awake: some to everlasting life, others to shame and everlasting contempt." (Dan. 2:2)[185] God holds man accountable to him for his actions, which will be revealed for better or worse in the judgment to come. "Nothing in all creation is hidden from God's sight. Everything is uncovered and laid bare before the eyes of him to whom we must give account" (Heb. 4:13).[186]

Moksha/Liberation/Salvation

A third contradiction of Christianity is that Hinduism promises any number of ways that a soul can achieve *moksha* or release from the endless cycle of life (lit. *samsara*). The four main *yogas* ("disciplines" and "yokes") or paths (*margas*) for attaining *moksha* are working for the Supreme (*Karma Yoga*), realizing the Supreme (*Jnana Yoga*), meditating on the Supreme (*Raja Yoga*) and serving the Supreme in loving devotion (*Bhakti Yoga*). In *Karma Yoga* one is said to achieve and maintain unity with the god within the devotee through the worshipful practice of selfless actions. It is action in accordance with one's duty (*dharma*) without regard to personal desires.[187] In Hinduism, karma (lit. "deed" or "act") is understood as the universal principle of cause and effect, action and reaction, which governs all human life throughout its multiple transmigrations/reincarnations.[188]

Karma Yoga

Essentially, *Karma Yoga* seeks to practice good karma actions so that subsequent lives can be free of negative karmic consequences, which can directly hinder *moksha*. In addition to careful attention to *karma*, the principle of *dharma*, or fulfilling one's duty and role in life (including within the caste system), is also incumbent on the worshipper. The problems of human deification and reincarnation aside, it is certainly appropriate for one's actions to be an expression of worship for God. Indeed faith without actions/works is criticized by James as vain and hypocritical. "What good is it, my brothers if a man claims to have faith but has no deeds?...faith by itself, if it is not accompanied by action is dead" (James 14, 17).[189] Though we are saved by grace (Eph 2:8-10) genuine faith will produce good works. The problem is when such actions (self-effort) are believed to achieve and maintain one's relationship with God as if our relationship depended on our performance of some kind.

On the other hand, the New Testament teaches that grace, or God's unmerited favor in Christ toward the undeserving, is the basis of our salvation. "For it is by grace you have been saved through faith—and this not from yourselves, it is the gift of God —not by works, so that no one can boast" (Eph. 2:8-9). Our response to God's grace in Christ is faith. Such faith is exercised to appropriate God's gift of salvation and to act in accordance with the new life we now profess in Christ. Three other biblical issues that could be raised over the Hindu concept of *Karma Yoga* are the notions of desire-less actions (in denial of our humanity and need for hope), the historic misuse of the caste system as a means of social oppression[190] in the name of *dharma*, and the lack of forgiveness within the construct of the inexorable law of karma.

Jnana Yoga

Jnana Yoga (lit. *path of knowledge*) is the assertion that knowledge acquisition is necessary to divine liberation. Such knowledge will enable one to discriminate between the real/eternal (Brahman) and the unreal/temporal (material world). With sufficient knowledge and intense concentration/self-control, the practitioner will be able to detach oneself from all that is temporary thus achieving Brahman consciousness—the release from all worldly limitations and distractions. In Christianity, knowledge of the truth in Christ is a liberating experience. "If you hold to my teaching, you are really my disciples. Then you will know the truth, and the truth will set you free" (John 8:31-32). However, the focal point of all knowledge acquisition is in Christ, "in whom are hidden all the treasures of wisdom and knowledge." (Col. 3:3) Such knowledge is necessarily rooted in a revelation of the grace (2 Pet. 3:18) of God that enables us to "deny ungodliness and worldly passions, and to live self-controlled, upright and godly lives in this present [evil] age, while we eagerly wait for the Lord's appearing" (Titus 2:11-13).

Notice how Christians are instructed to live godly lives and resist worldly passions in this present age. In other words, rather than denying our life in the world, we are rather exhorted to deny ungodliness and worldly lusts as we live out our lives in this present age or world. Jesus said that we should be *in* the world but not *of* the world in his prayer in John 17.

> ...but they are still in the world and I am coming to you...the world has hated them for they are not of the world any more than I am of the world. My prayer is not that you take them out of the world but that you protect them from the evil one [satan] (John 17:11, 14-15).

Furthermore, the Apostle John described the "evil sense" of the word *world* in three ways: the lust of the flesh (sensuous carnality), lust of the eyes (materialism), and the boastful pride of life (egoism).[191] It is the lust or "evil desire" of the flesh and the eyes—as well as the self-centered arrogance of life that should be denied. Beyond this, there is nothing intrinsically evil about the body, the eyes, or life itself.

Biblically speaking, this is the problem of Hinduism and all ascetically-oriented approaches to life. They tend to confuse the evilness of their fallen internal nature (the problem of sin) with the external world (nature), which was originally created by God for our good and meant for our grateful enjoyment. "So God created man in his own image...male and female...God blessed them and said, Be fruitful and increase...fill the earth and subdue it...God saw all that he had made, and it was very good" (Gen. 1:27-31). "...hope in God, who richly provides us with everything for our enjoyment" (1 Tim. 6:17). "For everything created by God is good, and nothing is to be rejected if it is received with thanksgiving, because it is consecrated by the word of God and prayer" (1 Tim. 4:4).

Speaking further on the issue of asceticism, Hinduism is deeply rooted in the belief of the efficacy of discipline, or the "negation of the flesh," as an aid to the attainment of spiritual liberation. Such spiritual liberation necessitates the shunning of all worldly attachments, including careers, homes, family, and friends in a quest of detachment from all that is worldly and transient be it possessions and/or pleasures.[192] As a sociological fact, such extreme self-renunciation is far too prohibitive for most young people in India today. Indeed, rather than attempt the arduous task of ascetic self-mastery, most young people generally choose to either wait until old age or even the next reincarnation cycle in order to "perhaps" provide them the opportunity for such all-consuming reflective and austere pursuits.[193]

The Apostle Paul addresses the issue of religious/Gnostic asceticism by arguing that such external rules have the "appearance of wisdom, with their self-imposed worship, their false humility, and their harsh treatment of the body, but they lack any value in restraining [internal] sensual indulgence" (Col. 2:23). The main problem, argues Paul, is the need to "put to death the earthly nature" and to "put on the new self, which is being renewed in knowledge in the image of its Creator" (Col. 2:1-10). In reality, the transformation that humanity needs is essentially internal, by spiritual rebirth (Titus 3:5-6, NIV), rather than a self-imposed effort to curb every deviation of the mind and body in one's attempt to achieve some specter of spirituality. Furthermore this transformation is a spiritual reality for all those who have died with Christ and been raised to walk in newness of life. Such a reality is affirmed in Christian water baptism where we are symbolically both buried and raised with Christ. The burial symbolizes our death to the power of sin in the flesh, whereas our rising up out of the water signifies our resurrection life in the power of the indwelling spirit.[194]

Raja Yoga

Raja Yoga is mainly concerned with the cultivation of the mind using meditation (*dhyana*) in the pursuit of *moksha* (liberation/salvation). However, in order to be fit to practice such meditation, the body must first be tamed through restraint (*yama*) such as celibacy, abstaining from drugs and alcohol, and being careful to control one's actions of body, speech, and mind. As mentioned previously, biblical teaching harshly rejects all manner of required celibacy as a precondition to spirituality.

> The Spirit clearly says that in the later times some will abandon the faith and follow deceiving spirits and things taught by demons...They forbid people to marry and order them to abstain from certain foods, which God created to be received with thanksgiving by those who believe and who know the truth (1 Tim. 4: 1, 3).

Beyond this prerequisite for the deeper realms of *Raja Yoga* is the "senseless" goal of descending to the quiet mind, the *Nirbija* or *seedless state*, in which there is no mental object of focus. Furthermore, this seedless state of mind is itself considered to be the starting point in the quest to cleanse *Karma* and achieve *Moksha*, or in the case of Buddhism, to attain *Nirvana*—the liberation from all that is false and unreal.

The kind of spiritual meditation (Ps. 119:97) that is encouraged in both the Old and New Testaments is a focused and prayerful concentration on God's word through which mind renewal can be facilitated. The result in mind renewal is the ability to perceive and hence cooperate with the will of God in one's actions and attitudes. "Do not be conformed any longer to the pattern of this world, but be transformed by the renewing of your mind. Then you will be able to test and approve what God's will is—his good, pleasing and perfect will" (Rom 12:1-2). Christian prayer and meditation does help bring a greater awareness of

God's presence, but its goal is not a mind void of objects but a heart that is filled with adoration and understanding—thus enhancing one's relationship with the Lord and a greater commitment to "please the Lord" by intentionally cooperating with his kingdom purpose (Matt. 6:33). "And we pray this in order that you may live a life worthy of the Lord and may please him in every way" (Col. 1:10).

Bhakti Yoga

Finally *Bhakti Yoga* is the discipline of cultivating loving devotion to a particular deity, or an aspect of the deity, selected by the devotee. In *Bhakti Yoga* there are nine forms of devotional service including hearing about the Lord,[195] glorifying the Lord,[196] remembering the Lord,[197] serving the Lord, worshipping the Lord (prayer), surrendering to the Lord, etc.

"Engage your mind always in thinking of Me, become My devotee, offer obeisances to Me and worship Me. Being completely absorbed in Me, surely you will come to Me." (Bhagavad-Gita 9.34)[198]

"One can understand Me as I am, as the Supreme Personality of Godhead, only by devotional service. And when one is in full consciousness of Me by such devotion, he can enter into the kingdom of God." (Bhagavad-Gita 18.55)

While loving devotion toward God is biblically commendable[199] the problem with this aspect of Hinduism is that such devotion is directed toward any number of gods of the Hindu Pantheon—especially Krishna, who is one of the ten avatars[200] of Vishnu. Vishnu, in turn, is one of the three major gods in postclassical Hinduism—the other two being Brahma (creator) and Shiva (destroyer). As a result, such devotion is essentially misdirected idolatry and thereby rejected in both Old and New Testaments.

> And God spoke all these words: 'I am the Lord your God, who brought you out of Egypt, out of the land of slavery. You shall have no other gods before me. You shall not make for yourself an idol in the form of anything in heaven above or on the earth beneath or in the water below. You shall not bow down to them or worship them' (Ex. 20:1-5).

> We know that an idol is nothing...and that there is no God but one. For even if there are so-called gods, whether in heaven or on earth (as indeed there are many 'gods' and many 'lords'), yet for us there is but one God, the Father, from whom all things came and from whom we live; and there is but one Lord, Jesus Christ, through whom all things came and through whom we live (1 Cor. 8:4b-6).

The Apostle Paul further connects idolatry with demon worship as justification for his strong prohibition against such involvement. "Do I mean that a sacrifice to an idol is anything or that an idol is anything? No, but the sacrifices of pagans are offered to demons, not to God, and I do not want you to be participants with demons" (1 Cor. 10:19-20). What is instructive about Paul's treatment on the subject of "eating meat sacrificed to an idol (1 Cor. 8:4)" is how he appeals to brotherly love as a basis for limiting one's freedom of conscience. After all, publicly eating meat sacrificed to an idol could be wrongly interpreted by some (either unbelievers or young/weak believers) as consent to engage in idolatrous worship. As a result, Paul passionately recommends that such misinterpretations of motives should be resisted—by the limitation of one's freedom rather than an argumentation about one's rights. Loving sensitivity and kindness is a higher principle than personal freedom and rights. In God's kingdom, loving kindness, grace, and wisdom must be exercised, not only towards young[201] Christians but also toward those that are lost—regardless of their idolatrous deception and behavior.

> But when the kindness and love of God our Savior appeared, he saved us, not because of righteous things we had done, but because of his mercy...through the washing of [spiritual] rebirth and renewal by the Holy Spirit, whom he poured out on us generously through Jesus Christ (Titus 3:4-6).

Chapter 6: Review Questions

1. What was the most interesting thing that you learned from Chapter 6 and why?
2. To whom do most scholars trace the beginning to Hinduism?

3. In what way is the Hindu concept of non-cognitive muttering of sounds (such as Aum) in quest of spiritual enlightenment, addressed by Jesus in relation to Christian prayer (See Matt. 6:7).
4. What is the difference between monism and dualism in the Upanishads?
5. How is the idea of salvation different between Christianity and Hinduism?

Chapter VII

-Buddhism-

The Origin of Buddhism

The founder of Buddhism was Siddhartha, of the Gautama clan[202], who was born in what is now Nepal, around 563 BCE. Tradition maintains that soon after Siddhartha's birth, a hermit-soothsayer prophesied that the child would grow to be either a great king (*Chakravartin*) or a holy man (*Sadhu*) based on whether or not he ever saw what are now called the "four sights." The four sights were an elderly man, a diseased man, a decaying corpse, and an ascetic monk. Since Siddhartha's father was himself a chieftain, he also wanted his son to have the same privileged lifestyle as he had lived. As a result, Siddhartha, though raised in opulence, was purposefully sheltered from the realities of the outside world, especially away from the "four sights," by his highly protective father—who even arranged for his marriage at around 16 years of age. Nevertheless, Siddhartha was still eventually exposed to the cruel realities of suffering, old age, and death. Such revelations ultimately caused him, at the age of 29, to reject his self-indulgent life, to leave his family[203] and friends, and to seek truth as a wandering and beggarly ascetic mendicant.

For the next six years Siddhartha practiced the most extreme form of asceticism possible, including self-mortifying practices such as nearly starving himself by eating only a leaf or nut or the smallest serving of rice per day, sleeping in graveyards, wearing extremely irritating garments, sitting in awkwardly painful positions for hours, etc. Finally, he was so weakened by hunger that he collapsed into a river while attempting to bath. Reflecting on the uselessness of such extreme asceticism, Siddhartha, thereafter sat under a Bodhi tree vowing never to arise from that place until he was enlightened by the truth. Such enlightenment was allegedly attained 49 days later, earning Siddhartha the title "Buddha" or literally the "Enlightened or Awakened One." This enlightened state occurred when he was 35 years of age. For the next 40 years Buddha taught the way of enlightenment (Dharma) until he finally died in 483 BCE at 80 years of age in the Indian State of Uttar Pradesh. So profound was Buddha's affect on Hinduism that he was accorded the title of one of the ten avatars (physical incarnation) of Vishnu—which/who is the preserver and sustainer aspect of God within the Hindu trinity or Trimurti: Brahma being the creator, Vishnu the sustainer, and Shiva the destroyer. The remainder of this article will consist of an exploration and critique of a number of the key foundational concepts of classical Buddhism including the Middle Way, Three Jewels, Four Noble Truths, Eight-fold Path, anatman (non-soulness), five aggregates, and Nirvana.

Interpreting Buddhism

Theravada and Mahayana Schools

When discussing the interpretation of Buddhism it is important to keep in mind the primary, and at times competing sects within Buddhism, specifically the Theravada (lit. "Way of the Elders") and Mahayana (lit. "Greater Vehicle)[204] denominations. Mahayana is further sub-divided into many branches including the East Asian sects of Pure Land, Chan/Zen, Nichiren, Shingon, etc., and the Vajrayana (lit. "Diamond Vehicle") especially popular in Tibet.

Basically, the Theravadans claim to be the closest followers of the original beliefs and practices of the Buddha and early monastic Elders.[205] Theravadans only accept the earlier text of the Pali Canon while rejecting the later Sutra texts of the Mahayanans. Theravada Buddhism is also much more exclusive—in that only a world-renouncing ascetic and/or fully devoted monk can ever become an *arhat* (or saint) thus achieving Nirvana. Conversely, Mahayana Buddhism is much more liberal and maintains that nirvanic liberation, beyond the exclusive domain of ascetics and monks, can be achieved by any layperson and perhaps in a single lifetime as well.[206]

The liberalism of Mahayanism is further reflected in its three cardinal principles including a). The belief that Buddha's teachings, though foundational, could also be expanded beyond what he originally taught b). Buddha was actually an eternal and divine-like being (hence worthy of worship), who was intentionally incarnated to assist/save mankind (much like Christ Jesus), and, c). Gautama Buddha was only one of countless Buddhas who have appeared throughout human history (Hofpe and Woodward, 2007, p. 132). Hence, all gods and religious leaders were simply heavenly or earthly incarnations of the Buddha. This clearly syncretistic nature of Mahayana Buddhism explains why its spread into China, Korea, Japan, Mongolia, Tibet, etc. was so prolific.

From a critical perspective, the polarization of conservative (Theravada) and liberal (Mahayana) factions within Buddhism is similar to nearly all major world religions including Judaism (conservative vs. reform), Christianity (Protestant fundamentalism vs. liberalism), Islam (Shia vs. Sunni), and Hinduism (Vedic ritualistic dualism vs. Vedanta philosophical monism[207]). And as is often the case, the conservatives are much more fundamentalist and orthodox in their devotion—insisting that theirs in the original intention of the founder. Furthermore, religious liberalism, of all stripes, is generally more popularly modernistic in its theological constructs.

The Hindu Cultural Context

One other important factor when interpreting Buddhism is the need to realize that Buddhism arose from the Hindu culture. In other words, Buddha understood life in Hindu terms—as attested to by the aforementioned Hindu embrace/coronation of the Buddha as an Avatar of Vishnu. In other words, such terms as karma, dharma, samsara, and Brahman long preceded Gautama Buddha's birth. As a result, Buddha had no desire or need to create a new religion. Rather, in a sense, Buddhism can be viewed as a renewal movement within Hinduism itself. This is certainly not to imply that Buddha approved of Hinduism as much as Hinduism approved of Buddha. Quite the contrary, Buddha rejected many fundamental truths and values of Hinduism including the original Vedic literature with its ritualistic preoccupation with priests and sacrifices, rampant polytheism (the gods were mortal and even subject to karma themselves), and the wholesale discounting of the caste system to name a few. Indeed, classical Buddhism was much more practical, relying less on religious constructs, and more on the personal pursuit of enlightenment through meditation and disciplined mastery of the mind and body. Rather than trusting in the grace of any god or sacrifice to achieve liberation, Buddhism posits salvation as an achievement of the practitioner over potentially countless lifetimes of gradual perfection.

Needless to say, this notion of self-righteousness is far from the biblical idea of salvation by grace through faith. "For it is by grace you have been saved through faith—and this not from yourselves, it is a gift of God—not by works so that no one can boast" (Eph. 2:8-9).

> But when the kindness and love of God our Savior appeared, he saved us, not because of righteous things we have done, but because of his mercy. He saved us through the washing of [spiritual] rebirth and renewal by the Holy Spirit, whom he poured out on us generously through Jesus Christ our Savior, so that, having been justified by his grace, we might become heirs having the hope of eternal life (Titus 3:4-7).

Some Key Foundational Concepts

The Middle Way

As previously mentioned, it was while meditating on the vanity of extreme asceticism that Buddha discovered the concept of the Middle Way or Path. Essentially, the Middle Way is a path of moderation between the two extremes of self-indulgence on the one hand and self-denial/mortification on the other hand. In the place of either extremes Buddhism teaches the practice of wisdom, morality, and mental cultivation. This concept of a middle way between two extremes is also endorsed in Christianity. The fruit of temperance or self-control is balanced with a call away from severe or harsh treatment of the body in at least the following verses: "But the fruit of the Holy Spirit is love, joy, peace, patience, kindness, goodness, faithfulness, and self-control" (Gal. 5:22). "Such regulations indeed have an appearance of wisdom, with their self-imposed worship, their false humility and their harsh treatment of the body, but they lack any value in restraining sensual indulgence" (Col. 2:23).

The Three Jewels

After becoming enlightened, Buddha formed the first community of monks called the *sangha*—thus completing the establishment of the Three Jewels or Refuges: The Buddha, the Dharma (Buddha's teaching), and the Sangha (community of disciples).[208] The Christian corollary would be finding one's refuge in Jesus Christ, his teachings on the Kingdom of God as recorded in the New Testament, and the church—the redeemed community of disciples-followers of Christ. However, because of many of the issues to follow in this article, including Buddhism's contradiction to the biblical necessity of the atoning sacrifice of Jesus Christ for the forgiveness[209] of sins, there can be no ultimate certainty of truth/liberation either in the Buddhist dharma or sangha. In other words, although the heartfelt devotion to the idea of truth and enlightenment within Buddhism is commendable, nevertheless, Buddhism's fundamental contradictions to the ultimate revelation of God in Christ render it inadequate to provide the universal salvation it seeks to assert in and through the person or nature of the Buddha.

The Four Noble Truths

The Four Noble Truths/Realities are one of the most fundamental concepts within Buddhism, and are said to be the essential truths Gautama Buddha realized during his initial experience of enlightenment. Each of these truths is mentioned in the Pali Canon as the following way:

1. The nature of suffering (*Dukkha*): All life is suffering. "Now this ... is the noble truth of suffering: birth is suffering, aging is

suffering, illness is suffering, death is suffering; sorrow, lamentation, pain, grief and despair are suffering; union with what is displeasing is suffering; separation from what is pleasing is suffering; not to get what one wants is suffering; in brief, the five aggregates subject to clinging are suffering."[210]
2. The origin (*Samudaya*) of suffering: We suffer because of craving/desire and ignorance. "Now this ... is the noble truth of the origin of suffering: it is this craving which leads to renewed existence, accompanied by delight and lust, seeking delight here and there, that is, craving for sensual pleasures, craving for existence, craving for extermination."[211]
3. The cessation (*Nirodha*) of suffering: We can be free from the endless cycle of life (samsara) through knowledge and practice. "Now this ... is the noble truth of the cessation of suffering: it is the remainderless fading away and cessation of that same craving, the giving up and relinquishing of it, freedom from it, nonreliance on it."[212] This is the ultimate reality/non-reality of Nirvanic existence/non-existence (More on this below).
4. The way (*Marga*) leading to the cessation of suffering: "Now this ... is the noble truth of the way leading to the cessation of suffering: it is the Noble Eightfold Path; that is, right view, right intention, right speech, right action, right livelihood, right effort, right mindfulness, right concentration."[213]

While considerable suffering in life is undeniably self-inflicted, the goal of the Christian is far from being delivered *from* suffering. In fact, in many instances, the Bible teaches that often we can only be delivered through suffering.

> No temptation [trial or test] has overtaken you but such as is common to all men. And God is faithful and will not allow you to be tempted [tested or tried] beyond what you can bear. But when you are tempted [tested or tried] he will provide a way out [or through] so that you can stand up under it (1 Cor. 10:13).

Indeed, Christians are taught that is it necessary to embrace suffering (Woodworth, 2001, p. 3:2-3)—especially when it is in accordance with the will of God.

It is better, if it is God's will, to suffer for doing good than for doing evil...Therefore, since Christ suffered in his body, arm yourselves also with the same attitude [a willingness to suffer for/with Christ], because he who has suffered in his body is done with sin...if you suffer as a Christian, do not be ashamed, but praise God that you bear that name (1 Pet. 3:17; 4:1; 5:16).

Furthermore, the Bible indicates that because God is trustworthy, we are able to respond to all of life's suffering (deserved or undeserved), with a genuine sense of joyful anticipation—knowing that God has promised to work in every circumstance of our lives to perfect our character and prepare us for even greater opportunities of service and reward.

"Consider it pure joy, my brothers, whenever you face trials of many kinds, because you know that the testing of your faith develops perseverance. And perseverance must finish its work so that you may be mature and complete not lacking in anything" (James 1:3-4).

"And we know that in all things God works for the good of those who love him, who have been called according to his purpose" (Rom. 8:28).

As a result, the Christian, though acknowledging the universality of suffering is never obsessed with the avoidance of the inevitable. Rather, our focus is on the will and glory of God—regardless of what we may need to endure.[214] The Lord will never abandon us, but rather, will faithfully deliver and/or comfort us through all our trials for the sake of his glory and the service of others.

Praise be to the God and Father of our Lord Jesus Christ, the Father of compassion and the God of all comfort, who comforts us in all our troubles, so that we can comfort those in any trouble with the comfort we ourselves have received from God. For just as the sufferings of Christ flow over into our lives, so also through Christ our comfort overflows. If we are distressed, it is for your comfort and salvation; if we are comforted, it is for your comfort, which produces in you patient endurance of the same sufferings we suffer. And our hope for you is firm, because we know that just as you share in our sufferings, so also you share in our comfort (2 Cor. 1:3-7).

Nirvana

Nirvana is a Sanskrit word that means to "extinguish" or to "blow out"—as when the flame of a candle goes out.[215] This extinguishing of all passions is used to describe the realization of enlightenment, peace of mind, and liberation from all afflictive states (*kilesa*). In Nirvana, or Nibbana (Pali language) one is no longer subject to human suffering, nor are any further rebirths necessary. In other words, the karmaic-bound consequence of *samsara* (reincarnation/birth, death and rebirth)[216] is nullified thus bringing one to a realization (vs. a state or place) of "deathlessness" and the ultimate release (*moksha*) from perceived personhood. As a result, any who achieve Nirvana are not spoken of as dying, but rather as "fully" passing away (*parinirvana*)—never to be reborn again. Hence, the ultimate goal and end of samsaric existence, according to Buddhism, is the realization of Nirvana. Whatever happens to a person after his *parinirvana* is purportedly unexplainable since such existence is beyond any conceivable experience or knowledge.

A central criticism of Nirvana is that it sounds like the goal of all existence is to cease to be—to become existenceless. So essentially, you spend your entire life striving not to live, in hopes that in the end you never will have been. This is not a definition of life or of living but a recipe of death and dying. And tragically, while avoiding suffering all of one's life, one suffers the greatest loss of all—life itself. Furthermore, the Bible speaks of living for a purpose in life, a purpose that if fulfilled promises both temporal and eternal reward. "But godliness has value for all things, holding promise for both the present life and the life to come" (1 Tim. 4:8). In other words, there is every reason and provision to hope in God in this present life while still remaining focused on the next.

Seeing that His divine power has granted to us everything pertaining to life and godliness, through the true knowledge of Him who called us by His own glory and excellence. For by these He has granted to us His precious and magnificent promises, so that by them you may become partakers of the divine nature, having escaped the corruption that is in the world by lust (2 Pet. 1:3-4).

It is true that Christianity does indeed call for a self and worldly-denial: "If anyone would come after me, he must deny himself and take up his cross and follow me" (Mark 8:34) and, "Love not the world nor anything that is in the world...the lust of the flesh, the lust of the eyes, and the boastful pride of life" (1 John 2:15-17). However, such denial is not an assault on the physical existence of either the world or our bodies. Rather, our "rebirth in Christ" (Titus 3:5, NIV) has provided us with a new internal spiritual power[217] to deny our fallen nature as well as to live for God's purpose in this present life.[218] In Christ, Christians have a new life, a new power, and a new purpose. And though Buddhism is a titanic attempt to relieve human suffering, from a Christian perspective, it is simply too hard and harsh of a solution when compared with the promise of life in Christ.

I came that you might have life and have it abundantly (John 10:10).

For God so loved the world that he gave his one and only Son, that whoever believes in him shall not perish, but have eternal life" (John 3:16).

By God's power he has saved us and called us with a holy calling, not according to our works, but according to His own purpose and grace which was granted us in Christ Jesus from all eternity, but now has been revealed by the appearing of our Savior Christ Jesus, who abolished death and brought life and immortality to light through the gospel (2 Tim. 1:9-10).

Chapter 7: Review Questions

1. What was the most interesting thing that you learned from Chapter 7 and why?

2. What the four (sights) that Siddhartha could not see in his youth or else he would be a poor, yet holy man.
3. What title did Hinduism award to Buddha as a result of his spiritual success? Hint: It is the name of one of the most popular science-fiction films in 2009 by James Cameron.
4. Discuss the difference(s) between the Theravada and Mahayana Schools of Buddhism.
5. Explain the three jewels of Buddhism.

Chapter VIII

Chinese Religions-Religious Thought

Any nation with over 1.3 billion people deserves a review of its religious culture in a text on World Religions. Unfortunately, Chinese religion has been suppressed and tightly controlled since the early Twentieth century by both the New Culture movement (1915) and the atheistic Communist party takeover (1949), which witnessed the extermination of 50-60 million Chinese citizens in the Mao political revolution.

However, there still remains a strong current of folk-religious sentiment throughout China, perhaps numbering up to several hundred million. This is the case, even though, in reality, the percentage of people who call themselves religious in China is the lowest in the world at just over 30 percent. In fact, in China today, the largest religions are Shenism (folk religion)-Taoism and Buddhism who collectively comprise about 30% of the population. Another 50% of Chinese are mostly agnostic and secular/non-religious; whereas those who claim to be purely atheistic are about 14%. Interestingly, there are 70 million communist party members in China today, which is less than 5% of the total population.[219]

The history of religion in China generally falls into five broad epochs

1. The beginning of recorded history (c. 3000 BCE) until the end of the Shang dynasty (1700-1046 BCE) in the Eleventh-Century BCE During this time Chinese religions consisted of a combination of polytheism and ancestral worship (Hopfe and Woodward, 2007, p.164).
2. The second epoch in the history of religion in China is from the development of the Chou dynasty (1066-256 BCE) in the Eleventh-Century BCE until around the birth of Christ (c. 4 BCE—Herod died in 4BC). Main developments during this era included a reverence for the Supreme God (*Shang Ti—Lord of Heaven*) above all other gods and spirits—who could be contacted by divination (See *Historic Elements* below). Interestingly, this was also a time of ethical morality of its leadership, which was very similar to historic Judaism.

During this same time period (between the Eighth and Third Centuries BCE) there was also the collapse of feudalism.[220] Into this vacuum of social uncertainty emerged a number of Chinese philosophical schools of thought (Hopfe and Woodward, 2007, p. 175) including:

- Taoists (*Lao-tzu*), who were pacifists and believed that the best form of government was as little government as possible;
- Confucians (Confucius), who favored a restoration of China's earlier feudal form of government;
- Legalists (rule of law; no specific leader) maintained that only a strong-handed central government was the best way to govern the evil and lazy inclinations of society[221];
- Mohists (*Mo-tzu*) were religious traditionalists, who believed the government should ideally operate from a position of love rather than coercive power.

Though all of these schools of philosophy had (and have) been impressed on the consciousness and culture of China, the most dominate systems of thought to emerge with religious connotations were Taoism and Confucianism—both of which will be covered in more depth in this monograph.

3. From the beginning of the Birth of Christ/Common Era until the Eleventh Century CE/AD[222] marks the time when Buddhism first entered China. As a result, the *religious triad* of China was established and comprised of Taoism, Buddhism, and Confuscianism .
4. From the Eleventh-Century to the early Twentieth-Century was marked by a heightening of religious scholarship, a greater simplicity in Confucian ceremonial life, and an era of continued synthesis of religions in China.
5. Twentieth-Century (1915+) to present has been marked by continual religious suppression. Essentially, the history of Twentieth-Century China is one of trying to "configure new systems of social, political, and economic theories aimed at reconstituting the nation as a whole after the collapse of dynastic rule."[223]

The New Culture movement (1915) and Communist Party (1949) takeovers spelled disaster for religion in China—including the martyrdom of thousands of believers. The backlash from this severe persecution of religions has resulted in a small measure of religious expression—at least for the five state-approved religions today, which include: Taoism, Buddhism, Islam, Protestantism, and Catholicism. From an earlier time of extreme state suppression, even Confucianism is also making a comeback as a *populist religious and traditional-ethical ideology*.

Four Major Historic Religious Elements in China

- *Polytheism (many gods) and animism* (individual spirits inhabit natural objects and phenomena—such as is popular among native Americans and in the 2009 movie by James Cameron called *Avatar*). Such spirits, in the mind of the ancient Chinese, needed to be placated by offerings, which were comprised of fruit, animal, grain, and even human sacrifices. Such human sacrifices ceased at the end of the Chou dynasty in 256 BCE. Both the *Kuei* (evil spirits of darkness) and the *Shen* (good spirits of light) were appeased or invoked during such sacrificial religious rites (Hopfe and Woodward, 2007 p. 166).

In comparing polytheism and animism with Christianity, a couple of observations could be made. First is the obvious contradiction between the monotheism of Christianity and the polytheism in Chinese early religious elements. Second is that animism is fear-based, whereby the worshipper must placate the spirits by offerings and sacrifices in order to appease the angry deities and spirits. In contradiction to this, Jesus affirmed that God was a loving Heavenly Father who sacrificed his Son to atone for the sins of humanity thereby making his gift of grace available to all who call upon his name in faith (John 3:16; Eph. 2:8-9).

- *Filial (family) piety and Ancestor worship.* Tangential to the notion of sacrifices to spirits is the Chinese concept of Ancestor worship. Such ancestral veneration was necessary because of the Chinese fearful concern that deceased ancestors would wonder around as ghosts—who could wreck havoc on the lives of their descendants who disrespected them in life and in death (Hopfe and Woodward, 2007, 167). Christianity, while encouraging honor (manifest respect) toward one's parents (Ex. 20:12) reserves worship for God alone. To direct ones reverential worship toward anyone or anything else but God is, according to biblical theology, an act of idolatry (Ex. 20:3-4).

In fact, in China today, stylized imitation paper money literally called *Hell Bank Notes* are specially printed, in very large denominations (from $10,000 to billions of dollars), and sacrificially burned at the gravesites of deceased ancestors. Such bank notes are believed to be powerful negotiation tools in escaping Hell's fire and gaining favorable access to Heaven in the afterlife. This superstitious merchandizing of religious fear is sad for Christians to consider because of the futility of anyone who would try to gain heaven by virtue of a financial transaction with imitation money—or on the merits of anyone other than Jesus Christ. "For there is no other name [than Jesus] which has given among men by which we must be saved" (Acts 4:12). "For it is by grace you have been saved, through faith—and this is not from yourselves; it is the gift of God—not by [human] works, so that no one can boast" (Eph. 2:8-9).

This is an important point to make—especially since there are even varieties of Hell Bank Notes now being printed with famous people on them such as John F. Kennedy (renown U.S. President), Albert Einstein (renown theoretical Physicist), and Marilyn Monroe (playboy actress)—none of which can grant anyone entrance to heaven based on their contrived spiritual notoriety before God.

- *Divination* is another frequently practiced religious-spiritual rite to access information about the future upon which many in China made/make important life decisions. Such Chinese divination originally involved reading the lines on bones or cracks on heated tortoise shells. However, divination reached its zenith in the Taoist Book of Changes called the *I Ching*, which was subsequently (and allegedly) edited by Confucius—thereby propelling it to national prominence (Hopfe and Woodward, 2007, p. 168). Essentially, the *I Ching* contains a very elaborate and complex reading of 64 hexagram patterns along with commentaries and analysis.

The I-Ching: Book of Changes

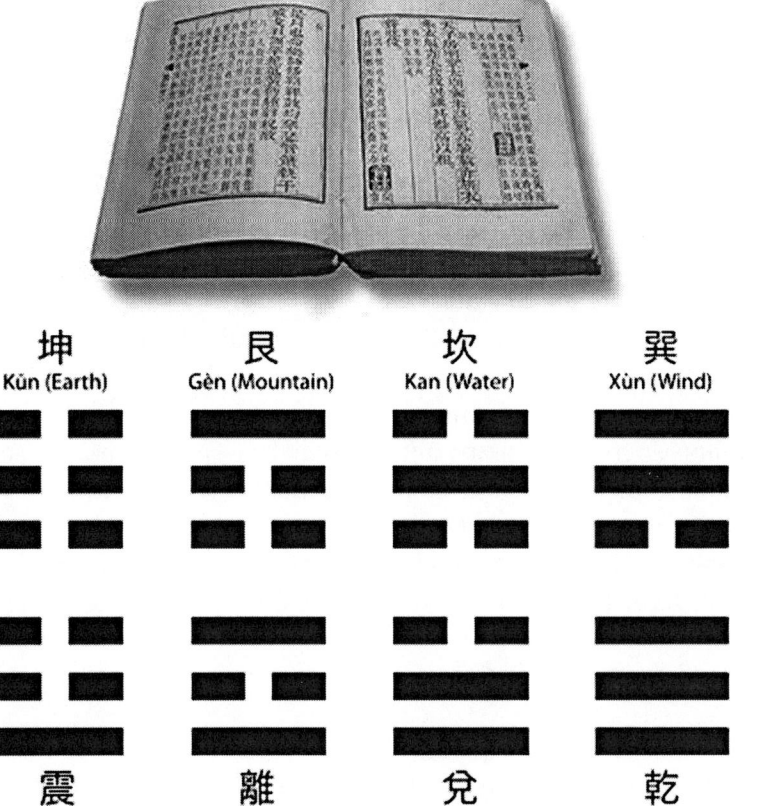

坤 Kǔn (Earth)

艮 Gèn (Mountain)

坎 Kan (Water)

巽 Xùn (Wind)

震 Zhèn (Thunder)

離 Lí (Fire)

兌 Duì (Lake)

乾 Qián (Heaven)

Psychoanalyst and religious mystic Carl Jung wrote a very affirming introduction to the *I Chang* for western readers in which he explained the way in which the book could be consulted as an oracle—thus exposing all his readers to occult (paranormal) practices, which are specifically forbidden in the Old and New Testaments:

There shall not be found among you anyone who makes his son or his daughter pass through the fire, one who uses divination, one who practices witchcraft, or one who interprets omens, or a sorcerer, or one who casts a spell, or a medium, or a spiritist, or one who calls up the dead (Deut. 18:10-11).

It happened that as we were going to the place of prayer, a slave-girl having a spirit of divination met us, who was bringing her masters much profit by fortune-telling. Following after Paul and us, she kept crying out, saying, 'These men are bond-servants of the Most High God, who are proclaiming to you the way of salvation.' She continued doing this for many days. But Paul was greatly annoyed, and turned and said to the spirit, 'I command you in the name of Jesus Christ to come out of her!' And it came out at that very moment (Acts 16:16-18).

As a result of these biblical cautions, all Christians should purposefully avoid any occult activities as obvious as witchcraft and necromancy (communicating with the dead)—or as subtle as toying with horoscopes and astrological signs. As entertaining as some of the occult may be, it is a path that leads to deception and spiritual bondage knowing that our adversary, the devil, comes to "steal, kill, and destroy. But I [Jesus] have come that you might have life in abundance" (John 10:10).

One further application here:

A similar caution could also be given regarding those who claim to move in the power of any legitimate expression of spiritual gifts from 1 Corinthians 12:

But to each one is given the manifestation of the Spirit for the common good. For to one is given the word of wisdom through the Spirit, and to another the word of knowledge according to the same Spirit; to another faith by the same Spirit, and to another gifts of healing by the one Spirit, and to another the effecting of miracles, and to another prophecy, and to another the distinguishing of spirits, to another various kinds of tongues, and to another the interpretation of tongues. But one and the same Spirit works all these things, distributing to each one individually just as He wills (1 Cor. 12:7-11).

Just the fact that these kinds of gifts are spiritual in nature, means that there is a mysterious dimension to their origin and exercise. However, all true gifts of the Holy Spirit, though a mystery, are never mystical in nature. Furthermore, true servants of the Lord Jesus should be careful about the authenticity of the exercise of such gifts, especially in relation to the minister's message, method, and motive. As a result, such spiritual gifts are therefore never to be used to manipulate honor from men; be it in ministerial notoriety or financial gain gimmickry. After all, the Gospel of Jesus Christ should never be merchandized as some cheap commodity on display at a discounted rate. I say this because there is a marked increase of false prophets/ministers and ministries today who are preaching God's kingdom for personal gain— rather than as a faithful and honored servant of the Lord Jesus himself (Matt. 24:24-25; 1 Tim.6:3-10; 2 Pet. 2:1-3, NIV). Beware!

- *Yin and Yang* is a symbolic circle of darkness and light representing complementary but opposing forces of the universe that generate all forms of reality, including nature, humankind, and events (Molloy, 2007, p. 219). The *Yin* is the negative force in nature encompassing darkness, coolness, femaleness, moon, and shadows. The *Yang* is the positive force in nature encompassing lightness, brightness, warmth, maleness, dryness and the sun. The Chinese do not hold either symbol as superior to the other, but rather as a necessary balance to the rhythm of all reality. Interestingly, in early Chinese philosophy (prior to the Christian Era), Daoism was considered as the *Yin* whereas Confucianism was thought to be the *Yang*.

  The notion that the *Yin* and the *Yang* are the two main opposing, complimentary, and collaborative forces in the universe; from which all creation is derived is problematic for a number of reasons. Genesis One and Two are quite clear that God alone (not the collaboration of the Yin and the Yang) created the universe. In other words, God has no equal or opposite—including satan, who is merely a fallen angel (Is. 45;5; 14:12-15; Ezek. 28: 14-17a). And while the idea of balance and symmetry is an observable fact of nature, such an observance should not lead to the unnecessary conclusion that nature can create itself.

The Origin of Taoism

The founder of Taoism is a legendary figure named Lao-tzu[224] meaning "old master"" or "old child" who was allegedly born of a virgin—but emerged from the womb as an old man of wisdom. The sacred text of Taoism is called the *Tao Te Ching* (lit. *The Classic of the Way and Its Power or Virtue*) which was doubtfully written by Lao-tzu, and compiled 100's of years after his death—or presumed bodily assumption into heaven. In fact, *Lao Tzu* is worshipped by many as the human incarnation of the *Tao* (the way of nature) as *Lord Tao*. The *Tao Te Ching* has 5,000 characters (20 typed pages) and 81 brief section/chapters/poems whose general themes include both political advice for rulers and practical wisdom for people—as well as reaching trace-like states of consciousness and thereby attaining invulnerability to harm, which is tantamount to the concept of reaching immortality.[225]

> The Christian concept of immortality denies that mortal people can ever attain immortality through a trace-like induced state of consciousness. Rather, immortality is a gift of God's grace by faith in Jesus Christ and the power of his resurrection alone (1 Cor. 15:20-56, NIV).

Additionally, the *Tao Te Ching* speaks about such things as the creative power and essence of the Tao (an impersonal, nameless, uncaring, and ineffable force behind the universe), the importance of always returning to the primordial, emptiness, knowledge and humility, the vanity of material wealth, living simply, victory in war should be mourned as devastation, flexibility and suppleness (as exemplified by water) are superior to rigidity and strength, the duality of nature, appreciating the differences of opposite polarities, etc. After the Bible, the *Tao Te Ching* is the most translated book in the world.

A Taoist scholar named Chuang Tzu has helpfully codified and clarified the following themes of Taoist philosophy:

- *Dao* (道, lit. "the way of nature") The basic unity behind the universe is a mysterious and undefinable force called the *Dao*—the way of nature, which will ultimately destroy all human achievements. Therefore, the major purpose of life should be understanding and ordering one's existence in harmony with the cosmic force that will ultimately destroy all things. In essence, the ultimately reality behind all existence for the Chinese Taoist is nameless, impersonal, unknowable, and uncaring. Such an austere belief falls far short of what Jesus taught about our heavenly Father, who could be prayerfully communicated with (Matt. 6:9-14), who is compassionate toward the world (John 3:16, NIV), and who has promised to meet all of the earthly needs of his family members by faith in Christ (Matt.6:31-33).

- *Life is the greatest of all possessions.* Life for life's sake is superior to striving to achieve fame, wealth, power, education, and family ties—which are all vain pursuits of illusions.

> In Christianity, life for life's sake is a form of idolatry. Rather, knowing Jesus Christ is the greatest of all possessions—for which we must be willing to sacrifice, or lay down our lives in loving pursuit of his kingdom purpose or will and that which glorifies him. (Phil. 3:7-14).

According to Tao philosophy, life should therefore be extended as long as possible by the use of moderation and magical practices—such as external and internal alchemy (the mystical quest to change baser metals into gold, to discover the panacea or the cure for all ills), and the concoction of the elixir potion of longevity), astral travel, divination, etc. Practicing magic, in any form, has been previously cautioned against by both Old and New Testament prohibitions (Deut. 18:10-11; Acts 16:16-18).

Note how the Daoist concept of worldly detachment is similar to the Buddhism teaching regarding the illusion of worldly desires and attachments. And even though the Bible cautions Christians about not loving the world (1 John 2:15-17), which is characterized by the lust of the flesh (carnality), the lust of the eyes (materialism), and the boastful pride of life (egoism/narcissism); we are still enjoined to engage the world as citizens of the kingdom of God/heaven who are here to declare the

Gospel of Christ with power, to build the church with grace, and to rescue the nations with compassion (Matt. 28:18-20, NIV). Essentially, we are on a mission that requires us to be simultaneously *in* the world but not *of* the world (John 17:11-17).
- *Life is to be lived simply.* Such a rationale is to express itself in attitudes of a distrust of education—leading to complexity/confusion of thought, asceticism (extreme self-denial), childlike innocence evidenced by the unquestioned acceptance of one's lot in life, and radical passivism—even to the point of submitting to foreign invaders in hopes of winning them by superior character. Taoists believed that a simple life is best pursued under the least amount of government as possible. In fact, a famous Taoist motto is "the least government is the best government."
Simplicity is a Christian value, but not to the point of denying that God could want us to pursue professional degrees for greater service of his kingdom and the culture in which we live. Furthermore, the apostle Paul specifically warns against asceticism or extreme self-denial as having any spiritual merit (Col, 2:20-23) . Regarding yielding to one's lot in life. We should not be excessively ambitious as this can bring untenable stress, but neither should we be fearful of our progressive calling and what that might require in relation to improving one's lot in life. Finally, the radical passivism of Taoist philosophy is at best naive and at worst a deadly mistake toward foreign aggression.
- *Wú wéi* (无为, lit. "no action or strain; effortlessness") is an important concept of Taoism with regard to understanding when to act and when not to act. The understanding is one of instinctive wisdom rather than exemplified by *natural action*, such as the planets orbiting the Sun; they *do* without *doing* — without ends or means, effort or error. Thus, understanding when and how to act is not knowledge in the sense of calculating the right time and way, what is free of toil and care does not hesitate and cannot falter. Action without action, *"wu wei wu"*, is effortless action.

The main problem with this above concept is that human beings are not like planets orbiting the Sun based on the Newtonian principle of the gravitational pull of larger bodies. Rather we are people created with free-will which requires us to learn to take responsible action in time of need. In other words, inertia (effortless motion and inaction often leading to sluggishness) is not a good principle to build the responses of one's life upon. On the other hand, the hyper-activity of a virtual *obsessive compulsive disorder* is no virtue either. Finally, to think that human effortlessness and inertia cannot hesitate or falter is patently false because of the human element. In other words, there is no observable corroboration to an unfaltering human being. We simply are not that perfect or programmed to be without fault. To think otherwise would itself be an error.

The Origin of Confucianism

Confucius is the Latinized name of *Kung Fu-tzu* (lit. Master Kong), who was born to an aristocratic family in 551 BCE (d. 479 BCE) in the state of Lu, modern Shantung (Hopfe and Woodward, 2007, p. 178). Confucius married and divorced at an early age (19-24) and left his wife and two young children (a son and daughter)—which seems curious for a philosopher who espoused the "ethical centrality of family obligations."[226] Even if he was morally enlightened later in life, this still would not explain why he would not include his children as part of his ethical obligation.

As the *Supreme Editor* of China's deliberate (or contemplative) tradition the two most important books associated with Confucianism are the *I Ching* (which predated Confucius) and *The Analects of Confucius* (a collection of moral and social teachings of Confucius) which was most probably later codified by his disciples.[227]

Confucius was said to be fascinated by the *I Ching* and kept a copy always tethered to his clothing for frequent reference. He once commented that if he had fifty years to spare, that he would devote them to the *I Ching*. In fact, in Confucius' commentaries he literally transforms the *I Ching* from a complex book of divination into a virtual "philosophical masterpiece," which has intrigued philosophers and scientists ever since.[228]

Key Terms and Concepts in Confucian teaching[229]

1. Jen (wren), is the principle of benevolent consideration of both oneself as well as others. *Jen* is an all encompassing love for not only every other person but also of oneself. *Jen* is the virtue of virtues, the supreme guide to all human action, and is the foundation of all human relationships. Translating the Chinese character *Jen* leaves us with the symbol for 'human being' and for 'two'. This translates loosely to loving others as you would love yourself, and in the West it could be best described as Confucius' Golden (or Silver) rule. However Confucianism states the Golden Rule in the negative- "Do not do unto others what you would not want others to do unto you."

2. ***Chun tzu*** (the superior man; the ideal person who is righteous of heart) The *Chun tzu* is one who lives by the ideal of Jen and is neither petty, arrogant, mean-spirited or vengeful. A *Chun tzu* is one who is comfortable with his or herself and is completely respecting to the people he or she meets. He/She is at home in the world, at the disposal of others, completely beyond personal ambition, is intelligent enough to meet anything without fear, and values personal relationships before anything else (i.e., before thinking, reasoning, or studying). Admittedly, few people will ever be able to attain to this ideal — a reality which cause communist leaders to accuse Confucianism of elitism. Finally, a *Chun tzu* was Confucius's solution to his historical situation. For if one can be righteous in the heart, then he will naturally bring about peace to his surroundings.

3. ***Li*** (lee), is the way things should be done — such as a concrete guide to human action as a clear sense of propriety. In *Li* one must be aware of the way one should act and function within a society. In *Li* one can best cultivate their character by understanding what it entails. *Li* encompasses most importantly the *Doctrine of the Mean*, and the *Five Constant Relationships*:

- *The Doctrine of the Mean* is the way in which one should make decisions in life, in which the best decision is always the middle between unworkable extremes. Taking the middle road as Confucius said would guide one to the way things should be done.
- *The Five Constant Relationships* outline how one should act in society, being the relationships between parent and child, husband and wife, elder sibling and junior sibling,

elder friend and junior friend, and ruler and subject. With these constant relationship guidelines, *Li* sets up a hierarchy between the two people and terms the accepted responses and actions between them:

- A parent is to be loving, a child obedient. An elder sibling is to be gentle, and younger siblings respectful.
- Husbands are to be good and fair, and wives understanding.
- Older friends are to be considerate, younger friends reverential.
- Rulers should be benevolent, and subjects loyal.

This concept of hierarchy would fashion Chinese society and government for thousands of years and builds into the next concepts of Confucianism.

4. *Yi* (yee); righteousness; *the moral disposition to do good* (also a necessary condition for *jen* or for the superior man). *Yi* connotes a moral sense: the ability to recognize what is right and good; the ability to feel, under the circumstances what the right thing to do is.

5. *Hsiao* (showe): filial piety; reverence. Parents are revered because they are the source of your life. They have sacrificed much for you. As a result, one should do well and make the family name known and respected thus bringing honor to your family. *Hsiao* also implies that you give your parents not only physical care but also emotional and spiritual richness. When the parents die, their unfulfilled aims and purposes should be the purposes of the children. Confucianism maintains that the beginnings of *jen* are found in ***hsiao*** (family life).

6. *Chih* (chee): moral wisdom; the source of this virtue is knowledge of right and wrong. *Chih* was added to Confucianism by Mencius (372 – 289 BCE), a Chinese philosopher[230] who was arguably the most famous Confucian after Confucius himself who believed that people are basically born good. In other words, man is a moral being for Mencius—who has great potential for good.

Note: Biblically speaking our potential for good has been marred by sin and the resultant fallen-ness within every human being which awakens at the relative age of moral accountability. However, when we come to Christ we have a new capacity to be and do good. Unfortunately, we still have the carnal/fallen nature (also called the *flesh*) which wars against the spirit — also called the *new man* (Gal. 5:16-26). It is only as we grow in grace and knowledge (by renewing our mind) that we can develop the character of Christ and produce more good fruit and works of righteousness (Matt. 5:16).

7. ***Te*** (day) is proper discharge of political power, which is to be exercised by the influence of moral example. *Te* establishes the guidelines for a just government and faithful subjects. Government should be virtuous while ruling, and must keep the confidence of the people — or risk being justifiably overthrown. In fact, for Confucianism, the whole art of government consists in the art of being honest. As a result, government is good if it can maintain economic sufficiency, military sufficiency, and confidence of the people. For their part, all subjects to the ruler must give their popular trust for a country to prosper.
8. ***Wen*** (the arts). *Wen* is Confucianism's respect for art for art's sake and for society's sake as well. Confucius saw that great and powerful nations have extensively cultivated their arts and intellectual endeavors. As knowledge grows, so does the country, leading Confucius to base his esteem of a country by the beauty of its art and the intellect of their philosophers.

These terms and concepts would guide China's culture and governments for thousands of years, and would ultimately help China out of its dark ages and into a period of growth and diversity. However, the rigidity and idealism of Confucianism could not adequately influence China on such a large scale in its original form. Modifications had to be made with the changing times to accommodate the changing perceptions and feelings of the eras. But, the basic principles remained constant throughout the ages.

The Challenges of the Modern World to Chinese Religion

The New Culture Movement of the mid 1910s and 1920s sprang from the disillusionment with traditional Chinese culture following the failure of the Chinese Republic founded in 1912 to address China's problems. New Culture scholars had a classical Chinese education but embraced the ideas of American pragmatism and began to lead a revolt against the Confucian culture.

Specifically, these new scholars called for the creation of a new Chinese culture based on global and western standards, especially democracy and science. Younger followers took up their call for: vernacular literature; an end to the patriarchal family in favor of individual freedom and women's liberation; an acceptance of China's place as a nation among nations (rather than the assertion of superiority of Confucian culture); the re-examination of Confucian texts and ancient classics using modern textual and critical methods (known as the Doubting Antiquity School); democratic and egalitarian values; and an orientation to the future rather than the past.[231]

During the final stage of the Chinese Civil War (1926-1949) the (atheistic) Communist Party of China claimed victory and subjugated mainland China under its rule.

Communist takeover of China

On October 1, 1949, Mao Zedong proclaimed the birth of the People's Republic of China—with the statement "The central government of the People's republic of China is established!"—before a crowd of 500,000 to 1 million people at Tiananmen Square.[232]

Mao's theoretical contribution to Marxism-Leninism, military strategies, and his brand of Communist policies are now collectively known as Maoism. Mao is attributed to having laid the economic, technological, and cultural foundation of modern China—transforming it from an agrarian society into a major world power. However, simultaneous to these accomplishments, Mao's political purges from 1949 until his death in 1976 have, by most estimates, cost between 50-60 million lives in China by one of the world's cruelest Chinese dictators. Since Deng Xiaoping assumed power in 1978, many Maoist policies have been abandoned in favor of economic reforms.

Part of Mao's rejection of religion resulted in the state's requirement that Christians join the three-self movement (self-governance, self-support, and self-propagation) in order to remove all foreign influence from Chinese churches (Hopfe and Woodward, 2007, p. 187). Then in 1952, all Christian missionaries were expelled and most indigenous Christian ministers were imprisoned and/or killed by the thousands—including Watchman Nee. Nee was a national spiritual leader, remarkable church planter, and renowned author Interestingly, Watchman Nee was originally offered the position of leadership over the newly emerging state church—if he would only become a communist. After being continually rebuffed by Nee, the communists imprisoned him and nearly one thousand of his leaders, from which none were said to have escaped—including Nee, who died after 20 years of captivity in 1972 (Kinnear, 1974).

During the Cultural Revolution in 1966, and as part of an ever-tightening noose of religious persecution, Moa implemented a severe repression of all Chinese religion's accusing them of being part of the "four olds," including:

a. Old ideas,
b. Old culture,
c. Old customs,
d. Old habits.

As a result, Confucius was called the number one criminal of feudal thinking (whose birth place was raided and temple destroyed); Taoism was considered an old and superstitious religion; and Buddhism became suspect as a foreign-imported ideology (Hopfe and Woodward, 2007, 186-187).

After the death of Mao, churches began to slowly reopen, the Bible was translated into a Chinese dialect, and the Center for Religious Studies was opened in 1979. However, religion is still limited and all state-approved religions, which are now Taoism, Buddhism, Roman Catholicism, Protestantism, and Islam, are still required to be free from foreign influence, remain officially authorized by the state, and must accept government censorship of all religious writings, state guidance in all clergy selection, and limit their religious activities to approved locations and times only (Hopfe and Woodward, 2007, 187).

Chapter 8: Review Questions

1. What was the most interesting thing that you learned from Chapter 8 and why?
2. What can be culturally discerned by the fact that only 5% of the 1.3 billion Chinese are ruled by atheistic communists?
3. What is the superstition surrounding burning paper money called Hell's Bank Notes at a person's funeral?
4. What does Carl Jung have to do with the occultic use of the I-Ching (Book of Changes)?
5. Discuss the value that modern Chinese place upon Lao-Tsz and Confucius.

Chapter IX

-Atheistic Evolution-

Dr. Dawkins,

As a religious studies scholar and a philosophical-theologian, I would like to respectfully (and briefly) address four main issues which have come to mind as I have reviewed, with great interest, your scientific-philosophical assumptions.

1. Negative Religious Stereotyping (NRS):

    a. While it is irrefutably true that certain religious people have done great harm to some societies, you fail to make a distinction between the abuse of religion itself rather than the proper use of religion—as the affirmation of faith, hope, and love (1 Cor. 13). After all, the same could be said of certain scientists who have abused science—thus reflecting poorly on the practice of scientific methodology, which is the current accusation against Intelligent Design scientific-proponents.

b. Religious stereotyping is also evident in your non-inclusion of what can be described as religiously zealous atheists who were some of the most egregious genocidal murderers of all time—such as Mao (50 million), Lenin (5 million), Stalin (23 million), Pol Pot (2 million, 30% of Cambodia), etc.
c. A final example of NRS is your assumption that most Christians believe in the young-earth/universe theory. On the contrary, only certain fundamental Christian groups, who are in the vast minority, maintain a literal interpretation of Genesis Chapter One. Most all Evangelicals and Roman Catholics believe in the old-earth theory, and the concept of the day-ages in Genesis Chapter One. As a result, the old-earth theory perfectly aligns itself with the geological time scales standards of the International Commission of Stratigraphy (ICS). When you verify this fact, your accusation of being *history haters* will no longer apply to the more than 1.5 billion Christians who are better informed today.

2. Misunderstanding of Biblical-Covenant Theology:

a. The assumption here is that the Law of God, as given to Moses in the Old *Testament* (lit. *covenant*) reveals a morally repugnant false deity who is intent on slaughtering Jewish non-conformists and Gentile nations—including the wholesale massacre of women and children. And while a sufficient explanation is difficult...*Such as God's ultimate judgment for those who wantonly indulge in indolatrous corruption, including sacrificing one's children to the pagan deities such as Moloch and Baal* (Lev. 18:21; 2 Chron. 28:3; Jer. 19:4-6). Such practice was doubtless a foreshadow of abortion on demand, which will ultimately incur the wrath of God on such heartless nations. *However,* the important thing to remember is that now, in Jesus Christ, God has inaugurated a new covenant of grace (Jer. 31:31-34).
b. Such a covenant, though foreshadowed in the Old Testament animal sacrifices, has now been fulfilled in the sacrificial atonement of Jesus—who died for our sin (which now physically separates us from God), but rose from the dead to

guarantee our own resurrection to eternal life in the presence of God. As a result, the Old Covenant is now superseded by the New Covenant; grace has fulfilled the law; and mercy has triumphed over judgment!

3. Scientific over-reach:

   a. My observation of scientific over-reach comes from your attempt to use biological evolution, or any scientific discipline for that matter, to disprove God's existence. My contention is that just as no one can use science to *prove* God's existence, so also can no one use science to *disprove* it either. Furthermore, as long as scientific inquiry is possible, which would be as long as matter exists; there can never be ultimate proof of God's non-existence. The truth is that God does exist, but in another dimension—biblically referred to as the realm of the spirit (John 4:24). Such a spiritual realm can only be discerned by faith, which is a truthful conviction concerning the nature of ultimate reality. In other words, the spiritual dimension of reality is not visible to sensory perception (Heb. 11:1).

   b. The point here is that scientific methodology (observation, hypothesis, controlled/repeated experimentation, theory construction) does not have the tools to quantify ultimate spiritual realities—including that of God's existences and activities. Hence, to attempt to use science to argue a *metaphysical* point is a misuse/abuse of science itself—by presuming that science can quantify a realm beyond its capability. Such an attempt to violate the boundaries of science will most certainly result in claims that more closely reflect science-fiction (alien panspermia) or scientism (the religion of science) rather than the truly scientific. And though it is possible to make strong inferences from scientific research, we should be careful not to make the patently false claim of scientific indubitability—especially regarding the question of God's transcendent existence and the issue of pre-material origins of the universe/creation.

c. An important observation that needs to be mentioned here is a little known or acknowledged fact in the history of science—that the original commissioning of science actually occurred at the end of Genesis Chapter Two, where God said to the presumed progenitors of the human race: "God blessed them and said to them, 'Be fruitful and increase in number; fill the earth and *subdue it*. Rule over the fish of the sea and the birds of the air and over every living creature that moves on the *ground*'" (Gen. 1:28). In this context the term *subdue it*, means to harness the earth's resources for productive human ends—which is the task and privilege of science. Furthermore, such scientific inquiry-discovery was to probe the three realms of physical existence: the ocean/water depths, the land surface of the earth; and the sky—implying the earth's atmosphere and the universal stars of outer-space.

d. In other words, God originally declared science as a blessing to humanity rather than an enemy of faith. However, during the Scientific Revolution of the 16th and 17th centuries science was suppressed by the Roman Catholic hierarchy, who felt threatened by a challenge to its revelation-based hegemony. And so began the long struggle between religion/faith and science/reason—which still persists today. In this regard, I have found the writings of Einstein quite helpful by his insistence that there is no necessary conflict between religion and science.[233] Indeed, Einstein's quote that "Science without religion is lame; religion without science is blind" at least suggests the possibility of a complimentary configuration where science deals with the *what* and *how*; and religion deals with the *who* and *why*.

4. Atheistic Evolution vs. Theistic Evolution:

a. In the argument above, I have sought to demonstrate the issue between the proper use and/or abuse of science. This is why I argue for the *religious neutrality* of evolution as an empirical science alone without reference for or against any religious, theological, or philosophical belief system. And since atheism is a statement against the existence of God, then the term atheistic evolution is oxymoronic and conveys an apparent incongruity. And though I am immensely appreciative of your life work in the fields of ethnology and evolutionary biology, I would appeal to you to reconsider your atheism as an unnecessary extension of evolutionary thought.

b. For example, even if I were to cede you the fact/truth of evolutionary theory as *you* now understand it, this would still not necessarily imply that God could have used the mechanism of evolution to bring about human existence over the 4.5 billion years of the earth's history. This is exactly what the notion of Theistic Evolution (TE) has done. And since the official Roman Catholic position is very close to TE, there is plenty of evidence in support of Christian willingness—including the majority of the 75 million evangelicals in the US, to embrace what you have been proposing throughout your life—however, without the unnecessary rejection of faith or religion.

c. And though I am personally not willing to embrace evolution as the total solution to the answer of man's origin, I, and others like me, am willing to at least admit the possibility that such a mechanism could have been employed by the God who commissioned scientific inquiry at the dawn of human history.

Sincerely, Dr. Ron Woodworth

p.s. The honor of any response would be greatly appreciated as would the opportunity to make your personal acquaintance at any place, time, and/or occasion.

Atheistic-Evolutionary Debate at Arizona State

A funny thing happened the other day when I decided to attend an atheist forum at ASU Grady Gammage Auditorium (3,000 in attendance) in February, 2012. After Dawkin's customary, and quite bombastic atheistic presentation explaining, among other things, why even though there is an unmistakable (re-)appearance of design in nature—

there simply cannot be a design because "we all know that there is no such thing as a designer"!

This kind of extreme bias was peppered throughout the evening, with other assertions, such as:

1. All scientists and American politicians are liars who do not publically admit that they are actually closet atheists.
2. The tacit denial of Einstein as one of the world's great scientists...but I knew the reason for Einstein's demotion. Einstein actually believed that religion and science could and should exist together. In fact, though an agnostic, Einstein actually criticized "fanatical atheists...[who] are like slaves...to their grudge against traditional religion...[rather Einstein] preferred the attitude of humility corresponding to the weakness of our intellectual understanding of nature and of our own being."[234]
3. We need to save the world by *evangelizing* it with the literature from Dr. Dawkins—who is the only one who really knows the truth.
4. It was remarkable how people actually shared rather emotionally charged *testimonies* to the *truth* of Dawkins books, which had literally, "set them free from all ignorance of religion and dependence on the futility of faith in any so-called god."
5. Both Mormons and Republicans deserve equal public ridicule.
6. We should reject all contradictory philosophy/philosophers and theology/theologians, who would ever challenge the notion that God does not exist.
7. Finally, the evening ended with a stunning call from Dawkins to the necessity of *atheistic self-deception*. The reason we need to lie to ourselves (and others) is because that is the only way we can give any meaning to our otherwise meaningless existence.

Well, I decided that I had had enough and went down to the open microphone waiting 20 minutes for the Q&A section to begin...

For the rest of the story, please listen to the recorded live interview of Dr. Woodworth on KPXQ 1360AM radio Monday, March 26, 2012 from 2PM-3PM. There is also an abbreviated link of the ASU event with Dawkins, Krauss, and Ron at RonWoodworth.Org.

The Creation and Evolution Debate

(Neo-Creationism vs. Neo-Darwinism)
-By Stan Reynolds-

The genius of Charles Darwin may have been his ability to notice the little details. Even before the science of genetics and the information carrying power of DNA had been discovered, he correctly observed that characteristics of animal populations changed over time in response to changes in their environment. With his books *On the Origin of Species* and *The Descent of Man*, he launched a revolution in thinking about human origins that reverberates today as the *Theory of Evolution*. As it has been extended by others, his theory has itself *evolved* over time. Because of Darwin's groundbreaking work, for the first time in history a thinking man or woman could postulate a pathway from molecules to man without invoking a creator god. In fact, atheism is now claiming to gain intellectual legitimacy from the theories of evolution. In addition, science's modern mandate to seek only naturalistic solutions in understanding the universe's phenomena seems to represent a decidedly atheistic approach. When coupled with the philosophy of atheism, evolution forms a comprehensive worldview that is the only serious alternative to Christian creation. This worldview attempts to answer life's most fundamental questions of origin, purpose and destiny.

Most proponents of this worldview would probably not consider themselves to be religious, yet it has many of the attributes of a religion. It has its revered *fathers of the faith* in Darwin and Wallace. It has its apologists in Richard Dawkins and Christopher Hitchens[235].

Like a church, there are orthodoxies of belief that are necessary for membership (some university academics have expressed dismay at allowing a commencement speaker who does not profess a belief in the full implications of evolutionary thinking[236]). And like any church there are different levels of commitment among its adherents. There are the *barely attenders* who cannot really articulate what evolution entails but are sure it must be true since somebody else has apparently worked it all out. There are the *consistent members* who find evolution's moral relativism fits well with their own desires and inclinations and can be counted on to show up whenever needed. And there are the *radical fundamentalists* who believe that those who think differently are actually dangerous and may need to be suppressed.

As a legitimate modern alternative to Christian creationism and as a powerful and growing worldview, we should examine its claims, review its critique of Christian creationism and provide a reasoned response. Unfortunately, the Christian church is largely fragmented into various creation/evolution camps at the present time and, in a moment, we will consider differences of opinion within the church before we formulate a reasoned response to the claims of evolution.

The Evolution of Evolution

Darwin's first book did not address the question of human origins but focused on the changes he observed in animal populations. He proposed that different animals had descended from common ancestral groups. After Darwin's time, as we began to understand how key information governing the development and expression of animal features were encoded as information in the DNA of all organisms, we realized the changes Darwin noted fell into two categories. The first types of changes were largely pre-programmed variability present in all animals. We would label these changes as *micro-evolution*, that is, changes within animal species that do not result in entirely different animal kinds but instead allow them to survive as the same animal kinds in the face of changing environmental conditions. Beaks of finches that vary in size and strength in response to rainfall conditions and coloration of moths that vary with pollutant-caused darkening of trees are classic examples.

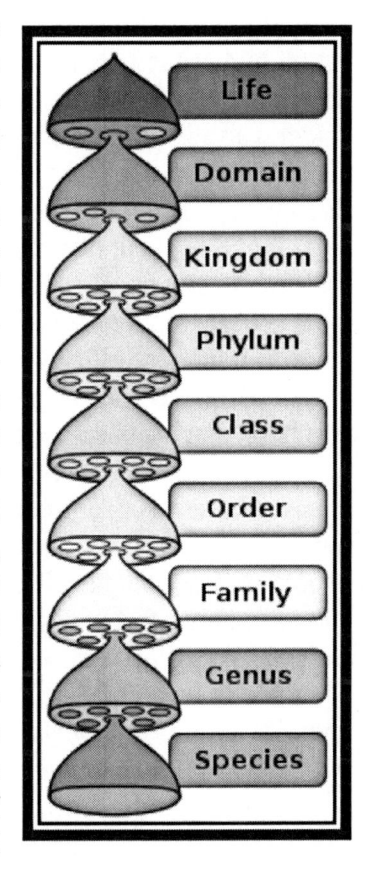

The second type of changes involve a modification to the DNA genetic programming due to copying error in the duplication of genetic material during reproduction or due to mutational change from environmental factors. The vast majority of these types of changes are fatal to the organism but a small fraction can result in a slight difference in a still functioning animal. If enough of these changes are evident, scientists may assign the animal to a separate species. This is generally referred to as *speciation*. Christians would not consider micro-evolution or even speciation to be particularly troubling. The ability of creatures to adapt to their changing world and to vary within broad kinds is drawn quite readily from the biblical creation passages. Variance within animal *kinds*, as well as their unique adaptability is highlighted within the creation material from the oldest book of the Bible, Job, and complements the Genesis material. The Bible indicates that animals were created to stay within their various *kinds*, which is a level of organization higher than species and more similar to the modern concepts of order or family.[237] While researchers might feel that certain changes in a spider warrant assigning it to a different spider species, it would still be considered a spider. Genetic variability and mutational change can have the power to bring Pekinese, dachshunds and St. Bernard dogs (*canis lupis familiaris*) out of an ancient wolf (*canis lupis*), but this leads only to different sub-species. Such **micro-evolution** is consistent both with what is observed live-time in nature and with what the biblical material asserts about variability within broad boundaries called *kinds*.

However, evolution has evolved. It was not long after Darwin's first book that his observations of micro-evolution were extended to the concept of *macro-evolution*. It was thought that if enough of these small changes were to accumulate successfully over time the animal would eventually become a completely different *kind* of animal. **Macro-evolution** asserted that all present, complex animals came from earlier, simpler animal forms. Something that could be observed in real-time (**micro-evolution**) was postulated to produce something that cannot be observed in real-time (**macro-evolution**). Micro-evolution deals with changes within, say, *worms*, for example, while macro-evolution deals with the proposed pathway of changes from soft-bodied, pre-cambrian, worm-like creatures into, eventually, humans.

In the modern dialog about human origins, the word *evolution* is used interchangeably when speaking of both micro-evolution and macro-evolution. Evolution's proponents may say *"evolution (micro-evolution) is a proven fact and anyone who doubts evolution (macro-evolution) is either ignorant or deceived"*. The switching of what is being referred to when using the same term of *evolution* makes reasonable discussion difficult.

Today, evolution has evolved again. In addition to purporting a pathway from one animal kind to an entirely different kind, *chemical evolution* asserts that a completely undirected and unguided pathway exists from *molecules to man* in the natural world. In other words, evolutionary theory has been extended from small changes within animal kinds (micro-evolution) to the descent of completely different animal kinds from simpler ancestors (macro-evolution) to a progression from non-living chemicals to living humans (evolution). This fully developed, all-encompassing, naturalistic pathway from molecules to man is what evolution now teaches.

The evidence for micro-evolution is directly *observable;* however the evidence for macro-evolution has only been *inferred* from nature. Evolutionary scientists believe the inference of macro-evolutionary change is well justified, even perhaps self-evident, given the body of material they review and given what they believe (erroneously) they would have to accept in an alternative, creationistic, explanation. However, because the macro conclusions of the theory of evolution are inferences, reasonable people can and do come to different conclusions. As of early 2010 there were 816 signers of the Scientific Dissent From Darwinism, which states, **"We are skeptical of claims for the ability of random mutation and natural selection to account for the complexity of life. Careful examination of the evidence for Darwinian theory should be encouraged."** Signers must either hold a Ph.D. in a scientific field such as biology, chemistry, mathematics, engineering computer science, or one of the other natural sciences; or they must hold an M.D. and serve as a professor of medicine.[238] Now, there are surely many times that number of qualified scientists and researchers worldwide who have great confidence in evolutionary theory. The point of citing the 816 signers to the Scientific Dissent from Darwinism is no to establish truth by the number of people who believe something to be true, but, rather, to document that trained and qualified people believe there are limits to what evolutionary mechanisms can actually accomplish in the natural realm.

Some believe the evidence is both clear enough and strong enough to *prove* the macro conclusions of evolution. Others currently believe that the tenants of modern evolution are correct but admit the body of evidence might not be conclusive for some. For example, Dr. Richard Leakey, a famed paleoanthropologist and son of respected researchers, Luis and Mary Leakey, has recently predicted that in 15 to 30 years he believes sufficient evidence will have accumulated to convince even the skeptics and the debate over evolution will be over. Not that he has any doubts himself, but, in saying this, he tacitly admits that the evidence, which he believes to be strong, is not yet fully conclusive but will be in the future.[239] Others believe that some evidence supports macro-evolution but cannot preclude the existence of a transcendent creator. And still others believe the evidence can be better interpreted in the framework of a purposeful creator acting progressively over time. The pursuit of evidence creates a kind of *moving target* as the progression of science complicates or resets positions with new data emerging regularly. Some Christians have reluctantly accepted aspects of macro-evolution based on scientific findings only to have subsequent investigations reverse earlier science opinions.

The Range of Opinion

The science related to evolution has emerged over 150 years or more. Some initial conclusions drawn from the data have had to be revised. Some conclusions have been completely reversed. Along the way Christians have attempted to respond to both the assumptions of macro-evolution and the underlying scientific findings. These Christian responses vary based on the information available at the time and the prior bias of the responder. As a result there are many different positions talked about today.

Dr. Hugh Ross, a PhD astronomer and Christian writer has noted...

> Over the past two hundred years, despite exponential growth in the body of data from which to develop a more thorough understanding of both natural history and relevant Bible passages, hostility and controversy seem to have intensified. What began as a skirmish over which explanation - natural process or

divine miracle - provides the best account of Earth's and life's existence and development has exploded into a multi-pronged battle. On the topic of creation alone, combatants include non-theistic evolutionists, young-earth creationists, day-age creationists, framework and analogical-day creationists, deistic and theistic creationists, advocates of 'fully gifted creation,' Genesis-as-myth creationists, Genesis-as-polemic creationists, evolutionary creationists, and the list continues to expand.[240]

In this chapter, we will attempt to highlight and summarize eight of these *options*. In doing so, some will feel we have neglected one position or another. Still others will feel we have assigned their positions to a category not of their liking. In citing certain individuals as representative of one position or another we run the risk of mischaracterizing them. Hence, for our purpose, we will use certain names merely as an indication of some degree of representation without any intention to academically/scientifically limit the individuals so designated.

The Creation-Evolution Debate
Eight Historical-Contemporary Options
(Woodworth & Reynolds)

1. Neo-Creationism—old-earth, day-ages of Genesis/ H. Ross	1. Neo-Darwinism—DNA/ Genetic traits E.O. Wilson/E. Scott
2. Theistic Evolution— F. Collins/ Vatican	2. Atheistic Evolution— Scientism R. Dawkins/C. Hitchens
3. Intelligent Design— religious inference/M. Behe	3. Scientific Evolution— religious neutrality S.J. Gould
4. Young-Earth Creationism— D. Gish/K. Hamm	4. Darwinian Evolution— extreme age, Natural Selection/C. Darwin

We will examine these in pairs starting with the fourth pair.

4. Young-Earth Creationism and Darwinian Evolution

Darwin's theory of evolution emerged in the primarily English-speaking, western civilization of the 1860's. The Christian apologists of the era were at a relative disadvantage in trying to address the findings from the rapidly emerging new sciences of geology, paleontology, archeology and biology. However, they knew that Darwin's proposed theory required a nearly inconceivable amount of time to work...if it worked at all. Although the Bible made no explicit statement about the age of the Earth and universe, in 1654 Bishop James Ussher, Archbishop of Armagh, Primate of All Ireland, had used the Bible lists of genealogies to propose a date for the creation of the earth in 4004 BC and had assigned corresponding dates for most of the major events of the Bible.

The popularity of Ussher's 1654 Chronology grew alongside the expansion of the use of the King James English Bible of 1611. Since Ussher's dates had become incorporated in the margins of many of their Bibles, by the 1860's many English-speaking, western civilization Christians assumed the Earth was quite young. Christian attempts to respond to the spread of the theory of evolution quickly centered on the lack of time available for evolution to work. Being ill-equipped to assess the scientific *possibility* of evolutionary forces, many Christians responded that there was simply not enough *time* for it to work. *Young-Earth Creationism*, while only one of several historic positions, became the more recognized and more vocal response to the challenge of evolution.

The view that *Creationism* meant *young-earth creationism* may have been strengthened one hundred years later, in the 1960's in America. Supreme Court decisions regarding religion and prayer in public schools prompted a significant growth of both private Christian schools and the Christian home schooling movement. These alternative schools desired alternative science textbooks as nearly all public textbooks adopted an evolutionary framework. Several *Young-Earth Creationism* organizations were among the first to create and provide science textbooks and a significantly large generation of young Christians in America were educated with a decidedly youth-earth creationist orientation. From the writings and speeches of the more intense proponents of evolution, it seems clear that *more than a few* average Americans believe that young earth creationism is the official position of the Christian church. In fact, the assumption is so prevalent that almost any use of the term *Creationism* means a belief the world and the universe came into existence between 6,000 and 10,000 years ago. Writers and speakers such as Ken Hamm[241] and Duane Gish[242] are examples of those who have promoted this view.

In the same way that we must clearly define what we are discussing when we talk about Evolution (micro-evolution within animal kinds **versus** macro-evolution of animals into entirely different kinds), we must also carefully define which model of Creationism we are discussing (young-earth that rejects current science data about the age of the earth **or** older-earth creationism that accepts the current data). Only then can we have a meaningful dialog.

Over the last twenty years many of the various evidences enunciated in support of a young earth have weakened or been set aside. Meanwhile, multiple, independent means for dating the age of the earth have been corroborated. This has been recognized by both courts and school districts as young-earth creationists have argued for equal time in science classes for the teaching of (young-earth) creationism. By and large, young earth creationism has been ineffective in being considered a scientific, as opposed to simply, religious endeavor.

It is quite interesting that the emerging confidence and consensus about the earth's age at around 4 billion years and the universe's age at around 14 billion years, has presented problems for both traditional *Darwinian Evolution* and *Young-Earth Creationism.* The kind of evolution envisioned by Darwin and the forces of natural selection would require trillions and quadrillions of years to unfold. This was no problem in the 1860s of Darwin's day as the universe was considered by most scholars to be infinitely large and infinitely old. Einstein's scientific revolution of 1905 shocked the intelligentsia by asserting the universe sprang into being a finite time ago. Our current best understanding of the age of the Earth does not provide enough time for all the ramifications of evolution via unaided natural forces…just as the early young-earth creationists argued. However, even at only a few billions of years old, the earth is far, far older than even the most liberal young-earth creationist would accept. *Our middle-aged universe poses big obstacles for both Extremely-Old-Earth Darwinian Evolution and Young-Earth Creationism.*

3. Intelligent Design and Scientific Evolution

Stephen J. Gould considered carefully the problem a middle-aged universe posed for the classical understanding of evolution handed down from Darwin.[243] Not only was the earth (at 4 billion years old) much younger than the universe (at 14 billion years old), but early earth conditions meant life did not have a chance to get started until quite a while after the earth formed. Meanwhile, the oldest date for the appearance of functional life on the earth kept being pushed farther and farther back. These two factors squeezed the time available for evolutionary forces to work, even if they could be shown to work at all, into mere millions of years. The scientific discovery of the information carrying function of DNA and its rare errors and mutations had provided support for how natural selection might actually function, but the growing fossil data showed that life had not arrived on the earth in the long, slow step-wise fashion proposed by Darwin. Gould proposed a modification to Darwinian evolution he called "punctuated equilibrium" where evolution was assumed to jump forward in rapid spurts and then settle into periods of prolonged stasis in response to environmental and climate changes.

His attempt was a recognition that the theory of evolution had to change to accommodate the new information. He is also known for proposing a resolution for the rancorous evolution/creation debate by suggesting that each view had its own area of authority, called a magisteria. His "non-overlapping magisteria"[244] concept let scientific evolution speak to the "what and when" while creation spoke to the "why and how." His desire was that scientific evolution should be 'religiously neutral.' His assertion that creationism had no authority to speak to the "what and when" did not sit well with creationists and did not gain much traction.

On the other hand, *Intelligent Design* proponents also attempt to avoid unnecessary religious implications by focusing on what scientific research could tell us about things designed versus things naturally evolved. Dr. Michael Behe of Lehigh University produced two very talked-about books (*Darwin's Black Box* and *The Edge of Evolution*)[245] and is representative of researchers who see evidence of design throughout the natural world that cannot be explained fully by naturalism but feel unable to scientifically identify who or what is the designer. They typically accept the current understanding of the age of the universe and urge researchers to follow the data wherever it leads... even if it leads away from naturalism and toward a designer. They generally accept many evolutionary principles but feel the evidence does not validate the full "molecules to man" pathway without the intervention of a designing intelligence. In short, they believe evidence points to limits in evolutionary theory and certain phenomena point to a designing intelligence. Although they may have individual opinions as to who or what the designer is, they simply urge other scientists to be open to design as an explanation. Many evolutionists feel the intelligent design movement is cover screen for introducing religion into schools.

2. Theistic Evolution and Atheistic Evolution

In another attempt to reconcile religious views (mostly based in multiple Bible passages describing the created realm) and non-religious research findings, *Theistic Evolutionists* propose that the forces of evolution are, indeed, able to bring about the human body from beginning to end by purely natural forces that God designed into the fabric and laws that govern this universe. In other words, God used evolution to bring humans about. Dr. Francis Collins, the well-respected head of the Human Genome Project that mapped the six billion programming characters of human DNA, believed that coding similarities between humans and chimps (as well as, other animals) showed that they must have descended from a previous common ancestor.[246] Shared similarities in errors in the DNA code even bolstered this view in their opinion.

For example, humans and chimps each have a "broken" (suppressed) gene that codes for production of Vitamin C. To avoid sickness and death from diseases like scurvy, they must both consume fruit on a regular basis to get the Vitamin C that other animals can manufacture internally. These kinds of DNA evidences are like a "smoking gun", they might say, pointing to common descent from an ancestor of both that had this defect. However, fruit bats also have this broken gene and must eat fruit...hence the name. Guinea pigs, as well, have the broken gene. No one suggests humans and fruit bats shared a recent common ancestor and no one holds that guinea pigs and humans are so closely related. Perhaps that gene is easier to 'break' than we allow.

In another example, vast portions of the six billion character programming code in the DNA for humans were initially found to have no function. Labeled as 'junk DNA', it was thought to be the unnecessary left over remnants of previous ancestors that now have no function. The random, hit-and-miss, start-and-stop processes described by evolution should result in a great many "failed attempts" and "false starts" that would populate the genetic code. Non-functional areas of the DNA would be predicted by evolutionary theory. Multiple animals actually have multiple regions of non-coding DNA in common...suggesting they share common ancestry. Theistic evolutionists attempt to deal honestly with this evidence while still holding to an ultimate Creator. However, recent research continues to astonish by finding that 'junk' DNA regions serve as command and control functions. While they do not code for production of proteins, they appear to control the functioning, or 'expression' of nearby genes that do. It is becoming evident that nearly every part of DNA may have function.

Nonetheless theistic evolutionists feel the evidence is still strong enough to justify their position. In allowing God a role in setting up the universe and endowing it with all the potential to evolve on its own to reach our present state, theistic evolutionists retain a belief in God and in life after death but usually deny much of the literalness of biblical creation passages. Adam and Eve are not seen as real individuals specially created by God but are viewed more as an allegorical or non-literal, poetic telling of God's purposes more than His actual acts.

On the other side of this comparison, *Atheistic Evolutionists* find no evidence for a creator god and allow no place for a divine foot in the door. We would put forward prominent biologist and writer, Richard Dawkins, as an example in this area. In their thinking, an intelligent designer or a divine creator simply limits and hinders man's exploration of the universe. Scientists must always pursue only natural causes for life's phenomena. The more militant of these atheistic evolutionists feel that any form of creationism is a hindrance to the scientific enterprise and may even be dangerous.

> "It is absolutely safe to say that, if you meet somebody who claims not to believe in evolution, that person is either ignorant, stupid, or insane."
>
> "Today the theory of evolution is about as much open to doubt as the theory that the earth goes round the sun."
>
> ## *Richard Dawkins*

Dr. William B. Provine, Professor of Biological Sciences at Cornell University, wrote honestly and directly about the logical and reasonable conclusions of atheistic evolution when he said...

> Let me summarize my views on what modern evolutionary biology tells us loud and clear... There are no gods, no purposes, and no goal-directed forces of any kind. There is no life after death. When I die, I am absolutely certain that I am going to be dead. That's the end for me. There is no ultimate foundation for ethics, no ultimate meaning to life, and no free will for humans, either.'[247]

Every comprehensive *worldview* provides answers to at least life's five great questions, which includes:

1. Origin..."Where did I come from?"
2. Identity..."Who am I?"
3. Meaning..."What is my purpose?"
4. Morality..."How should I conduct my life?"
5. Destiny..."What lies ahead?"

The worldview of atheistic evolution provides answers, as Dr. Provine so honestly listed for us above, but they are not very satisfying.

1. Progressive Creationism and Neo-Darwinism

Neo-Darwinism represents the best modern efforts to weave the elements of evolutionary theory into a comprehensive and cohesive science that embraces the emerging technologies, techniques and data. These researchers are utilizing the many new tools unavailable to Darwin, such as, genetics, bio-chemistry, cellular biology, astrobiology, physics and others. They look hopefully to the search for extraterrestrial planets for evidence of microscopic life to show that life from non-life should have happened multiple times in history of the universe. They seek evidence of randomness inside the cell and its programming code, DNA, and they look for naturalistic chemical pathways for life's origin.

Increasingly, the areas of research are quite specialized and require unique training. It is difficult for any one scientist to know well what is going on in other disciplines. Often each assumes the others have solved or are well on their way to solving any difficulties for evolutionary theory. The puzzling obstacles in their particular field will surely have to fall since evolution has been "proved" in so many other fields. In *"The Grand Design"* Dr. Stephen Hawking, physicist and author of the highest selling science book of all time, *"A Brief History Of Time"*, asserts that his mathematical model for the instant of the universe's appearance negates a need for God and he confidently states, "Darwin and Wallace explained how the apparently miraculous design of living forms could appear without intervention by a supreme being."[248] The brilliance of Stephen Hawking in the area of physics can hardly be overstated, yet he assumes biologists have answered all the questions in their area.

Nonetheless, assuming each scientific specialty has solved its evolution questions, a general consensus has developed within evolutionary theory that holds to certain hallmarks of belief.

*So, today we have the current **hallmarks of Neo-Darwinism**...*

1. Life is an emergent property of the universe.

Like the universal law of gravity, if the right materials and conditions exist together anywhere in the universe, then non-living chemicals will self-assemble into living, biological systems and will increase in complexity and information over time.

2. Life on the Earth is neither unique nor special.

Life is inevitable. Though statistically improbable, given enough time and enough places of opportunity, this progression "from molecules to man" is inevitable.

3. On multiple occasions life on Earth has replaced itself after mass extinctions.

Asteroidal impacts, environmental changes and other factors have wiped out more than 90% of life forms on the earth in short periods of geologic time on numerous occasions. New, novel and different life forms have appeared afterward to replenish the Earth. At times, then, evolution is hyper-efficient, producing results in astonishingly short geologic time periods.

4. Though impossible to detect in modern history, complete changes from one type of animal to an entirely different kind are present in the fossil record.

Darwin was concerned about the paucity of evidence in the fossil record for his theory but was confident that future study in these fields would uncover the proof. After another 150 years of diligent search of the earth, the fossil record still presents a picture of fully formed, fully functional creatures appearing seemingly out of nowhere. However, proponents of evolution insist that notable examples such as the horse and whale fossil records do outline the evolutionary progression.

5. Therefore, the extrapolation from the observation of micro-evolution to the proposed outcome of macro-evolution is not only justified but is self-evident.

Field observations show the characteristics within animal kinds (beak length, thickness of feathers or fur, coloration, body size) changing in subsequent generations in response to environmental changes. Under evolutionary theory this can and should be extrapolated and projected forward to the point that enough accumulated changes culminate in a creature that is an utterly different kind than the original.

6. Evolutionary theory is the central organizing theme of modern biology.

All biological discoveries and observations must fit into appropriate "cubbyholes" in the evolutionary cabinet. In other words, as we go out to observe the real world, each thing we note and each process we document should be interpreted within an evolutionary framework. If we find a fossil whose sophistication level would fit for a later date according to evolutionary theory but our dating techniques show is out of sequence time-wise then something is suspect with the dating technique. Discordant dates should be reanalyzed and reinterpreted and additional types of dating should be employed before reassessing what evolutionary theory would have predicted. A portion of the "how" evolution played out may be adjusted but the underlying assumption that that it "did" play out should remain intact. The data may be suspect, but the fundamental theory is not.

In contrast with Neo-Darwinism, *Progressive Creationism* does not believe the extrapolation from observable micro-evolution to an acceptance of macro-evolution is justified. Progressive creationism is a rapidly growing Christian initiative regarding the origins debate. Progressive creationists believe the Creator worked over long periods of time to place just-right life forms suited for certain epochs of earth's physical history and to progressively replace life forms that went extinct with new forms suited for the next phase of earth's development. God is aggressively and progressively involved in shepherding the process of life through the ages preparing the earth's biosphere for the introduction of man during the small window of time that advanced humans can exist on earth. The progressive creationist model benefits from a much closer alignment with the science data on the age and geologic history of the earth than young-earth creationism. At the same time it upholds much of the "literalness" of scriptural creation material that theistic evolution often denies.It does this by matching the words "and God said" or "then God made" from the biblical creation material to specific, progressive steps in their model and in evidence drawn from nature's record.

Just as the ancient Belgic Confession of 1561 asserts that Nature and Scripture work together to reveal God's activity and purposes, so too do progressive creationists believe that harmony between the record of nature and the record of Scripture not only exists but is best revealed when both are considered together. As such, progressive creationism views scientists and the scientific endeavor as allies rather than antagonists. They accept the scientifically established ages for the earth and the universe and, as such, are often labeled "old-earth creationists". They see the record of nature casting light on puzzling or difficult passages of scripture and they see scripture illuminating the purpose of parts of the natural realm. Like two gloves in a pair, neither functions fully complete alone and neither can fully substitute for the other in this matter of unveiling the creation.

In the words of theology, *General Revelation* (the record of Nature) shows us a portion of the Creator's plan in the what and when, while *Special Revelation* (the special revelation of Christ as recorded in Scripture) shows us the Creator's plan in the who and why. Progressive creationists assert that Nature (when correctly examined and understood) and Scripture (when all passages are fully integrated) will not be in conflict. Science is a human endeavor in the study and interpretation of the facts of Nature and occasionally gets things wrong. In like manner, Theology is a human endeavor in the study and interpretation of the facts of Scripture and also gets things wrong sometimes. Therefore, to progressive creationists, it is not surprising that we see conflict between Science and Theology, but open-minded study should produce cohesion between Nature and Scripture.

Progressive creationism believes the scientific enterprise can and does produce information that enriches the understanding of scripture. In accepting the "middle-aged" nature of the universe they believe both macro-evolution and young-earth creationism have significant problems. They see the choice of the 1611 King James translators of the English words "morning", "evening", and "day" for their original Hebrew counterparts (in place of at least two other literal definition translation choices available to them) may have inadvertently helped give rise to the young-earth creationists assumptions that all of the universe, earth, plants, animals and humans were brought into existence in six, consecutive twenty-four hour "days". In their opinion, the Genesis creation material, as originally delivered in Hebrew, allows easily for a literal (not metaphorical or poetic) translation into a chronology of events occurring during six long creation periods or epochs.[249] They, thus, believe that the passages of Genesis are more literal than theistic evolutionists or, even, many intelligent design proponents would allow, but are not chained to the rigid understanding of young-earth creationists. As such, they often take criticism from both evolutionist and creationist groups.

One Debate, Many Schools of Thought

As has been seen, both creationists and evolutionists fall into multiple camps. The differences between them can be great. However, there are some common areas of agreement that some might find surprising.

1. Both Sides Agree The Universe Was Created!

Though the notion of a beginning to the universe that we can measure and observe was repugnant to some scientists, the accumulation of vast data has forced a recognition that all the matter, energy, space and time of this universe sprang into being a finite time ago out of nothing that we can observe or measure. The Space-Time Theorems of General Relativity as postulated by Stephen Hawking and Roger Penrose lead to a corollary that the causal agent for the universe's existence must lie outside the space-time manifold. This means nothing within the universe could have brought the universe into being and, yet, it definitely came into being a finite time ago. ***The debate is no longer about whether the universe was created, but who or what was the creator.***

2. Both Sides Propose That An Invisible Agent Brought About The Universe!

Current theoretical work into the multiverse concept attempts to say that our universe is one of an infinite number of universes being spawned out of a sort of great universe-creating machine. Since such a phenomena lies outside the space-time limits of the universe to which we are confined, no direct evidence or observation is possible. Evolutionary proponents have been forced to the place of postulating, without perfect evidence, an invisible, impersonal mechanism that "spawns" universes. Christian creationism believes, without perfect evidence, in an invisible, personal being that creates a universe for purposes of His own.

3. Both Sides Acknowledge The Three Great Singularities!

We describe the universe as having begun in a "singularity." This means its appearance out of seemingly nothing a finite time ago is a singular event. It cannot be replicated and run as an experiment. Through the massive Hadrian collider and others we accelerate protons to nearly the speed of light and set up head-on collisions that are microscopically spectacular. They mimic, for an incredibly short period of time, the enormous energies and temperatures near the beginning of the universe. Though we can push back our insights about how the universe probably behaved in some of its earliest moments, we cannot push back to the precise initial instant when energies were essentially nearly infinite. In short, a "singularity" is a singular incident you can speculate about but have little hope of being able to prove since it cannot be replicated.

There are three such singularities in the physical world that have proven particularly thorny for researchers to explain...

i. Everything from Nothing... (Without A Creator)
ii. Life from Non-Life... (Without Help)
iii. Humanity from Animals... (Spirituality From Physicality)

When it comes to these three singularities, we will likely continue to be uncertain about lies just "before" each. Being creatures of this universe imposes limitations on us about what can be known for certain. Like the Heisenberg Uncertainty Principle in physics, it seems that a certain level of uncertainty is "baked into the cake" of our existence. When we correctly say that science can neither prove nor disprove the existence of the Creator God of the Bible we are making a scientifically accurate statement. Science *can* disprove the gods of Greek mythology for they were supposed to have created from within the universe. However, the Space-Time Theorems of General Relativity assure that the question of ultimate origins will remain a question of faith. Non-creationists and creationists alike recognize that there are singular barriers beyond which we cannot *know*, we can only *infer*. We are not saying that evidence from the record of nature can prove the existence of a Creator God. The same record of Scripture that brings us the words "in the beginning God created" also bring us the words "for without faith it is impossible to please God." We are asserting, however, that the record of nature (when properly examined) and the record of scripture (when properly interpreted) provide a concurrence and a reassurance that can take us much, much farther down the path than we have previously imagined. However, at the end of that path, when nature can take us no further, lies a step of faith. We believe it is reasonable faith and not "blind" faith, but it will require faith nonetheless. Evolutionists exercise faith in something about which they cannot have complete knowledge when they postulate that some kind of multiverse or other non-personal entity exists beyond the edge of our reality that initiated things here. Christian creationists, likewise, must exercise faith in that which may be illuminated by nature but cannot ever be fully known when they assert the personal Creator God of the Bible initiated (and participated in) the origin and development of our home and life.

Evolution's Critique of Christian Creationism

In a moment, we will consider some reasons people of reasonable and rational logic find it difficult to accept and adopt the fundamental conclusions of evolution in order to explain life on earth. First, however, let us consider evolution's critique of Christian creationism.

In many cases in recent years we have witnessed an increase in the stridency and forcefulness of the speeches and writings of prominent evolutionary atheism proponents. These writers leap quickly from scientific theory to transcendent truth claim - which is the domain of philosophy, theology and metaphysics. They have expressed dismay at the continuance of creationistic belief in the face of the scientific advances of the last 150 years. They further believe that a rejection of the conclusions of Neo-Darwinism is actually detrimental to the further advance of science. They reason that researchers will simply be ill-equipped to probe the mysteries of life on earth if they reject the primary driving factor that, in their opinion, shapes and directs both the origin and the development of life. However, they would not consider this "their opinion" but simply a statement of "self-evident truth".

They believe the short time periods presented by "classical" creationism (more on this concept later) are at odds with the mounting evidence of the much older age of the universe and of the earth presented by the disciplines of astronomy and physics. They believe that critiquing evolution's limited ability to fully explain all phenomena at this time is a weak argument. In a sense it is merely a form of the so-called *God -of-the-gaps* approach. They find the silence or the absence of the creator or our inability to measure or detect a creator further weakens creationist positions.

As they have considered the case for creation they have concluded that it is not rational in the face of current scientific knowledge and is, at its core, simply a religious belief. Some of these writers declare that this core religious belief shapes, colors and warps the way creationists view and interpret facts and data. While a pre-set commitment to naturalism biases evolutionary researchers as well, science has made great strides in the past by refusing to accept non-natural causes as explanations of phenomena.

For some years certain creation proponents have advocated presenting creation alongside evolution as equally viable theories in public school teaching sessions. Evolution proponents do not see this as some sort of "fairness" or "equal time" issue but, rather, are sincerely alarmed that a theory that seems to violate major tenets from chemistry, astronomy, physics, as well as, biology would want to be presented on equal footing with evolutionary theory. The well-entrenched, opposite positions seen at some school board curriculum meetings displays this quite well. Evolutionists are often genuinely astonished creationists could be so committed to their views in the face of what they perceive to be overwhelming evidence to the contrary. However, in biology and behavioral sciences like psychology and sociology, people come to radically different opinions about what they observe in nature. These systems are enormously complex with multiple, interacting variables and it is often very difficult to directly link cause and effect for certain observed phenomena. These sciences are referred to as the "soft" sciences. It often confuses laypeople that seemingly opposite conclusions can be drawn from data and research in these areas.

Soft and *Hard* Sciences

In some fields of research there are several or many possible explanations for observed phenomena. This is a "soft" science. In other areas, one and only one, answer arises from a solved problem. We would refer to these areas as the "hard" sciences.

In biology, behavioral psychology and even, economics, multiple interpretations and reasons are given for the outcomes of research and experiments. Well-meaning, sincere people can come down on both sides of an issue. However, in mathematics, physics, chemistry and astronomy, effects spring quite directly from certain accurately described causes that follow very consistent and repetitive, mathematically described physical laws. For these "hard" sciences, a direct link between cause and effect is usually evident and often a singular answer arises.

As Dr. Hugh Ross has observed, stars are far simpler than children. Using relatively straight forward physical equations we can accurately describe and predict the behavior of stars, that is, their birth, development and death in any part of the universe. However no such simple system of equations can predict the behavior of our sons or daughters at nearly any point in their lives.

In summary, evolutionists today generally believe that the theory of creation puts forth arguments that have been refuted by the sciences of chemistry, physics and astronomy and, therefore, cannot be seriously considered. They do not merely believe it is a difference of opinion over the findings of the *soft* sciences but an actual violation of the discoveries of the *hard* sciences.

Christianity's Critique of Evolution

Christians of reasonable faith are concerned that evolution's grand explanation of all things has failed to fully deliver on each of the three great singularities. The explanation of "Everything-From-Nothing" has become an exercise in metaphysics, whereby speculative, invisible, non-personal, non-testable forces are presumed to exist beyond the universe that bring it into being already pregnant with the possibility of stars, planets, plants, animals and humans. In addition, the explanation of "Life from Non-Living Chemicals" has been repeatedly frustrated. *(The reader is encouraged to see the addendum article **"Top Ten Things Nobody In The Know Believes Anymore"** for a greater discussion of the barriers encountered by origins-of-life researchers.)* Proposals speculated by origins-of-life researchers have encountered dead ends. While scientists in other fields may think this problem has been worked out, those in the know are aware that we are no closer than ever to a plausible way of explaining how non-living chemicals self-assemble themselves into complex, information-bearing, living systems. And finally, little significant work has been completed to explain the massively vast gulf between sentient, self-aware, spiritual humans and the animals of creation. No other creatures wonder about and seek answers to where we came from and what happens when we die.

Now, we are well aware that absence-of-proof is not proof-of-absence. We are not advocating a *god-of-the-gaps* argument here. We are not saying macro-evolution is proven false simply because of the questions it cannot presently answer. We do, however, say that people of good intelligence and reasonable intentions can and do find fault with the grand pronunciations that *evolution is a proven fact*. Proving that animal characteristics vary within their *kinds* in response to changing environmental conditions is "peanuts" compared to proving the three great singularities happened entirely by accident and without intervening direction or help of any kind.

Digging Down A Little Deeper...
10 Cracks in the Foundation of Evolution

1. The Growing Realization of the Appearance of Design

In "Disturbing the Universe" in 1979 Freeman Dyson wrote, *"The more I examine the universe and the details of its architecture, the more evidence I find that the universe in some sense must have known we were coming."*[250] Ever since Wm. Paley proposed that a watch found during your morning walk would always be considered a product of an intelligent designer, evolution's defenders have argued that the comparison is meaningless. Since mechanical systems like the watch are not biological systems like life then Paley must have been talking apples instead of oranges.

However, two hundred years of peeling the cover of nature back layer by layer have simply revealed deeper and deeper levels of complexity and integration. we now routinely refer to processes going on in every one of the trillion or so cells of our bodies as "factories" or "cities" with transportation systems for moving raw materials in and waste out and sensing systems to know the difference. The internal workings of the cell were unknown to Darwin but today we are struck with how they are organized in much the same way we humans organize our cities and factories. And from physics comes the realization that several hundred very distinct physical constants and laws must be perfectly set in place and "fine-tuned" to each other to even allow for the possibility of life to ever exist. Before the forces of "natural selection" could even work on a biological system, these hundreds of physical parameters had to be in precise arrangement. So great has grown the appearance of design that evolutionary biologists must constantly remind themselves to ignore it.

> *"Biologists must constantly keep in mind that what they see was not designed, but rather evolved."*
> Co-discoverer of the structure of DNA, Francis Crick
>
> *"Biology is the study of complicated things that give the appearance of having been designed for a purpose."*
> Richard Dawkins, "Climbing Mount Improbable"

Additionally, we now recognize the interdependence of many of these physical constants in allowing for life. It becomes increasingly hard to dismiss the appearance of design of such multi-contingencies. Finally, there is the puzzling observation that many of the very features needed for life's existence and survival also simultaneously make exploring and discovering the universe's secrets accessible to that very life. For example, due to radiation effects life cannot reside in any of the star dense areas of galaxy cores, and complex, human life needs to reside under a relatively thin, oxygen-rich atmosphere. By being positioned in the darker, outer areas of the Milky Way galaxy between two of its spiral arms and having a transparent atmosphere Earth just happens to be a nearly ideal platform on which to build telescopes to observe the cosmos. As a result, many of the things that make for habitability also allow and even enhance discoverability. That we, on such a small place in such a large universe, have been able to map the full size and scope and nearly all of the 13.73 billion year history of the cosmos, is a matter of no small wonder to many. In the light of these observations, one might modify Einstein's famous quotation ("The most incomprehensible thing about the universe is that it is comprehensible!") and rephrase it as..."The discovery that the universe is discoverable by mere humans is mind-boggling!"[251]

2. The Origin of Life Cannot Be Described Scientifically

Despite multiple decades of detailed proposals, hypotheses and tests, no random, naturalistic process has been discovered that can turn non-living chemicals and molecules into living, biological systems without the intervention of askilled, outside helper and the simultaneous injection of information. Biological life systems require both order and function that must be regulated through the use of information technology.

The details of how the Stanley Miller experiments of the 1950's resulted in biological precursor molecules (amino acids) actually show how critically necessary is the intervention of a clever, outside researcher. Without the clever trap arrangement, the amino acids produced by running sparks through a chamber of gases would only quickly decay away. In addition, more recent research reveals a different makeup of the primordial atmosphere than Miller assumed. Today's origin of life researchers are more frustrated than ever before.[252]

3. The Time Window for Evolution Keeps Shrinking

The universe is about 13.73 billion years old, but the earth is only about 4.6 billion years old. The evidence for the earliest life on earth is now pushed back to nearly 3.8 billion years ago. The time window for the process of chemical evolution to surmount the second great singularity...life from non-life...has now shrunk to only 800 million years. This is a mere blink of the eye in cosmic time.

However, the first several hundred million years of earth's existence contain the "hadean" (hellish) period where cosmic debris bombarded the planet. The craters of the moon still show what our planet went through. Any kind of pre-life chemistry was constantly interrupted in the hadean period. The earliest life's activity shows up almost as soon as earth exits this period. The time window to go from non-living chemicals to integrated, replicating, living systems of dozens and dozens of proteins has now shrunk to a few tens of millions of years. This is an inconceivably short, vanishingly small period of time.

For random chemicals to bump together in some primordial soup and accidentally self-assemble into the many dozens of just-right long-chain proteins in just the right orientation to each other has always been so improbable as to be considered statistically impossible by skeptical mathematicians, even in trillions of years. It is no wonder that a great scientist like Francis Crick, co-discoverer of the structure of DNA, argues that life here had to be brought for out there. He suggests "panspermia", the seeding of life here from somewhere else in the universe, as a reasonable solution. Perhaps life molecules hitchhiked here on

4. Macro-Evolution is not discernible in real time yet is hyper-efficient in the past

The forces of evolutionary theory involve undirected, random, chance encounters and turns of events, most of which turn out to be blind alleys. The vast majority of mutations and changes are unproductive and damaging and are discarded. Far more often than not, the mutation kills the organism and evolution must start over. It is hyper inefficient to the extreme.

The earth experienced multiple life exterminating events where 90% or more of the life forms on the planet were wiped out. These were followed by repopulating of the earth with completely new ecosystems of involving both plant and animal life within tens of millions of years. These evidences imply the forces of evolution must be hyper-efficient, producing millions and billions of successful DNA programming changes to organisms in short periods of time on multiple occasions.[254]

5. The Best Fossil Examples of Macro-Evolution are Animals Least Likely to Undergo Successful Evolutionary Change

While not discernible in real-time, macro-evolution says that the fossil

"In the Cambrian strata of rocks, vintage about 600 million years, are the oldest in which we find most of the major invertebrate groups. And we find many of them already in an advanced state of evolution, the very first time they appear. It is as though they were just planted there, without any evolutionary history. Needless to say, this appearance of sudden planting has delighted creationists."

Richard Dawkins, The Blind Watchmaker (New York: W. W. Norton, 1996), 229.

remains of both horse and whale creatures documents evidence of macro-evolution over past periods. However, among all animals, horses and whales are some of the least likely to derive benefits from the forces of evolutionary change.

Mutational change to the DNA programming core is highly negative. Scientists know that a chance mutation of your DNA is far, far more likely to improve your chances of cancer than it is to improve your career. This means random mutations will more likely kill you than help you and if you do not grow up quickly and have a lot of children they will shut down your entire family line.

This means negative mutational defects will kill off large-bodied, slow-growing creatures that have few offspring faster than they can reproduce and will drive them toward extinction. The forces of evolution involve an enormous imbalance between negative mutations (mistakes) and positive mutations (improvements). As such these forces might favor small-bodied, rapidly growing organisms that produce millions of offspring (think bacteria and the evidence of evolved bacterial resistance to antibiotics). However they will work the opposite way in large-bodied, slow-growing, limited-reproducing creatures, driving them repeatedly to extinction (like horses and whales).

The best series of fossils that can be arranged and presented as "evolving" in the fossil record are the creatures least likely to undergo successful evolutionary change even if the forces of evolution actually work! It is more likely these are the fossils of multiple species of whales and horses that have gone extinct than they are species that gave rise to each other.[255]

6. The Cambrian Explosion Impasse...Biology's "Big Bag"

Pre-Cambrian levels of the "geologic column" contain extremely low levels of fossil impressions while the Cambrian levels immediately above literally explode with fossil impressions of a wide and varied kind. Representative body types of nearly all 70 of the phyla (body plan) classifications used today appear suddenly in the sea life fossils of Cambrian rocks without noticeable precursors and in a fully formed and fully functional state. They exhibit an extraordinarily high level of organization and development despite the fact that they are the first appearances of higher level life in earth's history. Even our own body plan...chordates...appears in the Cambrian material. This is not what Neo-Darwinism would predict.

7. Probability Problems in Protein Production

The cell produces the very proteins that work to build and maintain cells. At a bare minimum several dozens of proteins must be in coordinated action for even the most minimal of life forms. Each protein consists of several hundred individual chemical units that must exist in their exact sequence. The mathematical probabilities against random, non-directed encounters of biological precursors in some ancient primordial soup producing such a suite of proteins at the same time have been calculated as being essentially impossible. In addition, in a random world the amino acid sub-units that must be used to build proteins each come in two varieties known as right-handed and left-handed. The cell uses only the left-handed versions in proteins and only the right-handed versions in sugars...a condition known as "homochirality". If the process were random and undirected, we would expect a roughly equal mixture of both versions used throughout biology. This is not the case and greatly complicates the case for the accidental development of the cell.

8. The Signature in the Cell...the 800 Pound Gorilla in the Room

In Darwin's time the inside of the cell was a mystery. The cell was viewed as a "black box". Things went into it and things came out but what went on inside was unknown. The phrase "simple, one-celled animals" referred to idea that they must be incredibly simple since the cell was seemingly a bag of mostly water and nutrients. Over the last 150 years we have learned differently.

That the cell is enormously well-organized and complex far beyond anyone's earlier predictions is well known. That the nucleus of the cell contains a material called DNA that operates like a modern day computer hard drive storage device is now also well known. One might perform a modern day update to Wm. Paley's watchmaker argument for the existence of a creator by assuming the stroller in the English meadow who finds a watch is a jogger on a California beach who stubs her toe against a computer hard drive just under the sand. She assumes it was made up the road in Silicon Valley by intelligent designers.

Evolutionists might argue that random forces acting through enormous time powered by the energy of wave action were responsible. And the arguments and symposiums could go on indefinitely.

But the 800 pound gorilla in the room is the fact that the computer hard drive of the cell is not just a marvel of engineering efficiency but comes pre-loaded to capacity with...information. All of our experiments and all of our experience teach us that information always comes from a mind. Suppose the California beach jogger managed to insert and operate the hard drive in a computer only to find it was full to capacity with pre-existing, pre-loaded information. Suppose she found that it was encoded with plans for a trillion-part, mobile mechanical robot that can operate on its own for 100 years extracting the energy it needs from plants and repairing itself when damaged. This changes the level of the intelligent design debate by orders of magnitude. Explaining that a complicated device like a hard drive came about by random, non-directed natural forces is one thing. Explaining the presence of pre-loaded information on the computer hard drive is quite another.[256]

9. *New DNA Studies Undermine Chimp/Human Similarity*

Media headlines trumpeted the initial results of comparative studies of the newly mapped six billion characters of human and chimp DNA. The reported number varied from 96% to 98% similar and certainly seemed to suggest the two must have derived from a previous common stock. However, these initial researchers compared only sections of the six billion letter code where chimps and humans were already most likely to be similar and extrapolated the results to the whole genetic code. Differences between humans and chimps in the vast areas of so-called "junk" DNA were ignored as this was thought to be a wasteland of discarded, non-coding, non-functioning remnants of previous evolutionary starts and stops. The presence of non-functional sections of DNA was thought to be the naturally predicted outcome of evolution's random activity over time.

Now, as we study and learn deeper, we find that "junk" DNA is not so junky. It is true these regions do not code for protein production but it now appears that they perform a command-and-control function in regulating the activity or "expression" of genetic characteristics. On September 5th, 2012, the results of the "ENCODE Consortium"

DNA research project were published. The Encyclopedia of DNA Elements (ENCODE) Consortium was initiated by the US National Human Genome Research Institute (NHGRI) in 2003 to seek to identify all functional elements in the DNA coding of humans. Nine years later, in 2012, a coordinated release of 30 research papers representing many scientists from over 30 institutes around the world revealed that so-called "junk" areas of DNA have far more function and complexity than previously thought. Among other things, these areas serve as control centers directing "expression" of the genes themselves...effectively turning genes "on" and "off" at different and crucial times in an organism. The direction research is headed suggests that no area of the genetic code is unused.[257]

When the whole six billion characters of the DNA data storage and retrieval machines for chimps and humans are compared, there are over one hundred million programming differences and the higher frequency of differences occur in the "command-and-control" sections of what was previously erroneously considered "junk". Even one difference in this region affects the expression of hundreds of programming units in a gene farther down the line.

Darwin thought that the differences between animals and humans were just a matter of "degree" and not a matter of "kind". Humans were a few more degrees around the evolutionary dial from animals, but still the same kind. Preliminary results from the budding science of genetic decoding were viewed by many researchers through the same eyeglass lens as Darwin...any differences would surely be just a matter of "degree" and a small degree, at that! However, we now know the differences are both of degree *and* kind. The physical, intellectual, vocal, social and spiritual differences between humans and chimps are exponentially enormous.[258]

10. New Fossil Finds Force Evolutionary Re-Thinking

Mathematical theory is a *hard* science. Each observation usually has only one truly correct mathematical formulation as an answer. Biology is a *soft* science. Each observation in the real world comes with a myriad of possible explanations complicated by another myriad of further complicating, interacting physical and biological ingredients.

Thus, no two observers tend to come to the same complete conclusion about a biological observation.

The initial simplicity of the evolutionary explanation for things has gotten decidedly complicated with increasing discoveries. While what we are about to say is hardly scientific, we note a high number of articles about fossil discoveries include some phrase about "needing to re-think or re-formulate previous theories". Phrases like, "Fossil brain size out of place...", "This is a game changer...", "Surprising fossil requires rethinking bipedalism...", "Everything we thought we knew may need to be changed..." often appear. Increasingly, biological charts of the "tree of life" resemble a weedy lawn. The "descent of man" charts increasingly resemble the convoluted paths of a circuit board rather than the straightforward mode once assumed. In good science a good initial hypothesis requires fewer and smaller changes as new data and tests emerge. It points increasingly accurately toward its predicted conclusion. In good science a bad initial hypothesis requires greater and larger modifications in order to accommodate discordant data and may have to be set aside entirely. New data seems to force larger changes to the evolutionary hypothesis.

Now we do know that sincere evolutionists would argue this point with us vigorously. However consider this illustration. Rube Goldberg was a cartoonist famous for drawing fabulously complicated machines to get things done. The game "Mouse Trap" illustrates Goldberg's ideas in making the simple matter of catching a mouse the result of dozens of sequential steps from dropping a ball that lights a match that fires a cannon that knocks away a barrier that allows a bowling ball to run down a curving track that triggers a release of a net that falls on the hapless mouse. Some things are complex, yet elegant. "Mouse Trap" is certainly complex but not at all elegant. The "evolution" of evolution has, for some of us, lost its simple allure and seems to resemble a Rube Goldberg machine more and more.

The mind of evolution is not dissuaded by how the rush of recent findings has complicated their charts and pictures. After all, in their approach, organized and efficient life as we see it presently is the result of unorganized and random processes. Therefore, they would say they expect to see many terminated side branches and ineffective false starts at many points along the path toward the present. They could easily wonder that others could be so naïve as to think it would be a simple system or process. However, they should not be dismayed when men and women of good will and sincere intent sense the present theory is getting a bit strained and looks more and more *Rube-like* as it attempts to make the new data fit somewhere on its framework.

Hence, the question must be asked, "why do Richard Dawkins' books continue to be best sellers?" Why has the overall general consensus popularized in the press and schools seemingly shifted to an unqualified acceptance of evolution and a rejection, even derision, of creationism? We believe this to be a faulty comparison of the claims of Darwinism with the claims of Creationism. Each side misunderstands the other. For our purposes, it is not sufficient to only point out the problems in evolutionary theory and application. As holding to Christian creationism, we have a responsibility to put forth a coherent model of creation that deals in integrity with what the truth of the world around us reveals. Non-Christians, both atheists and agnostics, deserve to hear a more unified presentation of creationism than they have been hearing. What is needed is a more proper comparison of the claims of Neo-Darwinism with Neo-Creationism.

Neo-Darwinism vs. Neo-Creationism...Reframing the Debate!

How is it that one side of the argument believes the other side is not merely mistaken but actually deluded, misled, ignorant and possibly even dangerous? We contend that this may result from a misunderstanding on one side of what constitutes creationism. For the most part, the term *Creationism* has become nearly universally linked in the minds of average modern Western Civilization members as referring to a model that is hopelessly out of touch with the findings of modern physics, astronomy, chemistry and biology and is, therefore, unscientific. Since God's **methods** of creation are suspect, they generally do not believe the Bible's message of God's **purposes** of creation. This is a great shame.

We, therefore, propose a new name is needed for a model of creationism that reflects on both the truths of science and the interpretation of scripture with integrity. We believe that ***Neo-Darwinism*** needs to consider *Neo-Creationism*. In much the same way that evolutionists would be critical of someone punching holes in Darwinism without considering the added information brought by Neo-Darwinism, we would also be critical of those who reject Creationism without considering the added insight brought by Neo-Creationism.

Neo-Creationism believes the resolution of the apparent conflicts between science and theology comes from carefully reviewing and integrating (more on this in a moment) what the facts of nature are really saying and carefully reviewing and integrating what **all** the various creation portions throughout Scripture are really saying.

Key Elements of Neo-Creationism

1. Nature and Scripture vs. Science and Theology

Scientists may or may not correctly interpret the facts of nature, while theologians may or may not correctly interpret the facts of scripture. Neo-Creationism expects to see conflict between Science and Theology. However, Neo-Creationism expects to find concordance between Nature and Scripture.

2. Time and Timing

Neo-Creationism sees the earth and universe as "middle-aged"... neither old enough to provide the nearly infinite time of classical Darwinian evolutionary models nor young enough to satisfy the *classical* young-earth creationists' models.

Since all known cultures of the world have varying creation accounts, we could fill countless books exploring these. However, we contend that modern science has done us a great service by helping sift out most of these from being legitimate options. We contend that the findings of Einstein and the equations of relativity support the notion of a limited, finite universe that came into being some 13.73 billion years. These findings are supportive of the biblical, Christian notion of creation (the universe was brought into being..."in the beginning") and they actually invalidate the eternal, cyclical, reincarnating notion of creation put forth by most Eastern religions. However, even when we restrict ourselves to considering biblically based, Christian creation we note differences of opinion and separate, even conflicting, models put forth.

These different Christian models of creation often arise from translation difficulties in moving a few of the key original Hebrew words of the biblical creation material into English. Biblical Hebrew, with just 3,000 words, is much more compact that modern English (with well over 100,000 words and rising). A word will often do double duty. The English words "son", "grandson", "great-grandson" and, even, "descendent" would all be handled by one Hebrew word (-ben). Likewise, the Hebrew word for father (-ab) serves also for grandfather, great-grandfather or, even, ancestor. These are *literal* translations, not allegorical or poetic. Thus, one is being both literal and accurate in biblical Hebrew to refer to their father as "-ab" and their grandfather as "-ab". To select a more descriptive English word, one must know the context or have other clues or information from another source to do so correctly.

This leads us to Christian creation models centered around time and timing. The Hebrew word "-yom" translated by King James 1611 interpreters as "day" in Genesis chapter 1, has a few other literal uses, such as, a 24-hour day, a 12-hour period (daylight) or a long, but finite period of time (epoch, era or period). Thus, a young-earth model of six 24-hour days *and* an old-earth model of six, consecutive epochs or eras are both *literal* translations. However, they cannot both be right and therefore contextual use and other clues or information from other sources help us discern the correct use.

Neo-Creationism would contend that God has given us a way to determine the correct model. The scriptural injunction to "put everything to the test and hold to what proves to be true and let go of what proves to be false" (I Thess. 5:21) encourages us to critically test these things. The scriptural principles of establishing truth based on two or more reliable witnesses (Deut. 17:6 and 19:15) also comes into play. The record of Nature, as the left over evidence of the Creator's activity, forms a second witness to the record of Scripture. Neo-Creationism asserts that science, as it studies and correctly identifies the facts of Nature, can help clarify competing creation models.

3. *The Problem of a Middle-aged Universe*

The truly *middle-aged* nature of the universe around us (billions of years) reduces the reliability of both young-earth models of creation (which assert thousands of years) and extremely old-earth models of theistic evolution (which require trillions or, even, quadrillions of years).[259] However, it increases the reliability of concepts from the progressive creationist models. The *middle-aged* nature of the universe supports both the evidence outside the earth (from astronomy/physics) and the evidence on the earth used to construct the geological column time charts.

4. The Need for Integration

Another foundation of Neo-Creationism is the need for integration within science and within theology. Let us consider science first. Scientists are often very isolated beings. In order to be truly excellent in their field a scientist specializes and studies deeply into their particular area. Bio-chemists, while being reasonably competent to have basic understanding of physics, or say, geology, will simply not have the time, interest, desire or ability to study those areas extensively. The bio-chemist is often simply not aware of what leading edge research is discovering in other fields. They can easily assume that what they learned or heard before is what geology or physics still regards as accurate. The geologist or physicist may assume some aspect of biological evolution is a proven fact, when, in actuality, it has already been set aside as false by current bio-chemical research. For instance, in the recent bestselling book "The Grand Design" physicist Stephen Hawking asserts "as Darwin and Wallace explained how the apparently miraculous design of living forms could appear without intervention by a supreme being, the multiverse concept can explain the fine tuning of physical law without the need for a benevolent creator who made the Universe for our benefit."[260] As a physicist Dr. Hawking is tremendously focused on his area of scientific specialty. However, he assumes that the biologists have worked out all the difficulties of Darwin's biological proposal. Being intelligent and well-read, Dr. Hawking probably knows more about biology then most laymen, but not being a specialist working deeply in the origins-of-life research field (which is, itself, a deep specialization within the area of biology) he is unaware or chooses to ignore the difficulties they are encountering. Darwin and Wallace may have *proposed* an explanation for life's apparently miraculous design but origins-of-life researchers and chemical evolutionists have certainly not proven and verified this explanation. This is an example of how each scientific discipline assumes the other disciplines have solved their problems.

In the sense that a true view of Neo-Darwinism must come from an integration of the findings of all the fields of science, Neo-Creationism insists that a true view of creationism and the Creator must come from integrating all of the creation material throughout the Bible. Some creationists can end up with a myopic view of what they think scripture says about creation by concentrating primarily on the classic creation chapter...Genesis Chapter One. One could safely say the Bible is primarily concerned about man's relationship with God and it gets quickly to the meat of the matter. After only 26 verses in Genesis 1, the scripture comes to man. In 26 short verses Genesis 1 quickly and elegantly covers billions of years of pre-human history. It is unreasonable to believe that all our questions can be answered fully and solely by this body of material. We receive a large amount of creation information from locations across the Bible, including Genesis 2, Psalms 104, Isaiah 44, Zechariah 12, Job 38 and 39, Jeremiah 31, Romans 1, Romans 8, Hebrews 4 and 11 and others. The level of creation material in the Bible is breathtakingly huge compared to that found in other religious texts of the world's religions. This information helps to "flesh out" the skeleton of information provided by Genesis 1. A useful and comprehensive model of Christian creationism such as Neo-Creationism must integrate and utilize all this information. Neo-Creationism suggests that a great degree of conflict within the Christian Church concerning origins can be resolved by carefully comparing and integrating all the creation scriptures and forming an explanatory model that is true to the sum of the scriptural knowledge available.

5. Neo-Creationism Views Science and Scientists as Valued Partners in the Pursuit of Truth.

Neo-Creationism is pragmatic. Either the universe was created or it was not. The truth of reality around us must find logical integration with the truth of the written Bible. Therefore, Neo-Creationism looks forward with excitement to the continued findings of science. As the model of Neo-Creationism is refined and tested by current scientific discoveries, it is able in turn to make testable predictions about the direction of future research and the nature of future discoveries. Science helps to not only validate the Neo-Creationism model but refine it, as well. We are not at war. We are excited partners in the unveiling of the Creator's actions, plans and purposes.

6. Neo-Creationism is Faith Affirming

The approach taken by Neo-Creationism has proven to be invaluable in resolving both the apparent conflicts that have tested the faith of many people and the conflicts that led to alienation among many groups. Christian students attending secular universities should no longer be disturbed by what they think are faith-destroying scientific pronouncements. Instead, through Neo-Creationism, they are informed and inspired as they have a model where this scientific data can be integrated into a cohesive understanding. Under an older understanding of 'classical-Western' Creationism the rapidly unfolding discoveries of science were often seen as threatening but with the revolutionary refinements of Neo-Creationism each new discovery is awaited with eagerness as we continued to be stunned by the accuracy of the information that has been embedded in the Bible accounts.

...An Overview of the Common Ground Both Scripture and Nature Record Sequentially.

1. The universe came into being out of things that cannot be seen or measured (a singularity) a fixed time ago and has been expanding under constant laws of physics
2. The early earth was hostile to life and empty of life and was surrounded by a dark, opaque atmosphere.
3. The earth's smotheringly thick and dark first atmosphere was replaced by a thinner, translucent one, possibly through a collision with an asteroid or planetoid such as the one posited as forming the moon.
4. A water cycle developed next with water exchanging from the oceans below with the atmospheric layers above.
5. Without a pre-biotic soup, living systems of life appear suddenly at the earliest possible time.

> 6. Land emerged above the watery covering through plate tectonics with plants (including cyano©bacteria and other microscopic organisms) appearing next in various waves and rollouts.
> 7. Plant vegetation, both land and sea based, helped produce the great oxygenation events, lowering carbon dioxide content and raising oxygen levels in the atmosphere, leading to a change from translucent to transparent. From the earth's surface observations of sun, moon and stars became possible providing a way to set the biorhythms of coming animal life.
> 8. The kind of animal life that would be visible to a human observer appeared in the oceans suddenly and in great numbers of fully formed and functioning formats. This life preceded visible life on the land.
> 9. Visible, land-based life came next. This life came in stages as the environment continued to develop. Some life appears at the earliest moments the planet might be able to support it. As the environment changed over time and life went extinct, the Creator introduced new life suitable to the new conditions.
> 10. Modern humans were the last new creature to be introduced. Since then the Creator has rested (ceased) from creating. No new "kinds" of animals have been introduced. Since the introduction of modern humans, the predominant fossil record would be one of extinctions.

Conclusion: The Neo-Creationist Model

Some may think what follows is an arbitrary assignment of scientific facts to fit scriptural statements. However, we are attempting to show how Scripture and Science can and do mutually inform one another. We believe that emerging scientific discoveries and understandings are complementary to this particular model of biblically-based, Christian creationism. Using the backbone of the Genesis 1 material as a basis for our creation skeleton, we will "flesh out" the structure by interweaving the additional creation material from other parts of the Bible and show how this corresponds to what science is telling us about the record from the natural world around us. As we have said before, we do not expect the accurate correlation of the scriptural accounts with the scientific descriptions of reality to form a proof of the Creator's existence or purposes. We do however believe it greatly enhances the perceived reliability of the biblical record of both history and nature. If the biblical information about history and nature are reliable and more accurate than any other religious text on the planet, then acting upon the biblical information about the Creator and His purposes and desires for us becomes more a step of reasonable faith, as opposed to blind faith.

1. *"In the beginning God created (bara) the heavens and the earth..." (Genesis 1:1)*

Scripture here affirms the universe was not and is not eternal in either size or time (In the beginning...), that it began at a singularity where the ability of physical laws to describe it breakdown (...God created...*bara*, something new that had not existed before), and the material that makes up all the universe was involved (...the heavens and the earth.). While this assertion was derided by many in the two thousand years from Socrates to just before Einstein, the study of Nature has confirmed all of the matter, energy, space, and even time that make up this present universe we experience sprang into being a very long but finite time ago (13.73 billion years ago). During the many generations where science erroneously held to the eternal universe position, Christians did not have the benefit of confirming data from the study of Nature and had to take these Scriptural statements by faith.

"By faith we understand that the worlds were prepared by the word of God so that what is seen was not made out of things that are visible..." (Hebrews 11:3)

That which we can see and detect was not made from that which we can see and detect. From Nature we now know that the material that makes up worlds is made from things that are invisible to the human eye. All that appears solid and sure is not at all. Solid walls and floors are merely collections of atoms with enormous relative levels of empty space inside them. Even these atoms and the protons, neutrons and electrons that compose them are made up of smaller component particles, leptons and quarks. If the theoretical work in sub-atomic particle physics proves to be confirmed, then, at some point as we go smaller still, the line between matter and energy fuzzes out as particles of 'matter' give way to the vibrating loops of energy of the quantum world of string theory.

From this quantum smallness, the universe from its singularity creation, expanded outward. Multiple Bible writers separated from each other by centuries and miles write about this and add more 'flesh' to the Genesis One summary 'skeleton'.

The heavens are telling of the glory of God; and their expanse is declaring the work of His hands. Day to day pours forth speech and night to night reveals knowledge. (Psalms 19:1).

Neo-Creationism asserts that Nature is a reliable witness and record of the Creator's activities. Eastern religions contend that life is an illusion, but Scripture says otherwise.

It is He who sits above the circle of the earth, and its inhabitants are like grasshoppers; Who stretches out the heavens like a curtain and spreads them out like a tent to dwell in. (Isaiah 40:22).

Isaiah speaks of the expansion of the universe as an ongoing process.

Who alone stretches out the heavens...He stretches out the north over empty space and hangs the earth on nothing (Job 9:8, 26).

Job also echoes the cosmic expansion and the invisible scaffolding of spatial gravity fields.

Thus says God the Lord, Who created the heavens and stretched them out...It is I who made the earth and created man upon it. I stretched out the heavens with My hands and I ordained all their host...You have forgotten the Lord your Maker, Who stretched out the heavens and laid the foundations of the earth. (Isaiah 42:5,12; 51:13).

Isaiah also speaks of the initial expansion as a past event.

It is He who made the earth by His power, Who established the world by His wisdom; and by His understanding He has stretched out the heavens. (Jeremiah 10:12).

Jeremiah says He stretched out the cosmos by His understanding. We now also understand that advanced human life is only possible in a universe that experiences ongoing expansion.

Thus declares the Lord who stretches out the heavens, lays the foundation of the earth, and forms the spirit of man within him. (Zechariah 12:1).

It is hard to imagine how one could more succinctly outline the establishment of a stable, expanding universe with a stable orbital cycle of the planet and the distinctive difference of humans above all animals...than how the inspired prophet Zechariah put it so many years ago.

These verses of the Bible assert that the Creator set matters in place so that the universe has rapidly expanded in the past and is continuing to expand today so that it can form a foundation for hanging the earth 'on nothing' and can form a 'spatial surface' in which humans may dwell. From the world of Nature we find perfect confirmation for these assertions. Einstein's revolutionary equations of relativity in 1905 and 1915 and 100 years of diligent testing involving solar eclipses, telescopes, satellites like Hubble and COBE and high altitude, Arctic balloons like the Boomerang program have shown the universe is, indeed, expanding and cooling from an initial creative event. Millions and millions of dollars have been diverted from other areas to be used in research that shows the 'fabric of space-time' is an invisible structure on which stars and planets appear to be hung on nothing and is, indeed, quite like a tent in which we dwell.

"...I have established the fixed laws of heaven and earth." (Jeremiah 33:25)

In multiple places, biblical writers assert that the laws that govern the universe were fixed by God, are stable and can be relied upon. Putting this biblical information together we find the universe had unique beginning point a finite time ago and has been expanding since then under fixed and constant physical laws. Physics and mathematics show us that any such expanding, closed system would be cooling down over time. Thus, the Bible predicts we will find the universe is finite, not infinite and is expanding and is cooling. This is precisely what the "Hot Inflationary, Big Bang" model of the universe describes...but the Bible said it first! No other religious book purporting divine authority that has ever appeared on this planet has ever come anywhere close to so accurately describing the reality of the created realm.

2. *"...And the earth was without form and void and darkness was on the face of the deep..." (Genesis 1:2a).*

Scripture moves forward to the next significant point in the creation narrative...the point at which the early earth was unorganized (without form) and empty of life (void) and no light reached the surface of the planet. We have covered about 9 billion years from the singularity at the universe's beginning through galaxy formation and two generations of star life cycles. The manufacture of the heavier elements and metals in the dying throes of star death has paved the way for planetary systems like our own Solar System. Studies of the Natural world have given a name for this time at which we have now arrived...the Hadean period. Taken from the Greek word for Hades, this hellish period was the time in the early solar system when excessive asteroids, meteors and other material bombarded the more fully formed planets. Some evidence of this bombardment can be seen on the Moon though most of Earth's scars have been covered by our active weather systems. Scientists believe that toward the end of the Late Heavy Bombardment, the Earth would have been inhospitable to any life (**...void...**), under an utterly opaque atmosphere (the makeup of which is still in dispute) of hydrocarbons, such as CH_4-methane and NH_3-ammonia, and CO_2-carbon dioxide (**...darkness was on...**), and uniformly covered under water (**...the face of the deep**).

> **Where were you when I laid the foundation of the earth? Tell Me, if you have understanding. Who set its measurements? Since you (think you) know. Or who stretched the line on it?...Or who enclosed the sea with doors when, bursting forth, it went out from the womb; <u>when I made a cloud its garment and thick darkness its swaddling band</u> and I placed boundaries on it and set a bolt and doors and I said, 'Thus far you shall come, but no farther, and here your proud waves stop'? (Job 38:4)**

Scripture fills in some details for us in the book of Job. The creator appears to communicate three distinctive things about the early earth... its size and mass were predetermined (set its measurements) and it was covered with water at the surface and a thick, dark atmosphere swaddled it like a garment. Like present day gas-giants, Jupiter and Saturn and Uranus and Neptune are still 'swaddled' under totally opaque atmospheres of primarily ammonia and methane. Their great size and mass (and, thus, their large gravity) tend to hold onto these gaseous molecules with little loss to surrounding space. The Earth went down a different path and today has an unusually thin, transparent atmosphere for which all astronomers give thanks. We will speak of some of the events that may have helped transform the earth's atmosphere later; however, early on the earth was "swaddled" with a suffocatingly thick, dark atmosphere.

While the stage was set for the darkness banding the earth to eventually change through natural processes, something else was about to happen on earth that would require more than natural processes. The second of three great singularities was about to happen...Life from Non-Life.

3. "...and the Spirit of God was brooding over the surface of the waters" (Genesis 1:2b)

Neo-Creationism asserts that life is too complex to happen spontaneously. Organized, living systems do not arise from non-organized, non-living molecules without help. All living systems display information content in the coding and storage device that directs their growth (the DNA). Aside from the incredible improbability of such a complex 'computer hard drive' (the DNA information storage molecule) arising by accident, the 800 pound gorilla in the center of the room that no one speaks about is the presence of information. Multiplied thousands of megabytes of information are contained in the DNA. The computer 'hardware' that is DNA is stunning in its design but the fact that it is pre-loaded with sophisticated, error detecting and correcting 'software' is a fingerprint of origin. Whenever we see a high level of organized information content in systems we always see that it was the product of a mind. Information content arises from a mind. No natural system has been found that allows for an increase in the information content without a mind being involved. Those few cases where it has seemed that information arose without a mind have been shown, upon later examination, to have been inadvertently introduced by the researchers themselves. Thus, the intelligent coding of informational content into the driving backbone of life (the DNA) without an external agent is the second of three great singularities in the universe. [As a reminder, these are...Everything From Nothing (the first moment of creation of the physical universe)...Life from Non-Life (the informational coding that directs non-living molecules in living systems)...and Spirit from Non-Spirit (the extra-dimensional nature of man's spirit).

In the verse above, we see the word "brooding" as it speaks of actions of the Spirit of God at the surface of the planet. Translated from ancient biblical Hebrew as "moving" by some, "brooding" carries the better feeling of what is meant. This Hebrew word is only used in a few other rare instances but does correctly connote how a mother chicken 'broods' over her offspring and nurtures and protects their young life. It would appear that to get life started on Earth required the intervention of an intelligent agent from outside the system and required a 'brooding' oversight to nurture its establishment on the somewhat hostile early earth.

Secular studies from Nature would probably identify this very first life as being cyanobacteria.

4. "God said, 'Let there be light (or, 'Let the light appear') and there was light (or, 'and the light appeared')...and God separated the light from the darkness" (Genesis 1:3,4)

At some point the atmosphere transitioned from opaque to translucent. The study of Nature is still a bit unclear as to the exact early makeup of the atmosphere before this transition and how the transition from opaque to translucent came about. NASA's ventures to the Moon in the 1970's revealed that it was gradually receding from earth and was, in the past, closer to the earth. The evidence for the spiraling away of the moon gave rise to the conjecture that it was formed out of a low-velocity, glancing collision of the earth with a Mars-sized body. This hypothesis explained the peculiar chemical makeup of the lunar rocks, the high metal content of earth's core, the slow spiraling away of the moon in its orbit and suggested that much of the earth's early atmosphere was ripped away in this collision. By comparison, Venus, our nearby "sister" planet has an atmosphere that is nearly 100 times as dense as ours. We would expect a thicker atmosphere for a planet of our gravitational size unless some past event had stripped much of it. Although no life was present on the Earth at the time of this proposed collision and no life would have survived the sterilizing effects of the energy blasts associated with it, an observer situated at the surface of Earth after the evaporated oceans re-condensed would have begun to note the gradually lightening of daylight hours through the now translucent atmosphere and the return to darkness during the nighttime cycle. While light could now reach the surface, a clear visual image of the sun, moon or stars could not. Earth's gravity was just light enough to allow some dissipation to space of remaining atmospheric levels of opaque gases of methane and ammonia (molecular weights 16 and 17) and just heavy enough to retain most of the water vapor (molecular weight 18). The gravity was still too great to release significant amounts of carbon dioxide in the air (CO_2, molecular weight 44) to space.

An atmosphere that would now be predominantly carbon dioxide would make a dense, unbroken cloud cover that allowed light to pass through to the surface but did not allow any clear view of the space beyond the Earth. So, the atmosphere had changed from being opaque (utterly dark at the surface) to being translucent (light can pass through but no clear images can be seen through it).

To this present day, the planet Venus is still stuck at this point of planetary development. We looked at Venus through our telescopes for years wondering what might lie beneath the continuous cloud cover until the robot probes of the 1970's pierced through and sent us video images of a stark surface. With a runaway greenhouse effect and 900 degree temperatures hot enough to melt lead, Venus's oceans and water cycle were nonexistent. What made the difference for Earth? Why had its translucent atmosphere eventually gone transparent, as it is now? Three primary things...lower temperatures than Venus due to its now less dense atmosphere and its location farther from the sun, a water cycle of H_2O movement from oceans to atmosphere and back, and the eventual introduction of plant life, which harvested translucent CO_2 gas from the atmosphere and returned transparent O_2 gas as its waste product.

5. *"Then the Creator said, 'Let there be an expanse in the midst of the waters, and let it separate the waters from the waters." He put the firmament structures into place and separated the waters which were below the expanse from the waters which were above the expanse; and it was so. God called the expanse heaven (or sky)" (Genesis 1:6,7,8)*

Given the knowledge framework and the language words available to the writer of this account, this is a remarkably succinct account of the beginning of the hydrological (water) cycle so vital to life on earth... water above, at and below the surface with active and ongoing movement among them. Planetary geologists tell us that widespread plant life only became possible because of this water cycle and the emergence of land masses above the ocean surfaces.

6. *"Then God said, 'Let the waters below the heavens be gathered into one place, and let the dry land appear....Let the earth sprout vegetation'" (Genesis 1:9 and 11)*

A geologically active planetary core, molten from the heat of radioactive decay of the excessive abundances of elements like uranium and thorium is very rare in all the parts of the universe we have been able to study deeply. The collision that may have formed the Moon would also have resulted in the Earth acquiring a disproportionate share of the heavier elements like uranium and thorium from the collider. This remarkable, just-right event assured the Earth the power plant engine for volcanism and plate tectonics which uplift and move land over time. It also provided the planet with a magnetic field whose radiating lines of force deflect incoming, life-exterminating cosmic radiation.

Fortunately for us, the earth has just the extremely delicate balance of elements and forces present in one place to produce all these effects.

Plate tectonics build up continental land masses while an active hydrological cycle tends to wear them back down. Eventually the ratio of land mass to ocean surface reached an equilibrium level. With land masses and a water cycle, cyanobacteria and plant life could flourish... and this is exactly what the fossil record shows and is precisely what the biblical record reports here. Interestingly, recent studies have pushed back the date of the appearance of simple cyanobacterial life on earth to the very earliest periods imaginable given the conditions of earth at that time. This suggests an economy and purpose to the Creator. Just as soon as the earth is capable of supporting early "simple" life (as if any living system, no matter how small, could be called "simple"!) we find evidence of its emergence. The Creator is moving ahead rapidly with His plan and for His purpose.

Some have suggested the long time periods of the universe (13.73 billion years) and the earth (4.5 billion years) somehow expresses wastefulness on the part of the proposed Creator. However, Neo-Creationists notice this quick and rapid transition at each step in the earth's development. The rapid appearance of cyanobacteria at the earliest time Earth could support it and the early explosion of more complex life forms in the Cambrian era just as soon as the planet ecosystem and free oxygen levels in the atmosphere were ready are examples. Neo-Creationists see a Creator not bound by time as we experience it yet moving forcefully and efficiently toward the creation and introduction of mankind. This tells us something of the Creator's character. Meticulous, detailed, purposeful, efficient and, given all that went into preparing a habitat for humanity, lavish.

With the emergence of land, both Scripture and Nature tell us, next came copious levels of plants. Plants could process wavelengths of light that pass through the translucent, carbon dioxide heavy atmosphere into energy. They would feast upon high CO_2 levels in a "greenhouse effect" and begin oxygenating the world. Over time, CO_2 levels would fall and O_2 levels would rise. In time, the rising levels of transparent O_2 gas and the falling levels of translucent CO_2 gas would lead to a transformation of the atmosphere. Objects in space would become visible at the surface of the planet.

7. *"Then God said, 'Let there the heavens to separate the day and the night, and let them be for signs and for seasons and for days and years...God (had previously) made the two great lights, the greater one to govern the day, and the lesser light to govern the night; (He had previously made) the stars also." (Genesis 1:14)*

With the remaking of the chemical composition of the atmosphere by the plants (reducing carbon dioxide levels, raising oxygen levels), the surrounding atmosphere went from translucent (light passes through but no objects are visible beyond) to transparent. From the position of an observer situated at the surface of the earth (which is the perspective identified for this narrative in verse 2...under the atmosphere at the surface of the deep), the sun, moon and stars would now be discernible. The original biblical Hebrew here has caused some confusion. Unlike English, which has more than one type of past tense action, biblical Hebrew has but one form to indicate completed action. Thus, at least two equally valid translations

Did God Make the Sun, Moon and Stars on the 4th Day?

English speaking, western civilization readers often come away with this understanding from reading Genesis chapter 1. An understanding of translation can help clarify.

Only one past tense exists in biblical Hebrew, the actual original language of this account. Thus, both the concepts of 'made' ("And God made...") and 'had made' ("And God had previously made...") are imbedded in the same Hebrew word. English translators must decide whether the simple past tense or the complex past tense was intended.

Thus, the text could legitimately be saying the sun, moon, and stars that had been previously made did not become visible from an earthbound perspective until the 4th Creation Period. So, which is correct? Here the record of Nature helps inform us. While it is true no human was there to observe these events, every measurement and test we can devise for Nature shows the sun, moon, and stars were in existence before the events of Creation Period 4.

Given two equally literal and valid translations for a text and variance of opinion among scholars, the second witness of Nature (the left over evidence of the Creator's activity) can offer clarity.

are possible...'God made the two great lights' or 'God had (previously) made the two great lights.' The facts of Nature help clarify for us which of the two is more correct. The sun, moon and stars had been made at several previous times but only became visible (appeared) at the surface of the earth after the introduction of plants that could oxygenate the atmosphere and render it transparent. The sun was not made after the plants although we can see how a cursory reading of the English versions of the Bible might lead one to assume this. In actuality, the Scripture does not demand one accept or believe such a thing.

As a primary sequence, then, wide-spread existence of plants came first, then the visibility of sun, moon and stars, then the main body of sea and land animals...according to the biblical sequencing. This matches very well with the main findings of modern science. In addition, sea and land animals and birds require sightings of sun, moon and stars in order to set and regulate vital biological cycles, such as, migrations, reproduction, and hibernations. Thus, most animal life would need to be introduced only after the plant life had helped move the atmosphere from translucent to transparent.

8. *"Then God said, 'Let the waters teem with swarms of living creatures, and let birds fly above the earth.' God created (bara) the great sea creatures and every living creature that moves..." (Genesis 1:20)*

Scripture reflects the creation and introduction of teeming swarms of sea creatures during the fifth creation period. Nature records for us a phenomenon scientists have called "the Cambrian Explosion" or, as some have dubbed it, "biology's big bang". The sudden and, from a neo-Darwinist evolutionary perspective, totally unexpected appearance in the fossil record of fully-formed, fully-functional, completely-complex sea creatures of virtually every phyla (animals categorized by body plan/type) on the planet. With no pre-cursers below them in the geologic column and no signs of transitionary intermediates, life explodes on the scene in the fossil record. This is an unexpected development from the evolutionary perspective where gradual appearance with abundant intermediaries would be the presumed norm. However, from a Neo-Creationist approach, this data comports quite well with the record here in Scripture. In fact, scientists say that Nature "exploded" (the Cambrian Explosion) with life in the seas prior to the appearance of land animals and Scripture here says that life in the seas "teemed" and "swarmed" into existence! A closer match of descriptive words could hardly have been chosen even on purpose! The use of the Hebrew verb "*bara*", meaning to create something new that had not previously existed, suggests that living creatures are not simply a collection of non-living chemicals but have been endowed with something new... life itself.

9. "Then God said, 'Let the earth bring forth living creatures after their kind'; and it was so" (Genesis 1:24)

In organizing and presenting the skeletal history of life's origin and progression on earth into six chronological steps, we come to creation period six and the introduction of the main body of land animal life. For purposes of this broad overview of the Neo-Creationism model it is sufficient to note that the bulk of the animal life in the sea preceded the bulk of the animal life on land. The Hebrew words used in verse 25 to elaborate on some of the kinds of animals suggest not only insects and reptiles but mammals, as well. Scripture here does not dictate that all land animals appeared at the same time and does not give a concise sequence of their appearance. Therefore, the Neo-Creationist model accepts that land animals came in various waves with periods where whole ecosystems went extinct (such as the dinosaurs due possibly to an asteroid collision and several other mass extinction events) and the Creator successively replaced them with new versions, each fine-tuned to the newer, changing, developing environment of the earth as it matured. This means the events of this Creation Period ("Day") spanned millions of years.

> **All your creatures look to you for their sustenance. You open your hand and they are satisfied. Then you turn away from them. They are dismayed and they expire (go extinct). Then you renew them again (creating replacements) Psalms 104 : 29, 30.**

Here in Psalms 104 David (through the coordinating inspiration of God's Spirit...as Neo-Creationists assert) gives us his review of the events of the six creative "days". He adds information about extinctions and re-introductions of life that is not covered in Genesis.

As well as they may be designed and suited for their environments, copying errors during reproduction and mutational errors tend to drive large bodied, slow growing animals extinct. This is because the vast majority of copying and mutational errors are negative. The few that just might be positive are overwhelmed by the many negative changes. Unless the organism can reproduce in extreme numbers and extremely rapidly, gradual accumulation of negative mutations will drive it to extinction. Over long enough periods of time, large-sized advanced life is doomed unless replaced. Neo-Creationism asserts and Psalms 104 (above) suggests the Creator progressively replaced life forms, as needed, during the first six chronological creation ages. Part of this process prepared the way for the humans, who were placed on an earth whose crust is packed full of bio-deposit resources, such as oil, natural gas, bitumen, coal and others. These "fossil fuels" from past mass extinctions allow our advanced, technological life and were pre-planned by the Creator.

10. *"The God said, 'Let Us make man in our image, according to Our likeness; and let them rule over the fish of the sea and over the birds of the sky and over the cattle and over all the earth, and over every creeping thing that creeps on the earth.' God created man in His own image, in the image of God He created him; male and female He created them." (Genesis 1:26)*

In attempting to give the reader an overview of Neo-Creationism, we cannot cover the many nuances of the record of Scripture in the original Hebrew but we should note here in this verse the use of "*asa*...to make or manufacture out of available materials" at the beginning of the verse and the use of "*bara*...to create something new that did not exist before" at the end of the verse. God made (manufactured) man's physical body from "the dust of the earth" (the physical materials from which the planet is also made) but He created something new in endowing man with a spirit, creating something new and different from the sea and land animals and birds, something uniquely like the image of the Creator Himself.

> ### In the Image of God
>
> Humanity's difference from all the other creatures is vast and breathtaking. The notion that we are just a 'human animal' is quite misguided. We possess and exhibit substantive, functional and relational differences, such as... self-consciousness, moral reflection, deliberative decision making, creativity, imagination, self-sacrificing love, purposeful existence, abstract symbolism (Maslow), self-transcendence (Frankl), free-will, rationality and spirituality. With the appearance of humans came the 'Cultural Explosion' of beads, jewelry, makeup, money, art, musical instruments, language and writing. This 'Cultural Big Bang' rivals the 'Physical Big Bang' of the initial creative event and the 'Biological Big Bang' of the Cambrian Explosion.

The great gap between the abilities and nuances of humans compared to any animal group on the planet should be apparent to the honest observer. Though some animals display a range of emotional responses and show some flashes of intelligence, the capability of the arts and of philosophy will always escape them. Only humans worry enough about our place in the world and the universe to be driven to build machines to seek out and map the great length and depth of the vast universe. Though an elephant may show emotional depression at the death of a mate, only humans can become depressed about our mortality and our potential eternal destiny. We are creatures with a spiritual element missing in the rest of creation. We have the brain size and organization to be able to express this spiritual nature to others but it is not merely the more intricately organized brain that gives rise to the spiritual side. We are not simply "super-animals" sitting at the pinnacle of an evolutionary process. The Scripture tells us we are created with and for a purpose. The accuracy of the Scripture's record about the rest of the created universe can give us a willingness to accept the Scripture's testimony about our spiritual nature and eternal purpose and destiny.[261]

So, in 26 short verses and only a few hundred words, the inspired author has compactly and correctly summarized the major events of earth's pre-history organized into six clear chronological sequences that match quite well with the record of Nature. While theologians in the past have sometimes misinterpreted the facts of Scripture and scientists have sometimes misidentified the facts of Nature, the convergence that is now emerging is somewhat breathtaking. As a result, it is our hope the reader will see why well-intentioned, reasonable, and educated people can and do strongly question the assumed conclusions of Neo-Darwinism. Rather, such scholars and scientists are finding the remarkable concurrence of both Scripture and Nature in the model of Neo-Creationism as a very compelling proposition.

Chapter 9: Review Questions

1. What was the most interesting thing that you learned from Chapter 9 and why?
2. Explain the critique of scientific over-reach in relation to atheistic evolution.
3. Discuss the difference between micro-evolution and macro-evolution.
4. Where would you locate your present understanding of the debate between evolutionism and creationism on the Eight Options chart of Woodworth & Reynolds?
5. How does the discussion between soft and hard sciences inform the evolution debate?

ADDENDUM ARTICLES

1. Oprah Winfrey: New Age Spirituality

2. Lady Gaga: A Christian Moral Response to Homosexuality

3. Twenty-Seven of the Most Important People and Events in Christian History

4. Top Ten Things that No One, in the Know, Believes Any More about Evolution

5. Secularism and the Misinterpretation of the First Amendment

6. Faith and Education: How to Get a Higher Education Without Losing Your Faith!

7. Ghosts and Other Occult Phenomena

8. How to Become an Authentic Follower of Jesus: Tips for Beginners

9. Twelve Reasons I Believe

Addendum 1.

-An Open Letter to Oprah Winfrey and Eckhart Tolle-

A Christian Response to Eckhart Tolle's:

A New Earth: Awakening to Your Life's Purpose

Introduction

I first heard of Eckhart Tolle when dear friends of ours mentioned they had, out of curiosity, ordered a copy of his latest book *A New Earth: Awakening to Your Life's Purpose,* after hearing of it advertised on the Oprah Winfrey show.[262] The more we discussed the content and popularity of the book the more certain I was that I should read, research, and write a response (rather than a reaction) from a Christian perspective.[263] My objective here is to present an article that is informed by my experience as a college and university Professor of World Religions,[264] a seminary graduate,[265] a published Christian apologist,[266] and a former senior pastoral leader.[267]

Please know that in the article that follows there is absolutely no judgmentalism, resentment or vitriol in my intention. In fact, I am quite certain that Tolle and Winfrey are both sincerely seeking to bring spiritual awareness to many of those who have felt alienated from the irrelevance of legalistic "religion," be it Christian or otherwise. I also share their concern. People are hurting and are on a quest for healing, wholeness (harmony and alignment), and true meaning in life. Hence, rather than engage in an argumentative debate, my hope is that this article will at least help to clarify some fundamental issues between the worldview and subsequent spirituality recommended by Tolle vis-à-vis the biblical worldview and attending spirituality taught by Jesus Christ.

Anyone who has read Tolle's book and/or intends to embrace his call to enlightened/awakened consciousness needs to be aware of these critical distinctions before choosing, or recommending a life-path whose destination may merge with a reality not initially intended. To that end I write to all who seek an understanding of authentic spirituality in the 21st century and beyond.

[Note: Please be advised that a few of the responses below may be somewhat difficult to initially understand, especially if one has not studied Tolle's book or is unfamiliar with eastern religious philosophy. As a result, I have purposefully summarized the information that follows into 10 main sub-points—all with a view to public readability.]

Brief Biographical Background of Eckhart Tolle

Eckhart Tolle was originally born (1948) as Ulrich Tolle, but later changed his name to "Eckhart," after one of his acknowledged mentors, the Catholic-Dominican mystic Meister Eckhart (1260-1327). This name change coincided with Eckhart's spiritual rebirth and new identity at the age of 29—which was itself the result of overcoming years of severe bouts of "suicidal depression." Ulrich's mother's constant fretting about his future career allegedly drove him to move to Spain and live with his father from ages 13 to 19—after which he moved to England. Ulrich had no public education during these teenage years choosing rather to pursue his own particular interests in preparation for his studies and presumed graduation at the University of London—followed by at least some level of doctoral research at Cambridge University.[268] Since 1996, Tolle has lived in Vancouver, British Columbia/Canada where he resides with his domestic-partner and associate Kim Eng, who is also an advocate of the awakening of consciousness through her "Presence through Movement" workshop.[269]

Addendum 1.

Major Influences on Tolle's Life and Philosophy

Tolle claims, as a matter of principle, to be non-aligned with any particular religion or tradition. However, he and others have acknowledged his "strong connections" and significant influences with at least the following spiritual teachers, texts and religious-philosophical belief systems. These influences will be mentioned and briefly described for the sake of gaining a perspective of the foundational thinking upon which Tolle's worldview is understandably predicated.

- J. Krishnamurti (1895-1986)…was an Indian philosopher and popular writer and speaker who, among many other things, taught that there is no path to truth and no set of beliefs to describe what can only be an "individual matter" alone. In essence, all truth is relative to each individual who makes their own path. However, Krishnamurti, in contradiction to relativism, advocated his own teachings "absolutely and unconditionally."
- Ramana Maharshi (1879-1950)…was an Indian sage who taught non-dualism (or monism), which maintains that there is only one reality and ultimate consciousness in the universe. In other words, all suggestions of dualism, like between creator and creation do not exist and are therefore delusions.
- Joseph Anton Schneiderfranken also called "Bo Yin Ra" (1876-1943)…was a German mystical author and celebrated abstract painter whose books on mystical reality were eagerly ingested by Tolle at the formative age of 15 years.
- Zen Buddhism is a particular sect of Mahayana (or liberal) Buddhism in which practitioners attain "awakening" through the use of meditation and experiential wisdom over theoretical or text-based learning. Especially notable is Zen's emphasis on the "present moment, spontaneous action, and letting go of self-consciousness and judgmental thinking."[270]
- Hinduism is one of the oldest and the 3rd largest world religion whose origin is traced in India. Hinduism (parent to Buddhism and Jainism) is based on karma, reincarnation and the concept of liberation (lit. *moksha*) from the endless cycle of life (birth, death, and rebirth).

- A Course in Miracles (ACIM) is a book written by psychologist Helen Schucman (1909-1981) who insists that she was channeling (through "inner dictation") Jesus Christ who is simply an evolutionary elder brother. The Course text is built on "Eastern religious philosophy but uses traditional Judeo-Christian terminology even though it contradicts Christian doctrine—and is most popular among those have been disillusioned by organized/institutional Christianity."[271] J.G. Melton and W. Hanegraaffof, secular scholars of alternative religions—including the New Age movement, have called the A Course in Miracles the "sacred scripture" of the New Age movement.

Thematic Review and Biblical Response to Tolle's Predominant Ideas

1. The New Age and the Biblical Concept of the "Antichrist"

As a religious studies scholar-professor, I would classify Tolle's book as a form of New Age spirituality with a westernized version of Zen Buddhism at its core. For those unfamiliar with New Age spirituality, it can basically be described as a "decentralized social phenomenon and a Western socio-religious movement that combines aspects of spirituality, esotericism[272] and religious-philosophical practices from many eastern (Asian and Indian) and western traditions across the world."[273]

Several key characteristics of New Age spirituality include eclecticism,[274] relativistic individualism,[275] Gnosticism,[276] and universalism[277]—including a strong aversion to creeds (doctrines or belief systems) from historic and/or institutionalized religious traditions.

As a Christian theologian, the main problem with the New Age is that many of the sources it consults either contradict, or in Tolle's case, replace the biblical revelation that "God was reconciling the world to himself in Christ" (2 Cor. 5:19). In other words, Christianity starts (and ends) with Christ Jesus the Son of God who was/is the Lamb of God that "takes away the sin of the world" by the sacrifice of himself on the cross at Calvary (John 3:16; John 1:29; Heb. 9:26).

Addendum 1.

In Tolle's "theology" there is no mention of the need for sacrificial atonement of Jesus Christ because of his alignment with historic Buddhism which is a non-theistic religious-philosophy of the 6th century BCE. However, before one embraces Buddhism as an operative world view, it is important to know a couple of historic facts about Buddha himself. Born 563 BCE, Siddhartha Gautama (d. 483 BCE), later called Buddha (lit. "Enlightened one"), grew up in the culture of polytheistic Hinduism, which he came to view as superstition and futility. This helps to explain his aversion to the notion of God in favor of a non-theistic philosophy. Hence, Buddha's concept of salvation (the freedom from endless human suffering) was a self-derived personal matter apart from the belief in any specific mythological god offered by Hinduism in Buddha's lifetime. This also helps explain his rejection of dualism (god vs. creature) in favor of monism—in which there is only one ultimate reality.

If Buddha would have had the advantage of knowing about the atoning death of Jesus Christ for the salvation of all human suffering, one can only wonder how it would have influenced his perspective. Hence, before adopting Buddhism as a *modern* world view, one should understand the implications of its historic distance from the revelation of God in Christ. Indeed, why make a conclusion about one's ultimate destiny without the serious consideration of what Buddha, by no fault of his own, had no conception of himself when he was alive? After all, just think of what a difference the reality of flying would have made to all who lived 600 years before its invention by the Wright Brothers in the early 20th century!

Nevertheless, "modern" Buddhism argues that humanity's problem is not "sin" (requiring atonement) but rather "ignorance" needing enlightenment, or what Tolle calls awakening. This is clearly an atheistic, or god denying proposition. However, rather than offend the theistic sensitivities of western culture, Tolle intentionally avoids the use of the term atheism. Rather than denying god he simply replaces the notion of deity by suggesting, in monistic/Buddhist terms that we are our own "God," our own Being, Presence, Source—even our own "I Am" (Tolle, 2005, p. 251).[278]

In Christian terms, this deification of humanity finds a direct corollary with the concept of the "antichrist." The word anti-Christ literally means two things: "in place of," and/or "against" Christ. The New Testament uses the term five times to indicate the spiritual opposition (some kind of global influence—be it doctrine, philosophy, or a person) who deceives the world by seeking to usurp the title, power, and prerogatives of the Lord Jesus Christ.[279]

> But every spirit that does not acknowledge Jesus [as having come in the flesh/incarnate, 2 John 7] is not from God. This is the spirit of the antichrist, which you have heard is coming and even now is already in the world (1 John 4:3).

It is not that I am suggesting that Tolle is himself the "antichrist," but there is a curious connection between what he is teaching and what the Bible warns as the "spirit of the antichrist" that will globally emerge as a major deceptive force in the last days.[280]

2. Religion vs. Spirituality

Tolle rightly argues that there is difference between being religious and being spiritual (Tolle, 2005, p. 17-19). This truism is reflected in the statement: True Christianity is not a religion with rituals, rules, and relics, but a relationship with the living God through faith in his Son, the Lord Jesus Christ. The problem, however, with Tolle's statement is that he unjustifiably jumps to the conclusion that true spirituality has nothing to do with beliefs or thinking at all. Instead, a set of beliefs necessarily leads to mind-dominated judgmentalism of others in order to protect our belief system, which has unfortunately become an extension of our own personal or form-based identity. In fact, what Tolle is advocating here is that no one can be truly spiritual if they embrace a set of beliefs that engage the mind in a rational process. Furthermore, all such religious people are always insecure and judgmental of others.

This is simply not the case. There are many people who are as spiritual as Tolle and at the same time embrace an historic set of beliefs (the incarnation of Christ Jesus, his miraculous ministry, atoning death for sin, confirmed bodily resurrection and ascension, and outpouring of the Holy Spirit on the Jewish feast of Pentecost, ca. 30AD) that undergird their personal practice of transformational faith and loving relationships with others. One does not need to reject their rationality to be spiritual. Indeed, echoing the Old Testament command, Jesus taught that we should love the Lord our God with all our heart, soul and *mind*—and to love your neighbor as yourself (Deut. 6:5; Luke 10:27).

3. *The Egoic-Self and Immortality*

Tolle defines the ego as "the illusory sense of self" (Tolle, 2005, p. 27-28), which must be exposed in order for the illusion of the egoic-self, and all of its form-based identifies (thinking, feeling, wanting, owning, our bodies, etc.) to be dissolved. Such a dissolution of the egoic-self is necessary to realize the "I Am-ness" of our eternally present existence, which is another term for our awakened consciousness. In fact, much of Tolle's book is devoted to detecting and thereby dissolving the bondage of the egoic self—be it individual or collective. However, this radical denial of the "egoic" self, as well as the impossibility of "losing one's self-life" (Tolle, 2005, p. 128) is at the same time a misunderstanding of New Testament spirituality as well as a logical extension of Tolle's monistic (non-duality) assumptions.

The words of Jesus are quite clear: "If anyone would follow after me, he must deny himself and take up his cross daily and follow me. For whoever wants to save his life will lose it, but whoever loses his life for me will save it" (Luke 9:23-24).

First, what Tolle fails to see is the distinction between denying THE self (monism) versus denying ONEself (Christianity).[281] In other words, Jesus admitted that there was such a thing as a personal self that needed to be denied in the daily practice of following him as Lord. Essentially this means to surrender one's self-centered claims of autonomy in order to live *from* Christ (the regenerated spirit within)[282] and *for* Christ (rather than for fame, fortune, happiness, etc.) throughout one's life from conversion onward. Jesus further described this manner of spiritual life when he encouraged his followers to, "Seek first the kingdom of God and his righteousness and everything you need in this life will be provided for you as well" (Matt. 6:33; Phil. 4:19). Furthermore, this kingdom-centered style of living is a continual source of Christian empowerment and has as its goal the "fruit of the spirit," which is "love, joy, peace, patience, kindness, goodness, faithfulness, gentleness, and self-control" (Gal. 5:22).

Second, Jesus also specifically acknowledges the need to "lose one's life" in order to gain it. Again, this plainly implies that each person must make a deliberate choice[283] to lay down (surrender) one's own life for the sake of serving the purpose of God and hence gaining a reward/blessing "in this present life and also in the one to come" (1 Tim. 4:8).

It should be pointed out here that Christians also believe in the immortality of every human being. Such a belief however, is not based on Tolle's "incontrovertible" (Tolle, 2005, p. 127) argument of monistic inseparability, but on the reality of the spark of divine-eternal life in every human being who has been created in the "image of God" (Gen. 1:27). And though every human being will live forever, the question is: in which state? Tolle's answer is in the state of the ultimate-universal consciousness in which there is no life to be gained or lost. The biblical answer is either in the presence or absence of God. And though ultimate judgment is left to God, who alone knows the secrets of all men's hearts,[284] there is however a certainty of hope based on the promise of God to all who have sought refuge in God's free gift of righteousness to all who believe in Christ Jesus.[285] In other words, while Christians cannot (and should not) conclusively speculate regarding the eternal state of others (1 Cor. 4:5), what we can (and should) proclaim with full conviction is the forgiveness of sin and the promise of eternal life in the Lord Jesus Christ (Acts 2:38-39; John 17:3).

4. *The Pain-Body and the Presence of the Lord*

Tolle defines the "pain-body" as an "accumulation of old [negative] emotional pain" (Tolle, 2005, p. 140), which feeds on and/or is triggered by such things as your thoughts, emotions, relational drama, and negative forms of entertainment. Prime examples of negative emotions are fear, anxiety, anger, bearing a grudge, sadness, hatred or intense dislike, jealous, envy, and the quintessential negative emotion of the them all: unhappiness. (Tolle, 2005, p. 136) A predominate theme in Tolle's writing, the pain-body is initially heavier in some than others—especially the great spiritual reformers and enlightened master teachers.

The pain-body is also generationally transferable, and is the basis of a sense of alienation and victimization through such things as the historic suppression of women (the feminine principle), as well as the collective identity of certain nations (Germany and Japan) and racial groups, such as Jews, Native Americans, and Black Americans (Tolle, 2005, p. 154-160). Tolle's solution to the pain-body is to break the pattern of accumulating and perpetuating the old emotional pain of the past (Tolle, 2005, p. 141). We do this by acknowledging the reality of the pain-body itself, accepting the presence of the negative emotions that surface (Tolle, 2005, p. 184), and then shifting one's consciousness through the practice of Presence (Tolle, 2005, p. 161)—which can be immediately accessed by the awareness of one's breathing (Tolle, 2005, p. 246).

Tolle then concludes chapter six by citing Jesus' teaching in Matthew 5:48 (NIV), "Be ye whole, even as your Father in Heaven is whole" as evidence in support of the notion that our inner God-nature emerges as we accept "the is-ness of the Now" (Tolle, 2005, p. 184), thereby ensuring the ultimate dissolution of the pain-body.

> Note: Contrary to Tolle's re-interpretation of the Greek text, the Greek word for "whole" is actually *holos*. However, the word used here is *teleios* and literally means "to reach an end/goal" i.e. to "complete" and by

extension to be perfect or mature. In other words, it is simply inaccurate to insist, as Tolle does, that "perfect" is a "mistranslation of the original Greek word."

From a Christian perspective, though the term "pain-body" may not be a biblical word, yet the idea of needing to overcome negative emotions that are generationally transferable, serve as a collective identity, tied to past trauma, reinforced by obsessive thinking, are the basis of much human unhappiness, and yet may serve as a catalyst for spiritual enlightenment[286] are all compatible with Christian psychology and spirituality. Furthermore, the idea of living in the present, rather than the past or future is a familiar biblical theme.

Do not worry about tomorrow, for tomorrow will take care of itself. Focus your energies instead on today's concerns (Matt. 6:34).

Do not be anxious about anything, but in everything, by prayer and petition, with thanksgiving, present your requests to God. And the peace of God, which passes all understanding, will guard your hearts and your minds in Christ Jesus (Phil. 4:6-7).

The difference is that Tolle's version of Presence is not the presence of the Lord, where there is joyful refreshing,[287] but a breath-induced state of consciousness of the God-nature within all things. This pantheistic view (God is the universe and the universe is God) of reality is foreign to the biblical worldview of a loving heavenly Father, who sent Jesus Christ his Son, to restore humanity to a right relationship. Such a relationship enables God's presence to permeate every aspect of our earthly existence by the gift and power of the Holy Spirit. The Holy Spirit provides guidance, comfort, healing, strength, and wisdom to overcome our past wounds and present temptations as we live in moment by moment communion with Him.

Hence, the idea that we should get in touch with our godlike true selves by deep breathing falls far short of God's gracious and abundant provision in Christ—the promised gift of the Holy Spirit. Furthermore, our inclusion in the kingdom (eternally present spiritual rule) of God (Col. 1:13-14) fills us with comforting assurance that though we do not know *what* the future holds, we do know *who* holds the future. In other words, the presence of God, confidently accessed and maintained by faith in Christ (Eph. 3:12, NIV), is an eternal reality for all those who willingly believe in the Lordship of Jesus. Why accept any other substitute?

5. Transformation of Consciousness, the Kingdom of God and the Power of Free-will

When Tolle asserts that the "central message" of Jesus (Tolle, 2005, p. 6) was the transformation of consciousness he is, from a Christian perspective, "half right" and "half wrong." He is half right to describe the radical need for human transformation in order to shape a better world. Unfortunately however, such a transformed world cannot be fully realized in this present age. Rather, the present heavens and earth must undergo a radical regeneration (rebirth) in order for the ultimate-eternal next age to begin.[288] But he is also half wrong to assume that this was Jesus' "central teaching." In fact, Matthew makes an unequivocal statement regarding Jesus' main message and central focus in his entire earthly ministry: "Jesus went throughout Galilee, teaching in their synagogues, preaching the good news of the kingdom, and healing every disease and sickness among the people" (Matt. 4:23).

Theologically speaking, the kingdom of God is the presence of the future invading human history—the eternal intersecting the temporal in the person of Christ Jesus; the establishment of God's rule in the hearts and lives of all who embrace its reality[289]; the dethroning of all the spiritual forces of evil aligned against humanity (Col. 2:15); the removal of the consequences of sin, including death and all that diminishes human life (2 Tim. 1:10; John 10:10); and the creation of a new universal order of righteousness and peace for redeemed humanity.[290]

Furthermore, the kingdom of God not only transforms the believer's present identity (in keeping with the reality of Christ within us), but, as stated above, it will also ultimately regenerate the physical structures of the universe in which we now live.

> But the day of the Lord will come like a thief. The heavens will disappear with a roar; the elements will be destroyed by fire, and the earth and everything in it will be laid bare...But in keeping with his promise we are looking forward to a new heaven and a new earth, in which righteousness dwells (2 Pet. 3:10, 13).

This is where Tolle's transformational vision does not go far enough. Rather than simply an awakening of human/universal consciousness through dissolution of the egoic self's dependence on form-based reality, the Bible calls for the need for a physical dissolution of the present heavens and earth as a necessary precursor for the ultimate revelation/manifestation of the kingdom of God. Such a manifestation will specifically coincide with the central theme of the New Testament writers—the resurrection from the dead (1 Cor. 15:50-57).

Again, this is where Tolle's text is absolutely silent. Predictably, this is because in Buddhism, death is an illusion that gives way to innumerable reincarnations.[291] And for Tolle, reincarnation is the implied (and necessary) mechanism for human evolution to occur—hopefully resulting in a universal consciousness and consensus. The only problem is that for this to occur would mean that every human being would ultimately have to arrive at fully awakened consciousness. This would imply that, among many other human dysfunctions and delusions not-with-standing,[292] every monotheist on the planet now, of which there are over 3.3 billion,[293] will, in multiple lifetimes to come, have to abandon their belief in God and embrace Tolle's philosophy in order for it to become a global reality of the newly evolved human species. Needless to say, the chances of this happening are beyond any reasonable calculation, which is undoubtedly why Tolle's monistic utopianism (Tolle, 2005,

p. 308) must be based on the wholesale denial and/or rejection of rationality.

However, what Tolle has not accounted for, and which is destined to be the undoing of his utopian ideal, is the biblical concept of free-will.[294] And even if the freedom of the individual is denied for a season, it will eventually emerge to cast off the constraints of those who seek to control it. Free-will, after all, is an inexorable aspect of our divine origin. Even the kingdom of God can not violate freedom of individual choice—which is why the Bible repeatedly invites the voluntary participation of "whosoever will" (Rev. 22:17).

6. *The Impermanence of Form, Eternal Life and Divine Purpose*

A key part of Tolle's argument is that our egoic-self is attached to forms, be they material or otherwise in its insatiable thirst for what ultimately leads a false sense of identity. It is only through the realization of the instability of all forms (structures) that peace arises within.[295] This is because, according to Tolle, "the recognition of the impermanence of all forms awakens you to the dimension of the formless within yourself, that which is beyond death. Jesus called it 'eternal life.'" (Tolle, 2005, p. 81)

Though the concept of the impermanence of this-worldly form-based structures does find a degree of resonance within the New Testament,[296] the notion that eternal life is somehow associated with the awakening to formlessness within oneself is not even remotely a consideration of Jesus, or any other biblical writer. On the contrary, Jesus specifically taught that eternal life was a gift from a loving God mediated through him[297] to all who would behold and believe in the salvation accomplished by his death on their behalf.

> Just as Moses lifted up a snake in the desert [through mounting it on a pole so that anyone who was bitten could look upon it and live, Numbers 21:4-9], so the Son of Man must be lifted up, that everyone who believes in him may have eternal life. For God so loved the

> world that he gave his one and only Son, that whoever believes in him shall not perish but have eternal life (John 3:14-16).

Notice that the context for God's gift of eternal life is by the acknowledgment of Christ's sacrificial death for sin. Allegorically, the result of the snake-serpent-satan's "bite" has resulted in the poisoning of humanity's personality as well the eventual reality of physical death. Such a terminal condition can only be effectively neutralized by "ingesting-believing" in Christ's resurrection life. Indeed, the "antibody" of Christ's life alone is sufficient to overcome the terminal condition of sin. Furthermore, such antibody is available to all who believe in his name. For to earnestly invoke the name (nature and authority) of the Lord Jesus Christ is to access the presence and power of God with confidence and certainty (Eph. 3:12; John 14:13-14).

In the final analysis, the biblical alternative to an idolatrous preoccupation with the passing forms of this world is to lovingly devote oneself to serving the will (purpose and intention) of God on earth.

> Do not love the world or the things in the world. If anyone loves the world, the love of the Father is not in him. For all that is in the world, the lust of the flesh[-carnality] and the lust of the eyes [materialism] and the boastful pride of life [egoism], is not from the Father, but is from the world. The world is passing away, and also its lusts; but the one who does the will of God lives forever (1 John 2:15-17).

Tolle's assertion is that the "reason for our existence" (Tolle, 2005, p. 166) is to bring an awareness of our own universal connectedness (or consciousness) to the planet. However, the divine call and destiny for a Christian is undoubtedly and essentially reflected in a whole-hearted commitment to what is called "the great commission." The great commission has a number of essential components, which should at least include the following: the special empowering of the Holy Spirit (Luke 24:49;

Acts 1:4-5); being "built together" as a living expression of the Body of Christ on earth[298]; going forth into all of the nations of the world with the intent to share the good news of Christ's atoning sacrifice for humanity (Luke 24: 46-47); baptizing those who repent and believe the Gospel as a public profession of their faith in Christ Jesus (Matt. 28:19); instructing-nurturing believers in spiritual growth (Matt. 28:20); and trusting the Lord to confirm his word by any number of signs that he may choose to grant (Mark 16: 17-20; Heb. 2:3b-4).

Any lack of dynamic Christian spirituality can be traced to a loss of one or more of these essential kingdom characteristics-objectives. Furthermore, fulfillment of these objectives will most assuredly catalyze a Christian version of a global spiritual awakening (especially among the youth), a transformation of consciousness and character, and a counter-awakening backlash of persecution. All such events will collectively signal that the end of the age is upon us.[299] "And this gospel of the kingdom will be preached in the whole world as a testimony to all nations, and then the end will come" (Matt. 24:14).

7. *The Problem of Evil*

In Tolle's worldview the problem of evil is only one of misperception. Indeed, evil only exists (in relative terms) in those who are currently unenlightened-unawakened and thereby unconscious to the delusion of evil, which operates through the form-based identification of the egoic-mind (Tolle, 2005, p. 22). This is why Tolle insists that the only "perpetrator of evil on the planet is human unconsciousness" (Tolle, 2005, p. 160). Essentially, the unawareness of our universal connectedness coupled with our egoic identification with forms[300] is what Tolle refers to as the "original sin"—resulting in suffering and delusion (Tolle, 2005, p. 22). And since evil only has a relative (vs. absolute) reality among the unconscious, when we are finally awakened we realize the futility of judgment and resistance— thus enabling us to forgive all offenses automatically. After all, if no evil offense was perpetrated against us then there is no need to retain judgments against others. Hence, forgiveness flows without effort from the heart of the awakened.

This notion of pacifism toward the presence of evil is based on a philosophical fatalism that embraces everything that happens to us, regardless of the appearance of evil, as a necessary part of "the greater whole" to which we are all connected (Tolle, 2006, p. 286). In other words, evil itself will work to awaken us to the truth that there is actually no such thing as evil—we were only dreaming it was evil (Tolle, 2005, p. 208). And when once awakened we now see the light that resistance to the illusion of evil is futile.

First observation: From a biblical perspective, the concept of "original sin" springs from the rebellion of Adam and Eve in the Garden of Eden (Gen. 3), which resulted in the "fall of man" and subsequent power of evil in the world. (Rom. 5:12-19). Needless to say, this is a far cry from Tolle's idea that "original sin" is forgetfulness of our ultimate connection with the universe (Tolle, 2005, p. 22).

Second observation: Though Jesus did advocate that we "turn the other cheek" (Matt. 5:39) in our attitude toward dealing with personal offenses, most commentators doubt that this was an unqualified endorsement of the doctrine of pacifism. Rather, the command goes to the heart of a self-defensiveness that escalates too quickly to confrontation (litigation) and violence. Such caustic behavior would indicate a lack of trust in God whose forgiveness, protection and favor is fundamental to those who confess faith in the Gospel of Christ. In addition, this injunction cannot be construed to disallow the resistance of evil in relation to the assault of others. For to do so would be a violation of civil law, which according to the New Testament is given by God for the protection of social order.[301] Finally, the apostle Paul clarifies that the ultimate source of evil is not people, but "spiritual forces of evil in the heavenly realms." Here Paul speaks of the devil/satan, who, as the archenemy of God must be firmly resisted by all who believe the truth in Christ (Eph. 6: 10-17; 2 Cor. 10:3-5).

8. *The Cure for Unhappiness*

According to Tolle, all unhappiness is the result of not being aligned with the present moment (Tolle, 2005, p. 172) Indeed, the secret of living, success, and happiness is to be "one with life"...one with the present moment (or now) (Tolle, 2005, p. 115). As a result, all unhappiness, is simply a state of the egoic-mind which must be overcome by a denial of—or what Tolle prefers to call a "disidentification" (Tolle, 2005, p. 117) with, the power of the illusion. Of course, the illusion is whatever appears to be the cause of the mental or emotional suffering, which can be painful issues from the past or desires regarding the future. Hence, both the past and the future must be equally resisted, or disidentified with, in order to live in the now of the present moment and be free of all unhappiness.

There are several things here that require response from a Christian perspective. First is the issue of misalignment. Tolle proposes that in order to find happiness and peace that we align ourselves with ourselves—albeit in a universally transcendent way. This of course is in direct contradiction to the idea of the ultimate transcendence of God alone. The Bible teaches that only God is the eternally self-existent one, which is the meaning of "I Am" (Ex. 3:14; John 8:58). Therefore, to suggest that we can align ourselves with someone or something that does not exist is, biblically speaking, an exercise of futility and self-deception.

Second is the issue of the denial. In Tolle's perception of reality he borrows heavily from what are called the Four Noble Truths of Buddhism, which are built around the concept that all life involves suffering—that can only be "extinguished" (lit. *Nirvana*) by the cessation of desire. Such desire is the motivation for attachment to things that can provide only temporary satisfaction. Hence, in order not to suffer ultimate disappointment we should refuse all attachments by attaining and perfecting a passion-less (or dispassionate) existence.[302]

Biblically speaking, God created the earth to bless and sustain human life (Gen. 1:28-31). The New Testament again affirms, even with the reality of the "fall of man" and the entrance of sin, that there is still an intrinsic goodness in God's creation which should not be rejected by those who know and believe the truth (1 Tim. 4:3-4). It is instructive that in the context of this affirmation of the goodness of God's creation that marriage—one of the most basic and passionate relationships of humanity is mentioned (1 Tim. 4:3). In other words, rather than avoid disappointment by shielding oneself from temporal loss, we are encouraged to embrace life to its fullest trusting that one can express worship to God in the normal affairs and relationships of everyday life.

Furthermore, the hope of a future resurrection life mediates any and every sense of loss we might experience in this life" (1 Thess. 4:1-18). Though the believer in Christ is wary of the temptation of evil, nevertheless, the Christian occupation is not one of reservation but rather celebration; not one of denial but of affirmation; not one of withdrawal but of engagement; not one of dispassion but of cheerfulness. "The kingdom of God is righteousness, peace and joy in the Holy Spirit" (Rom. 14:17).

Finally there is the issue of unhappiness itself. As mentioned above, Tolle's solution to unhappiness is simply to live in the present moment alone—the eternal now-ness of being. And while learning to live one day at a time (moment by moment/thought by thought) is also a vital aspect of Christian spirituality (Matt. 6:34; 2 Cor. 10:5). there is biblically much more involved in comprehensively addressing the causes and cures for unhappiness.

Specifically, happiness flows to those who have been blessed by God by aligning themselves with the kingdom values as taught by Jesus in the "Sermon on the Mount": Blessed (lit. "happy") are the poor in spirit...blessed/happy are those who mourn...blessed/happy are the meek...blessed/happy are those who hunger and thirsty for righteousness...blessed/happy are the merciful...blessed/happy are the pure in heart...blessed/happy are the peacemakers...blessed/happy are those who are persecuted for the sake of righteousness (Matt 5:3-12).

Happiness also flows to those who have an optimistic attitude, which reveals itself in a positive spirit of gratitude, thankfulness, and cheerfulness rather than negativity, pessimism, and cynicism.[303] Happiness flows to those who have learned the "secret of contentment" (Phil.4:11-13) with what they have rather than by always requiring more. In other words, they have embraced a limitation (rather than an ascetic "moratorium") regarding the necessities of life—purposefully and persistently shunning greed and materialism (1 Tim. 6:6-10). Happiness flows to those who prayerfully trust in the Lord to intervene on their behalf—regardless of what the future may bring.[304] Happiness flows to and through those who have learned to patiently forgive—themselves and others (Luke 4:4, NIV).

9. Popular Psychology and Interpreting Jesus

Similar to how Tolle approaches the cure to unhappiness—by disidentification-denial of the past and future in favor of cultivating the presence of Now, so too are many of his prescriptions to the fundamental struggles of life. Such struggles include physical illness (Tolle, 2005, p. 124), addictions (smoking, drinking, gluttony (p. 246), emotional negativity (pain-body), judgmentalism, guilt (p. 204), unforgiveness, resentment (p. 65), victimization, depression (234), anger (p. 136), fear, greed (p. 12), etc. All of these, and many more are, according to Tolle, basically symptomatic of the need to connect with our higher consciousness through acknowledging, accepting, and dissolving the awareness of our reactive lives (p. 65).

The problem with this remedy is that it simply fails to address the complex nature of (and solutions to) the great variety of physical-psychological infirmities of the human race. In other words, it is going to take a lot more than "deep breathing" exercises (Tolle, 2005, p. 247), and the denial of temporal realities, in order to effectively deal with destructive issues like cancer, paranoia, heart disease, murder, rape or genocide. Granted that one's attitude and awareness can help in the healing process, there is however, so much more involved in the quest for wholeness than offered by a "Zen version of popular psychology."

As to "interpreting Jesus," though Tolle specifically refers to Jesus thirty-one times,[305] he nevertheless insists that Jesus is often mis-interpreted by those who are not aware of his "deeper-mystical meaning." Such deeper meaning however, is generally in direct contradiction to the biblical context of Jesus' own words.

For example, when Jesus said that he was/is "the way, the truth, and the life" (John 14:6a, NIV), Tolle insists that what Jesus meant was that like himself, so too do all life-forms share the collective-universal identity of the Way, the Truth and the Life (p. 71). Jesus is simply an archetypal representation (Tolle, 2005, p. 144) of a transcendent reality that we should all claim as our own. The problem here is the last half of the same verse, "No one comes to the Father except through me" (John 14:6b). Here Jesus is clearly conveying his ability to mediate between humanity and God, his Father (1 Tim. 2:5). This mediation is biblically based on his atoning sacrifice through which we have redemption, the forgiveness of our sins (Col. 1:14).

In other words, Jesus Christ is the unique Son of God who has been divinely-prophetically identified as the Savior of humanity by virtue of his historical birth, life, death and resurrection. This means that any righteous person (who "fears God and does what is right," Acts 10:34-35), and from any era of human history, is welcomed without partiality to God on the basis of the finished-eternal work of Christ. This is because the "work of atonement" was foreseen by God before the foundation of the world, but revealed in the "fullness of time" in the person of Christ Jesus.[306] Essentially, God summed up the past (Eph. 1:10) and inaugurated a "new and living way," through Christ's death for sin and physical resurrection from the dead. The way is now open, whereby men of all nations can receive the gift of salvation apart from all previous religious systems of good works—be they Jewish or Gentile, Eastern or Western.[307] Suffice it to say, a Christian interpretation of Christ is stunningly different than the mystical alternative proposed by Tolle (Tolle, 2005, p. 16).

10. *A New Heaven and New Earth and the Lordship of Jesus Christ*

Inspiration for the title of Tolle's book came from a Bible prophecy in Revelation 21:1 and Isaiah 65:17, which both speak of the future creation of a new heaven(s) and a new earth (Tolle, 2005, p. 23). For Tolle, the new heaven is a "transformed state of human consciousness," and the new earth is an unspecified "reflection in the physical realm."[308] Again, Tolle admits that he derives this idea, not from biblical hermeneutics, but from "esoteric"-mystical inference.[309] As previously explained in point number five above, the kingdom of heaven[310] has both a present and future dynamic. And though the present manifestation of the kingdom of heaven does indeed involve a "global spiritual awakening," such awakening however, is not to a universal consciousness of a monistic (non-theistic/"god-less") reality.

Rather, the biblical prophecies clearly reveal that, as a result of the supernatural resurrection of Christ from the dead, the Father has poured out the gift of the Holy Spirit upon "all people."[311] This gift (infilling) of the Holy Spirit has even now been personally experienced by, what Harvard Professor Harvey Cox calculates to be, in excess of 500 million people worldwide—with no sign of receding.[312] Furthermore, the central revelation of this global empowerment is the transcendent reality of the eternal kingdom of God, over which Jesus Christ is Lord of all.

> This is what was spoken by the prophet Joel; 'In the last days, God say, I will pour out my Spirit on all people. Your sons and daughters will prophesy, your young men will see visions, your old men will dream dreams...I will show wonders in the heaven above and signs on the earth below. The sun will be turned to darkness and the moon to blood before the coming of the great and glorious day of the Lord. And everyone who calls on the name of the Lord will be saved (Acts 2:16-21 c.f. Joel 2:28-32).

He [Christ Jesus] became obedient to death—even the death on a cross! Therefore God exalted him to the highest place and gave him the name that is above every name, that at the name of Jesus every knee should bow, in heaven and on earth and under the earth, and every tongue confess that Jesus Christ is Lord, to the glory of God the Father (Phil. 8-11).

The seventh angel sounded his trumpet, and there were loud voices in heaven, which said: The kingdom of the world has become the kingdom of our Lord and of his Christ, and he will reign forever and ever (Rev. 11:15).

Conclusion

This article was conceived as a Christian response (not reaction) to the published and "prophetic vision"[313] of Eckhart Tolle in his book entitled, *A New Earth: Awakening to Your Life's Purpose*. The content of Tolle's text has been unreservedly promoted (and even co-taught) by beloved American icon, Oprah Winfrey.[314] Such an endorsement has affected millions, both Christian and non-Christian alike.

As a result, and given my previously mentioned background, I felt a "prophetic prompting" of my own to objectively evaluate Tolle's assertions (1 Cor. 14:29). What I have discovered has been briefly enumerated here for all to assess in light of biblical revelation and contemporary Christian spirituality.

And while I would agree that the general state of institutionalized Christianity has been sadly lacking a dynamic and integrated faith, what I would recommend is not a rejection-replacement, but a spiritual renewal-revival[315] of the original Christian message and power. Furthermore, where ever this dynamic Christian spirituality is lacking, a vacuum or void has been created. Such a void will attempt to be filled by those offering an alternative for humanity's deepest longing for meaning and purpose.

In place of this dynamic Christian spirituality, what Tolle is recommending is that we all let go of our rational thinking in favor of an awareness that is a "consciousness without thought." (p. 259). In other words, an uncritical awareness that finds no need for divine intervention...no need for the atoning sacrifice of Christ...no need for the resurrection from the dead...no need for Christianity itself.

Such an alternative is unacceptable to the proliferating hundreds of millions of us who have experienced the power of the Spirit of Christ and believe in the integrity of his word.[316] And while Tolle insists that humanity must either "evolve or die," (Tolle, 2005, p. 21) the Christian messages remains the same: "repent and live!" (Luke 24:46-49)

> This grace...has now been revealed through the appearing of our Savior, Christ Jesus, who has destroyed death and has brought life and immortality to light through the gospel (2 Tim. 1:10).

> Whoever is thirsty, let him come; and whoever wishes, let him take the free gift of the water of life...even so, Come, Lord Jesus (Rev. 17, 20).

Addendum 2.

A Christian Moral Response to Homosexuality

Lady Gaga, Monster Ball

Born this Way, Lady Gaga

"...A different lover is not a sin...no matter gay straight or bi, transgender life...I'm beautiful in my way 'Cause God makes no mistakes...I'm on the right track baby I was [you were] born this way..."

Recently, the state of New York became the sixth state in the United States to legalize same-sex marriage. Although actions like these are deemed justified by secular ideologies,[317] such laws need to be challenged by a rational argument of biblical morality[318]. Though laws should not be used to legislate morality, they can and should be used to protect society from the dangers of immorality, as the apostle Paul taught. "But we know that the Law is good, if one uses it lawfully, realizing the fact that law is not made for a righteous person [See Gal. 5:22-23], but for those who are lawless..." (1 Tim. 1:8-9a, New American Standard Bible, NASB).

As a result, the law should primarily be used to restrain the evil of those who would intentionally threaten, harm, or endanger the lives of themselves or others (See *Criminal Law*). This is why Jesus' teaching regarding the two greatest commands is such a compelling idea statement:

Jesus replied: 'Love the Lord your God with all your heart and with all your soul and with all your mind. This is the first and greatest commandment. And the second is like it: Love your neighbor as yourself. All the Law and the Prophets [the entire Old Testament] hang on these two commandments (Matt. 22:34-40).

In other words, if people followed these two laws there would be no need to legislate against criminal or immoral behavior. However, it is biblically impossible for unregenerate people, as well as immature Christians to live by the law of love because of the fallen nature of humanity and the resultant *principle of evil* that resides within all of us.

For the good that I want, I do not do, but I practice the very evil that I do not want. But if I am doing the very thing I do not want, I am no longer the one doing it, but sin which dwells in me. I find then the principle that evil is present in me, the one who wants to do good (Rom. 7:19-21).

In this regard, it is also important to realize that the Old Covenant Law of Moses, though not destroyed, has been fulfilled and hence superseded by the New Covenant of Grace in Jesus Christ (John 1:17, Heb. 8:13, NASB). This means that there is now no reason that Christians need to embrace the legal system and penalties of the Old Testament—especially regarding sexual violations, religious law, family offenses, and violent crimes, as well as any other illegalities of the Old Covenant/Testament.

However, this does not imply that such offenses should be deemed as insignificant, especially by the Church. As a result, in the realm of the state, Christians, like any other citizens, need to make a moral argument for establishing legal violations and penalties that are based on both the biblical enlightenment of the truth in Jesus Christ as well as compelling rational argumentation. Such truthful enlightenment enables the believer to understand the existence of evil, the *fallen-ness* of human nature, the appropriate use of law (to protect society against evil), as well as the promise of forgiveness and healing in Christ—leading to a new life free from the tyranny of satan, sin, sickness, and death (John 10:10, NASB).

Here then is a Christian moral response to what most Christians would understand as the destructive consequences of the legalization of homosexuality. Though secularists will *ipso facto* resist any such moral arguments it is still our legal right and Christian responsibility to speak the truth as we perceive it—so help us God.

Homosexuality should not be legalized (in any form) because it contributes to:

1. The corruption of the culture at large by the violation of God's original design for marriage between members of the opposite sex. Such violation results in a sexually disordered lifestyle—hence lowering the norms for propriety and the dignity of our sexual identity and behavior (Gen. 2:7, 20b-22, Today's New Living Version, TNLV).
2. The danger of the spread of deadly diseases in tandem with the extremely high cost of medical treatment of homosexuals who have the highest incidents of STD's such as Syphilis, Hepatitis B, oral gonorrhea, gay bowel syndrome, AIDS, other very serious diseases.[319]
3. The harmful and especially overwhelming temptations for children and youth who are not prepared to be exposed to such a serious degree of moral depravity at a young age (Matt. 18:6, NASB). For instance, many youth consider it *cool to be gay or bi-sexual* because of poor example of certain celebrities they respect without understanding the harmful consequences of such a lifestyle. As a result, they begin to feed on gay pornography and sexually exploitive entertainment leading to experimentation and entrapment in compulsively degrading behavior—for which they cannot extricate themselves from such addictive behavior.
4. The emotional and psychological confusion, guilt, shame, and hopelessness leading to greater suicidal contemplation and action—all the while placing blame on *Christians* for their religiously harmful moral beliefs[320] (John 10:10, NASB).
5. The hardening of one's heart toward truth resulting in even more perverse and de-humanizing behavior (Rom. 1:18-32, TNLV).
6. The abuse of minors by specifically predatory homosexual adults[321] (Mark 9:42, NASB).
7. The shortening of one's lifespan by as high as 20 years—for the active homosexual.[322]

These arguments, and others like it, can help provide a basis for a reasonable, compassionate, and yet truthful response to the debate about pro-homosexual legislation (James 3:17-18). And even though a few permissive states may have already legalized homosexual marriage; if the voting majority of Christians (nearly 80%) continued to stand firm against the spread of homosexuality—such efforts would fail and/or at least be greatly hindered—all for the protection of those who do not yet understand the power of evil or of God's love for them in Jesus Christ (John 3:16, TNLV).

It must also be acknowledged here that our Christian efforts to restrain evil must be linked with an equally passionate ministry of caring for those who seek to be released from the devastation of homosexuality, including personal brokenness, relational confusion, emotional bitterness, physical disease and death, deception, pride, and rebellion that such a lifestyle inevitably engenders. In other words, the suffering of the homosexual is never an issue for mockery (of any kind); but rather an opportunity to demonstrate the truthful-compassion, care, and the love of Jesus Christ toward those who are lost without him—as we also once were lost ourselves without him (Eph. 2:1-5; 2 Cor. 6:9-11).

As a result, the church must have a similar pro-active (truthful and yet compassionate) response to homosexuality as it has had toward abortion. More than just an issue for public debate, our commission is a call to action on behalf of those who desperately need practical, emotional, physical, and spiritual help and nurturing. My plea is that Christians in cities throughout the nation would link with proven homosexual ministries and/or begin their own redemptive outreach to homosexuals in their own localities. May the Lord Jesus give us grace and generosity of heart to respond to this call to action.

Lady Gaga Reprise...

> "...A different lover is not a sin...no matter gay straight or bi, transgender life...I'm beautiful in my way 'Cause God makes no mistakes...I'm on the right track baby I was [you were] born this way..."

- Having a homosexual lover is a *sin*—which simply means that we have all missed the mark of God's best design for our life... but you can still change! Yes you can!
- You are beautiful (!) but God did not make you a homosexual. The *fallen-ness* of the world has caused brokenness in all of our lives. Although some may have a genetic predisposition toward homosexuality you can be born again (1 Cor. 6:9-11, NASB). Yes you can!
- You can be on the right track if you willingly accept God's forgiveness extended to you in Jesus Christ—who died and rose again to bring us the hope and power of eternal life. Yes he did!

Have I any pleasure in the death of the rebellious, declares the Lord GOD, and not rather that he/she should turn from his/her way and live? (Ezek. 18:23, English Standard Version, ESV).

Don't you see how wonderfully kind, tolerant, and patient God is with you? Does this mean nothing to you? Can't you see that his kindness is intended to turn you from your wayward style of life? (Rom. 2:4, New Living Translation, NLT).

Do not be deceived: for neither fornicators, nor idolaters, nor adulterers, nor homosexuals [notice how many other things are listed along with homosexuality], nor cheats (swindlers and thieves), nor greedy graspers, nor drunkards, nor foulmouthed revilers and slanderers, nor extortioners and robbers will inherit or have any share in the kingdom of God. And such were some of you. But you were washed clean (purified from all defilement), and you were consecrated (set apart, dedicated), and you were justified [pronounced righteous, by trusting] in the name of the Lord Jesus Christ and in the [power of the] Spirit of our God (1 Cor. 6:9-11, Amplified Bible, AMP).

> But he [Jesus] was pierced for our transgressions, he was crushed for our iniquities; the punishment that brought us peace was upon him, and by his wounds we are healed (Isaiah 53:5, NIV & NLT).

Addendum 3.

Twenty-Seven of the Most Important People and Events in Christian History

-From the Early Church; to the Papacy; to Eastern Orthodoxy; to the Protestant Reformation; to the Settlement of America to the Twenty-First Century & Beyond-

1. The birth, ministry, death and resurrection of the Lord Jesus Christ[323]

2. The birth of the Church at Pentecost and its early development[324]

The apostolic ministries of Peter, to the Jews, and Paul, to the Gentiles are recorded in the Book of Acts. Peter's primacy is from Acts Chapters 1 to 12. Paul's primacy is from Acts Chapters 13 to 27 with his conversion recorded in Acts 9. Most historians say that Peter was first the bishop of Antioch and then later of Rome. The reason for Paul's primacy in Acts is undoubtedly due to the fact that the author of Acts, the physician Luke, was a close traveling companion of Paul (2 Tim. 4:11; Col. 4:14). Both Peter and Paul were ultimately martyred in Rome—Paul being beheaded as was the privilege of Roman citizens and Peter being crucified upside down allegedly claiming he was unworthy to be crucified like his Lord.

3. The development of the New Testament scriptures (mid 50's to 250)

Most scholars say the New Testament was written between the early 50's to as late as 95 AD. Other scholars insist that most all of the New Testament was written before the destruction of Jerusalem in AD 70, since such an event would certainly not go unnoticed and noted by those who knew of Jesus' ominous warnings about Jerusalem's destruction.[325] The various books/letters of the New Testament were circulated among the local congregations soon after they were written. However, the official canon of the New Testament was the result of years of development as evidenced by writings from such men as Ignatius (who was martyred in AD 110)[326], to Marcion the heretic (ca. AD 150), to the Muratorian Canon (ca. AD 170); to Origen's canon (ca AD 185-254), etc.[327]

4. Christian persecutions by the Roman Emperors (AD 67 to 303)

The techniques of torture employed by a number of the Roman Emperors included beheadings, dipping in wax and burning them for garden parties, sowing them in animal skins and feeding them to wild beasts, burning them at the stake, pouring hot tar on their heads, submerging them in boiling water, forcing them to be seated on red-hot metal thrones, subjecting them to racks, scourges, daggers, poisons, etc. *Foxes Book of Martyr's* chronicles ten (10) mass persecutions by the Roman Emperors Nero (AD 67), Domitian (AD 81), Trajan (AD 108), Antoninas (AD 162), Severus (AD 192), Maximus (AD 235), Decius "Deny or die!" edict (AD 249), Valerian (AD 257), Aurelian (AD 274), and Diocletian (AD 303). In fact, it was through witnessing the courageous suffering of these faithful Christian martyrs that the Roman citizens were in large part won to Christ! In retrospect, most biblical scholars now identify one of the primary purposes of the Book of Revelation as seeking to prepare the early Christians for the next two centuries of the agony of martyrdom.[328]

5. Constantine I and the Edict of Milan (AD 313)

The Edit of Milan officially ended Christian persecution in favor of religious tolerance. Constantine is called the first Christian Roman Emperor who made way for Christianity to become the official religion of the Roman Empire. He was also instrumental in provoking the Council of Nicaea (AD 323) and moving the capital of Rome to Constantinople in AD 330.

6. Augustine of Hippo (AD 354-430)

Augustine is one of the most important figures in the development of Western Christianity. His early education in philosophy (the art of persuasion) and rhetoric (public speaking) won him the "most visible academic chair in the Latin world"[329]—that of professor of rhetoric for the imperial court at Milan. He subsequently left Milan to serve Christ as a monastic priest in the city of Hippo until his death. As one of the most prolific Latin writers (100+ separate titles), Augustine combined Christian revelation with Greek philosophy to articulate doctrinal ideas such as original sin, salvation and grace, predestination, just war theory, ethics and the role of the will, exegetical articles (Genesis, Romans) and especially apologetic arguments against heresy. Two of his most popular books were *Confessions* (considered the first western autobiography) and *The City of God* written after the fall of Rome.

"Thou madest us for Thyself, and our heart is restless until it finds its rest [repose] in Thee." (Confessions I, i, 1)
"Nothing conquers except truth and the victory of truth is love"
(*Victoria veritatis est caritas*)

7. Rise of the Roman Papacy (Third to Sixth centuries)

The Roman Catholic Church *theologically* claims that based on their interpretation of Matthew 16:18, the first "Pope" was Simon Peter—who was later Bishop of the church in Rome prior to his death. However, Protestant theologians (as well as most secular scholars) dispute this claim of Catholic supremacy and to Peter being the rock upon which Jesus would build his church by, among many other arguments, the following:

i. Peter (Greek, *petros*) means small/detached stone whereas the bedrock (Greek, *petra*) of the body of Christ is Jesus alone—the head of the Church, his body (Eph. 1:22-23). Hence, the "rock" is the *revelation* given to Peter by God the Father regarding Jesus' identity as the Christ/Messiah. In fact, both Peter and Paul subsequently agreed that the only sufficient foundational cornerstone was none other than Jesus Christ (1

Cor. 3:11; Eph. 2:20; 1 Pet. 2:4-7). Peter never accepted nor conferred any title of preeminence over the other apostles (Mark 10:42-45).

    ii. Just 5 verses later (Matthew 16:23), Jesus sternly rebukes Peter for his spiritual ignorance in seeking to hinder Christ from his work of atonement.

    iii. The Roman Catholic Church also claims that based on the doctrine of *apostolic succession* they alone are the legitimate heirs of Peter's throne and therefore all spiritual authority on earth resides with them. The pope is himself now called the *vicar*, or chief representative of Christ on earth.

The problem with this claim of exclusivity is that the New Testament contradicts it with the apostle Paul unequivocally indicating that his call and authority were from God and not man (Gal. 1:1, 12, 2:6-10)—especially implying Peter, whom he publicly rebuked for hypocrisy (Gal. 2:11-14). Truth be told, even Peter warmly commends Paul's writings on the same level of authority as the scriptures themselves[330] (2 Pet. 3:15-16). It is clear that both Paul and Peter regarded each other as no more or less than fellow apostolic bond-servants of Jesus Christ (Rom. 1:1; 2 Pet. 1:1)—neither deriving their authority from the other, but from Christ himself.

The rise of the Roman papacy, as we know it today, was the result of a process that took literally hundreds of years to develop. At every turn there was opposition to this universal imposition by the bishop of Rome—undergirded by the force of the Roman Emperors, and leading eventually to the Great Schism of 1054 and the Protestant Reformation in 1517 (more below). However, even today Roman Catholics are still arguing for their right to rule all of Christendom from the Holy See in Rome.[331]

On the other side of the argument regarding the rise of the papacy are the proponents of the papacy including Ireneaus' list of apostolic succession (c.189); Stephen I's claim to Rome's primacy in writing (254-257); Damasus I's (366-384) insistence in Rome's primacy based on Peter's foundational rule; Leo the Great (440) [*the first generally recognized pope by historians*] who claimed to speak "with the voice of Peter" as he asserted the doctrine of papal authority; the Council of Chalcedon (451) which, though rejected by Rome, sought to give equal honor to both the Bishop of Constantinople and the Bishop of Rome, etc. Hence, one can rightly observe that:

The power of the Bishop of Rome increased as the imperial power of the Emperor declined. Edicts of the Emperor Theodosius II (401-450) and of Valentinian III (425-455) proclaimed the Roman bishop 'as Rector of the whole Church.' The Emperor Justinian, who was living in the East in Constantinople, in the sixth century, published a similar decree. These proclamations did not create the office of the Pope but from the sixth [6th] century onward the Bishop of Rome's power and prestige increased so dramatically that the title of "Pope" began to fit the Bishop of Rome best.[332]

8. The Great Schism of 1054

As mentioned above, the split between the Western (Latin) and Eastern (Greek) segments of the Church was primarily over the issue of papal authority. At the time, Pope Leo IX (1049-1054) claimed that he held authority over the other four leading Eastern patriarchs of Constantinople, Alexandria, Antioch, and Jerusalem. Additionally, the Roman Bishop authorized the insertion of the filioque clause[333] into the Nicene Creed—which was seen as another attempt of the unwarranted extension of his presumed authority. The Orthodox argument is that the "primacy" of the Patriarch of Rome was only honorary—which did not include a right to unilaterally change the decisions of the Ecumenical Councils like Nicaea. As a result, mutual excommunications were exchanged in 1054 and the Great Schism, which still persists today, began.

9. Thomas Aquinas (c. 1225-1274)

Thomas Aquinas was an Italian priest who is one of the 33 Doctors of the Church and considered by many to be the Catholic Church's "greatest theologian." In fact, by order of the Council of Trent, Aquinas's Summa Theologica[334] was placed next to Bible on the altar of the Church.[335] Pius X (1903-1914) even asserted that the teachings of the Catholic Church cannot be understood scientifically without the philosophical underpinning of Aquinas.[336] Vatican II (1962-65) remarked that Aquinas thought was the "perennial philosophy" of the Roman Catholic Church.[337]

Aquinas was a preacher, philosopher, and theologian in the scholastic tradition. He masterfully blended Greek philosophy (Aristotelian) and Christian doctrine suggesting that rational thinking and the study of nature, like revelation, were valid ways to understand God.[338] In addition to being a major classical proponent of natural theology.[339] Aquinas wrote extensively (in the *Summa Theologica* and elsewhere) about the proofs of God's existence (prime mover, efficient cause, necessarily existent being, category source, and intelligent design), ontology (the nature of being and meaning), cosmology (understanding the universe), psychology, theodicy (the problem of evil), the nature of law, sacramental theology, etc.

It is ironic that such a seminal philosopher and theologian was (earlier in his educational career) actually called the "dumb ox" because of his large and bulky frame, quiet demeanor, difficulty in public debates, and awkwardness in personal communication. Indeed, some of his fellow-students were said to have taken special pity on him because of his apparent dullness—that is until his remarkable intellectual gifts began to be evident to all.[340]

> Every contingent being at some time fails to exist. So if everything were contingent, then at some time there would have been nothing — and so there would be nothing now — which is clearly false. So not everything is contingent. So there is a necessary being. This is God. (Aquinas)

> "Love takes up where knowledge leaves off."
> (Aquinas)

10. The Crusades (1095-1291)

Historically, the Crusades were a series of nine (9) military campaigns[341], initially authorized by the Pope Urban II of Rome, and stretching over nearly 200 years. The purpose of the crusades was to liberate Jerusalem from the hands of Muslim rule—and was originally launched in response to a call from the Eastern Orthodox Byzantine Empire for help against the expansion of the Muslim Empire (Seljuq dynasty) into Anatolia (modern Turkey).[342]

Viewed broadly, the Crusades were an expression of militant Christianity and European expansionism. In essence, they dangerously combined religious ideology with secular ambitions and military enterprise.[343] The crusades have been simultaneously lauded by the Catholic church (as elevating European civilization to universal cultural icon)[344], romanticized by western European nations (heroic adventures by noble countrymen)[345], criticized by secular historians (greed and intolerance in the name of God)[346], and demonized by Muslims (as militant Christo-European aggression), Eastern Orthodox Christians (for the savage sacking of Constantinople during the 4th Crusade), and Jews (who were massacred along the way in Germany, France, Palestine, etc.).

In the final analysis, the crusades, either directly or indirectly, produced at least the following four results:

1. They failed to secure the ultimate liberation of Jerusalem.
2. They confronted Islamic aggression with European might.
3. They created a pathway for diverse inter-cultural exchange and enrichment.
4. They provided historic justification for the separation of church and state—leading to the political dethronement of the Roman Catholic Church and the eventual launching of the American democratic experiment.

11. The Protestant Reformation (1517)

On October 31, 1517, Martin Luther nailed his *Ninety-Five Theses On the Power and Efficacy of Indulgences* to the door of the Wittenberg Castle Church. This action, combined with his public denial to recant before the Diet of Worms in 1521 served to symbolically initiate the Protestant Reformation.[347]

Unless I am convicted by Scripture and plain reason —I do not accept the authority of popes and councils, for they have contradicted each other— my conscience is captive to the Word of God. I cannot and will not recant anything, for to go against conscience is neither right nor safe... Here I stand. I can do no other. God help me. Amen (Martin Luther, Diet of Worms, 1521).

Preceded by Peter Waldo (d. 1218, Waldensians), John Wycliffe (c. 1320-1384, Lollards) and John Huss (c. 1369-1415, Hussites) Luther and a fellow reformer, Ulrich Zwingli (1484-1531, Switzerland), were protesting Pope Leo X's sale of indulgences for the construction of St. Peter's basilica in Rome.[348]

The main Protestant criticisms of the Catholic church during the Reformation were indulgences (paying for release from purgatory suffering), simony (paying for church offices), clergy corruption (materialism, sexual immorality, lust for secular power), Marianism (excessive devotion to Mary), the intercession of deceased saints, the sacraments—especially as mediated by the catholic hierarchy, pilgrimages to holy sites, the authority of church tradition over biblical revelation, and the primacy of the Pope in all matters of faith.[349]

Other historic factors in the origin and rise of the Protestant Reformation include the rise of nationalism, the breakdown of the monastic institution and Scholasticism, peasant uprisings (poverty and disease), Papal scandals (Avignon Papacy, 1308-1378 and the papal schism, 1378-1416), Renaissance humanism, moveable type, etc.

Three of the major results of the Protestant Reformation:

1. The end of the ecclesiastical supremacy of the Pope in Western Christendom by the legal establishment of Protestant churches.

2. The end of the political dominance of the Pope by the redistribution of power and wealth previously held by the feudal nobility and the Roman Catholic hierarchy—now passed to the middle classes and to monarchial rulers of nation states.[350]

3. The emergence of the ideal of democratic governments based on the notion of the "consent of the governed" and the foundation of the future doctrine of the "separation of church and state."

The major criticisms arising from the Reformation include the accusation that Protestantism is a "reactionary theology." For instance, the Five Sola's of the Reformation are *solus Christus* (Christ alone), *sola scriptura* (scripture alone), *sola fide* (faith alone), *sola gratia* (grace alone), and *Soli Deo gloria* (glory to God alone).[351] However, postulated as reactions to the Catholicism, Protestants are often seen as radically individualistic and independent[352]; as against tradition and hence historically impoverished; as so fearful of works that grace and faith are often hollow and unconfirmed by actions[353]; and as emphasizing God's sovereignty to such a degree that it excuses man from any responsibility to align his will with the purpose of God on earth, respectively.

Secondly, the Roman Catholic Church still criticizes Protestants for a heretical "subjective arbitrariness" as evidenced by its rampant denominationalism, [354]which can only be remedied by the "return of all dissenters to the Catholic Church."[355] However, another solution would be that Roman Catholics embrace their Protestant brethren as a legitimate part of the larger Body of Christ and relinquish their claim to be the only legitimate church on earth. After all, divisions, according to the apostle Paul, can serve a necessary purpose when they expose and correct error[356]—leading to repentance.[357]

A third criticism is that both Protestant and Roman Catholics are so intransigent that they seem deaf to the Lord's call to mutual repentance and restoration.[358] One wonders how Christians will ever be able to make peace among the nations if they cannot make peace within their own household.[359] May the Lord lift off this reproach of perpetual division from the Body of Christ by giving us a heart of humility and a vision to "rebuild the ancient ruins and restore the places long devastated" (Isaiah 61:4; 58:9-12).

> "Be completely humble and gentle; be patient, bearing with one another in love. Make every effort to keep the unity of the Spirit in the bond of peace. There is only one body and one Spirit—just as you were called to one hope when you were called—one Lord, one faith, one baptism; one God and Father of all, who is over all and through all and in all" (Eph. 4:2-6).

12. John Calvin (1509-1564)

The Frenchman-lawyer John Calvin was arguably the greatest theologian of the Protestant Reformation.[360] Although Calvin, being a generation younger, never met Luther, he nevertheless resonated with Protestant ideals.[361] In Geneva, Calvin actually forged a "working model" of how civic and church government (Presbyterianism) should interact—all based on biblical principles utilizing a literal-pragmatic interpretation.[362] Among other things, Calvin undertook the establishment of a municipal school system for children which developed into a full university for those showing academic promise, promoted the value that became known as the Protestant work ethic[363], helped lay the foundation for Capitalism[364], and was even instrumental in the later development of "separation of powers" doctrine resulting in the three (3) branches of the American government: Executive, Legislative, and Judicial.[365]

So compelling were Calvin's ideas that by the mid 1550's Geneva was virtually the "Protestant Rome" of the Reformation. Indeed, other Reformers throughout Europe (France, England, Scotland, and the Netherlands) used Calvin's theology to model their own reformation ideologies and applications.

Prominent among these reformers were such men as John Knox[366] in Scotland, the Puritans in England, Jonathan Edwards in the American colonies[367], Francis Schaeffer (American Evangelical theologian, philosopher, and Presbyterian pastor, 1912-1984), and even Karl Barth (1886-1968)—who in the 20th century argued from Calvin's view of God's supremacy versus human insufficiency in his defense against biblical liberalism.[368]

Calvin was a systematic theologian whose *Institutes of the Christian Religion* (1536)[369] originally written to defend the French Huguenots against persecution, immediately promoted Calvin to the forefront as a Reformation-Reformed theologian, practitioner, and spokesman. The *Institutes* follow the outline of the then popular Apostles' Creed—addressing the Father, Son, Holy Spirit, and Church, respectively.[370]

Calvin's theology is generally summarized by the acronym T.U.L.I.P.[371], which stands for Total Depravity, Unconditional Election, Limited Atonement, Irresistible Grace, and Perseverance of the saints.[372] Unfortunately, theocratic over-lording and the unmerciful execution of the popular Spanish Protestant theologian and physician Michael Servetus (who was dubbed an anti-Trinitarian heretic) have, among other things, been a major source of reproach on the record of Calvin's rule in Geneva.[373] A weary ecclesiastical-social reformer, John Calvin died in Geneva May 27, 1564 (age 55) and was buried, by his request, without witness or ceremony in a virtually unmarked grave bearing only the initials "J.C."[374]

13. The Council of Trent (1545-1563)

The Council of Trent was the 19th Ecumenical Council of the Roman Catholic Church which finally convened (after much political wrangling)[375] by Pope Paul III to counteract the spread of the Protestant Reformation. In so doing Roman Catholicism was able to articulate its essential dogmas (salvation, sacraments, biblical canon) and initiate a general reform of the Church that lasted until Vatican II (1962-1965).[376]

The Council of Trent took on a decidedly anti-Protestant posture[377] by refusing to directly address the main issue of the role of the papacy in the Church; by affirming (in contradiction to *sola scriptura*) church tradition as a co-equal source of Christian truth; by determining (in contradiction to Protestant vernacular translations) the Latin Vulgate to be the only true sacred canon; by insisting that the Catholic church alone had the ability to rightly interpret Scripture; by proclaiming seven (instead of two) sacraments; by supporting the veneration of the saints, relics, and the Virgin Mary; by modifying and continuing the sale of indulgences, etc.[378]

From a Catholic perspective, the Council of Trent served to revitalize Roman Catholicism by accepting the Nicene Creed; endorsing the Latin Vulgate version of the Bible; standardizing the mass; delineating the nature and consequences of original sin; rejecting Luther's doctrine of *sola fide* (justification by faith); confirming "transubstantiation" (the physical presence of Christ in the Eucharistic bread and wine); enacting moral reforms of convents; prescribing the education and discipline of the clergy; curtailing the extravagance of bishops, etc.[379]

Trent also helped create the highly effective counter-Reformation Society of Jesus (Jesuits) under the able leadership of Ignatius Loyola (1491-1556), whose absolute obedience to the Pope, scholarship, Spiritual Exercises retreats, and missionary zeal are highly renown in Catholic history.[380] The doctrinal determinations of the Council of Trent[22] are divided into decrees (*decreta*) or positive statements of Catholic dogmas and short canons (*canones*), which condemn the opposing Protestant views with the concluding "*anathema sit*," or... Declaration: "Anathema to all heretics." Response: "Anathema,

anathema." The official Vatican article on the Council of Trent in the *Catholic Encyclopedia* closes with the following:

> Although unfortunately the council, through no fault of the fathers assembled, was not able to heal the religious differences of western Europe, yet the infallible Divine truth was clearly proclaimed in opposition to the false doctrines of the day, and in this way a firm foundation was laid for the overthrow of heresy and the carrying out of genuine internal reform in the Church.

Protestants would interpret the Council of Trent more as a patronizing rejection of an historic appeal to reform. With both Protestants and Catholics now firmly polarized, a seething hatred later erupted in the 30 Years War (1618-1648), which was one of the "most destructive conflicts in European history."[381] The Thirty Years' War finally ended with the Peace of Westphalia in 1648 affirming the sovereign right of European nation-states to determine their own religious preference, be it Catholic or Protestant. Christianity had now been finally divided into its three major enduring expressions: Roman Catholic, Eastern Orthodox, and Protestant.

14. The Church of England (Anglicanism) & King Henry VIII

The Church of England was officially established in 1534 by the "Act of Supremacy," which made the English Monarch (then King Henry VIII) head of the English Church. Four main factors that contributed to England's break from Rome included the rise of Renaissance learning, English sympathy with the Protestant Reformation, the historic political struggle for autonomy from church-rule, and King Henry VIII's consternation at the refusal of Pope Clement VII to annul Henry's marriage to Catherine of Aragon.[382] It is hard to imagine that just 13 years earlier Henry had been awarded the Catholic medal of honor by Pope Leo X as "Defender of the Faith" (*Fidei Defensor*). The text (undoubtedly co-authored by the scholar Thomas More) that garnered Henry such recognition was called *The Defense of the Seven Sacraments*—in which he counters Luther's attack on the Catholic Church for the sale of indulgences. So treacherous were Henry's disloyalties toward his six wives (2 were divorced and 2 beheaded) and colleagues, that at Sir Thomas Mores' principled refusal to accept Henry's claim to be the supreme head of the Church of England, Henry had him executed as a traitor.

A major influence of Henry VIII and of Anglicanism itself was Thomas Cranmer (1489-1556) who was Archbishop of Canterbury. Cranmer is credited with the authorship of both the *Book of Common Prayer* and the *Thirty Nine Articles*, together which provided the foundation for Anglican liturgical tradition for over four centuries. After Queen Mary reunited the Church of England with the Church of Rome, Cranmer was summarily executed for heresy. Henry's eventual death signaled a period of continuing political instability caused by the religious preference (Catholic or Protestant) of the heirs to the English throne. Hostilities finally erupted in the English Civil War (1642-1651) and again in the Revolution of 1688. These conflicts resulted in at least two major developments, (a) the limitation of the British monarch, who would not be allowed to govern without the consent of Parliament. This ultimately led to the modern implementation of a constitutional-parliamentary democracy, where it remains intact in the United Kingdom today and (b) the specific prohibition of a Roman Catholic monarch (such as James II of England had been) ascending the English throne in the foreseeable future. Nonconformist (non-Anglican) Protestant groups were given a limited toleration until the Test and Corporation Acts passed in 1662 were finally repealed by the parliament in 1828.[383]

Today, the Church of England (Anglicanism) sees itself standing in both the Reformed and in the Catholic tradition. To some, Anglicanism represents a non-papal Catholicism, whereas for others, it represents a dynamic form of Protestantism but without a dominant reformation leader. The *sine qua non* (essential requirements) of the Anglican Communion is condensed to four points: 1. The Holy Scriptures as containing all things necessary to salvation 2.The Creeds (Apostles' and the Nicene Creeds) as sufficient statement of the Christian Faith

3. The sacraments of Baptism and Holy Communion 4.The historic episcopate, locally adapted.[384]

Among the global Anglican Communion, the Archbishop of Canterbury is recognized as *primus inter pares,* or first among equals. As the recognized "spiritual head" of the Communion, he maintains a certain moral authority and has the right to determine those provinces and primates who qualify for Communion admission. He also provides leadership in ecumenical dialogue, in which capacity he speaks on behalf of Anglicans worldwide.

The Puritans King James Oliver Cromwell The Mayflower

15. *Puritanism* was a theological-cultural movement rather than a designation for a particular religious sect or denomination. It arose in the Church of England in the latter part of the 16th century in objection to the Elizabethan Religious Settlement (1559) which mandated a *via media*, or middle way between Roman Catholicism and Protestantism. Puritans felt this accommodation to Catholicism rendered the Church of England in need of further purification from the "taint of popery."[385]

16. The King James Bible

In response to a request by the Puritans, King James I of England (VI of Scotland) authorized an English version of the Bible, now called the King James Version (KJV), first published in 1611. Unfortunately, several Protestant groups still act as if the KJV is the only authoritative translation that all Protestants should use.

17. The English Civil War/Puritan Revolution

Tensions between the Puritans and the pro-Anglican monarch King Charles I erupted in the English Civil War, also called the Puritan Revolution (1640-1660). Defeated by the Puritan military commander Oliver Cromwell, King Charles I was convicted of treason by the puritan dominated Parliament and beheaded. Olive Cromwell had ruled a republican Commonwealth as *Lord Protector* with a one-house Parliament until King Charles II was restored to monarchial rule in 1660.

18. The Mayflower and Massachusetts Bay Colony

The early Pilgrims were Puritan separatists who sailed on the Mayflower in 1620 and established one of the first English colonies in North America at Plymouth, Mass. The Great Migration of Puritans to New England was to the Massachusetts Bay Colony where some 21,000 relocated between 1629 and 1643—transforming the colony into a magnet for industry, family, democratic self-rule, and theocratic ideals.[386] However, such theocratic ideals became far too restrictive for future emigrants who were forced to flee from puritan persecution. So harsh was the Puritan concept of non-affectionate parenting (aimed at breaking the will of the child in preparation for salvation) that in the 1660's they were forced to implement the half-way covenant (partial church membership) for their children and grand children who were noticeably waning from spiritual concern. The Salem (Massachusetts) Witch Trials in 1690's further tarnished the reputation of the puritans, who were ousted from direct political control of Massachusetts by 1700.

19. Pietism

Puritan ideology became a strong trans-continental religious force known as Pietism in late Seventeenth and Eighteenth century Europe and English colonies. Pietism was a combination of the Lutheran emphasis on biblical doctrine with the Reformed (and especially Puritan) emphasis on *individual piety* and a vigorous Christian life. Pietism was to become the foundational impetus of John Wesley (1703-1791) and the Methodist Church.

20. Presbyterian, Baptist, and Congregational legacy

The theological momentum for Puritanism came from the Reformed/Calvinist tradition and led to the founding of Presbyterian, Baptist, and Congregational churches in North America.

21. John Wesley (1703-1791) and Methodism

Schooled at Oxford, John and Charles Wesley (along with George Whitefield) formed an insignificant *Holy Club* (1729-1735) for the purpose of mutual encouragement, accountability and Christian service. This group was pejoratively labeled *Methodists* for their rather methodical pursuit of God which included, weekly communion, Bible study, singing, sharing personal testimonies, mutual confession of sins, open air preaching, fasting, no amusements or luxury, visiting the poor, sick and imprisoned, etc.[387]

It is important to note that Methodism was originally a renewal movement within the Church of England. And although Wesley's theology was critically viewed by many, Wesley himself viewed his efforts as well within the bounds of the Anglican Church[388] and even maintained his Anglican priestly status throughout his life.[389]

Wesley's theology included a strong emphasis on the necessity of a "new-birth"; justification by faith; sanctification as a "second work of grace,"[390] the free-will ability of the lost to choose Christ (pervenient grace)[391]; informal church services (low-church), a disdain of the educated clergy; the formation of small group "societies" along the lines of the original Oxford *Holy Club*; enthusiastic preaching as modeled by Whitfield; congregational singing—often adapted from popular *bar room melodies*;[392] a passion for social justice, etc.

Using Wesley's idea of "circuit riding preachers," Methodism grew rapidly until by the 1840's Methodists were the largest Christian denomination in the United States. Today, the United Methodist church has 10.4 million members, second in size only to the Southern Baptists. In 2006 worldwide membership in the Methodist Church totaled 75 million.

Though originally suspect of "educated clergy" the Methodist church has since established seminaries at Boston University, Vanderbilt,

Emory, Duke, etc. There is however a major division within contemporary Methodism regarding the embrace of liberal theology[393] with its favorable predilection toward homosexuality.[394]

Beyond the worldwide Methodist Church, the legacy of Methodism can also be seen in two significant theological-ecclesiastical developments:

1. Pentecostalism, which argues for an additional baptism in the Holy Spirit—subsequent to salvation and evidenced by speaking in tongues.
2. The Holiness movement, which is more pronounced in its view of entire sanctification and Christian perfectionism vis-à-vis the Church of the Nazarene the Salvation Army.

22. The Great Awakening (1720-1750)
Jonathan Edwards (1703-1758)

The *Great Awakening* was a series of revivals that took place throughout the American colonies from the 1720's through the 1750's. The revival began under the ministry of Jonathan Edwards in Northampton, Massachusetts and spread throughout the other colonies through the powerful preaching gift of George Whitefield, a Methodist traveling evangelist. The focus of the revival was on the experience of conversion and was accompanied by passionate preaching, emotional worship, and cross-denominational involvement. In fact, a division occurred between the anti-revivalists ("Old Lights") who felt the revival was too emotional and the "New Lights" who justified emotionalism/enthusiasm as evidence of a response to the immediate presence and power of the Holy Spirit. The Great Awakening established revivalism as a key component of American Protestantism and made evangelicalism the nation's *dominant religious impulse*.[395] Many historians also see a link between the emerging colonial identity of the Great Awakening and the American War of Independence (1775-1783).

23. *The Second Great Awakening (1800-1830's)*
Charles G. Finney (1792-1875)

The *Second Great Awakening* (1800-1830's) was also a series of revival-renewal type camp meetings throughout the United States but with Charles Grandison Finney (1792-1875) becoming the dominate figure. Finney was an extemporaneous preacher who emphasized free-will over the Calvinist doctrine of sovereign predestination. This conviction enabled Finney to lead literally hundreds of thousands of people (est. 500,000) to salvation as a response to an immediate crisis on conscience.[396] He also believed that a revival was a result of "human initiative" as opposed to Edwards' conviction that revival was a miraculous "surprising work of God" alone. Furthermore, Finney was an abolitionist who preached against slavery from the pulpit—even refusing communion for slave owners. This gave the revival a decidedly *social renewal dynamic* that resulted in non-denominational movements to address prison reform, women's voting rights (suffrage), alcoholism (temperance), and the abolition of slavery—contributing to the public debate that ultimately led to the American Civil War (1861-1865).

It was during the Second Great Awakening that Baptists and Methodists, who shared Finney's Arminianist tenets (man's free-will), grew in numerical strength to that of the denominations prominent in the colonial period—the Anglicans, Presbyterians, Congregationalists, and Reformed. Evangelical ideals, though still debated, were (and are) having an undeniable impact on the mindset and heartbeat of American Protestantism.

24. *Frontier Cults: Mormons and Jehovah's Witnesses*

It was also the result of the Second Great Awakening that restorationist movements were born, including the Mormons and Jehovah's Witnesses. Restorationists were able to "capitalize" (intentionally or unintentionally) on the new found emphases of a dynamic *personal* faith, a desire to change the moral climate of the American culture, and a discontent with denominational rigidity. Indeed, this anti-denominationalism (except for their own religious structures) accompanies restorationism with its idealistic attempt to get back to (restore vs. reform) the original pattern of the church in the New Testament. For instance, Mormonism goes to great lengths in claiming "apostolic succession" by insisting that Peter, James, and John actually appeared and laid hands on Joseph Smith Jr. in order to pass on the only modern apostolic legacy of authenticity.[397] This alleged "apostolic ordination" occurred very near the time that Smith officially organized the Church of Jesus Christ of Latter Day Saints (1830).

25. Christian Fundamentalism: 19*th* & 20*th* Centuries

John Nelson Darby   Billy Graham
(1800-1882)   (b. 1918)

Christian Fundamentalism is a conservative Protestant movement that began in Britain and the U.S. in the late 19*th* and early 20*th* centuries in reaction to modernistic thought, including Darwin's theory of evolution, German biblical criticism, liberal theology, Freud's psychoanalysis, Marxist socialism, etc. The Roman Catholic Church issued a decree condemning both biblical criticism and modernism on July 3, 1907.[398] Although fundamentalism has no single founder, its origins can be directly traced to the American revivalism of the 18*th* and 19*th* centuries. A number of evangelicals also paved the way for the rise of fundamentalist values and theology, including Martin Luther (1483-1546)[399], American evangelist Dwight L. Moody (1837-1899)[400] and the British preacher and "Father of Dispensationalism," John Nelson Darby (1800-1882). [401]

Whereas theological liberalism pursued a course of radical accommodation to scientific thought[402]; fundamentalism was much more of a militant reaction against what was perceived as the wholesale abandonment of biblical truth. As a result, certain fundamental beliefs of Christianity were articulated by various denominational scholars, which included five essentials:

1. Biblical inerrancy[403]
2. The virgin birth of Jesus Christ
3. The doctrine of substitutionary atonement
4. The bodily resurrection of Jesus
5. The authenticity of Christ's miracles—including his promised second coming

"*The Fundamentals*" as they were called, were published and freely distributed, by a grant from two wealthy Christian businessmen, throughout the United States in 1909 reaching a circulation of some 3 million copies. Christian fundamentalists also established Bible Institutes in places like Chicago (Moody) and Los Angeles in order to counter the secular orientation of higher education. Fundamentalism was growing in strength, numbers, and political clout until the John Thomas Scopes "monkey" trial of 1925 in Tennessee, which ultimately served to undermine the fundamentalist effort to enforce laws against the teaching of evolution in public schools. The political backlash of this case was enshrined in the popular epic Broadway play and film called *Inherit the Wind*.

From the growing social reaction against fundamentalism came a renewal of evangelicalism, called Neo-Evangelicalism that was/is more moderate in its response to modernity. Indeed, the new evangelicals, for the most part, are still theologically conservative, but place much more importance on higher education (evangelical seminaries), rational-scientific debate (Intelligent Design), social service involvement (Habitat for Humanity Intl.), world missions (Lausanne Congress), and mass media productions—especially radio (Salem Communications), television (CBN, TBN, Daystar), and publications/journals (Zondervan publications, Christianity Today, Charisma, Leadership Journal).

A leading evangelical, American evangelist Billy Graham, came from a fundamentalist background, but was repudiated by many Christian fundamentalists because of his decision, in the 1950s, to cooperate with other non-fundamentalist Christian groups and leaders in his popular mass evangelism campaigns.

26. The Rise of Evangelicalism in the 20*th* & 21*st* Centuries

Evangelical comes from the Greek word *euangelion* meaning Gospel or Good News—from which we derive "evangelist." Martin Luther originally used the term "evangelical church" *evangelische kirke* (German) to characterize his reformation movement ideals. Such an evangelical church would be faithful to the message and ministry of the Gospel (or Evangel).

In America, evangelicalism sprang from the revivals of the 18th century onward led by such notable figures as George Whitefield (1715-1770), John Wesley (1703-1791), Jonathan Edwards (1703-1758), Charles G. Finney (1792-1875), Billy Sunday (1863-1935), Dwight L. Moody (1837-1899), Billy Graham (1918-present), et al. However, Evangelicalism, though indebted to these leaders, cannot be characterized as *either* Armenian (free-will) *or* Calvinist (predestination) perspectives since they both are deemed to contain important aspects of biblical truth. A number of evangelicals are also merging the Wesleyan-Pentecostal-Charismatic idea of a "second work of grace" or "baptism of the Holy Spirit" with an updated Calvinist orthodoxy with its emphasis on church councils and systematic theology.

Prior to the civil war (1861) evangelicals were largely credited with helping to reshape American society through such reforms as temperance, the early women's movement, the establishment of various organizations to help alleviate social suffering, the abolition of slavery, etc. In modern times, evangelicals have been very influential in U.S. elections, the debates over abortion and homosexuality—and most recently the controversy over Creationism and/or Intelligent Design vs. Evolution.

Evangelicals generally hold to certain biblical *fundamentals* including the inspiration of the Bible, the deity of Christ, salvation as gift by grace through faith, the importance of a vital relationship with Christ (the head) and the Church (his body), a commitment to help fulfill the Great Commission, and the victorious return of Jesus Christ who will judge the world and make visible his eternal kingdom.

Though there is an undeniable link between evangelicalism and fundamentalism, there are however, some important distinctions that need to be made between them as well. Generally speaking, fundamentalism is often perceived as a militant reaction against modernism whereas evangelicalism is much more committed to the validity of scientific investigation, social service, and the use of the media in promoting the Gospel.

Today, evangelicalism is a broad designation encompassing any number of Protestant churches and ministries that value the principle of denominationalism: an *inclusive* theory that no single ecclesiastical structure can represent the whole church—as opposed to the *exclusive* claims of certain sects and cults. As such, evangelicalism is now a cross-denomination phenomenon.

27. Twenty-first Century Neo-Protestantism (NP) [404]

"Go into all the world and preach the Gospel" (Mark 16:15)

In harmony with evangelicalism's cross-denomination influence, there is a new wave of Protestantism, which has been emerging on the scene of global Christian renewal, in the wake of the Charismatic Movement (1960-1990's). This Neo-Protestantism is *somewhat* of a convergence/confluence (or at least an important influence) between three streams, which include Evangelical-Reformed[405], with its primary emphasis on the Scripture but with a cessastionist[406] background; Charismatic, with its emphasis on spiritual gifts and independence/non-denominationalism; and Pentecostal, with its emphasis on experience, emotion, and mission within a denominational context. Neo-Protestantism could even mean that there is a determined refusal to embrace the ancient acrimony between Protestants and Catholics—signaling the promise/potential of a hopeful dialogue between historic arch-rivals, in the cause of Christ's larger Kingdom mission on earth. "Thy kingdom come. Thy will be done in earth, as *it is* in heaven" (Matt. 6:10).

Addendum 3.

In this section, rather than a prolonged narrative, an attempt will be made to briefly highlight a number of key characteristics-issues regarding and/or accompanying the emergence of this Twenty-First Century Neo-Protestant (NP).

1. The Empowering Holy Spirit and Charismatic/ Pentecostal Charlatans

Twenty-First Century Neo-Protestants (NP) have experienced an undeniable empowering ("baptism") of the Holy Spirit, generally as a result of some acquaintance/association with the Pentecostal outpouring (1906+) or the Charismatic renewal (1960+; see Acts 1:8; 2:1-4). There is debate over the manifestation of speaking in tongues[407], but all NP are quite comfortable acknowledging the validity of spiritual gifts for today—including tongues, prophecy, healing, etc. [See 1 Cor. 1:7 for Paul's expectation that charismatic gifts would continue (vs. cease with the biblical canon) right up until the return of Christ.]

However, NP also have a general, if not strong distaste for how sensationalized the charismatic gifts and ministries have become in the name of Christian television, radio, and the printed media. Too many charismatic charlatans are masquerading as *powerful ministries*, which have in fact become little more than a front for financially fleecing the flock of God with a distorted version of the *seed money* doctrine— promising financial gain, marriage partners, obedient children, salvation of family members, supernatural healing from disease, new cars and clothes, ad nauseam in return for obedience to the "command of God" requiring them to "get off the sofa now and go to your phones!"

"In their greed these teachers will exploit you with stories they have made up." (2 Pet. 2:3)

Please note that the *falsity* of false teachers and prophets is not that what they are preaching is blatantly unbiblical, but rather that their motives and methods are skewed resulting in a *prosperity gospel* that creates an anxiousness about one's material means rather than a trusting submission to pursue faithful service to Christ—regardless of the status of one's earthly bank accounts. (1 Tim. 6:5-10; Matt. 6:19-21) It is not that prosperity is not taught in Scripture, it's just that these ministers make money (and material possessions) the primary objective and measure of faith...Beware!

This reproach of the charismatic gifts and ministries is the reason why the charismatic renewal has been virtually replaced by a huge migration of former independent or *recovering charismatics* to the more historic and reputable evangelical encampment and/or the larger and more reputable Pentecostal denominations, such as the Four Square or the Assemblies of God.

2. Kingdom-Centeredness and Christian Unity

Twenty-First Century Neo-Protestants can be described as being *Kingdom-centered* in their perspective and practice[408]. For them the Kingdom is both now and still to come; present and yet future[409]. In other words, the transforming power of God's Kingdom (be it personal, family, church, or cultural-social) does not necessarily await a future physical reign of Christ on earth. Jesus is Lord of all (!) is a dynamic truth to be optimistically pursued, at every dimension of human existence and interaction, although that undisputed Lordship will not be fully realized in this age because of the presence of sin. Nevertheless, an optimistic-realism still describes the *modus operandi* of the mission and lifestyle of the NP.

This kingdom reality does affect the way NP see the doctrine of the end-times, or eschatology. And though there is *still irresolvable debate*, a number of NP are now leaning away from dispensationalism (secret rapture; 7 year tribulation; 2nd stage of the second coming; 1,000 year reign of Christ with a rebuilt Third Jewish Temple including reinstituted animal sacrifice, etc.). As a result, NP are more open to the amillennial perspective of the Reformed tradition, which tends to embrace the kingdom as now and not yet; they also believe in a less literal rendering of prophecy; and more emphasis on the church's role in declaring the gospel of the kingdom to all nations, etc.)[410] "And this gospel of the kingdom will be preached in the whole world as a testimony to all nations, and then the end will come" (Matt. 24:14).

It is also in the context of Kingdom-centeredness that the biblical call to unity (Eph. 4; Phil 2; John 17) finds a priority in the mind of NP. For since the Kingdom of God is the foundational reality of the Church[411], all disciples of the "King of the Kingdom" (the Lord Jesus

Christ) share equal access to its rule, rights, and responsibilities—regardless of their denominational affiliation, or lack thereof. After all, there were multiple tribes in the one nation of Israel just as there are permissibly multiple historic distinctions between denominations in the universal Church[412]. Indeed, NP are convinced that it will ultimately take a united church to reach a divided world. Of course, this unity will be the mutual recognition of our relational oneness in the spirit of Christian love (Eph. 4:3; Phil. 2:2; John 13:34; Co. 3:14) rather than an organizational imposition of a single monolithic entity.[413]

3. Flexible Structures and Mega-Churches

Neo-Protestants (NP) generally embrace a more flexible and creative church structure. Theirs is an organization that is more relational than hierarchal, more dynamic than static, more creative than traditional, more diversified than uniform. As a result, NP utilize networks, affiliations, and associations in addition to, or in place of, denominational structures in fulfilling their kingdom commission.

A mega-church is a church from 2,000 to multiple tens of thousands of attenders. Additionally, most of these mammoth local churches tend to use more of a business model rather than a traditional church structure for governance and management. It should be noted here that part of the complaint with mega-churches is that they can tend to be "numbers-driven" in their attempt to manage ministry to the crowds—using a kind of mass marketing and commerce approach to succeed in the "business of ministry." They do this, say their detractors, at the expense of the more personal (vs. institutional), relational (vs. organizational), and spiritually dynamic (vs. corporate objectives) as reflected in the New Testament.

Having served four years on the senior staff of a reputable mega-church[414] I can attest to the fact that these tensions are very real in such an organization-professional culture. The simplicity and purity of devotion to Christ must always be maintained in dynamic tension with the ambition to succeed, which should mean to be faithful and fruitful in ministry (2 Cor. 11:3).

Regarding large church structures, here are a couple of functional definitions that can help the church stay on target in its developmental priorities:

The mission of the local church is to help make disciple-followers of the Lord Jesus Christ by reaching upward (in prayer and praise), inward (in care and training), outward (in service and witness), and forward (in vision and courage).

The church is a Holy Spirit empowered assembly of disciple-followers of the Lord Jesus Christ who have lovingly committed themselves to a shared-way of life together, and whose mission is to declare the gospel of the kingdom in their attempt to rescue fallen humanity.

Note that this "shared-way of life together" is the essence of Christian community which can only be realized as meaningful relational connections are intentionally and creatively cultivated. This life-sustaining community of Christ (the Church) is the key objective in all NP priorities in their efforts to build up the Body of Christ (Eph. 4:15-16).

4. Contemporary Apostolic and Prophetic Ministries

Many NP are convinced that one of the key safeguards of such structural-ministerial innocence and integrity is the collaborative involvement of contemporary "post-ascension" apostolic and prophetic ministries—regardless of what their organizational and/or denominational titles may be (Eph. 4:10-12).[415] In other words, all of the leadership gifts of the ascended Christ should be brought to bear on the building up of the Body of Christ—be it locally or trans-locally[416].

For instance, the nature of apostolic ministry is to provide expertise in structural design[417] keeping people from discouragement and confusion as the church grows. The passion of prophetic ministry is to seek to nurture continued dependence (personally and collectively) on the Holy Spirit—saving people from the weariness of structural and theological idolatry. Churches without apostolic vision lose their way, whereas churches without prophetic vision lose their heart along the way. Apostles are like building inspectors—ensuring the edifice is up to "kingdom building code" prior to divine occupation. Prophets are like electrical inspectors—ensuring the wiring is properly installed so that the entire edifice does not burn down when the power is turned on.

This is why it is so important to understand that "character is the conduit for the power of God." Unfortunately there are too many churches and ministries who have learned this lesson too late to save structures which took them years to build—only to see them crumble due to poor structural foundations (wrong people) or the "faulty wiring" of carnal character in time of trial.

Suffice it to say that NP apostolic and prophetic ministries have the vision, proven discernment, and organizational skills necessary to provide the church with a dynamically empowered structure—a living structure that is built upon people with the right gifts, calling, and character to stand the test of time without calcifying (by institutional idolatry) or imploding with relationally destructive conflict.

"As a coal to embers and as wood to fire; so is a quarrelsome man for kindling strife." (Proverbs 26:21)

5. Higher Education and Cultural Engagement

Unlike their fundamentalist predecessors NP value higher education/graduate degrees—partly to be further equipped for effective ministry but also to engage the culture at large. Cultural engagement means embracing the reformation-reformed ideal of the sacralization of every vocational pursuit in life, not just ecclesiastical, or "church-related" work.[418]

It has been observed that there are at least eight interdependent and legitimate spheres of western culture, each needing intentional engagement and influence from members of the Body of Christ. These spheres include: the family, the church, business and commerce, the arts/entertainment/sports, science and technology, education, the media (broadcast and print), and government/politics.[419]

NP realize that higher education is often needed to effectively engage these cultural spheres in ways that can have a maximum impact for the kingdom of God. To this end, NP are envisioning their children with this same "philosophy of engagement" so that they can be positioned, albeit earlier in life, to make a difference in their world for Christ. However, regardless of how noble such lofty goals may be, cultural engagement for NP is just as much, if not more, about ministering to the poor and needy[420]—as it is to ascending the cultural halls of power (Luke 7:22; Gal. 2:10; James 2:5).

This issue of cultural engagement is also seen by NP as a direct parallel between the biblical idea of incarnational ministry (the "word becoming flesh") and the universal Christian calling to be "salt and light" in a dark and depraved world system (Matt. 5:13-16). Hence, NP shun isolationism as ambassadors of reconciliation (2 Cor. 5:19-20). They actively engage the world (without becoming part of it) believing that their mission is an extension of the ministry of Jesus Christ, who was set apart and sent into the world in order to actively seek and to save those who are lost (John 10:36).

> It is a trustworthy statement deserving of full acceptance that Christ Jesus came into the world to save sinners (1 Tim. 1:15).

> As the Father has sent me, so am I sending you (John 20:21).

A word about the children of NP

The vision about strategically influencing an entire generation through cultural engagement is why there will always be such a fierce spiritual battle over the youth of each generation. Satan hopes to quench the NP fire of spiritual revival-renewal by captivating our children (a holy seed) thus rendering them incapable of hearing and responding to the call of God for their generation (Acts 13:36a). Parents, take heart, and remember how Jesus was sought with destructive intent while still in his infancy in Bethlehem and yet how God repeatedly rescued him for his ultimate purpose (Mtt. 2:7-23).

Verses for weary parents:[421]

> "Let your work appear to your servants; [but please show] your majesty to our children [the little ones]." (Psalm 90:16)

> Prayer: Lord Jesus, we will gladly do your work, but please remember our children in the process.

"Here am I, [oh Lord] and the children God has given me." (Hebrews 2:13b)

Prayer: Father, you have given us these children and we will never hand them over to the enemy—no matter how fierce may be the fight. Strengthen me oh my God.

"The youth will flock to you in droves—blanketing the earth like the dew of the dawn—in the day of your glorious conquest [final triumph]" (Psalm 110:3).

Prayer: Holy Father, please remember our children for the day when you visit the earth in power.

6. World Evangelization and Strategic Church Planting

This idea of cultural engagement also includes the classic priority of evangelical passion—global missions and world evangelization. From an empowered church where every disciple is envisioned to reach their sphere of influence NP actively seek to purposefully extend the ministry of the local church to the city, the state, the nation, and the world (Acts 1:8). Furthermore, humanitarian relief is just as much a part of their strategy to communicate the gospel as is the proclamation of the Word of God itself. For just as Jesus physically fed the crowds that he ministered to, so also is the church called to address the physical as well as spiritual needs of humanity.

> "By all means preach the gospel, and if necessary use words." (St. Francis Assisi)

Twenty-First Century Neo-Protestants also see strategic church planting as an essential part of the great commission. The critique of simply holding mass evangelism rallies without adequate follow up is that they often produce "spiritual orphans" who are both unconnected to and unprotected by God's spiritual family, the Church. Such unrelated believers are prey to discouragement, temptations, and entrapment by the cults.

Hence, NP see a pattern in Acts 8 where Philip's successful evangelism campaign was followed up by the apostles in Jerusalem, who sent Peter and John to confer the gift of the Holy Spirit and to confirm the foundations of the fledgling community (Eph. 2:20). Interestingly, the NIV footnote for Acts 8:14 affirms this observation by indicating that *"the Jerusalem church assumed the responsibility of inspecting new evangelistic efforts and the communities of believers they produced."* In this way, the fruit of Philip's evangelistic work was apostolically incorporated into a viable community of believers rather than wasted on a harvest without an appropriate "processing plant"—the local church.

7. Theological Balance and a Hermeneutic of Grace

The theological and philosophical perspective of NP is informed by multiple streams/inputs including fundamentalism (Trinity, biblical authority, Lordship of Jesus, etc), classic evangelicalism[422] (Kingdom-centered, educated, socially engaged, etc.), the charismatic renewal (Spirit-empowered, non-cessasionist/pro-spiritual gifts," renewal-restoration minded, etc.), the Pentecostal outpouring (spirit-filled denominations and global missions)—as well as a thoughtful discussion with contemporary culture (history, philosophy, social sciences, biology, etc.).

As a result, although NP are passionate truth-seekers they tend to be less dogmatic and more dialectic—where balance is found between "being" and "doing"; where the word (Bible) and power (Spirit) provide a new ecclesial paradigm for the Twenty First century[423]; where "the opposite of a profound truth may very well be another profound truth" (Niels Bohr, Nobel Prize physicist, 1922). As a result, rather than argue from an "either-or" position they prefer the "both-and" as a more inclusive option; instead of seeing only black and white the world is full of colors and other nuances that are not readily apparent to the casual and careless observer.

This is not to argue that NP are relativists but rather that in their absolutism they make room for applications that may be legitimately moderated by circumstances. Similarly the epistemology of NP can be described as comprising the binary propositions of "foundational eclecticism" and "integrated dualism."[424] Again the idea is one of seeing reality as multifaceted rather than only singular in composition.

Probably the best example of this is the Trinity, which is at-the-same-time both one (God) and yet three "persons" (Father, Son, and Holy Spirit). Too much emphasis on the oneness of God leads to an indistinguishable monism whereas too much emphasis on the three-ness of God leads to the error of tri-theism (three Gods). This mystery of the nature of reality is what enables NP to simultaneously embrace both the Reformed and Arminian positions where God's sovereign determination does not preclude him from granting free-will to humanity.[425]

Three other important theological descriptors of NP is that they are pragmatic, relational, and grace-based. They are pragmatic in that theological truth must have practical applications and productive consequences. They are relational in that Christianity is less about doctrinal abstractions and more about supportive relationships in the context of a nurturing community, or family of faith. They are grace-based in that biblical hermeneutics must be approached with a thorough grasp and pursuit of the dynamic of grace.[426]

Grace is both a positional reality (being in Christ, 1 Cor. 1:30) and yet a personal-spiritual empowerment for daily living (Phil. 2:12-13). Grace is both the means and the end of salvation; both our beginning point and yet our ultimate objective. Grace delivers from condemnation, judgmentalism and the need to control others. Indeed, grace is how our relationship with God and all others is initiated and sustained. "For the law was given through Moses, but grace and truth were realized through Jesus Christ" (John 1:17).

Conclusion

The objective of this article has been to briefly highlight a number of key characteristics-issues regarding and/or accompanying the emergence of what we have termed Twenty-First Century Neo-Protestants (NP). Those characteristics at least include the empowering Holy Spirit, kingdom-centeredness, flexible structures, contemporary apostolic and prophetic ministries, higher education, cultural engagement, world evangelization, strategic church planting, theological balance and grace.

In a real sense NP are heirs of Christian renewal movements that have graced the Church throughout her history. But rather than repeat some of the mistakes of history, NP are committed to help constructively steward the "purpose of God in their generation" (Acts 13:36a).

That purpose can be characterized as to declare the kingdom with power, to equip the church with grace, and to rescue the nations with compassion. To that end, Neo-Protestants are emboldened with a sense of divine destiny believing, by grace, that they too have come into the kingdom "for such a time as this" (Esther 4:13-14).

Addendum 4.

Top Ten Things No One, In The Know, Believes Anymore About Evolution
(by Stan Reynolds)

Evolutionary research is proceeding in increasingly specialized areas of study. Many researchers, as well as the general public, may not realize that there are many things those in the know no longer believe about evolutionism. Let's look at what has been happening lately.

1. "Mister, Have You Got The Time?"...Cosmology and Cosmic Time

Although old in the way we would think about it, the universe is far too young to justify the possibility of the chance evolution of life by unassisted, random processes as articulated in Darwinism. In addition, as we learn more about the physical history of the planet earth, we realize that life has not had even the 13.73 billion years currently calculated as the age of the universe to get going. The earth is only 4.6 billion years old, lowering the amount of time available to evolution. During the early years the earth was incredibly hostile to the chemical processes and reactions that under gird all life, thus further closing the window available for the right proteins to randomly appear in the right place.

Finally, we have discovered that life had to effectively *restart* many times due to mass extinctions as the earth settled into its present epoch of more life-friendly conditions. Therefore, evolution had to efficiently and repeatedly reproduce its results during increasingly smaller and narrower time frames. No one truly in the know believes enough time is available in earth's history for life to appear and develop unassisted by the processes enumerated in evolutionary theory. Life must have been assisted by a natural process we have yet to discover or life must have been brought here from somewhere else in the universe.

Sir Francis Crick, famed co-discoverer of the structure of

DNA, is one of many who have recognized this problem. He has proposed the theory of "panspermia", meaning life here must have arrived via an outside source. His has suggested that alien beings, for purposes of their own, may have "seeded" the first life here. This has been popularized by the media in television shows, such as, "Star Trek, Next Generation" and in recent movies, such as, "Prometheus".

2. "No Pre-Biotic Soup for You!"

The first living systems emerged through a random association of chemicals in a pre-biotic "soup" warmed by the tectonic plate activity of early earth and powered by lightning or some other, unspecified energy source. This is the commonly held belief of people who believe Neo-Darwinism accurately describes the appearance and development of life on Earth. In one of the Star Trek Next Generation episodes, the character Q takes Captain Picard back in time to the edge of just such a warm pool of water frothing with chemicals that could be used for life (pre-biotics) and urges him to watch Picard's earliest ancestors crawl into the world. The "pre-biotic soup" idea, while light on details, continues to be taught in schools and mentioned by various scientists, authors and media personalities with conviction. The only problem is that no one who is really in the know believes this anymore!

Origin-of-life researchers have known for some time that the chemical formation of the supposed pre-biotic building blocks of life cannot proceed in the presence of either oxygen or ultra-violet light. If the earth, at the time of life's appearance, were rich in oxygen then pre-biotic chemistry does not proceed. If the earth were oxygen poor then ultra-violet light would pass readily through the atmosphere (as it would lack a protective ozone layer under oxygen poor conditions) and quickly breakdown any pre-biotic molecules even as they might form. Under any possible scenario of early earth, pre-biotic chemistry does not work.

In addition, origins of life researchers have found unique chemical trace signatures in the earliest rocks that show with high certainty that no pre-biotic chemicals were ever present. Only biotic sources (life that already exists) are responsible for the chemical residue and signatures in the earliest rocks. No pre-biotic reservoir of chemicals could come into being and, indeed, the fossil rocks show that none ever did. As a result, all eyes are focused on finding life beyond the earth. If it could

Addendum 4.

not and did not originate here then it surely must have come here from out there. After 50 years of failures in the survey of the heavens by the SETI (Search For Extraterrestrial Intelligence) project using the world's greatest telescopes, satellites and computers, the program soldiers on since life's origin here on earth has been shown to be impossible. The growth of the science of astrobiology (the search for life out there) is directly attributable to the utter failure of the "pre-biotic soup" hypothesis.

3. Standing On Their Own Four Feet...Tetrapods Won't Stay Put

Evolutionism believes land life emerged from sea life. As such, the transition from finned to footed is of great interest, particularly the emergence of tetrapods (four-footed land creatures). Neo-Darwinistic researchers had put together a number of ancient fossil finds to build a reasonably coherent presentation of tetrapod development. From the Panderichthys and Tiktaalik (375 million years ago) to the Ichthyostega (365 mya), including a number of "intermediates" along the way, everything seemed to fit together in one of the better examples of possible Darwinian evolution in action.

Image 1 Life restoration of Tiktaalik roseae, a transitional fossil between sarcopterygian fishes and tetrapods from the late Devonian period of North America. Zina Deretsky, National Science Foundation Source: redOrbit (http://s.tt/161aB)

However, recent discoveries in Poland reveal fully developed tetrapods, reliably dated to 395 mya, apparently hunting in a developed ecosystem on land fully 10 million years or more before the "intermediates" of the classically proposed evolution. The process of explaining fin-to-foot development must begin anew. Either the old paradigm must be discarded or an attempt must be mounted to "re-date" the various finds to get the "square" data to fit the "round holes" of current theory.

4. Archaeopteryx...the bird-dinosaur intermediate that never was

Just one year after Darwin published his "Origin of Species" a magpie-sized fossil was discovered that had feathers and a wishbone like a bird but had the teeth, tail and three-fingered hands like a dinosaur. Archaeopteryx was considered to be the first bird for 150 years and spawned the legend that dinosaurs did not really disappear entirely but became the modern birds of today. The movie "Jurassic Park" made several uses of this theme.

The original 1860 fossils continued to be used as evidence for transitionary evolution. However, in October of 2009 paleontologist Gregory Erickson of Florida State University and the American Museum of Natural History and his colleagues showed that Archaeopteryx was far less bird and far more dinosaur than had been believed. Microscopic examination of bone chips revealed a dense and slow growing structure where those of birds are porous, light and fast-growing. "Arch" could have only performed very limited aerial maneuvers. Rather than being a "missing link" or a transitionary intermediate, Arch was merely a hybrid...a dinosaur with feathers. Modern biologists do not consider the penguin to be a transitionary intermediate between birds and fish. They also do not consider the duck-billed platypus of Australia to be a transitionary intermediate between birds (fowl) and mammals. In the same way, modern biologists who are up to date with the latest research do not consider Archaeopteryx to be transitionary between dinosaurs and birds any longer.

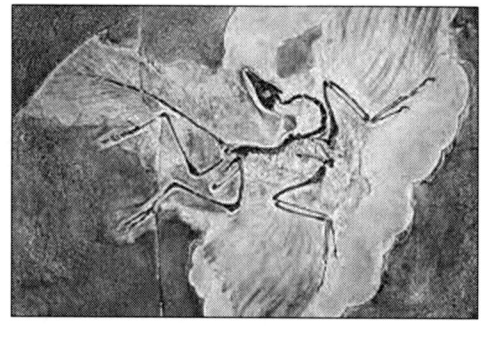

Addendum 4.

In 2010 and 2011 many more fossil finds of creatures similar to Archaeoopteryx have emerged from China. Researchers are currently swinging from whether what we have here are bird-like dinosaurs or dinosaur-like birds. (Readers wanting more detail may wish to review the July, 2011 National Geographic for coverage of this controversy and cross-links for deeper research.) Since it can take up to 40 years for scientific findings that upset the current status quo to become accepted mainstream and make their way into high-school and college textbooks, we suspect pictures of Archaeopteryx as a "missing link" will erroneously remain in biology books for some time.

5. "I Was In The Right Place But It Must Have Been The Wrong Time"

In the movie "Capricorn One" the first manned space flight to Mars turns out to be impossible because cost cutting and shoddy workmanship has rendered the craft incapable of supporting the astronauts there and back. To maintain their jobs, their program and their pride, mission directors secretly remove the astronauts right before launch and send the craft to Mars and back under remote control. The astronauts even help prepare false videos as if broadcasted live from Mars. The plan is to secretly insert them into the capsule after it has returned so they can emerge victorious to the waiting public. They could really go to Mars later when the proper changes have been made to the spacecraft. However, upon reentry an error causes the robot craft to burn up before the camera eyes of the world. As far as the world is concerned the astronauts died at that moment. Mission directors realize the astronauts must never be seen again and the rest of the movie is about their attempt to escape and tell the world the truth. The mission directors deemed it better to change the truth rather than let the truth radically change all they had spent their lives building.

This temptation is an underlying pressure in scientific research. When an ancient fossil is discovered, it must be assigned and fit into the proper place in time on the evolutionary progression. Various dating methods can and do result in differing possible dates for the fossil. Sometimes the same dating method produces different dates depending upon where and when performed and depending on the pre-conceived expected date. Now, please do not think this is a refutation of dating techniques on our part. Our model of Neo-Creationism accepts most of the major dating information that modern research is producing about the universe, the earth and the appearance of ancient and modern life. Still, it is an interesting point to consider...what would happen if a fossil was found entirely in the wrong "expected" time strata? This may happened with the human skull KNM-ER 1470.

Marvin L. Lubenow in "Bones of Contention" documents the history of the thoroughly modern skull that was found in a dating stratum that simply would not fit the mold of Neo-Darwinism. It was almost akin to Sherlock Holmes in the 1800's finding the criminal used a Taser to get past the guards. Something anachronistic. Totally out of its place in time. It makes for fascinating reading to see how the poor skull and samples from the surroundings where it was found are subjected to test after test after re-test as arguments and accusations fly among respected researchers. They simply must find a way to force the square peg of the fossil into the round hole allowed by the Neo-Darwinistic theories. Surely the original discoverers erred in documenting their find. Perhaps the labs erred in doing the dating tests. Perhaps the skull itself really is not modern human. In the end, over ten years, tests are repeated, modified and adjusted until one produces in a date that could be moderately accommodated in the theory and it is quietly put to rest outside the eye of scrutiny. It is hard for the fickle public world of journalism to stay interested in an arcane story of arguing bone testers over ten years so the skull resides, forgotten, in an office drawer somewhat like Indiana Jones' Ark of the Covenant was filed away in a huge government warehouse, effectively as lost as if it had never been found.

6. Lucy in the Sky with Diamonds

In 1974 as archeologists toiled in the hot sun of African fossil zones an extra special find was about to see the light of day. They say that the Beatles' song "Lucy in the Sky (with diamonds)" was playing on the radio that day for the ancient skeleton of a hominid was nicknamed Lucy. At the time, Lucy was the most complete skeleton of so ancient a creature ever found. Even though it was only 40% complete after the months of careful extraction from the ground, the bilateral symmetry of most animals allowed them to hypothesize and visual a lot more of the creature. Having one part of one arm, leg or face bone would allow them to imagine (through the use of computer techniques) what the mirror image on the other side of the body or head would have looked like.

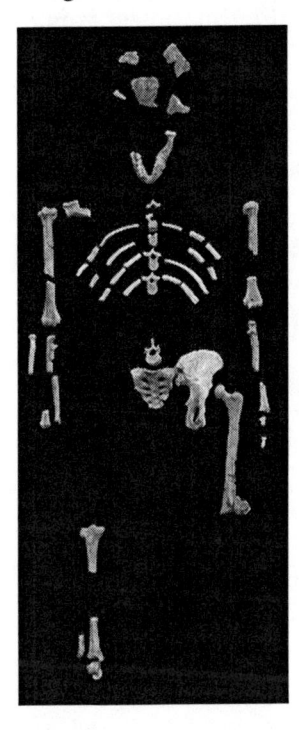

Within short order Lucy was hailed as a direct ancestor of modern humans. She was assigned to the species australopithecus afarensis and was quickly on the cover of national magazines. She was 3 ft, 7 in tall, about the size of a small modern day chimpanzee and may have weighed about 64 pounds. Her braincase was somewhat smaller than researchers might have expected and could have housed a brain the size of 375 to 500 cc. It would have been better for the prevailing theory if she had been a bit bigger so it was assumed she was a female and young and thus a smaller specimen of what the species probably really looked like.

Good science is a gradually correcting process and now, after nearly forty years, the gradual accumulation of other bones representing other members of Lucy's extinct species and the increasing mountain of coincident material found with the bones have given rise to the new line of conjecture (by specialists in the know) that Lucy and her kind are not part of Neo-Darwinism's envisioned path to modern humans after all. A 2007 study published in Proceedings of the National Academy of Sciences by Rak, Ginsburg and Geffin concluded that Lucy's jaw is more "gorilla-like" than other early hominid bone finds and should be linked with Australopithecus robustus rather than in a direct path from hominids to humans. In many textbooks still in use, Lucy and her line of Australopithecines are presented as part of the direct lineage of modern humans when, in fact, cutting-edge research is assigning them as an evolutionary offshoot path leading to a dead end. She is still considered an important part of the study of the development of bipedalism but even that status is diminishing as finds like Ardi in 1994 (more on that in a moment) upset the current bipedalism models.

7. IDA...Are You My Mother?

With all the fanfare of a media event unveiling the latest Apple, Inc. electronics gizmo or the official signing of a pro athlete, on Tuesday, May 19, 2009 researchers held a press conference to reveal the most complete fossil primate ever found. They named it "Darwinius masillae", but they gave her the nick name "Ida".

Ida was dated at 47 million years ago and with prevailing evolutionism contending that the human line of descent separated from the other primates about 6 million years ago, this small, cat-sized skeleton found in Germany was considered representative of an ancestor group that gave rise to the higher primates. They stopped short of referring to her as our great-great-great-grandmother but more like our great-great-great-aunt. The staging as a media event/press conference and the use of great catch phrases like this one resulted in major coverage in news outlets around the world. The very next day Ida's story and beautiful picture was even on the cover of the Wall Street Journal sharing the lead position with an article on "Credit-Card Fees Curbed". It even starred in a book, "The Link: Uncovering Our Earliest Ancestors" and appeared in a TV documentary shortly thereafter.

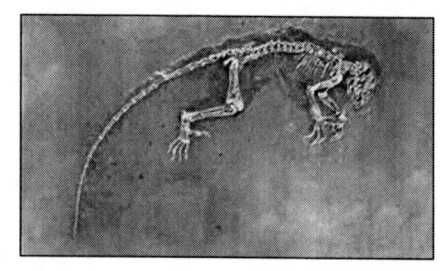

Assuming the dating of the fossil was correct, Ida then represented (in the minds of the original research team) one of the earliest ancestors to modern day primates and, by extension, an ancestor of modern man. However, many other members of the worldwide paleontology community criticized the release of data by the original research team directly to the public without giving access and time for other professionals to verify and confirm their conclusions. Many, well-meaning advocates of evolutionism knew that it really did their cause no good to have things erupt in fanfare only to be proven incorrect later. The public press has a tendency to add terms like "missing link" to articles even when the scientists may not have said the same at that time. Setting a set of fossil bones up on such a high pedestal is almost asking for disappointment.

Addendum 4.

Sure enough, by Wednesday, October 21 of that same year the Associated Press carried the follow-up story. It was titled, "'Missing link' primate isn't a link after all...Expert: Ida is as far from monkey-ape-human ancestry as primate can be." A team of researchers had carefully examined 360 specific anatomical features of 117 living and extinct primate species and compared them to Ida's features. They had submitted their research for peer review and it was accepted for publication in the journal "Nature" at which point it was picked up by the Associated Press. While the original discovers said they were not claiming Darwinius (Ida) was a direct ancestor of monkeys, apes and human they did argue it belonged to the same major evolutionary grouping and that it showed what an actual ancestor "might" have looked like. Unfortunately, the new analysis said Darwinius (Ida) does not belong in the same primate category as monkeys, apes and humans but, rather, it falls in another major grouping which includes lemurs. Other experts agreed. So, on the inside pages of a few newspapers that chose to run the Associated Press article and a few online sources like MSNBC.com, Ida was quietly demoted and removed from the human origins lineage. The find from May 2009 that would "revolutionize evolution" has now been reassessed and demoted by scientists worldwide.

8. ARDI...Well I'll Be A Monkey's Uncle!

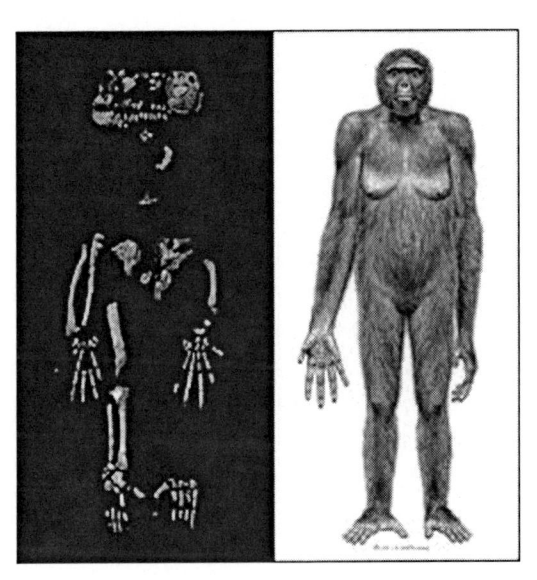

It seems that 2009 was a watershed year from sensationalistic reports from Neo-Darwinism. Perhaps being both the 200th anniversary of Darwin's birth and the 150th anniversary of the publishing of his work "Origin of Species" gave added interest to the stories. In October a team of researchers released a series of papers in the journal Science about the oldest, most complete skeleton of an ancient hominid they named Ardipithecus ramidus, but quickly became known to all as "Ardi". Found in Ethiopia and dated at an estimated age of 4.4 million years ago, Ardi was a full million years older than the celebrated hominid fossil "Lucy" and a much more complete skeleton. Anthropologist C. Owen Lovejoy of Kent State University said this older skeleton reverses the common wisdom of human evolution. Ardi was not a small, cat-like skeleton like Ida but resembled a chimpanzee-like shape. Evidence from the pelvis and hip showed the gluteal muscles were positioned so Ardi could have walked more or less upright for extended periods of time.

At an estimated four feet tall and possibly 110 pounds when fully grown, this older skeleton had been carefully assembled from 125 pieces and meticulously studied for nearly fifteen years since its find in 1995 before the team released their conclusions in 2009. Unlike the other 2009 superstar, Ida, Ardi's discovers had meticulously marshaled their research over time and published in the peer-reviewed journal of Science. The Associated Press quickly released a news article titled, "World's Oldest Human-Linked Skeleton Found...'Ardi' predates Lucy by a million years, changes scientific view of origins."

Within days, newspapers around the world carried the diagrams and colorful artists' recreations of what Ardi must have looked like and expounded on this new part of the Neo-Darwinism story. The cable channel Discovery prepared and aired a special for Ardi and National Geographic, with its editorial board's strong commitment to an evolutionary worldview, obliged with a cover story in July 2010. However, as 2010 progressed voices of dissent emerged from the evolutionary community. If Ardi's bi-pedalism (ability to walk upright on two legs) was correct then he was in the wrong place at the wrong time and his brain was too small to match the prevailing framework of evolution. Bi-pedalism had been conjectured to have come along with increasing brain size and the transition of primates from forested woodlands to open savannas. The need to stand upright to see predators coming from a distance in the grassland savannas was said to be the environmental factor pressuring for evolutionary change and the increased brain size and capacity could support the programming changes needed. However, here was Ardi with a very small braincase, living in a woodland environment (where climbing skills of apes are more favored over walking upright skills of humans) and possibly having bipedalism. No wonder, as mentioned earlier, those in the know said this discovery overturns current evolutionary theories and prompts the need to formulate new speculations.

In May, 2010 the journal of Science would publish new studies by Ardi's discoverers' peers who would contest the original findings. It was suggested that Ardi, rather than being ape-like, was an ape…an early, extinct ape. The original discoverers have responded with interpretations of the soil samples and seeds found at the site to buttress their first conclusions. Controversy in the field is not unusual. Indeed, many would say the back-and-forth, give-and-take discussions are a part and parcel of the scientific process.

For our part, we would contend that Ardi once again illustrates how initial conclusions about fossil finds are spread widely by the media. If it were a court of law we would say there was a "rush to judgment". Artists are marshaled to produce depictions of what skin, fur and eyes might have looked like. The eyes of these chimpanzee-looking creatures are usually given "whites" (a characteristic only of modern humans, not apes or chimpanzees) resulting in that eerie "human" look. But the "devil in the details" is often only seen in the follow-ups that find their way into the back pages in smaller print. Secondly, Ardi is a good example of new data confounding the prevailing framework forcing larger and larger revisions to the original plan. Instead of the actual evidence requiring smaller and smaller refinements to the original hypotheses, the field results call for larger and more convoluted shifts to the theory to allow a niche in which to park these findings. In other scientific areas, this tendency is an indication something is wrong with the hypothesized theory near its core.

9. Neanderthal….DNA extraction studies remove him from family

The original "ascent of man" charts usually included Neanderthal as a precursor to modern man. However, unlike the bones of earlier creatures which are transformed by fossilization into rocks, the bones of Neanderthal are actual bones, being recent enough to survive as organic material without being changed by mineralization. Through the creative and diligent work of researchers worldwide, we have coaxed the DNA out of the marrow of some of those bones from specimens originating in Europe, Asia and the Middle East. As early as 1995, DNA profiles were developed and refined from Neanderthal individuals that date from the beginning of their presence on the earth to near the time of their extinction. Over the next 15 years more exacting studies have confirmed and extended our understanding of Neanderthal. What we now know is that, whatever he was, he contributed no significant genetic information to modern humans. The differences in the DNA are so pronounced that he has been removed from the family tree of modern man and assigned as an evolutionary dead-end tree branch. Not only is his DNA dissimilar to modern humans but it is remarkably similar across the whole spectrum of Neanderthal specimens that span nearly 100,000 years between them. This means they experienced stasis...no internal evolution was going on within their species...across time and across half a world of geographic dispersion. Once again we have no ability to document real-time evidence of successful macro-evolutionary change.

Even the long held assertion that Neanderthal used tools similar to the earliest modern humans is now suspect. In October of 2010, Thomas Higham and a team of European researchers reported that tools associated with Neanderthal fossils at Grotte du Renne (a French site) actually belong to a later time and are a contamination. Published in Proceedings of the National Academy of Sciences, these careful and exacting carbon dating tests show artifacts in lower layers are younger than those of higher layers...meaning, the layers have been disturbed and mixed. The assumption that artifacts in lower layers are older than those in higher layers does not hold in this case. Neanderthal may not have used tools as we thought and made no significant contribution to the DNA history of modern humans.

10. Darwin's Famous Finches

Darwin noted the finches of the Galapagos Islands had changed enough from their ancestors on the South American mainland to justify being assigned separate species. They were still *finches*, but considered a different species. More modern researchers have noted that beak length and structural strength varies with changing periods of wet and drought on the islands. This has been touted as "evolution happening before our eyes". No one in the know among biologist really believes this anymore.

Beak length and structural strength actually vary regularly in finches over generations through the reshuffling of the DNA coding during reproduction. Natural selection does indeed result in some dying early and some living longer as rain and drought trends change on the islands. However, it is merely the proportions of the numbers of the individuals within the finch population exhibiting each characteristic that is changing. It is not the emergence of novel, new genetic information but only the expression of the present variability already encoded in the DNA. This variability does not allow the finch to change over time into an entirely different creature, but actually allows the creature to continue surviving in a changing environment and being what it had always been…a finch.

Addendum 5.

Secularism and the Misinterpretation of the First Amendment

First Amendment of the United States[427]

"Congress shall make no law respecting an establishment of religion, or prohibiting the free exercise thereof..." (The First Amendment to the Constitution of the United States, James Madison, 1789)

Abusing the First Amendment in Establishing a Secular State

In early Twenty-First century American life, the First Amendment is being misinterpreted and therefore misapplied, as a justification to politically marginalize and legally minimize any and all religious-faith convictions, references, or influences. Amazingly, this intolerance is especially being directed toward Christians, who seem to keep forgetting that they still comprise an overwhelming majority of the voting population (near 80%).

More on that later, but if/as this religious discrimination trend continues, the U.S. will soon become a functioning *secular state*—even without the official title, as is only claimed in the Constitutions of France (Article 2) and Russia (Article 14). It is also of interest to know that the person who invented the word *secularism* (George J.

Holyoake, 1850) was himself an atheist whose intention was to create a secular society based on scientific reason rather than religious revelation. Although one can be sensitive to the intellectual struggle against bigoted dogmatism, the wholesale abandonment of faith in God is an unnecessary leap—*a bridge too far.* [428]

This brief monograph will further caution against the slide toward secularism and indicate what people of faith can do to help personally and democratically address this issue in the context of their ultimate mission—to declare the present spiritual reality of God's eternal kingdom (Col. 1:13-14 New American Standard Bible, NASB).

The sacred-secular dichotomy

The word *secular* originally comes from the Fourteenth century Latin word *saeculum*, which means the *present world*. Synonyms for secular are nonreligious, temporal, and profane; whereas antonyms include words like religious and sacred. Even though the modern concept of profane (lit. marked by contempt or irreverence for what is sacred) has a negative connotation, the origin of the Latin word *profanous* simply meant *outside of the temple*. Furthermore, Roman Catholics still use the term *secular clergy* (deacons, priests, and bishops)—to specifically indicate the *location* of a clergyman's ministry—among the people/laity rather than as members of a cloistered monastic order, such as monks and abbots.

The Sixteenth century Protestant reformation had a profound effect on popular sentiments regarding what constituted the sacred-secular dichotomy. For instance, Luther rejected the notion that there was a clergy-laity distinction in the Bible, thus placing all believers on the same spiritual level. He demonstrated this parity before God by proclaiming the priesthood of all believers and by further encouraging marriage between ex-catholic priests and ex-nuns. Luther himself married an ex-nun, named Katharina von Bora—whose loving companionship, industry, and motherhood of six children were renowned.[429]

Essentially, for Luther, the *sacred* was not reserved for religious rites performed in a temple or cathedral, but in the human heart of every individual believer who was/is justified by grace through faith (Eph. 2:8-10, NASB). Furthermore, the *secular* was a realm in which we all live our daily lives and is referred to in the New Testament as the *world* consisting of both legitimate this-worldly concerns and needs (Matt. 6:25-34, NASB) as well as a sphere of human existence in which evil darkens and dominates the fallen soul of humanity (1 John 2:15-17, NASB).

In fact, the classic phrase that Christians are "both saints and sinners at the same time" points to the theological dichotomy in us all whereby we simultaneously have the potential for good and/or evil behavior (Rom. 7: 14-20, NASB). Of course, the more we mature spiritually the more consistently righteous will our character, words, and actions become (1 Pet. 2:2, NASB).

The point is that there is no such thing as a clear dividing line between the secular and the sacred. As a result, you cannot push religion into a church building neither can you keep it out of the Court(s), Congress and the White House—or any other sector of society. After all, faith in God, regardless of talk of the separation of church and state, has and will always operate in every sphere of human interaction. Like Mark Twain, whose obituary was reported in the New York Journal before he died, so also the reports of God's death have been greatly exaggerated![430]

> The separation of church and state is one thing; but the separation of God from the daily lives and concerns of all believers, in any nation, is quite another.

A Wall of Separation

In addition to the notion of the demarcation between the secular vs. the sacred, the First Amendment is also being misinterpreted by an almost instinctive reference to the Jeffersonian phrase of the *"(wall of) separation of church and state."*[431] The analogy is quite graphic when one pictures the Great Wall of China or the Berlin Wall—which were intended to separate one people group from another for the sake of political hegemony. However, since walls divide and bridges unite, the Jeffersonian idea of a wall would perhaps have been better depicted by the concept of a bridge.[432]

> We build too many walls and not enough bridges! (Isaac Newton)

A similar issue with the metaphorical notion of a *separation* (between church and state) is the fact that a marital separation can often lead to *divorce*. Hence, the very nature of a separation is often based on a serious relational conflict of some sort, which if not healed can be further wounded and/or even broken. Of course, this perceived tension between the church and the state might actually have been intended by the framers of the Constitution from the very foundation of the Republic. Like a pendulum which swings between opposites; with perhaps neither one meant to win over the other in their *dance of opposing interests*—so can the perennial conflicting nature of the relationship between church and state be conveyed. However, so long as there is a vital democracy, the church cannot (and should not) win over the state and the state cannot (and should not) win over the church. These two great realities are destined, by nature—and nature's God (!) to be either contradictory or complimentary[433]. In other words, an overlording state will hear it from the believing public—as will a dictatorial fundamentalism hear it from the state.

Christian Theocracy or Dual Citizenship

It is important to confirm that no American (Christian or otherwise) should worry about, or need to conceive of the establishment of a this-worldly Christian theocracy—as is a central feature of Islam.[434] For to reinvent the theocracies of old would be an ill-formed denial of the political lessons of our European heritage and specifically violate the clear teachings of Jesus Christ who declared tht:

> My kingdom is not of this world. If my kingdom were of this world, then my servants would be fighting [so that I might not die]; but as it is, my kingdom is not of this realm (John 18:36, NASB),

Note here that Jesus *is* making a claim to a domain over which he rules; but that such a kingdom is not to be established, maintained, or extended by the might of men—but by the love, truth and grace of God (Eph. 4:15, NASB). In other words, God's truth operates—not by the imposition of human force but by the freedom which love empowers

(John 8:32, New International Version, NIV). As a result, Christians have dual citizenship—in heaven and on earth (Phil. 3:20; Matt. 6:10, NASB).

And though many people's *religion* may be unrelated to their daily lives; the essence of true Christianity is more about a dynamic *relationship* of grace rather than a dogmatic compliance to religious laws. Hence, to try to restrict the free expression of one's religious perspective is an affront to one's personal liberties and freedom of speech, which is the second part of the First Amendment...

"[Congress shall make no law]...abridging the freedom of speech, or of the press; or the right of the people peaceably to assemble, and to petition the Government for a redress of grievances" (First Amendment conclusion).

However, to say that Christianity is not about following religious laws does not imply that Christians are anarchists who resist laws *ipso facto*, but rather that they have discovered the highest *law of love* (for God, others, and self; Matt. 22:37-41)—thereby fulfilling the spirit, or principle of the noblest virtues of relational interaction. In other words, Christians are not here to dominate or overlord anyone, but to lovingly serve all humanity, within their sphere of influence, by the witness of their lives in word and deed so as to bring honor to the Lord Jesus Christ—who gave his life as a ransom for all (1 Tim. 2:6; James 3:17-18, NASB).

As a result, even though Christians should not *politicize their faith*, by equating their belief system with temporal political realities, neither should they abandon their responsibility and rights as citizens who would seek to engage in the political process in any way that the love of God and the laws of our land would indicate. Such engagement could even involve attempts to reform such laws that are deemed in conflict with Christian/religious convictions—from whatever source they have been derived, be it in a church, synagogue, mosque, school, home, or from some form of literature.

Addendum 5.

A Closing Case in Point

"The only thing necessary for evil to triumph is for good men to do nothing."
(Edmund Burke, British Statesman and Philosopher, 1729-1797)

This popular inspirational quote by Edmund Burke is now in dispute by proponents of secularism who, in deference to political correctness, would refuse to admit to the reality of evil—even when discussing terrorism. Their secular rational is that if we admit that evil is real, then we might also be admitting to the reality of good; and if good exists—then we might be implying that God could also exist; which might even be a tacit admission to the reality of heaven and hell...which must be a flagrant violation of the separation between church and state—perhaps evening bordering on *hate speech* toward those who might be offended with such extremely offensive religious language! This example is just as insane as a recent television report in which some educators were suggesting that children in grade school should not be allowed to use the pronouns *he* or *she* when describing children of the opposite sex. The reason? It is sexist to do so.

Make no mistake, when secularism takes hold of a nation it will gradually lead to atheism—where no talk of God or dynamic expression of faith is allowed except as regulated by the state, such as is the case in China today with its 1.3 billion citizens. What is interesting in China is that the ruling atheistic communist party only consists of 5% of the population, which in large measure has to do with the fact that 50% of the general population in China consider themselves secular (agnostic and non-religious); whereas the total number of Chinese who say they are religious is only 30%.[435]

Practical Steps of Action

Some of the best ways that Christians can, and should, influence the American culture is by following the practical suggestions as listed below:

1. Love and serve the Lord Jesus Christ with greater conviction, humility, and passion (1 Pet. 3:15, NASB).
2. Become an active part of a vibrant Christian community of believers (Acts 2:38-47).
3. Be discerning and resist the pollutions and temptations of this fallen-world (James 1:27; 1 John 3:15-17—specifically carnality, materialism, and egoism).
4. Pray for America. One of the best prayers about politicians and malevolent forces in our culture is: "Lord Jesus, please raise up the righteous and root out the wicked" (D. Prince).
5. Study/learn more about how faith can engage the public sector.[436]
6. Be courageous and vote without timidity or apathy. Remember the story of history:

Ballots are always better than bullets. Do not be intimidated with secular arguments that seek to marginalize your religious/faith-based convictions. Each and every informed Christian has just as much power in the voting booth as any atheist—and there are millions more of us than of them. Let us exercise our freedom while we still have it. Collectively, the Christian majority in America has an important right and responsibility to politically respond so that the voices of secularism and atheism will not be able to corrupt the entire culture without objection. Remember: If secular ideas devolve into a functional secular state then our Christian liberties will be silenced or controlled, and we will have become like salt that loses its savor; or like a candle that has been extinguished...

> You are the salt of the earth. But if the salt loses its saltiness, how can it be made salty again? It is no longer good for anything, except to be thrown out and trampled underfoot. You are the light of the world. A town built on a hill cannot be hidden. Neither do people light a lamp and put it under a bowl. Instead they put it on its stand, and it gives light to everyone in the house. In the same way, let your light shine before others, that they may see your good deeds and glorify your Father in heaven (Matt. 5:13-16).

Addendum 5.

7. Run, as a Christian, for a political office or support an informed Christian candidate who does, or adopt a social issue and/or cause for which God has given you a heart
8. Have more children—through either natural birth and/or adoption. In a democracy, since the issue(s) with the most votes wins, we should seek the Lord about having more children to whom we can entrust the heritage of our Christian values.
9. Make sure our children are educationally grounded in the Christian faith rather than secularized by an education system and/or non-Christian teachers. This will most definitely include establishing charter schools, Christian schools, and home-schooling options to the amorality or immorality of public education—at least until our children are strong enough to engage (by a compelling apologetic of truth, grace, and love) the worldliness around them (1 John 2:15-17).
10. Encourage our youth to perhaps pursue a political career or at least a professional vocation in which they can have more of an influence in the court of public opinion—and through which they can sense and pursue God's calling and service.
11. Be more *salty* at work by praying for our co-workers, showing integrity, serving others, inviting them over or out to dinner some time, and using opportunities to share our faith wisely and with appropriate courage.

"When the righteous rule, the people rejoice; when the wicked rule, the people groan."
(Proverbs 29:2)

Addendum 6.

Faith and Education:
How to Get a Higher Education Without Losing Your Faith!

(Written Originally for Grand Canyon University/ Used by Permission)

As a child I received instruction both in the Bible and in the Talmud. I am a Jew, but I am enthralled by the luminous figure of [Jesus] the Nazarene....No one can read the Gospels without feeling the actual presence of Jesus. His personality pulsates in every word. No myth is filled with such life. —Albert Einstein. ("The World's Smartest Man," n.d.).

Alexander, Caesar, Charlemagne, and I have founded empires. But on what did we rest the creation of our genius? Upon force. Jesus Christ founded His empire upon love; and at this hour millions of men would die for Him—Napoleon Bonaparte. ("Tentmaker Quotes," n.d.).

Coming to Faith

I personally came to faith in Jesus Christ as a result of growing distress over needing to choose a career pathway after high school. Despite a number of seemingly viable options, I simply could not make up my mind. After all, how could I be sure which career to pursue at such a young age? What if I made the wrong choice? Was there something-anything that I was supposed to do with my life of which I was unawae?

> "You have made us for yourself, O Lord, and our hearts are restless until they find their rest in you" (St. Augustine of Hippo, 354-430AD)

In retrospect, what I now understand is that I was becoming progressively awakened to the fact that my life was empty and without any over-arching purpose. Furthermore, that emptiness had turned into a profound thirst for the truth about life itself, the meaning of my own existence, and the peace of mind that such a discovery might hold. Little did I know that my search for purpose, truth, and peace would all be found by placing my faith in the Lord Jesus Christ—which I did at a Billy Graham and Bill Bright Conference. My old life was now gone, and a brand new life had come at last (2 Cor. 5:17, New American Standard Bible, NASB)!

What is Faith?

Faith is:

A. A hopeful certainty about what is not seen.
B. Divine confidence in action.
C. A conviction concerning the nature of ultimate reality.

Faith is a hopeful certainty

Regarding a hopeful certainty about what is not seen; the Bible specifically mentions that "Faith is being sure of what we hope for and certain of what we do not see" (Heb. 11:1, Today's New International Version, TNIV). As a result, faith involves the non-empirical dimension of existence. Hence, the realm in which faith operates is not subject to the purview of scientific inquiry. Metaphysically, faith's focus is on the transcendent—toward things which are above, beneath, and beyond the scope of material existence.

Some people talk about taking a *leap of faith*—which is actually a fairly descriptive metaphor of the experience of those who live by faith. Such believers have been enabled to leap off, or move away from the limitations of their own rationality to the possibility that God could exist in another dimension beyond what their senses can now perceive. In fact, rather than argue about the scientific legitimacy of transcendence, a majority of scientists and theologians, have come to the conclusion that science can neither prove nor disprove the existence of God. God does exist, believers insist, but in another dimension, which is only accessible by faith. In fact, the writer of Hebrews confirms that "Without faith it is impossible to please God, because anyone who comes to him must believe [two things] that he exists and that he rewards those who earnestly seek him" (Heb. 11:6, TNIV).

Faith is divine confidence in action

Regarding divine confidence in action; God promises to empower all people of faith to be confident and courageous by the gift of the Holy Spirit (Acts 2:38-39, NASB). In Proverbs 28, the author declares that although the wicked may flee in fear, the righteous are bold as a lion (Prov. 28:1, NASB). By the way, the Hebrew word for *bold*, in this verse, also means to be *confident*. Speaking about confidence, there is an amazing story about a 40 year old man who had been lame since his birth, who was healed by Peter and John (Acts 3, NASB). When interrogated by the Jewish ruling council the Bible records that "Now as they observed the confidence of Peter and John and understood that they were uneducated, untrained, and [ordinary] men, they were amazed, and [took note that these men had] been with Jesus" (Acts 3:13, NASB & TNIV).

People of faith are empowered by the Holy Spirit to become emotionally and mentally confident and courageous. They have an internal strength of character which enables them to be bold in the face of all F.E.A.R.→False Evidence Appearing Real.

Addendum 6.

Faith is about ultimate reality

Faith can also be defined as a conviction concerning the nature of ultimate reality. This is more of a general definition of Eastern Pantheism, with which Christians would also be in agreement—although with quite a different interpretation. For instance, the main difference would be that Eastern Pantheism cannot be certain of what the ultimately reality is, because such a realm is completely impersonal (as in Hinduism) and/or completely unknowable (as in Buddhism).

However, a clear objective of both Hinduism and Buddhism is to escape the endless cycle of suffering: birth, life, death, rebirth—also called reincarnation. Hinduism calls the escape from such a cycle *moksha* or liberation, which allows the soul to join with the Impersonal Universal Divine Force called Brahman, or God. Buddhism, on the other hand, calls such a release from the endless cycle as entering the state of *Nirvana*, which literally means to extinguish as a candle's flame—suggesting the complete loss of self-consciousness forever ("Buddhism and Hinduism," n.d.).

> People of Eastern faith believe in an ultimate reality with which they hope to be joined after this earthly sojourn of suffering.

What does faith do for us?

Faith justifies us before God

> Faith justifies [just-as-if-I had never sinned] us before God.
> If you declare with your mouth, 'Jesus is Lord,' and believe in your heart that God raised him from the dead, you will be saved. For it is with your heart that you believe and are justified, and it is with your mouth that you profess your faith and are saved" (Rom. 10:9-10, TNIV).

In other words, rather than trying so hard to be a good person, or trusting in our good works, faith alone enables us to receive God's salvation as a gift of grace rather than an accomplishment of any man—except one, Jesus Christ (See also Eph. 2:8-9).

After all, just knowing that you are accepted by God, by grace through faith, can continue to nurture your mind and heart with courage to keep trying your best—regardless of your performance, or lack thereof. In other words, faith can sustain you through your academic learning process by motivating you to believe that you can do all things through Christ who is daily strengthening you from within (Phil. 4:13; 2:13; 1 John 4:4).

Faith comes by hearing God's Word

Faith comes to us by listening with our heart to God's word (Rom. 10:17, TNIV). God's word can be heard in any numbers of ways, including in music, art, teaching, reading, studying, preaching, memorizing, meditating, praying, etc.

> "Prayer is faith's first breath."

As you daily practice communicating (listening and speaking) with God, your faith will grow and your ability to walk in his strength will steadily increase. This is good news for all of us who, at times, feel that we are too weak to continue to reach for our dreams and goals. However, the Bible actually states that it is in our weakness that God's grace and power are even more readily available to us. After all, strong, rich, and healthy people are presumably not as aware of their need for God as are the weak, poor, and broken.

This is why the apostle Paul said, "Therefore I will boast all the more gladly about my weakness, so that Christ's power may rest on me...for when I am weak, then I am strong" (2 Cor. 12:9-10). This certainly does not mean that God wants to keep everyone weak, poor, and broken. Rather, as we become increasingly strong, wealthy, and healthy, we should always remember to be thankful to God for his gracious blessings and yet sensitive to others, who are where we once were ourselves.

Tested faith produces proven character

Tested faith produces proven character. Not only are we justified by grace through faith, but we are also learning to joyfully triumph in our trials and troubles. We can do this because we know that pressure, affliction, and hardship produce perseverance (lit. to persist through severity). As a result, we can celebrate in our trials because we know that such endurance and fortitude develops proven character that has passed the test. The result is a joyful and confident hope of eternal life that can never be shaken (Rom. 5:2-4, Amplified Bible, AMP & James 1: 2-4, New American Standard Bible, NASB, Adapted).

Two Biblical Heroes of Faith

Hebrews chapter 11 is called the *Faith Hall of Fame* because there is a list of people there who are recognized as having displayed exemplary faith throughout the history of biblical times. However, such champions of faith were also beset with personal weaknesses, which nevertheless did not disqualify them for inclusion in such a prestigious company of the faithful. Let's look at two such examples, one from the Old Testament and one from the New Testament.

1. *Abraham* is called the father of all those who believe (Rom. 6:16, New Living Translation, NLT). In fact, all monotheistic religions claim Abraham the father of their faith, including Muslims, Jews, and Christians. Abraham's merits include leaving his polytheistic homeland to a promised place of inheritance for his descendents who would become a mighty nation; establishing a monotheistic covenant with God; wholeheartedly believing God to such an extent that Abraham was considered as righteous before God; displaying a willingness to sacrifice his son Isaac in obedience to God's request [note: this potential sacrifice was a prophetic foreshadowing of the crucifixion of Christ, on the same mountain range as Mount Moriah some 2,000 years later!]; finally, Abraham was called the friend of God.

Some of Abraham's demerits were that he lied by implying that his wife was in fact only his sister—thus exposing Sarah to potential abuse and harm in the home of a clansman ruler. In other words, Abraham acted fearfully and dishonorably. Furthermore, Abraham impregnated Hagar, his wife's maid-servant in order to fulfill God's promise which was made over 20 years earlier. In other words, Abraham became impatient.

> Part of the moral of this story is that even though you may be fearful or impatient at times, you can still be powerfully used by God to affect the course of nations, while at the same time being called a friend of God.

2. *Peter* was a fisherman who Jesus called to be his disciple and a mighty apostle. Some of Peter's merits include his willingness to instantly respond to the call of Jesus to be his disciple-follower; he boldly asked Jesus if he could walk on the water with him—and he did!; he was the first disciple to declare that Jesus was the Messiah; he was a very powerful and compelling preacher—whose first sermon on the day of Pentecost resulted in the conversion of 3,000 people; he was used by God to display mighty miracles of healing—to such an extent that even his shadow would heal people (Acts 5:12-16); Peter was courageous, faithful, and humble until the end—as is evidenced with his request to be crucified upside down, as being unworthy of the same manner of crucifixion as was his Lord.

    Peter's demerits include his despicable denial of Jesus three times during Jesus' grueling legal trials; his impetuous and impulsive mannerisms for which he was rebuked by Jesus and the other apostles; while walking on the water with Jesus he lost faith and began to sink; he actually tried to discourage Jesus from speaking about his death in Jerusalem and subsequent resurrection from the dead; finally, Peter was publically reproved by Paul for his racial hypocrisy regarding avoiding Gentile companionship in the face of law-promoting Jewish believers.

> Part of the moral of this story is that even though you may have been unfaithful, impulsive, outspoken, or a racist, you too can find forgiveness for your most grievous sins and learn how to bring miraculous healing to the lives of others in Jesus' Name.

Now that you have heard about faith for perhaps the first time—what should/can you do about it?

Here are what could be called the *Top Ten Habits of Faith-Filled People*. "We are what we repeatedly do. Excellence, therefore, is not an act but a habit" (Aristotle, 384-322 BC).

Top Ten Habits of Faith-Filled People

1. Hear God's word (Rom. 10:17, TNIV). Get to some place, and with some people, where you can hear the inspirational message about faith, grace, hope, and love. Keep a journal to record your adventures as a follower of Jesus!
2. Believe with all of your heart and confess your new found faith to others (Rom. 10:9-10).
3. Pray, praise, and obey. You will be amazed of how God will lead you in small hidden ways at first and then larger (even perhaps public) ways, as your faith increases (Phil. 4:7-8, AMP).
4. Learn about God's Kingdom purpose for the world—as well as how you might fit into his purpose by discerning your gifts, talents, desires, calling, and career (Acts 13:36a; 1 Pet. 4:10, TNIV).
5. Make a strategic plan to accomplish your goals! (Prov. 16:9; 21:5, NASB)
6. Confirm your plan with wise consultation (Prov. 15:22, AMP).
7. Implement your plans; take action to both plan your work and work your plan. Remember that faith, like love, is a noun and a verb, which is both a state of *being* and *doing*. (James 1:22-25).
8. Persevere with joy knowing that though trials will come—God will always make a way for you to overcome. Remember, there can be no *testimony* without passing a *test* (1 Cor. 10:13, TNIV).
9. Adjust your plan as necessary as you proceed without wavering in unbelief (James 1:5-8, NLT).
10. Celebrate your success with family, friends, and key supporters. Enjoy the reward of faithfulness, which is the maturity of hope, the character of Christ, and the blessing of the Lord (Prov. 10:22; 10:4; 28:20).

The Community of Faith at Grand Canyon University

In this final section of exploring our topic about Faith and Education, it would be important to survey a few ways in which faith is used in the founding documents of Grand Canyon University (GCU)—Arizona's premiere private Christian University.

The first thing to note about Faith at GCU is that 'faith is defined from the context of our Christian heritage" ("GCU Statement of Faith," n.d.). This implies that the Gospel (lit. *Good News*) about Jesus Christ is central in what we believe. As a result, it is our sincere prayer that all who come to GCU, be they students, faculty, staff, or alumni will genuinely take some time to explore, or re-explore the foundation of the Christian's faith in Christ Jesus—"who brought life and immortality to light through the Gospel" (2 Tim. 1:10, TNIV).

However, more than having a mere mental assent to some religious doctrine, a Christian is a person who actually has a growing personal relationship with Jesus Christ. With such a relationship, the believer can develop in both academic competence and personal character, as they participate in the broader Christian community at GCU. Such a community of faith wholeheartedly embraces people of every Christian denomination—believing that our mutual love for God in Christ is well able to hold us all together in the perfect bond of unity (Col. 3:14).

Furthermore, since Jesus taught us to reach out and share his love with people throughout the world's various cultures (Matt. 28:18-20, TNIV); it is also our privilege to purposefully open our doors to all those of other faiths or those with no faith at all. Our hope is that such an expression of inclusion in GCU's community of faith will enable all of us to experience more of God's presence and purpose as we demonstrate his love in service and share his gracious truth with kindness. In fact, already, a significant number of people from the larger global community are finding GCU to be a preferred educational choice, because of stellar *accreditation*, academic rigor, inclusive philosophy, and an emphasis on moral character (2 Pet. 1: 3-8).

Finally, there is a GCU faith statement which says that, "God has a purpose for our lives and He prepares and calls us to that purpose" ("GCU Values," n.d.)—meaning that we each have a destiny which we are privileged to pursue in our quest to honor God, by bearing enduring fruit both internally (in personal character) and externally (in service

Addendum 6.

that we provide to others). As a result of this hope, there is always reason for optimism—regardless of how dark our life circumstances may become at times. After all, we may not know what the future holds; but we do know who holds the future (Romans 8:38-39, TNIV)!

Addendum 7.

Ghosts and other Occult Phenomena: A Biblical Perspective

Introduction

On a popular news show the other night the entire program was dedicated to interviewing a psychic who is best known for communicating with the dead relatives of his audience members. The commentator showed unusual intrigue as he consulted with the psychic about certain of his own paranormal sensations—all the while belittling the warnings of concerned television viewers (by way of email) against such occult preoccupations. During the course of the interview, the psychic informed the commentator that there was no such thing as the devil and furthermore, that psychic knowledge was unfortunately labeled occult (lit. hidden, secret, clandestine) by those who just did not understand how helpful it really can be. He even admitted sitting for hours at the library researching occult literature, which later became the foundation of his knowledge and practice as a professional psychic-medium.

The Scriptural Prohibition against Occult Practices

> When you enter the land which the LORD your God gives, you, you shall not learn to imitate the detestable things of those nations. There shall not be found among you anyone who makes his son or daughter pass through the fire, one who uses divination, one who practices witchcraft, or one who interprets omens, or a sorcerer, or one who casts a spell, or a medium, or a spiritist, or one who calls up the dead. Anyone who does these things is detestable to the LORD; and because of these detestable things the LORD your God will drive them out before you (Deuteronomy 18:9-12).

Interpretation:

* Anyone who makes his son or daughter pass through the fire—human sacrifice to the Ammonite god, Molech (See also Lev. 18:21).

* Divination—seeking to foretell the future by omens, oracles, or supernatural powers

* Witchcraft—black or white; the use of magical powers for seductive charm

* Omens—interpreting of certain signs (flight of birds, black cats, astrological signs) with reference to future events

* Sorcerer—a man skilled in the power of magic and the manipulation of evil spirits

* Casts a spell—words or chants to control others

* Medium, spiritist, or one who calls up the dead—those who pose as intermediaries between the living and the dead.

Note that both mediums and psychics claim to have extra-sensory perception. The difference is that mediums claim that their perception is aided by information provided by spirits in general or of the dead in particular—whereas psychics[437] claim their abilities are intrinsic such as clairvoyance, psychometry, precognition, or psychokinesis. It is also helpful to know that the study of such paranormal abilities is called parapsychology.[438]

I share this as the context for a discussion about ghosts because a ghost is a disembodied spirit (evil or otherwise) or presumably a disembodied personality of a dead person.[439] The question that most often arises when dealing with the issues of ghosts is whether or not the spirits (or souls) or dead people are really walking around on the earth seeking revenge or otherwise completing some unfinished task prior to their release from the earthly realm. Furthermore, is it really possible for a medium or spiritist to conjure up the dead or is this simply some kind of parlor trick of would-be psychic entertainers? Or could this necromantic activity actually be a demon that is impersonating a deceased person and lying to both the psychic and those who consult their trade?

What is interesting is that a synonym (though not necessarily an equivalent) for the word ghost is *demon*, which is also a disembodied evil spirit. This is why many biblical commentators have linked the psychic activity of communicating with the dead to that of conversing with demons whose main task is deceiving humanity.

> "...in the last days some will abandon their faith and follow deceiving spirits and things taught by demons" (1 Tim. 4:1).

As a result, it is definitely feasible that demons are indeed impersonating the dead with an intent to deceive humanity from believing the biblical teaching of the separation between the righteous and unrighteous at death and beyond at the final judgment. After all, if there is no separation at death (with everyone still floating around) then perhaps there's no eternal separation either. Hence, there is no need to believe in heaven or hell because the dead are all going to a "place of light" because that's what communication with the dead has revealed to us.

The Witch of Endor

Before I share some conclusions, there is a chapter in the Old Testament that deserves some attention in this regard. In 1 Samuel 28 King Saul consults with a medium-witch at Endor in order to bring up from the dead his mentor, the prophet Samuel. Without theological comment, the text states, that the woman did indeed conjure up Samuel who was quite perturbed at being "brought up" from the ground, which would be a reference for the place of departed spirits (*Sheol* in Hebrew and *Hades* in Greek). Saul then entreats Samuel for his prophetic direction since the Lord was not communicating with Saul through the normal ways, specifically, dreams, Urim (a priestly lot cast for divine direction), or prophets. Samuel denounces Saul's efforts as misguided and predicts his impending death the next day—which actually happened (1 Sam. 31:6).

This text is admittedly hard to interpret and should therefore not be made central in the development of doctrine. A careful student of Scripture can only conjecture (not conclude) that, on the basis of this chapter, and though condemned by God, communicating with the dead may be possible. Hence, the adamant denial of psychic phenomenon (particularly necromancy or conversing with the dead) must at least be moderated to make room for what the Bible mysteriously alludes to itself. Again, this is not to ever give endorsement for what the Bible clearly condemns, but it does allow the thoughtful Christian to reinterpret people's fascination with the subject. After all, there could be some basis in fact for occult practices, but the practices themselves are nevertheless strongly condemned for God's people—who are enjoined to communicate directly with the Lord rather than indirectly through demons and/or the dead—the distinguishing of which is never certain whenever occultic means are employed.

Bottom line: Occult practices, though containing some basis in fact, are intended by the "devil...who is the father of lies," (John 8:44) to replace people's worshipful devotion to God by suggesting that there is *reliable knowledge* of the spiritual realm through some other source than that of Scripture, the resident Holy Spirit, the community of believers, ordained ministers, and authentic spiritual gifts.

A Global Fascination with the Supernatural

There is no doubt that people are intrigued by the supernatural and/or paranormal. After all, part of the fascination that people had with Jesus was his ability to do miracles and bring healing to suffering of all kinds—not to mention the incredible claim of his resurrection from the dead! In fact, one of the main reasons the church at large (especially in its historic denominational expressions) has lost its appeal is because of its absence and/or wholesale denial of the supernatural power of God—leaving little other than superstitious tales of the saints of old, or the theology of cessation (the doctrine that since we now have the Bible—we no longer need the supernatural power gifts and ministries) of the Holy Spirit. To these the admonition of Scripture itself would appear appropriate:

> But mark this: In the last days difficult times will come. People will be lovers of themselves…money…[and] of pleasure rather than lovers of God—holding to a form of godliness although they have denied its power. Have nothing to do with them. (2 Tim. 3:1-5 NIV & NASB).

In my mind, this vacuum of the supernatural is and will continue to be filled in ever increasing intensity and paranormal manifestation by the occult—against which God has always had a superior Spirit which he promises to give to all believers (Luke 11:13; Mark 16:17-18), especially as the last days continue to unfold.

> In the last days, God says, I will pour out my Spirit on all people. Your sons and daughters will prophesy, your young men will see visions, your old men will dream dreams…I will show wonders in the heaven above and signs on the earth below…The sun will be turned to darkness and the moon to blood before the coming of the great and glorious day of the Lord. And everyone who calls on the name of the Lord will be saved. (Acts 2:17-21).

Notice that God's intention in all of these supernatural manifestations is that men might be saved—what a great and compassionate God we serve!

Ecstasy: Drug or Endowment

> When the day of Pentecost came, they were all together in one place. Suddenly a sound like the blowing of a violent wind came from heaven and filled the whole house where they were sitting. They saw what seemed to be tongues of fire that separated and came to rest on each of them. All of them were filled with the Holy Spirit and began to speak in other tongues as the Spirit enabled them. (Acts 2:1-4)

While studying this text one day I noticed an amazing corollary between the drug *ecstasy* and the phenomenon of *speaking in tongues* as mentioned above. The connection was that nearly all of my biblical references defined the supernatural gift of tongues in terms of an *ecstatic* utterance of some sort.[440] I found myself wondering if the drug[441] *ecstasy* was in fact a kind of demonic counterfeit for the authentic power of God (represented by the phenomenon of speaking in tongues) which many Christians had written off years ago as an emotional excess of Pentecostal *holy-rollers*. However one feels about Pentecostalism, one thing is certain: the youth of today are under an unprecedented onslaught of demonic activity and manifestations that can only be countered with a personal experience of the authentic power of God. We must not deny a generation any and every tool necessary to combat the forces of darkness at the end of this age.

Lord Jesus,

Raise up a mighty army from among our youth who are empowered by the Holy Spirit to take the Gospel of the Kingdom (Christ's dominion) into all the earth and hasten the day of your return. Even so, Come Lord Jesus.

The Lord will extend your mighty scepter from Zion [the royal center of the Messiah's universal rule]; you will rule in the midst of your enemies [through your assembled army]. Your troops will be willing on your day of battle [to stand with you regardless of the cost]. Arrayed in holy majesty, [with a heart of worship] from the womb of the dawn you will receive the youth like the dew [they will be too numerous to count] (Psalm 110:2-3).

Year of the King

(Song by Ron Woodworth; to the 21st century spiritual *army* of God)

Chorus: We are the Lord's generation,
We've come to worship and sing.
Now is the time of salvation—
This is the year of the king.
This is the year of the king.
Verse 1: We've been ransomed from our sinful lives;
Cleansed by the blood of the Lamb.
Clothed in the power of holy light.
The sword of truth is in our hand.
Bridge: Shout for joy you royal priesthood.
Raise the battle cry.
Press the fight into the stronghold.
The enemy's word is a lie—
Jesus is Lord is our cry!
Chorus
Verse 2: We've come to liberate your captives,
Set the prisoner free.
Crush the power of the serpent's curse—
and loose all humanity.
Bridge: Shout for joy you royal priesthood;
Raise the battle cry.
Press the fight into the stronghold,
The enemy's word is a lie—
Jesus is Lord is our cry.
Chorus: We are the Lord's generation,
We've come to worship and sing.
Now is the time of salvation,
This is the year of the king!
This is the year of the king!
This is the year of the...
Shout for joy you royal priesthood—Yeah!

Finally, here are four verses that should both humble and motivate every authentic minister (and believer) in the Body of Christ in order

Addendum 7.

to keep the supernatural dimension of the ministry central to the proclamation of God's Word.

> But he was pierced for our transgressions, he was crushed for our iniquities; the punishment that brought us peace was on him, and by his wounds we are healed (Isaiah 53:5).

> Is anyone among you sick? Let them call the elders of the church to pray over them and anoint them with oil in the name of the Lord. And the prayer offered in faith will make the sick person well; the Lord will raise them up. If they have sinned, they will be forgiven. Therefore confess your sins to each other and pray for each other so that you may be healed. The prayer of a righteous person is powerful and effective (James 5:14-16).

> My message and my preaching were not with wise and persuasive words [alone] but with a demonstration of the Spirit's power, so that your faith might not rest on men's wisdom, but on God's power (1 Cor. 2:4).

> And coming to His home town He began teaching them in their synagogue, so that they became astonished and said, 'Where did this man get this wisdom, and these miraculous powers?' (Matthew 13:54, NASB)

Addendum 8.

Becoming an Authentic Follower of Jesus: Tips for Beginners!

Dear Friend,

Congratulations on making Jesus the Lord of your life! The Bible says that the moment you believed in your heart and confessed with your mouth your faith in Christ you were saved. "...if you confess with your mouth that Jesus is Lord and believe in your heart that God raised Him from the dead you shall be saved" (Romans 10:9). Although you may not have felt or seen anything *physically*, I can assure you that many things instantly happened *spiritually*!

- The debt for all your sins was paid in full by Christ's death on the cross at Calvary. Everything God had against you has now been purged from His records by the blood of Christ! (Rev. 1:5; I Cor. 15:3)
- You were born into the family of God. You are now a child of your Father in heaven (Matt. 6:14).
- You were transferred from Satan's authority into God's Kingdom. Jesus is now your official representative to God. As a citizen of the Kingdom of Heaven, you must pledge to Christ your total allegiance and are therefore qualified to receive his sovereign protection (Col. 1:13; I Tim. 1:5).
- You died *spiritually* to all that bound you in this life, "...The lust of the flesh (carnality), the lust of the eyes (materialism), and the boastful pride of life (egoism/narcissism)" (1 John 2:16).
- Your inner man became spiritually alive by the power of the Holy Spirit. Now you are able to live a pleasing, productive, and holy life for God (Romans 6:3-6).

How did I learn these things? The same way you are going to—by prayer, study of the Bible, obedience to the Holy Spirit, becoming part of a Christian fellowship, and sharing your faith with others. Let's look at each of these vital keys to spiritual growth for a moment.

Prayer

Now that God is your Father, He desires to talk with you about everything. He loves you and wants to help meet your every need. But remember the four secrets to effective prayer:

- Faith – Keep believing God is listening to you and desires to give you the best, even when things are not going very well.
- Perseverance – Some things just cannot be solved overnight. So keep at it.
- A thankful attitude – God does not appreciate an ungrateful, demanding, and critical attitude. Remember: He is not manipulated by temper tantrums.
- A listening ear – Do not just talk to God, but learn to listen to His responses. It will change your prayer life for sure. Start a journal.

Do not be anxious about anything, but in everything, by prayer and petition, with thanksgiving, present your requests to God. And the peace of God, which transcends all understanding, will guard your hearts and your minds in Christ Jesus (Phil. 4:6-7).

Study of the Bible/Mind Renewal

The Bible is the most tested and trusted source of God's written Word in the world. If you ever hope to mature spiritually, you must renew your mind with the word of God. You see, the mind is like a computer. It operates according to the way it has been programmed. As you prayerfully study God's word, the Holy Spirit will help you to see how you have been thinking wrongly or rightly about things in your life. As you practice right thinking, you will then be able to speak and act rightly as well. In this way you will be able to find and fulfill God's will for your life.

Sow a thought, you reap an action.
    Sow an action, you reap a habit.
        Sow a habit, you reap a lifestyle.
            Sow a lifestyle, you reap a destiny.
                (Ralph Waldo Emerson)

DO – Begin a regular Bible study program today! [Note: Your local Christian bookstore is loaded with great Bible study resources. Visit it as soon as possible to get started. Make sure also to load up on alternative Christian music.]

> Therefore, I urge you brothers, in view of God's mercy to offer your bodies as living sacrifices, holy and pleasing to God – which is your spiritual worship. Do not conform any longer to the pattern of this world, but be transformed by the renewing of your mind. Then you will be able to test and approve what God's will is – His good, pleasing and perfect will (Romans 12:1-2).

Obedience to the Holy Spirit

In order for the Word of God to have its desired effect, the Spirit of God must accompany it. Without the power of the Holy Spirit energizing God's Word, Christianity becomes just another legalistic and death-producing religion. The truth is, though millions may try, you and I cannot live the Christian life in our own strength. This is where naturally gifted and strong people are especially vulnerable to error. Whereas weak people know that they cannot do it on their own, the strong tend to last longer on sheer will power. But do not worry, God has a way of breaking us all from trusting in ourselves and teaching us to rely on His grace to work in us "both to will and to work for His own good pleasure" (Phil. 2:12-13).

Allow me to suggest four ways that you can avoid the pitfall of legalism as you seek to grow in grace:

- <u>Acknowledge</u> God's word to you when you hear it, even if you do not like what he says.
- <u>Admit</u> to yourself and Him that you cannot perform His will in your own strength.
- <u>Ask</u> the Lord to give you His strength.
- <u>Act</u> on your faith now, trusting that He is working in you (Philippians 4:13).

If you should fail do not backslide! Confess your fault to God and He will forgive you (John 1:9). Then try again. After a while you will grow stronger in spirit and will not make such obvious/foolish mistakes. If on the other hand, you succeed the first couple of tries, praise the Lord! But do not congratulate yourself too quickly. (Maybe you had beginner's luck!) Just remember, it is those who finish the course who win the race, not just those who start. In God's school you only graduate when you can prove your learning by how you *live* and not just by what you think you *know*.

> He has made us competent as ministers of the new covenant – not of the letter but of the Spirit: For the letter kills, but the Spirit gives life (2 Corinthians 3:6).

> The man who thinks he knows something does not yet know as he ought to know (1 Corinthians 8:2).

Becoming Part of a Christian Fellowship/Church

The moment you became a Christian, (by receiving Christ) you also became a part of the family of God. You are not alone anymore (Psalm 68:6). And like any responsible father, your Heavenly Father has provided a home for all of his children to come and live. It's called the *Church*. Not just a building, but also a body of believers who are seeking to learn how to lovingly relate as fellow members of God's household. I say, *learn to lovingly relate* because some of us may have had less than a loving family experience in the past.

For those with a troubled family background, it may be a little harder and take a little longer for you to be healed of past hurts and offenses; especially if someone in the church should act just like those who wounded you in the past. Cheer up, God may be providing a repeat experience (in a controlled environment) to help you learn how to rightly respond to situations that would have devastated you before. So be patient with yourself and with others. After all, only Jesus is the perfect elder-brother into whose likeness we are all being conformed by the Spirit of Grace.

DO — Go and ask the person who led you to Christ which church (and additional small group) they would suggest you join so you can begin to learn to love and be loved by the family of God.

Sharing your faith with others

Now that you have come to know the truth of God in Christ you will naturally want to share such exciting news with your family and friends. However, as you will soon discover, not everyone is as equally excited about your new faith as are you. Some may be intimidated by the radical claims of Christ, or jealous that you might be rejecting them, or defensive against religious hypocrisy, or too wounded by life to care, or too deceived by counterfeit philosophies to hear your words.[442] This can be discouraging unless you understand that all of these reactions can help teach you how to be more of a gracious, truthful, and wise witness for Christ Jesus. Remember: The more you allow God to deeply work *within* you (your character, attitudes, and actions)—the more he will be able to effectively work *through* you. The best way to share your faith with others is by "show and tell." This means that we should not just say with our words that we are Christians, but we should equally show with our lives that we truly care about Christ and others—even those who do not yet believe. Always remember this verse: *"It's the kindness of the Lord that leads people to repentance"* (Romans 2:4). Learn more of the truth in Christ,[443] pray for others to be open, be genuinely caring and friendly, invite those you are sharing with to *appropriate* Christian functions, and be patient.

Do—Begin to pray daily for the top three people in your life that you would love to see come to faith in Jesus Christ. Then follow the tips above and watch how God works in their lives.

Two Other Important Foundations

There are two other things you will want to consider in order to lay a good foundation for your new life in Christ:

1. Water Baptism – This is a testimony to your personal identification and appropriation of the death, burial, and resurrection of Jesus Christ. Through water baptism you are signifying that you have died to your old life and have been raised to live the rest of your life on earth to do God's will alone.

DO—Ask the Pastor of the church you are joining to baptize you as soon as possible.

2. Receive the gift of the Holy Spirit – This is another important foundation to establish early on in your walk with Christ. The first gift God gave you was His Son, the Lord Jesus. Now the Father and Son (the Lord Jesus) want to give you the gift, or baptism of the Holy Spirit. Note: Even though all believers in Christ already have the Holy Spirit within them, the gift (or baptism) in the Holy Spirit is when the power of God comes upon us to help us to be more consistent in our behavior and bold in our faith and witness to others.[444]

DO—Ask the Pastor of the church you are considering joining to help you receive the baptism/gift of the Holy Spirit. Note: If you receive an unfavorable response about the gift of the Baptism in the Holy Spirit (and spiritual gifts in general), let me suggest that you study Biblical Christianity 101—especially Lesson #6 on *The Person and Power of the Holy Spirit* and decide for yourself. Most mature pastors will allow some doctrinal latitude to their church members so long as they maintain a respectful attitude toward others who differ. If you continue to receive a cold reception to your request then you probably have not found your church home yet. Keep looking, or contact me and I will be glad to help you find a church home in your area of residence. Remember: In the final analysis, Christ-like character is the ultimate test of any doctrine and those who teach Bible doctrine should be the best examples of such character (James 3:13-18).

Allow me to pray with you now...

Father God, thank you for loving and accepting my precious brother and/or sister in Christ. Lord, I ask that you grant them your grace to obey, your hope to endure, and your wisdom to discern. Please enable them to let go of the things in their life that would hold them back from becoming all that you have intended them to be. I break the power of the enemy over them now in Jesus' name! Heal their hearts from all wounds and help them to be merciful to others who are ignorant of defiant. Speak peace to their troubled soul and bring healing to any sickness in their body. Lord, place within their heart an undying love for you and an uncompromising conviction for the truth in Christ. Equip them to fulfill their ministry in your kingdom. Prosper them financially and teach them to give cheerfully and generously of their time, talents, and treasures. May they bear much fruit and lead many others to your pathway of life as faithful followers of your Son. In the name of Jesus Christ I pray. Amen.

God bless you my friend. I hope this article has been helpful. Make sure to re-read it every day for the first month of your new life in Christ (2 Cor. 5:17). Now may the Lord Jesus take you gently by the hand and guide you safely into the paths of righteousness for His Name's sake (Psalm 23).

Addendum 9.

Twelve Reasons I Believe in God and in the Gospel of Jesus Christ

-A Response to Bertrand Russell-

1. A Creator is the best answer for questions about the pre-material origin of the universe. (Outward evidence)
2. The historical record of Jesus' life, ministry, death and resurrection ("No mere myth is filled with such life." Einstein, about the Gospel of Jesus Christ)
3. The existence of the moral faculty of conscience, which convicts me of good and evil.
4. The rationality of my mind convinces me to believe. (A Christian worldview makes sense; sin, salvation, God's Kingdom)
5. The scriptural record. (Origin, translation, transmission and preservation)
6. The existence and influence of the Christian Church. (A global force of 2.4 billion people)
7. Bible prophecy fulfillment. (Micah, Psalms, Isaiah)
8. Confirming archeological evidence. (The Bible actually historically happened)
9. The authentic testimony of others I know and respect. (I have seen it in the lives of others)
10. The power of prayer. (Healing, miraculous intervention, supernatural provision)
11. My personal experience. (The truth has set me free and infused my life with meaning)
12. Global comparisons with other religious truth claims. (Beyond a religion; Christianity is a relationship with God by grace through faith in Jesus Christ—the Son of God.

"For God so loved the world that he gave his only Son; that whosoever would believe in him, would not perish, but have eternal life" (John 3:16).

A response to Zeitgeist: the Movie, See "AlwaysBeReady.com"

References

A.C. Bhaktivendanta Swami Prabhupada, *Bhagavad-Gita*. California: Bhaktivedanta Book Trust International, 1989.

Ankerberg, John, and John Weldon. *The Facts on World Religions*. Oregon: Harvest House Publishers, 2004.

Armstrong, Dave. *The Catholic Verses*. New Hampshire: Sophia Institute Press, 2004.

Barker, Kenneth L. and John R. Kohlenberger III, eds., *Zondervan NIV Bible Commentary Volume 2 New Testament*. Grand Rapids: MI. Zondervan Publishing House, 1994.

Barker, Kenneth L. *New International Study Bible*. Grand Rapids: Michigan, The Zondervan Corporation, 2002.

Barnes, Albert. *Barnes' Notes on the Old & New Testaments Vol.1*. 18th edition. Michigan: Baker Book House, 1981.

Behe, Michael. *Darwin's Black Box*. New York: The Free Press, 1996.

Benner, David, and Peter C. Hill. 1999, *Baker Encyclopedia of Psychology & Counseling*. 2nd ed. Michigan: Baker Books, 1992.

Berger, Peter L. *The Desecularization of the World: Resurgent Religion and World Politics*. Michigan: William B. Eerdmans Publishing Company, 1999.

Berkhof, Louis. *Summary of Christian Doctrine*. Grand Rapids: WM. B. Eerdmans Publishing, 1938.

Bickel, Bruce, and Stan Jantz. *World Religions & Cults: A Guide to Spiritual Beliefs*. Oregon: Harvest House Publishers, 2002.

Boice, James M. *Foundations of the Christian faith*. Illinois: InterVarsity Press, 1986.

Borg, Marcus J. *The Heart of Christianity*. San Francisco: Harper Collins Publishers, 2003.

Bruce, F. F. *The New Testament Documents: Are They Reliable?* 5th ed. Illinois: Inter Varsity Press, 1982.

Buddhism and Hinduism: Differences and Similarities (n.d.). Retrieved August 28, 2011, from http://www.thebuddhagarden.com/buddhism-hinduism-difference.htm.

Cairns, Earle, E. *Christianity through the Centuries*. Rev. Ed. Michigan: Zondervan Publishing House, 1967.

Capps, Walter H. *Religious Studies: The Making of a Discipline*. Minneapolis: Fortress Press, 1995.

Conner, Kevin J. *The Church in the New Testament*. Australia: K.J.C. Publications, no date).

Cox, Harvey. *Fire from Heaven*. Massachusetts: Addison-Wesley Publishing Company, 1995.

Cox, William. *Biblical Studies in Final Things*. New Jersey: Presbyterian and Reformed publishing Co., 1966.

Dendo, Kyokai, B. *The Teaching of Buddha*. Tokyo: Kosaido Printing Co., 1966.

D'Aubigne, Merle. *The Life and Times of Martin Luther*. Chicago: Moody Press, 1980.

Esposito, John, Darrel Fasching, and Todd Lewis. *World Religions Today*. New York: Oxford University Press, 2006.

Ellsworth, Robert S., and Barbara A. McGraw. *Many Peoples, Many Faiths: Women and men in the World Religions*. 8th ed. New Jersey: Prentice-Hall, 2005.

Erickson, Millard J. *Contemporary Options in Eschatology*. Michigan: Baker Book House, 5th printing, 1985.

Fee, Gordon, and Douglas Stuart. *How To Read The Bible For All It's Worth*. 2nd ed. Michigan: Zondervan Publishing House, 1993.

Flannery, Austin, O.P. *Vatican Council II: The Conciliar and Post Conciliar Documents*. New York: Costello Publishing Company, 1975.

Flowers, Robert T., and Ronald B. Miller. *Toward Benevolent Neutrality: Church, State, and the Supreme Court*. 5th ed. Texas: The Markham Press Fund of Baylor University Press. 1996.

Geisler, Norman. *Baker Encyclopedia of Christian Apologetics*. 4th ed. Michigan: Baker Books, 2000.

Gore, R. J. *Outline of Systematic Theology*. 5th ed. Indian: Trinity Press, 2003.

Grand Canyon University (n.d.). *A Christian University that Values Spiritual Growth*. Retrieved August 21, 2011, from http://www.gcu.edu/Spiritual-Life/Christian-Position.php.

Grand Canyon University (n.d.). *Statement of Faith: Theological Position*. Retrieved August 20,

Grudem, Wayne. *Systematic Theology: An Introduction to Biblical Doctrine*. Michigan: Zondervan, 1994. See Greg, Steve. *Revelation: Four Views: (A Parallel Commentary)*. Nashville: Thomas Nelson Publ., 1997.

Hanegraaff, Hank. *The Apocalypse Code*. Tennessee: Thomas Nelson Publishing, 2007.

Hopfe, Lewis, and Mark R. Woodward. *Religions of the World*. 8th ed. New Jersey: Prentice Hall, 2001.

House, W. Wayne. *Charts of Christian Theology & Doctrine*. Michigan: Zondervan, 1992.

Islamic Community Center of Tempe. *Islam*. Indiana: The Islamic Book Service, 2007.

Johnson, Phillip. *Darwin On Trial*. 2nd ed. Illinois: Inter Varsity Press, 1993.

Kittel, Gerhard, and Geoffrey W. Gromiley (translator). *Theological Dictionary of the New Testament*. 11th ed. Michigan: WM. B. Eerdmans Publishing, 1981.

Langmuir, Gavin I. *History, Religion, and Antisemitism*. California: University of California Press, 1990.

McDowell, Josh, and Don Stewart. *Handbook of Today's Religions*. California: CCC Publishers, 1992.

McDowell, Josh. Evidence that Demands a Verdict. California: Campus Crusade for Christ International, 1972.

McGrath, Alister C. *The Christian Theology Reader*. 2nd ed. United Kingdom: Blackwell Publishing, 2001.

Milbank, John. *Theology & Social Theory: Beyond Secular Reason*. Massachusetts: Blackwell Publishers Inc., 1990.

Molly, Michael. *Experiencing the World's Religions*. 4th ed. New York: McGraw Hill, 2008.

Montgomery, John W. *Faith Founded on Fact*. 17th ed. Indiana: Trinity Press, 2002.

_____. *The Suicide of Christian Theology*. Indiana: Trinity Press, 1970.

Moser, Paul, and Arnold vander Nat. *Human Knowledge: Classical and Contemporary Approaches*. New York: Oxford University Press, 1995.

Mushaf Al-Madinah An-Nabawiyah. *The Holy Quran*. Saudi Arabia: King Fahd Holy Quran Printing Complex, no date.

Napoleon Bonaparte. (2010). In *Quotes about Jesus*. Retrieved August 20, 2011, from http://www.tentmaker.org/Quotes/jesus-christ.htm.

New American Standard Bible. (1995). La Habra, CA. Lockman Foundation

New Living Translation. (2007). Carol Stream, IL. Tyndale House Publishers, Inc.

Packer, J. I. *Knowing God*. Illinois: InterVarsity Press, 1973.

Paul, R. and Elders, L. *A Miniature Guide to Critical Thinking : Concepts and Tools*. The Foundation for Critical Thinking publishing, 2006.

Peters, B. (2011). *St. Augustine*. Retrieved August 20, 2011, from http://www.liturgy.co.nz/reflection/632b.html.

Prothero, Stephen. *Religious Literacy: What Every American Needs to Know—and Doesn't*. New York: HarperCollins Publishers, 2007.

Reymond, Robert. *A New Systematic Theology of the Christian Faith*. 2nd ed. Tennessee: Thomas Nelson Publishers, 1998.

Routledge. *Concise Routledge Encyclopedia of Philosophy*. New York, 2000.

Richards, Lawrence O. *The Revell Bible Dictionary*, Grand Rapids, MS: Fleming H. Revell, 1990.

Shelley, Bruce L. *The Church in History*. Texas: Word Publishing, 1995

Smith, Joseph Jr. *The Book of Mormon: Another Testament of Jesus Christ*, Utah: The Church of Jesus Christ of Latter Day Saints,1985.

_____. *Journal of Discourse*. Utah: The Church of Jesus Christ of Latter Day Saints Publications, (n.d.)

Smith, Wilfred C. *The Meaning and End of Religion*. Minneapolis: Fortress Press, 1991.

Soccio, Douglas, J.. *Archetypes of Wisdom*. 4th ed. California: Wadsworth/Thomson Learning, 2001.

Stott, John R.W. *The Message of the Sermon on the Mount*. Illinois: Inter-Varsity Press, 1978.

Swartley, Keith E. *Encountering the World of Islam*. Colorado: Authentic Media, 2005.

The Amplified Bible. (1987). La Habra, CA. Lockman Foundation

The World's Smartest Man Believed in Jesus and in God. (n.d.). Retrieved August 20, 2011, from http://gentleislam.com/love/pages/einstein.htm.

Tillich, Paul. *A History of Christian Thought: From Its Judaic and Hellenistic Origin to Existentialism*. New York: Simon & Schuster, 1968.

Today's New International Version. (2005). Biblica. Grand Rapids, MI. Zondervan Publishing.

Tweed, Thomas A., Editor. *Retelling U.S. Religious History*. California: University of California Press, 1997.

Veith, Gene. *Postmodern Times: A Christian Guide to Contemporary Thought and Culture*. Illinois: Good News Publishers, 1994.

Vos, Howard F. *An Introduction to Church History*. 3rd ed. Illinois: Moody Press, 1984.

Nee, Watchman. *The Normal Christian Church Life*. Colorado: International Students Press, 1938/Chinese & 1969/English.

Wayne House. *Charts of the New Testament*. Michigan: Zondervan, 1981.

Wentz, Richard E. *The Culture of Religious Pluralism*. Colorado, Westview Press, 1998.

_____. *Religion in the New World*. Minneapolis: Fortress Press, 1990.

Woodworth, Ron. *For Such a Time as This: Lessons in Discernment for the Thinking Christian*.
    Second edition. Washington: Pleasant Word Publishers, 2009.

_____. *Finding Your Place in God's House*, Arizona: Grace Commission International (GCU) Publishing, 2002.

_____. *Biblical Christianity 101*, Arizona: Grace Commission International (GCU), 2001.

Endnotes

1 My fulltime pastoral ministry tenure was from 1979 to 2004.

2 Isaacson, Walter (2008). *Einstein: His Life and Universe*. New York: Simon and Schuster, pp. 390.

3 Unless otherwise indicated all biblical references are from the New International Version, NIV.

4 In *The Meaning and End of Religion* (1991), Wilfred C. Smith insightfully suggests that perhaps the most adequate definition of religion should embrace the two essential aspects of *cumulative tradition* and *personal faith*.

5 During my tenure as an Adjunct Professor at Mesa Community College (2004-2007), I would make this statement at the beginning of each semester in all of my Major World Religions classes.

6 Norman Geisler concludes an argument against relativism by asserting that the only way a relativist can keep from the dilemma of relativism is to "admit that there are at least some absolute truths...most relativists believe that relativism is absolutely true and that everyone should be a relativist. Therein lays the destructive nature of relativism. The relativist stands on the pinnacle of an absolute truth and wants to relativize everything else." Norman L. Geisler, *The Baker Encyclopedia of Christian Apologetics* (Grand Rapids, MI: Baker Book House Company, 2000), 743-44.

7 Transcendence is defined as a divine attribute, existing above and independently of the material world. Jonathan Z. Smith, ed., *The Harper Collins Dictionary of Religion* (San Francisco: Harper Collins Publishers, 1995), article on "Transcendence," 1086.

8 Falsifiability, or falsificationism, as posited by Karl Popper (1902-94), requires that all scientific propositions must be able to be empirically critiqued. In other words, without the possibility of negation by observation there is no criterion for testability—which is essential in the scientific enterprise. *Concise Routledge Encyclopedia of Philosophy* (New York: Routledge, 2000), 693-94.

9 Summary of theory of truth @ http://instruct.westvalley.edu/lafave/Truth_theories.html.

10 Pre-suppositional truth-claims are a part of every major world religion and all manner of transcendent and metaphysical thinking. As a result, at least in the case of Christianity, it is impossible (at least in our current space-time continuum) to use the

Addendum 9.

mechanisms of scientific inquiry, to either try to prove or disprove the reality/existence of God, the creation of the universe, the incarnation of Jesus Christ, the miracles of Moses and Jesus, the resurrection from the dead, the outpouring of the Holy Spirit at Pentecost, etc. Biblically speaking, the only way for anyone to discern the truth is by faith (See Heb. 11:1, 3, 6). Nevertheless, Old and New Testament claims of truth include references such as Psalm 119:142, 151; John 1:17; 4:24; 8:31-23; 14:6; 17:17; Eph. 4:21; 1 Tim. 3:15; 1 Pet. 1:22, etc.

11 I constructed this definition by expanding the original description in *Religions of the World,Tenth Edition by Hopfe & Woodward* (page 1) and from my own academic and theological research over the past 30 years.

12 See Major Religions @ http://upload.wikimedia.org/wikipedia/en/2/21/Major_religions_2005_pie_small.png.

As a world religions professor, I am aware of the general misgivings about Wikipedia as an academic source due do its original lack of peer-review. However, as a religious studies scholar, I have personally reviewed hundreds of citations on the topic of this text from all kinds of sources. As a result, where articles have been deemed credible (by exhaustive comparison and contrast with other historical documentation), I have elected to use in an academically responsible manner.

13 These numbers have been update in 2013 in the range of a world population of over 7 billion.

14 See article on "Sir Francis Crick, DNA, and ID" @ http://www.cross-currents.com/archives/2005/10/26/sir-francis-crick-dna-and-id/.

14b "History of Civilization" @ http://www.historyworld.net/wrldhis/plaintexthistories.asp?historyid=ab25

15 See "Intelligent Design" article @ http://en.wikipedia.org/wiki/Intelligent_design.

16 See "Definitions of Intelligent Design on the Web" @ http://www.google.com/search?hl=en&rls=SUNA,SUNA:2005-46,SUNA:en&defl=en&q=define:intelligent+design&sa=X&oi=glossary_definition&ct=title.

17 Throughout this document my refusal to capitalize the archenemy of God is predicated on my unwillingness to confer any elevated status to satan (devil, adversary) other than that of a fallen angel whose destiny in the lake of fire is the due penalty of his betrayal (Is. 14; Ezek. 28; Rev. 20:10).

18 This partnership with the demonic can be either knowingly or unknowingly. For instance, renowned psychic-necromancer Jonathan Edwards actually insists that there is no such thing as the devil and that the occult is a perfectly benign spiritual reality. Such a proposition contradicts the teachings of Jesus in John 10:10, where he argues for the malevolent reality of the devil: *"The thief [synonym for the devil] comes to kill, steal, and destroy; but I came that you may have life in abundance."*

19 See "What is the Occult" at http://www.christiananswers.net/q-eden/edn-occult-defn.html.

20 Trinity Seminary Orientation Manual, "How to Write a Critical Paper," Tab 5, (Newburgh, IN), 33.

21 18 See *critical thinking* definition from "Chapter II: The Nature of a Critique." See also the following two websites: Northeast Texas Consortium and the Center for Educational Technologies at

22 http://www.netnet.org/students/student%20glossary.htm, Accessed 29 December 2011&

23 "Critical Thinking" article, http://en.wikipedia.org/wiki/Critical_thinking, Accessed 23 December 28, 2008.

24 See the addendum article called 21st Century Neo-Evangelicalism in this text above.

25 Two of the key verses that evangelicals use to justify the doctrine of inspiration are 2 Tim. 3:16 and 2 Pet. 1:20-21. See James M. Boice, *The Foundations of the Christian Faith*, Part II, The Word of God, (Illinois: Inter Varsity Press, 1986), 38-39 for an excellent exegesis of 2 Tim. 3:16.

26 It is telling that the Chicago Statement of Biblical Inerrancy redefines inerrancy in order to assert that Scripture must necessarily be inerrant. "Scripture is inerrant, not in the sense of being absolutely precise by modern standards, but in the sense of making good its claims and achieving that measure of focused truth at which its authors aimed. The truthfulness of Scripture is not negated by the appearance in it of irregularities of grammar or spelling, phenomenal descriptions of nature, reports of false statements (for example, the lies of Satan), or seeming discrepancies between one passage and another. It is not right to set the so-called "phenomena" of Scripture against the teaching of Scripture about itself. Apparent inconsistencies should not be ignored. Solution of them, where this can be convincingly achieved, will encourage our faith, and where for the present no convincing solution is at hand we shall significantly honor God by trusting His assurance that His Word is true, despite these appearances, and by maintaining our confidence that one day they will be seen to have been illusions." See "Chicago Statement on Biblical Inerrancy" http://www.spurgeon.org/~phil/creeds/chicago.htm, Accessed 30 January 2008. For a more probing analysis of the Inerrancy and Fundamentalism see Christian Fundamentalism @ http://www.ronwoodworth.org/archives-Fundamentalism.aspx Accessed 25 December 2011.

27 T. Norton Sterrett, *How to Understand Your Bible* (Illinois: InterVarsity Press, 1974), p. 49-89.

28 See *Reasons to Believe* article on "Does Old-Earth Creationism Contradict Genesis 1?" http://www.reasons.org/resources/apologetics/other_papers/greg_moore_does_old_earth_creationism_contradict_genesis_1.shtml, Accessed 3 February 2008.

29 See Footnote for Rev. 16:13, Kenneth L. Barker, ed., *New International Version Study Bible* (Michigan: Zondervan, 1984), 1983.

30 There is no separation of church/religion and state in Islam. Rather, the entire way of life is governed by Sharia Law, based on the Quran, which dictates "beliefs, manners, ethics, worship, social relations, commercial transactions, and the justice system." Islamic Community Center, *Islam: The Basics of Islam* (Arizona: Islamic Community Center of Tempe Arizona, 2005), 5.

31 The First Amendment to the Constitution of the United States says, "Congress shall make no law respecting an establishment of religion, or prohibiting the free

exercise thereof." It appears obvious to many that based on this amendment the founders did not want to have an official state religion, nor did they want to have people's religious convictions thwarted. Rather, each one was to be free to worship, or not to worship, according to the dictates of each person's conscience—without either the religious or non-religious having the upper hand in political debate. The enthronement of secularism and/or the marginalization of religious proponents are perceived by many to be an extreme misinterpretation of the intent of the First Amendment.

32 Roman Catholic conflicts over the Protestant Reformation ended with the Peace of Westphalia in 1648—affirming the sovereign right of European nation-states to determine their own religious orientation whether Roman Catholicism, Lutheranism, or Calvinism. The Latin phrase *cuius regio, eius religio*, the "religion of the ruler was the religion of the ruled" was the principle that expressed the result of religious toleration—at least between Catholics, Lutherans, and Calvinists. Rejecting this principle, Anabaptists were either exterminated or relocated to the New World. See http://en.wikipedia.org/wiki/Cuius_regio,_eius_religio

33 See the *Catholic Encyclopedia* @ http://www.newadvent.org/cathen/12700b.htm

34 See article on the Protestant Reformation at http://en.wikipedia.org/wiki/The_Protestant_Reformation

35 "The decline of the political power of the Roman Catholic Church can best be attributed to the Reformation, and the rise of renaissance ideas in Europe, which resulted in independent secular nations—Nation-states free from Catholic Rule and the peace of Westphalia" The Decline of the Political Power of the Catholic Church Http://www.associatedcontent.com/article/345079/the_decline_of_the_political_power.html?ca

36 See Reformation article at http://encarta.msn.com/encyclopedia_761562628_3/Reformation.html#s12

37 See Protestant article @ http://en.wikipedia.org/wiki/Protestant

38 Carl Jung once observed that it was the Protestant devaluation of the confessional booth which actually facilitated the emergence of the "secular" psychiatric profession.

39 Luther was actually hesitant to include the book of James into the canon of Scripture because of its perceived "over-emphasis" on works. See http://en.wikipedia.org/wiki/Biblical_canon#Reformation_Era

40 See Catholic Encyclopedia article on "The Reformation" at http://www.newadvent.org/cathen/12700b.htm. The most important denominations that directly emerged from the Reformation were the Lutherans, Reformed (Calvinists/Presbyterians), Anabaptists, and Anglicans. See also, Woodworth, For Such a Time as This (2009). Article 26: Why are there so many denominations? 26, p. 162-163

41 See New Advent: Catholic Encyclopedia article on "Sect and Sects" at http://www.newadvent.org/cathen/13674a.htm

42 Ibid.

43 See New Advent: Catholic Encyclopedia, article on "Apostolic Succession," http://www.newadvent.org/cathen/01641a.htm, Accessed 28, December 2011.

44 Pope Leo I, was an aristocrat who was Pope of Rome from 440 to 461. He is the first widely known pope, and even sometimes assigned the title "first pope." See Leo the Great at http://orthodoxwiki.org/Leo_the_Great

45 The Eastern Orthodox Church *is* now recognized by the Vatican as possessing apostolic succession—but still lacking in ecclesial authority by failing to embrace the primacy/supremacy of the Bishop of Rome, the Pope.

46 New International Version Study Bible (2002) footnotes on 2 Peter 3, p. 1943-44.

47 See Religion Facts: Persecution in the Early Church at http://www.religionfacts.com/christianity/history/persecution.htm, Accessed 23 December 2011.

48 Democratic weaknesses include secularism, moral corruption, false philosophies and religions, relativism, capitalist selfishness and greed—to name a few.

49 See article on Liberal Christianity at http://en.wikipedia.org/wiki/Liberal_Christianity

50 See article on "Heliocentricism" in Wikipedia at http://en.wikipedia.org/wiki/Heliocentricism, Accessed 19 December 2011.

51 U.S. Geological Survey, See "Radiometric Time Scale," http://pubs.usgs.gov/gip/geotime/radiometric.html, Accessed 19 December 2011. It should be noted that some "young earth creation theorists" argue that the decay rates of radioactive isotopes is inconsistent and therefore unreliable. In response, such theorists are accused of faulty geochronology experimentations, biased results, and a lack of any peer-reviewed publications. http://en.wikipedia.org/wiki/Rapid-decay_theory#Rapid-decay_theory

52 Ibid.

53 See "The Dinosaur Dilemma: And Lessons from Galileo," http://www.ronwoodworth.org/archives-DinosaurDilemma.aspx, Accessed 20 December 2011.

54 The six prosperity gospel preachers and ministries are Paula and Randy White (now divorced), Benny Hinn, Joyce Meyers, Creflo Dollars, Eddie Long (now embroiled in homosexual scandal and impending divorce), Kenneth and Gloria Kopeland.

55 "Prosperity Gospel and the IRS," http://theo2011.blogspot.com/2007/12/prosperity-gospel-and-irs.html, Accessed 15 February 2008.

56 "The New Evangelicals (1990's+)" article, http://www.ronwoodworth.org/archives- MajorReligions3IEvangelicals.aspx, Accessed 20 December 2011.

57 Viva Catholic, "Forbidding Marriage is the doctrine of demons (1 Tim. 4:1-3)." See http://vivacatholic.wordpress.com/2007/09/22/forbidding-marriage-is-the-doctrine-of-demons-1-timothy-41-3

58 Michael Molly, *Experiencing the World's Religions, 4th Edition,* (New York: McGraw Hill, 2008), 296. Note also that secular scholars prefer the designation C.E. for Common Era instead of the usual A.D. for Anno Domini, in the year of our Lord. I use both designations depending upon the religious context about which I am speaking.

59 Christian Reformed theologians see the destruction of the second temple in 70 A.D. as a pivotal prophetic fulfillment of Jesus' warnings in Matthew 24. They

Addendum 9.

also insist that appreciation of the significance of this event will radically affect one's eschatological perspective, especially with regard to the Old Covenant with Israel—which they view as having been ostensibly subsumed within the New Covenant.

60 Yahweh comes from the four Hebrew letters (the tetragrammaton) usually transliterated YHWH or JHVH that form a biblical proper name of God.

61 Muslims insist that the account of Genesis 22 has been corrupted by the Jews and should read that Abraham took his son Ishmael, not Isaac, to be sacrificed on the hill of Marwa, in Saudi Arabia, rather than mount Moriah in Jerusalem. See *The Holy Koran: English translation of the meanings and Commentary* 37:103, p. 1357, Footnote 4101. See also mounthttp://www.religioustolerance.org/isl_feast.htm and http://www.religioustolerance.org/isl_feast.htm.

62 Another major fulfillment of the Abrahamic covenant was that "all of the peoples of the earth" would be blessed through his seed or descendant, which the New Testament (Gal. 3:6-14) identifies as Jesus Christ, the Savior of the world.

63 See the Old Testament book of Judges.

64 See 2 Sam. 7:4-13; Matt. 1:1-2; Acts 2:29-36.

65 See 2 Chronicles 36:15-23. Also see http://en.wikipedia.org/wiki/6th_century_BCE.

66 Antiochus sacrificed a pig on the altar in Jerusalem and dismembered the Jewish men present who refused to eat it. This and many other atrocities were aimed at forcing Greek paganism on the Jews. This pagan desecration of Judaism is what many interpret as the "abomination of desolation" referred to in Dan. 9:27. See http://en.wikipedia.org/wiki/Antiochus_IV_Epiphanes. Also see the Catholic Encyclopedia @ http://www.newadvent.org/cathen/01046a.htm and the Jewish Encyclopedia @ http://www.jewishencyclopedia.com/view.jsp?artid=1589&letter=A.

67 To more clearly identify the time and function of the various "Herodian" rulers (King Herod, Archelaus, Antipas, Phillip, Agrippa I & II, etc.) during the time of the New Testament see http://catholic-resources.org/Bible/History-RomanEra.htm#Herod and http://catholic-resources.org/Bible/History-RomanEra.htm#Herod, Accessed 12 April 2008.

68 Though the second temple was destroyed by Rome in 70 AD, there was a subsequent Jewish revolt that was crushed in 135 A.D.—resulting in the expulsion of Jews from Jerusalem. The Roman Emperor Hadrian then demolished Jerusalem and rebuild a Hellenistic city named "Aelia Capitolina" ("Aelia" in his honor and "Capitolina" because it was to contain a Capitol for the Roman gods) in its place. See http://www.christusrex.org/www1/jhs/TSsptemp.html. Note: The second temple was often referred to as Herod's Temple because of the elaborate renovations King Herod the Great undertook during his reign.

69 As covered more in the text below, the Hebrew Scriptures, or the Tanakh, is the Jewish reference to what Christians call the Old Testament. Such Scriptures comprise the Torah/Law, the Prophets, and the Writings.

70 The Mishnah was the first written record of the oral law as championed by the Pharisees from AD 70-200.

71 "Medieval Period" at http://www.thirteen.org/edonline/teachingheritage/lessons/index_medieval.html, Accessed 22 December 2011.

72 Saladin became famous for having recaptured Jerusalem in 1187, thus signaling the turning point in the history of the Crusades.

73 Moses Maimonides also wrote (in Hebrew) the *Mishnah Torah* in which he summarized the Talmud and other rabbinic writings—even listing the Thirteen (13) Basic Principles of the Jewish Faith. Michael Molly, *Experiencing the World's Religions, 4th Edition* (New York: McGraw Hill, 2008), 323, 329.

74 See also article on Religious Tolerance at http://www.religioustolerance.org/chr_cru1.htm, Accessed 6 April 2008.

75 The Gnostic idea of "emanation" is the belief that the origination of the world was by "a series of hierarchically descending radiations from the Godhead through intermediate stages to matter." See http://mw1.merriam-webster.com/dictionary/emanation, Accessed 22 December 2011. The most famous book of the Kabbalah is the *Zohar* ("splendor"). At its height Kabbalahism was considered even more authoritative than the Talmud.

76 The transposing of words into numbers is called "gematria" and is related to the mathematical branch of geometry. See also http://www.straightdope.com/mailbag/mbiblecode.html for a basic refutation of the Bible Code. It is interesting that the recent preoccupation with a "Bible Code" is actually historically associated with Jewish mysticism and, in the author's opinion, is to be disqualified as a legitimate way to interpret the Bible.

77 Note that that Spanish Inquisition led to the expulsion of the Jews in 1492—on the same month when Columbus was commissioned to undertake his historic expedition leading to the "discovery" of the Americas. See http://www.jewishvirtuallibrary.org/jsource/Judaism/expulsion.html.

78 Referred to as the "third Moses" after Moses, the biblical lawgiver, and the medieval Moses Maimonides.

79 The following three definitions of the main branches of Judaism are drawn in large part from entries in the Merriam-Webster Online Dictionary @ http://www.m-w.com/home.htm. Also, the idea for the chart came from *Experiencing the World's Religions, 4th Edition*, p. 339.

80 See the U.S. Department of State article on "Roadmap for Peace in the Middle East: Israeli/Palestinian Reciprocal Action, Quartet Support @ http://www.state.gov/r/pa/ei/rls/22520.htm, Accessed 6 April 2008.

81 Dispensationalism is a "method of interpreting the Bible that divides history into separate eras or 'dispensations' in which God deals with man in a distinctive way...A leading feature of dispensationalism is the sharp division between ethnic Israel and the church of Jesus Christ." For instance, dispensationalists maintain two separate prophetic plans for Israel and the Church—emphasizing a two-phase rapture of the Church; followed by a 7-year tribulation period ending with a second Jewish holocaust (anti-Christ, 666); followed by the Second Coming of Christ; followed by a 1,000 year "millennium kingdom" (third temple); followed by the final judgment and new creation. Dispensationalists arrive at most all of these conclusions by insisting that the Book of Revelation was written well after 70 A.D. (around 95 AD). This later date enables them to avoid the apparent conflict with their "prophecy charts" and the seminal importance of the destruction of the second temple and the disper-

sion of the Jews as historically traced by this article. For to suggest a date earlier than 70 AD opens the real possibility that much of Jesus' "end-time prophecies," including those of the Book of Revelation, might well have been directed toward the cataclysmic events that changed the history of Judaism forever. Hence, evangelical scholars are becoming increasingly more convinced that the dispensational view, though containing a measure of interpretive justification, is nevertheless lacking when it comes to attributing sufficient historical and prophetic weight to those outcomes marked by the prophetic warnings of the New Testament. See http://www.google.com/search?hl=en&rls=SUNA,SUNA:2005-46,SUNA:en&defl=en&q=define:Dispensationalism&sa=X&oi=glossary_definition&ct=title. Also see *The Apocalypse Code* (2007) by Hank Hanegraaff and "The New Evangelicals" at http://www.ronwoodworth.org/archives-MajorReligions3IEvangelicals.aspx. One of the most helpful and balanced texts on Bible Prophecy is by Steve Greg's *Revelation: Four Views (A Parallel Commentary)*. (Nashville: Thomas Nelson Publ., 1997).

82 See "The Hebrew Scriptures and the Old Testament" at http://www.bibles.com/brcpages/thehebrewscriptures, Accessed 8 April 2008.

83 Apocrypha means "hidden" and generally implies to non-canonical Old Testament books as opposed to deuterocanonical which means "belonging to the second canon." Though such canonical distinctions exist in Catholic and Orthodox theology, Protestants have rejected both the Apocrypha and Deuterocanonical books as non-canonical.

84 See John 3:16 and Matt. 1:16 respectively.

85 See Catholic doctrinal article on " The Blessed Trinity" at http://www.newadvent.org/cathen/15047a.htm, Accessed 12 April 2008.

86 Old Testament References: Gen. 1:26-27 (plural form); Deut. 6:4 (composite ref); Is. 9:6 (Son/Mighty God); Is. 63:10 (personality of Holy Spirit). See http://www.biblicalresources.info/pages/ot1/trinityot.html, Accessed 23 December 2011. New Testament References of Father, Son and Holy Spirit: Matt. 3:16-17; 28:19; 2 Cor. 13:14; Luke 1:35; Heb. 9:14.

87 See The DaVinci Code: A Christian Response Part 2: Answering the Attacks, page 3 at http://www.ronwoodworth.org/Download/Articles/The%20Da%20Vinci%20Code%20A%20Christian%20Response%20Part%202.pdf, Accessed 16 April 2008.

88 See Judaism 101, "Moshiach: The Messiah" at http://www.jewfaq.org/moshiach.htm & Jews for Judaism, "Messiah: The Criteria" at http://www.jewsforjudaism.org/jews-jesus/jews-jesus-index.html, Accessed 20 December 2011.

89 See "The Genealogy of Jesus: Focusing on His Family Tree from the Gospels of Matthew & Luke" at http://www.zianet.com/maxey/reflx231.htm, Accessed 20 December 2011.

90 See All About the Truth, "Messianic Prophecy" at http://www.allabouttruth.org/messianic-prophecy.htm, Accessed 23 December 2011.

91 See over 300 Messianic prophecies filled in Jesus Christ listed at http://www.jesus-is-lord.com/messiah.htm, Accessed 23 December 2011.

92 The Catholic Encyclopedia, Article on "Kingdom of God" at http://www.newadvent.org/cathen/08646a.htm, Accessed 21 December 2011.

93 The Kingdom of God and the Kingdom of Heaven are synonymous in the New Testament. The main reason for the different designation is because the Book of Matthew was written to a Jewish audience—who may have been offended by an inappropriate the use of God's Name (Ex. 20:7). Hence, Matthew used the term *Kingdom of Heaven*, whereas Mark, writing to a predominately Gentile audience used the phrase *Kingdom of God*.

94 The Jewish Encyclopedia, Article on "Kingdom of God" at http://www.jewishencyclopedia.com/view.jsp?artid=225&letter=K&search=kingdom%20of%20God, Accessed 26 December 2011.

95 See Voices of Wisdom at http://books.google.com/books?id=Kpr2e-QobwdkC&pg=PA523&lpg=PA523&dq=in+the+world+to+come+there+is+neither+eating+nor+drinking+nor+procreation&source=web&ots=EUDt-dWQ8Lz&sig=4nTnP7O6_Z03F2DXsA9SvHNlQ7I&hl=en, Accessed 26 December 2011.

96 Roman Catholics teach transubstantiation, where the bread and wine are literally transformed into the physical presence of Christ. Lutherans argue for consubstantiation, where the presence of Christ is manifest along with the communion elements but not physically evident within them. Symbolism maintains that the communion elements are wholly symbolic of the crucifixion of Jesus without regard to the sacramental idea of the real presence of Christ.

97 See Acts 2:41, 47; 5:14; 6:1, 7; 9:31; 11:21; 21:20.

98 See Acts 4:1, 3; 5:17, 41; 7:1; 8:1.

99 See Acts 2:43; 4:33; 5:12-16.

100 Throughout the Middle Ages in Europe there was full-scale Jewish persecution in many places, with blood libels, expulsions, forced conversions and massacres. See article on "Jews in the Middle Ages" at http://en.wikipedia.org/wiki/Jews_in_the_Middle_Ages, Accessed 26 December 2011.

101 *Nostra Aetate, Declaration on the Relation of the Church to Non-Christian Religions*. Second Vatican Council, p. 4 at http://www.ewtn.com/library/COUNCILS/v2non.htm, Accessed 23 December 2011.

102 Luther, Martin. *On the Jews and Their Lies*, 154, 167, 229, cited in Michael, Robert. *HolyHatred: Christianity, Antisemitism, and the Holocaust*. (New York: Palgrave Macmillan, 2006), 111.

103 See article "On the Jews and their Lies" at http://en.wikipedia.org/wiki/On_the_Jews_and_Their_Lies#cite_note-0#cite_note-0

104 Ibid.

105 Christians and Jews: A Declaration of the Lutheran Church of Bavaria, November 24, 1998, also printed in *Freiburger Rundbrief*, 6:3 (1999), p.191-197 at http://www.jcrelations.net/en/?item=993, Accessed 28 December 2011.

106 See article "Examples of anti-Semitism sentiment in the Arab and Muslim World" at http://www.intelligence.org.il/eng/sib/4_04/as_egypt.htm, Accessed 28 December 2011.

107 5,313,800 or 40.6% of Jews live in Israel whereas 5,275,000 or 40.3% of Jews live in the United States. The next nearest Jewish population center is in France where 491,500 or just 3.8% of Jews live. See "The Jewish Population of the World"

Addendum 9.

at http://www.jewishvirtuallibrary.org/jsource/Judaism/jewpop.html, Accessed 28 December 2011.

108 See Pew Global Attitudes Project on "Islamic Extremism: Common Concern for Muslim and Western Publics" at http://pewglobal.org/reports/display.php?ReportID=248, Accessed 28 December 2011.

109 Note: all of these "facts" are approximations based on extensive reading of diverse sources as indicated in the bibliography of this research document.

110 A.D. signifies a Christian-Gregorian meaning of "in the year of our Lord," whereas C.E. generally means "the common era," which is preferred by secular writers.

111 Quran 5:3. Note all references in the Quran can be viewed in an online text at http://www.al-sunnah.com/call_to_islam/quran/pickthall/surah47.html.

112 See "Sunni's Outnumber Catholics" at http://blog.beliefnet.com/news/2008/03/muslims- more-numerous-than-cat.php, Accessed 28 December 2011.

113 "Why do Jews and Arabs/Muslims hate each other?" at http://www.gotquestions.org/Jews-Arabs.html, Accessed 28 December 2011.

114 Mushaf Al-Madinah, *The Holy Koran: English translation of the meanings and Commentary.* (King Fahd Holy Quran Printing Complex, not dated), Surah 37:99-107, p.1355-58, Footnotes 4095-4103.

115 "The Islamic Calendar" at http://webexhibits.org/calendars/calendar-islamic.html. Accessed 29 December 2011.

116 Ibid.

117 "Who Was Muhammad" at http://www.666soon.com/who_was_muhammad.htm, Accessed 29 December 2011.

118 "Khadijah" at http://www.rasoulallah.net/subject_en.asp?hit=1&parent_id=5&sub_id=247,

119 Ibid.

120 "Aisha" at http://mb-soft.com/believe/txh/aisha.htm, Accessed 15 April 2008.

121 "Muhammad's wives" at http://en.wikipedia.org/wiki/Muhammad's_wives#cite_note-4 Accessed 29 December 2011.

122 John Esposito et al, *World Religions Today, 2nd ed.*, (New York: Oxford University Press, 2006), p. 206.

123 Muslim's themselves believe that Muhammad was illiterate, which proves that the Koran was indeed a genuine miracle. After all, how could an illiterate man/prophet produce such a vast literary work without the direct intervention of God/Allah. See "Muhammad and Miracles" at http://www.answering-islam.org/Responses/Azmy/mhd_miracles.htm

124

125 "Who Wrote the Quran" at http://wiki.answers.com/Q/Who_wrote_the_Koran Accessed, 29 December 2011.

126 "Call to Islam: Translation to the Quran" at http://www.al-sunnah.com/call_to_islam/quran/pickthall/introduction_to_the_koran.html, Accessed 29 December 2011.

127 Joseph Smith Jr., *The Book of Mormon: Another Testament of Jesus Christ*, (Utah: The Church of Jesus Christ of Latter Day Saints,1985), Introduction,

128 "History of Muhammad" at http://www.historyworld.net/wrldhis/PlainTextHistories.asp?historyid=aa55, Accessed 29 December 2011.

129 "Banu Qurayza" at http://en.wikipedia.org/wiki/Banu_Qurayza, Accessed 29 December 2011.

130 "History of Muhammad" at http://www.historyworld.net/wrldhis/PlainTextHistories.asp?historyid=aa55, Accessed 29 December 2011.

131 "The Last Sermon of Prophet Muhammad" at http://www.everything2.com/index.pl?node=The%20Last%20Sermon%20of%20Prophet%20Muhammad, Accessed 29 December 2011.

132 "The History of Islam" at http://www.barkati.net/english/#07, Accessed 29 December 2011.

133 "Umayyad" at http://en.wikipedia.org/wiki/Umayyad. Accessed 29 December 2011.

134 "Islam" at http://en.wikipedia.org/wiki/Islam, Accessed 29 December 2011.

135 "Reconquista" at http://www.britannica.com/eb/article-9062907/Reconquista. Accessed 29 December 2011.

136 "Partitioning of the Ottoman Empire" at http://en.wikipedia.org/wiki/Partitioning_of_the_Ottoman_Empire, Accessed 37 December 2011.

137 "Muslim History" at http://en.wikipedia.org/wiki/Muslim_history, Accessed 7 May 2008.

138 PBS Frontline article on Wahabbism at http://www.pbs.org/wgbh/pages/frontline/shows/saudi/analyses/wahhabism.html, Accessed 29 December 2011.

139 The author heard these death chants on the evening news in the US during the ordeal.

140 "Caricatures and stereotypes that disguise the truth" at http://www.voltairenet.org/article136203.html, Accessed 29 December 2011.

141 Viktor Frankl is the author of *Man's Search for Meaning* where he challenges Abraham Maslow's *Hierarchy of Needs*. Frankl's challenge is that rather than accept Maslow's call to self-actualization; the ultimate meaning in life is to transcend oneself by serving others. This idea of self-transcendence is a direct corollary to the New Testament call of Jesus Christ to deny oneself in the loving service of God and others.

142 *The Declaration of Independence* at http://www.ushistory.org/declaration/document/index.htm, Accessed 12 May 2008.

143 "Israel and Palestine: A Brief History" at http://www.mideastweb.org/briefhistory.htm, Accessed 29 December 2011.

144 "A brief history of OPEC" at http://www.opec.org/aboutus/history/history.htm, Accessed December 30 2011.

145 Time Magazine blog on "The Middle East: American's it's okay to bomb Iran" at http://time-blog.com/middle_east/2007/11/re_americans_its_ok_to_bomb_ir.html#comment-446168, Accessed 30 December 2011.

146 "The Hadith of Gabriel" at http://www.salaam.co.uk/themeofthemonth/june02_index.php?l=5, Accessed 30 December 2011.

147 "Islam—It's Creed" at http://www.apologeticsindex.org/607-islam-creed, Accessed 30 December 2011.

Addendum 9.

148 "Allah the Moon-God" at http://www.biblebelievers.org.au/moongod.htm, Accessed 30 December 2011.

149 See Deut. 4:19;17:3; 2 Kings. 21:3,5; 23:5; Jer. 8:2; 19:13; Zeph. 1:5.

150 "Sufism" at http://www.google.com/search?hl=en&rls=SUNA,SUNA:2005-46,SUNA:en&defl=en&q=define:Sufism&sa=X&oi=glossary_definition&ct=title, Accessed 30 December 2011.

151 Shia Muslims can combine their prayers into three times per day: morning, afternoon, and evening. See http://www.bbc.co.uk/religion/religions/islam/subdivisions/sunnishia_4.shtml, Accessed 30 December 2011.

152 "How to Perform Wudu: Islamic Ritual Ablution" at http://muslim-canada.org/wudu.html, Accessed 28 December 2011.

153 USA Today at Q&A on Islam and Arab-Americans at http://www.usatoday.com/news/world/islam.htm & http://www.islamfortoday.com/7conditions.htm, Accessed 30 December 2011.

154 In 1Corinthians 11:1-16 Paul makes an argument for women wearing head coverings—especially in public worship. However, most Christian scholars acknowledge that this was more of a matter of a cultural custom than a universal mandate for all future generations. This cultural precondition to women wearing head coverings is specifically referenced in 1 Cor. 11:16, where Paul's defense of the practices is an appeal to the conventional norms of the day as demonstrated in the churches over which he had apostolic authority. One could also read into this apostolic injunction a Gentile need for sensitivity to the historic-biblical-cultural norms of Judaism, which was a considerable concern among the leadership of the early church. (Refer to the decision of the Jerusalem Council in Act 15:19-21 and the circumcision of Timothy in Acts 16:1-3)

155 "The financial obligation upon Muslims" at http://www.islam101.com/dawah/pillars.html, Accessed 25 December 2011.

156 See Malachi 3:8-10 where the Lord/Yahweh rebukes the entire nation of Israel for neglecting the law of tithing and thus "robbing God."

157 "Fasting" at http://www.islamicarchitecture.org/islam/fasting.html, Accessed 28 December 2011.

158 Ibid.

159 "The Night of Power" at http://www.submission.org/ramadan/nightpower.html, Accessed 28 December 2011.

160 Note that even though the Quran does not specifically here that Abraham's son was Ishmael nevertheless all Muslim scholars agree that is must be so since he was the "first born." It is further argued that since Isaac is mentioned immediately after this section, that the only other son of Abraham to whom the story could possibly indicate would be Ishmael.

161 "164 Jihad Verses in the Koran" at http://www.answering-islam.org/Quran/Themes/jihad_passages.html, Accessed 30 December 2011.

162 Rueven Firestone, *Jihad: The Origin of Holy War in Islam*, (England: Oxford University Press, 1999), 17. Also see "What is Jihad" at http://www.answerbag.com/q_view/156250. Accessed 30 December 2011.

163 "The Islamic Concept of a Political Order" at http://www.geocities.com/khyber007/islpol.html, Accessed 27 December 2011.

164 "Just War Doctrine" at http://www.catholic.com/library/Just_war_Doctrine_1.asp, Accessed 31 December 2011.

165 See Col. 2:15; 55-56.

166 An average of dozens of the comparative world religion dates of origin show that Hinduism and Judaism are the oldest religions dating from around the time of the Jewish patriarch Abraham about 2,000 BCE and the Aryan migration to India around 2,500 BCE, respectively.

167 "Indus-Sarasvati Civilization" (pre-Aryans) at http://www.aarweb.org/syllabus/syllabi/g/gier/306/prearyan.htm, Accessed 14 May 2008.

168 "Indian Caste System" especially the "social historical theory" at http://www.hotathrandom.com/IndianCaste.htm, Accessed 30 December 2011.

169 Around 1500 BCE.

170 "Mantras" at http://www.sanatansociety.org/indian_music_and_mantras/sounds_of_tantra_mantras.htm, Accessed 30 December 2011.

171 See Acts 2:1-4, 8:14-17; 9:17-18, 10:44-48; 11:15-18; 19:1-7; 1 Cor. 12-14.

172 In *Fire from Heaven: The Rise of Pentecostal Spirituality and the Reshaping of Religion in the 21st Century*, Harvard Professor Harvey Cox has indicated that there are over 500 million Christians worldwide who have personally experienced the "Pentecostal" infilling of the Holy Spirit as in the days of the New Testament.

173 The interpretation of tongues can be given by either the one who speaks in a tongue or to others present who have the spiritual gift of interpretation of tongues. See 1 Cor. 12:10; 14:13, 27.

174 In 1 Cor. 14 Paul shows the distinction and yet compatibility between speaking in tongues and the gift of prophecy. Tongues are spoken in spiritual languages whereas prophecy is spoken in discernable languages. The combination of tongues with the interpretation has the same effect as prophesy.

175 The baptism in the Holy Spirit was a specific "promise of the Father," which would be poured out upon all believers on behalf of Jesus Christ and his kingdom mission on earth. See Luke 24:46-49; Acts 2:33, 39; 1:4-5, 8.

176 Classical Hinduism deities included *Indra, Crtra, Agni, Varnuna*, etc. The three major post-classical deities are *Brahma, Shiva, and Vishnu*.

177 The Vedic language was the predecessor of early Sanskrit.

178 "Essays on Brahman" at http://www.hinduwebsite.com/brahmanmain.asp, Accessed 30 December 2011.

179 See 1 John 1:3, Acts 2:42-48, and Matt. 28:18-20.

180 "The Heart of Hinduism" at http://hinduism.iskcon.com/concepts/106.htm. Accessed 30 December 2011.

181 "Eternal Progression, Part 1" at http://www.angelfire.com/ms/seanie/mormon/adam_god.html. Accessed 30 December 2011.

182 Latter Day Saints Publications, Joseph Smith Jr., Journal of Discourse 6:1-11.

183 Lorenzo Snow, Mormon President, (1898-1901), Ibid.

184 "Perspectives on Reality: An Introduction to the Philosophy of Hinduism," at http://books.google.com/books?id=8dRZ4E-qgz8C&pg=PA157&lpg=PA157&d-

Addendum 9.

q=countless+transmigrations&source=web&ots=DuTnnHpKlH&sig=FjRSaWfze-1hVvxjxFljsX09TjnM&hl=en, Accessed 30 December 2011.

185 See John 5:24-29 regarding the authority the Father gave the Son to render judgment to humanity. Such judgment will result for those who have done gone, in a resurrection to life—or, for those who have done evil, in a resurrection to condemnation.

186 See Matt. 25:46 and Rev. 20:11-15 for the "fiery" finality of eternal judgment.

187 "Karma Yoga" by Sri Swami Sivananda at http://www.dlshq.org/teachings/karmayoga.htm, Accessed 31 December 2011.

188 Animals and young children are generally not karmic bound because of their incapacity to discriminate between right and wrong. See http://en.wikipedia.org/wiki/Karma_in_Hinduism.

189 People are justified by faith alone, but not by a faith that is alone. (John Murray) at http://www.powerofchange.org/blog/docs/twelvetruths/leaderguides/Ltruth7justification.pdf, Accessed 30 December 2011.

190 See "Indian leader likens caste system to apartheid regime" at http://www.guardian.co.uk/world/2006/dec/28/india.mainsection, Accessed 30 December 2011.

191 Woodworth, For Such a Time as This (2007), p. 40 and 1 John 2:15-17.

192 "Hinduism asceticism" at http://www.oldandsold.com/articles25/hindu-15.shtml, Accessed 30 December 2011.

193 "Moksha: Liberation/Salvation" at http://hinduism.iskcon.com/concepts/106.htm, Accessed 30 December 2011.

194 See Rom. 6:1-14 and 8:1-14.

195 "Hearing about the Lord" comes through listening to stories, singing, and chanting.

196 "Glorifying the Lord" means to describe God's attractive features.

197 "Remembering the Lord" involves meditation on God's form, activities, and personality.

198 The Bhagavad Gita (lit. "Song of the Blessed Lord"—Krishna) is an epic Sanskrit poem within the Upanishads regarded by many as the most important text in Hindu philosophy.

199 Jesus declared that the entire Law and Prophets could be essentially reduced to the two commandments: *"Love the Lord your God with all of your heart and with all your soul and with all your mind... [and to] Love your neighbor as yourself."* (Matt. 2:37-40).

200 The "10 Avatars of Vishnu" at http://hinduism.about.com/od/godsgoddesses/a/10avatars.htm, Accessed 30 December 2011.

201 The "young" in this context are those who are weak in their conscience by virtue of their spiritual immaturity.

202 Buddha's names are generally Siddhartha Gautama or Gautama Buddha.

203 Buddha's son was named *Rahula* meaning "fetter" and indicates that Siddhartha had come to see his family as an impediment to the quest for spiritual liberation. After his enlightenment, Buddha did return to convert his family to Buddhism, but thereafter lived as a celibate monk for the rest of his life.

204 The Mahanyanans pejoratively named the Theravadans the "lesser vehicle" because it was too restrictively orthodox and exclusive for many to follow.

205 "Religious Facts: Theravada Buddhism" at http://www.religionfacts.com/buddhism/sects/theravada.htm, Accessed 30 December 2011.

206 "Religious Facts: Mahayana Buddhism" at http://www.religionfacts.com/buddhism/sects/mahayana.htm, Accessed 30 December 2011.

207 Vedanta philosophical monism is most popularized in the later Vedic literature of the Upanishads including especially the Bhagavad Gita.

208 John L. Esposito et al, *World Religions Today, second edition*, (Oxford: Oxford University Press, 2006), p. 342.

209 Buddhism views the primary problem of the human condition not as sin in need of a sacrificial atonement but as suffering due to craving and ignorance thus requiring knowledge and self-control.

210 "Four Noble Truths" at http://en.wikipedia.org/wiki/Four_Noble_Truths#cite_note-BodhiDhammacakka-7. Quoted from Dhammacakkappavattana Sutta (SN 56.11), trans. Bodhi (2000), pp. 1843-47,

211 Ibid.

212 Ibid.

213 Ibid.

214 "Principles of Christian Suffering" at http://www.ministryhealth.net/mh_articles/016_principles_of_suffering_outline.html, Accessed 31 December 2011.

215 "Nirvana" Online Etymology Dictionary at http://www.etymonline.com/index.php?term=nirvana, Accessed 31 December 2011.

216 Indian thought views samsara as a curse whereby countless lives of suffering must be endured in order to "burn out" the negative karmaic consequences of one's unenlightened existence. See Hopfe and Woodward, 2007, p. 81.

217 This internal power is the gift of the Holy Spirit, who thereafter takes up his residence in the life of every believer who has received Christ Jesus as Lord. See Acts 1:8 and Rom. 8:10-12.

218 God's purpose is his will, which the believer must seek as the first priority of his life. See Matt. 6:33; Rom. 12:2; 1 John 2:17.

219 See Religion in China at http://en.wikipedia.org/wiki/Religion_in_China

220 Feudalism was the dominant social system in medieval Europe, in which land granted by the Crown to the nobility was in turn held by vassals. A vassal was a person who held land from a feudal lord and received protection in return for homage and allegiance. In turn, the land a vassal held in trust was actually worked by peasants, with each group owing homage and service to that above it. (See Encyclopedia.com & The Free Dictionary by Farlex)

221 The legalists theory of leadership was similar to Machiavellianism, which was the political doctrine of Machiavelli (1626), which denies the relevance of morality in political affairs and holds that craft and deceit are justified in pursuing and maintaining political power. (Online Dictionary by Farlex)

222 CE stands for the Common Era and is used by secular scholars who were/are averse to using the term AD, which means in the year of our Lord (lit. *anno domini*). Interestingly, Jews mark the beginning of their calendar during their Exodus from

Addendum 9.

Egyptian bondage under Moses' leadership (Ex. 12:2). Whereas, Muslims begin their calendar in the year Hijrah (622 AD) when Muhammad fled from Mecca to Medina.

223 Information on the 20th Century in China can be seen at http://en.wikipedia.org/wiki/China

224 Most scholars now doubt that Lao Tzsu was ever a person. Rather, the writings attributed to his name are probably a composite of many writers, scholars, and sages over hundreds of years.

225 See the Interpretation and Themes of Tao Te Ching at http://history.cultural-china.com/en/180H8541H13150.html.

226 How Confucian was Confucius? at http://www.chinatravel.net/forum/How-Confucian-was-Confucius/1782.html.

227 I Ching and the Analects of Confucius at http://www.world-religions-professor.com/iching.html.

228 I Ching's Influence at http://en.wikipedia.org/wiki/I_Ching%27s_influence.

229 Confucianism at http://library.thinkquest.org/12255/temple/confucianism.html & Oriental Philosophy: The Main Concepts in Confucianism at http://philosophy.lander.edu/oriental/main.html.

230 See Chinese Philosophy at http://en.wikipedia.org/wiki/Chinese_philosophy

231 The New Culture Movement at http://history.cultural-china.com/en/34History7207.html

232 The communist takeover of China at COMMUNISTS TAKE OVER CHINA@ http://factsanddetails.com/china.php?itemid=74&catid=2&subcatid=6]

233 Isaacson, Walter (2008). *Einstein: His Life and Universe*. New York: Simon and Schuster, p. 390.

234 Albert Einstein, *"Science, Philosophy and Religion: a Symposium", 1941 US (German-born) physicist (1879 – 1955)*.

235 Hitchens, Christopher. (2007). "God Is Not Great", Hachette Book Group. Also, Dawkins, Richard. (2006) "The God Delusion", First Mariner Books.

236 The Baltimore Sun, May 13, 2012; "Ben Carson and the evolution-morality debate." Reporter: Richard Weikart. Emory university faculty and students express dismay that their commencement speaker does not toe the ideological line when it comes to evolutionary biology. Renowned Johns Hopkins neurosurgeon, Dr. Ben Carson, does not believe in the full implications of evolutionary theory and some suggest he should not be allowed to speak at a university commencement.

237 Dr. Michael Behe has been among those suggesting the power of evolution as modernly conceived has limits that ought to be explored through more research. He suggests the forces ascribed to evolution comport well with actual field observations of biological changes at the species and genus levels of the traditional classification scheme but are ill-equipped and even unable to bring about changes at higher levels. Behe, Michael (2007). *The Edge of Evolution; The Search for the Limits of Evolution*. New York: The Free Press.

238 Discovery Institute, see website http://www.dissentfromdarwin.org. Now, with an estimated 40,000 to 50,000 scientists in the United States, we are not saying that 816 dissenters to classic Darwinism is relevant based on numbers. We are

pointing out that not everyone sees the present evidence as incontrovertible as some writers assert.

239 *"Paleoanthropologist Richard Leakey predicts end is near on debate over evolution."* Associated Press and Washington Post, May 26, 2012.

240 Ross, Hugh. (2011). *"Hidden Treasures in the Book of Job; How the oldest book in the Bible answers today's scientific questions"*, Baker Books.

241 Hamm, Ken; www.answersingenesis.org.

242 Gish, Duane; Institute for Creation Research, www.icr.org.

243 Eldredge, Niles and S. J. Gould (1972). "Punctuated equilibria: an alternative to phyletic gradualism" In T.J.M. Schopf, ed., *Models in Paleobiology*. San Francisco: Freeman Cooper. pp. 82-115. Reprinted in N. Eldredge *Time frames*. Princeton: Princeton Univ. Press, 1985, pp. 193-223.

244 Gould, Stephen Jay (2002). *Rocks of Ages: Science and Religion in the Fullness of Life*. New York: Ballantine Books.

245 Behe, Michael (1996). *Darwin's Black Box; The biochemical challenge to evolution"*. New York: The Free Press.

246 Collins, Francis S. (2006). *The Language of God: A Scientist Presents Evidence for Belief*. New York: The Free Press.

247 Provine, William B. (1994). Writing in "Origins Research."

248 Hawking, Stephen and Mlodinow, Leonard. (2010). *"The Grand Design"*, Bantam Books.

249 Ross, Hugh. (2004). *"A Matter of Days"*, NavPress.

250 Dyson, Freeman. (1979). *"Disturbing the Universe"*, New York, Basic Books.

251 Gonzalez, Guillermo and Richards, Jay W. (2004). *The Privileged Planet: How our place in the cosmos is designed for discovery*. Washington, D.C., Regnery Publishing, Inc. Also, the reader should consider...Ward, Peter and Brownlee, Donald. (2004) *"Rare Earth; Why complex life is uncommon in the universe"*, Copernicus Books. Also...Ross, Hugh. (2001). *"The Creator and the Cosmos"*, NavPress, 3rd ed.

252 Colson, Charles and Pearson, Nancy. (1999). *How Now Shall We Live"*. Pp. 71-79, Tyndale House. Also... Ross, Hugh and Rana, Fazale. (2004) *"The Origins of Life"*. NavPress.

253 Rana, Fazale. (2011). *"Creating Life In The Lab; How new discoveries in synthetic biology make a case for the creator"*. Baker Books.

254 To research deeper, the reader can consider the following books. Certain of our cited works may contain portions and conclusions with which we don't agree but many good points await the reader. These readable works contain further cross-references to detailed studies and journals to go even further..."*No Free Lunch; Why Specified Complexity Cannot Be Purchased Without Intelligence"* by William A. Dembski, Rowman and Littlefield, 2002; *"The Icons of Evolution"* by Jonathan Wells, Regnery Publishing, 2000.

255 Behe, Michael. (2007). *"The Edge of Evolution; The search for the limits of Darwinism"*. Free Press.

256 Meyer, Stephen C. (2009). *"The Signature in the Cell; DNA and the evidence for intelligent design"*. HarperCollins.

Addendum 9.

257 The reader may learn more about the ENCODE Consortium results at the National Human Genome Research Institute at http://www.genome.gov/10005107.

258 Rana, Fazale. (2005). *"Who Was Adam? A creation model approach to the origin of man"*. NavPress.

259 The assertion by Young-Earth Creationists that the Bible record mandates an earth and universe of only a few thousands of years of age is, perhaps, the area where the greatest amount of criticism is directed by non-creationists. Over the last 40 years the volume of evidence coming from multiple lines of inquiry as to the billions of year's age of the earth has continually strengthened while the evidences put forth for the thousands of year age have continually weakened. While some might argue the point, we know of no scientist who has independently arrived at a thousands of year age for the earth from the evidence alone, without having a pre-conceived notion that the Bible record requires such a belief. It is no wonder that the effort to have creationism taught in public schools as a *scientific* alternative to evolution has failed in every court case when it involves the young-earth creation model. At the other end of the spectrum are the assertions of Darwinism and, also, the old-earth/old universe Theistic Evolutionists. These theories need trillions and, even, quadrillions of years to work, if they work at all. Chemical evolution of life's proteins would have to have occurred prior to biological evolution. While the power of natural selection is invoked to help biological evolution overcome probability obstacles, natural selection does not exist in the pre-biotic world. Only random encounters and chance collisions of atoms and molecules can be invoked as a factor to change non-living chemicals into self-replicating proteins needed to build cells and life. The mathematical possibility of the successful random chance assemblage of even one 250 unit long protein chain is essentially zero in anywhere at any time in the 14 billion year history of the universe. At least trillions, quadrillions or more years would be needed to have a non-zero chance of the self-assemblage of one long-chain protein. Ross, Hugh. (2008). *"Why The Universe Is The Way It Is"*. Baker Books.

260 Hawking, Stephen and Mlodinow, Leonard. (2010). *"The Grand Design"*, Bantam Books.

261 The modern scientific method had its birth in the scripturally-influenced society of Europe. The Bible presented a worldview that truth was knowable and that nature contained and revealed truth. The worldview of Eastern religions that the world around us is an illusion did not lead naturally to studying and testing Nature to find truth. Out of the biblical worldview came the scientific method...a way of trying minimize bias and eliminate as many conflicting interpretations of the results of scientific experiments as possible. Two key ingredients before starting any experiment were to identify the initial conditions and the perspective of the observer. If the experiment heated up the room, you needed to know what temperature existed before the experiment was conducted (initial conditions). If the observer recorded the flash of light the experiment created but did not note the flash of heat, he was not lying if you understood that he had been standing outside the room behind the protection of safety glass (position of the observer). The short and concise description of the main events of several billions of years of the earth's early history would be described quite differently if the observer were looking on from the surface of

the moon instead of the surface of the earth. We find a precise description of both the initial conditions (the earth was without organization and no life existed and it was dark) and the perspective of the observer (darkness was upon the surface of the waters of the oceans). That the Bible writers, perhaps without consciously realizing it, provided the exact information any scientist would need to evaluate the validity and outcome of any field observation is a testimony to the reality of the inspiration of the Scriptures. "All scripture is given by inspiration (Gr: 'theospneustos'..meaning 'God breathed') of God and is suitable for teaching, for reproof, for correction, for training in righteousness." 2 Timothy 3:16

262 Winfrey and Tolle's association rapidly grew as a result of Tolle's book being selected in 2008 for Oprah's Book Club. Thereafter, Winfrey even led a free ten-week online webinar with Tolle, which was attended by some 35million people. Tolle's New Age Spirituality now provides the foundation for Winfrey's public rejection of Christianity in favor of becoming one's own god.

263 As will be explained later, this should not be interpreted as a wholesale acceptance of the state of Christianity at large. Refer to my recent text on "A Christian Critique of the Major World Religions" where I critique Christianity as well as Judaism, Islam, Hinduism, and Buddhism @ www.RonWoodworth.Org.

264 As a Doctor of Religious Studies, I worked as adjunct professor of World Religions at Mesa Community College (Arizona) for 3 years, from 2004 to 2007. I have also been an Online instructor (for three years) with the University of Phoenix teaching Critical Thinking. Finally, as of 2009 I have also been both an Adjunct Professor and now a Fulltime Online Professor for Grand Canyon University, where I teach Christian Worldview.

265 Trinity Seminary, Indiana.

266 *For Such a Time as This: Lessons in Discernment for the Thinking Christian*, Pleasant Word Publications, 2007. Available online at Amazon.com

267 I have formerly served in the capacities of church planter, senior pastor, and mega-church associate pastor, in a full time capacity from 1978 to 2005.

268 Tolle's major emphasis in study was literature, languages and philosophy.

269 See Kim Eng's Biography and endorsement by Eckhart Tolle at http://eckharttolle.com/kim_biography

270 See "Definitions of Zen Buddhism" at http://www.google.com/search?hl=en&defl=en&q=define:ZEN+BUDDHISM&sa=X&oi=glossary_definition&ct=title.

271 See "A Course in Miracles" at http://en.wikipedia.org/wiki/A_Course_in_Miracles.

272 Esotericism implies special inner-mystical knowledge available only to the enlightened.

273 See "New Age" article at http://en.wikipedia.org/wiki/New_age.

274 Eclecticism is that which is composed of elements from various/diverse sources.

275 Relativistic individualism is claiming oneself as the ultimate authority of truth.

276 Gnosticism literally means "to know," and suggests special spiritual knowledge known only by those who have been initiated into enlightenment.

Addendum 9.

277 Universalism maintains the ultimate/divine interrelatedness of all creatures.

278 "I AM" is the divine name in the Jewish Scriptures and also the title Jesus claimed as his own identity (Ex. 3:14; John 8:58). Note Tolle's use of capital letters to underscore his assertion that we, not a "transcendent God" or Jesus Christ, are the ultimate reality. Indeed, we are the god (the notion of divinity) that all historic religious traditions have been seeking and that all ancient spiritual masters, including Jesus, have been prophesying would come.

279 See 1 John 2:18, 22-23, 4:3, 2 John 7; 2 Thessalonians 2:3-4 and http://en.wikipedia.org/wiki/Antichrist.

280 See Matt. 24:4-5; 2 Thess. 2:4 and Rev. 13.

281 See Matt. 16:24; Mark 8:34 and Luke 9:23.

282 See Titus 3:5; 2 Pet. 1:4; and John 3:3-6.

283 The faculty of human choice is theologically a result of the biblical idea of free-will.

284 See Rom. 2:16 and Acts 10:34-35.

285 See Heb. 6:13-20; Phil. 3:9 and Rom. 3:22-24.

286 See Hebrews 6:4 and John 8:12.

287 See Ps. 16:11 and Acts 3:19.

288 See 1 John 2:17 and 2 Pet. 3:10-13.

289 Entrance into the kingdom of God biblically requires "repentance," which is literally "a change of mind." In other words, kingdom enlightenment does require a radical change of mind. However, such a change/renewal never implies a denial, dissolution or "disidentification" of/with the mind itself. See also Matt. 4:17; Rom. 12:1-2; Eph. 4:17-24.

290 See Rom. 14:17; 2 Pet. 3:13 and Rev. 21:4. Also see the NIV footnote to Matt. 3:2 which includes a number of the items I've listed as descriptive of the kingdom of God.

291 Reincarnation is the Hindu term *samsara* and refers to the "transmigration of the soul" across countless lifetimes. Furthermore, the force that binds the soul to *samsara* is the inexorable law of *karma*.

292 Such as the task of dissolving the egoic-mind of over seven billion people.

293 This number includes 2.4 billion Christians, 1.5 billion Muslims, and 14.3 million Jews.

294 See Joshua 24:15; John 1:12; Acts 2:41 and Rev. 3:20.

295 Such internal peace implies a cessation of striving. However, the end of striving, according to Psalm 46:10, is not in the knowledge of the impermanence of all structures, but rather the certainty that an eternally transcendent God is in control of the world and of all those who have entrusted their lives to him as well. See also Prov. 3:5-6 and Isaiah 26:3.

296 See 1 Cor. 7:31; 1 John 2:15-17 and Heb. 12:26-28.

297 See 1 Tim. 2:5.

298 The Body of Christ is also called the Church in the New Testament. See Eph. 2:19-22 and Eph. 4:15-16.

299 See Acts 2:17-21; 2 Pet, 3:11-12 and Matt. 24:9-14.

300 Forms, for Tolle, include physical, mental-thought, or emotional structures of identity.

301 See Rom. 13:1-7 and 1 Tim. 1:8.

302 See "The Four Nobles Truth" of Buddhism at http://www.thebigview.com/buddhism/fourtruths.html.

303 See Prov. 15:13, 15; 17:22 and Col. 3:15-16.

304 See Prov. 3:5-6; Isaiah 26:3-4; Psalm 23 and Matt. 6:34.

305 See pages 6, 13, 23, 43, 61 (2x's), 66, 71(3x's), 81, 89, 104, 144 (2x's as Christ), 184, 191, 192, 215, 216, 234, 254, 259, 267, 268 (3x's), 303, 305, 309 (2x's).

306 See 1 Pet. 1:17, 20-21 and Gal. 4:4.

307 See Heb. 10:20; Eph. 2:8-9; Rom. 2:6-16 and Heb. 6:1. Note: The NIV footnote for Heb. 6:1 says that "repentance from 'dead works'" are "deeds or rituals that cannot impart life."

308 This quote is also on p. 23.

309 Ibid.

310 It may be of some interest to know that the "kingdom of God" is synonymous with the "kingdom of heaven." This is demonstrated by the historic fact that Matthew was written to a predominately Jewish audience who would be offended with directed references to God—stemming from the commandment not to take the name of the Lord your God in vain (Ex. 20:7). Mark, on the other hand, was written to Gentiles (non-Jews) who would have no such religious-cultural sensitivity.

311 See Acts 2:33, 39 and Acts 2: 16-21.

312 See *Fire from Heaven: The Rise of Pentecostal Spirituality and the Reshaping of Religion in the Twenty-first Century.* Addison-Wesley Publishing Company, 1994. Also see Acts 2:33, 39; Acts 1:4-5 and Acts 2:1-4.

313 On page 307, Tolle indicates that "teachers of Being," like himself, are what he calls "frequency holders"—whose function is to "anchor the frequency of the new consciousness on this planet," until it takes hold in the broader global population. Another word I would propose for "frequency holders" would be "Prophets of the New Age" who are proclaiming another Gospel than originally represented in Christ Jesus. In fact, Tolle even uses the term "good news," which is the literal meaning of the word "Gospel," to describe his message (p.28, 52). See also Gal.1:6-9; Matt. 24:4 and 2 Pet. 2:1.

314 Oprah Winfrey's rejection of Christianity began when she mistakenly interpreted the verse in James 4:7 and/or Exodus 34:14 about God being a jealous God—as if God were a petty deity who is resentfully envious of others. The truth is that all of God's emotional attributes are perfect in their essence and expression rather than corrupted by sin—as in the case of fallen human beings. As such, God's jealousy is a loving affection that seeks only our good by drawing us to himself and away from the harmful distractions of the world, which are the lust of the flesh (carnality), the lust of the eyes (materialism), and the boastful pride of life (egoism). See 1 John 2:15-17.

315 Such a revival should not be equated with manipulated emotionalism, human striving, or gimmicky.

316 This would include believers from virtually all Christian denominations be they Catholic, Eastern Orthodox, or Protestants. And while there are some 2.2 billion

Christians in the world today, a sizeable number of those either do not believe in or are not experiencing a "dynamic Christian spirituality" such as recommended in this article. See my article on "Empowered Evangelicals" at www.RonWoodworth.Org

317 See *Secularism and the Misinterpretation of the First Amendment* by Ron Woodworth.

318 A former example of a violation of biblical morality was in 1972 when the Supreme Court ruled in favor of abortion on demand, which has so far resulted in the loss of over 50 million unborn children in the United States. See *For Such a Time as This: Lesson's in Discernment for Thinking Christians*, (2009), p. 233-239.

319 *Sexually transmitted disease among homosexuals* (n.d.). Retrieved August 30. 2011, from http://www.ncbi.nlm.nih.gov/pmc/articles/PMC1876122/?page=1 and *Homosexuals and Fisting* (n.d.). Retrieved August 30, 2011, from http://www.homosexinfo.org/Sexuality/Fisting.

320 *The Religion Virus* (n.d.). Retrieved August 30, 2011, from http://religion-virus.blogspot.com/2010/03/elton-john-gay-lovers-suicide-was-from.html.

321 *Homosexual recruitment: Homosexual Recruit Public School Children* (n.d.). Retrieved August, 30, 2011, from http://www.traditionalvalues.org/pdf_files/TVCSpecialRptHomosexualRecruitChildren.P DF.

322 *Homosexual lifespan* (n.d.). Retrieved August 30, 2011, from http://theroadtoemmaus.org/RdLb/22SxSo/PnSx/HSx/hosx_lifspn.htm.

323 Most scholars believe Jesus' birth was around 4 B.C. because Herod the Great presumably died that year. See Matthew 2:1-19

324 Acts 2 is generally referenced as the birth of the church with the outpouring of the Holy Spirit on Pentecost.

325 See the previous article on World Religions (Part 2) called Judaism: In History and Prophecy.

326 "Ignatius." Retrieved from http://www.ntcanon.org/Ignatius.shtml.

327 "Thus, while there was a good measure of debate in the Early Church over the New Testament canon, general sources such as the *Cambridge History of the Bible* claim the major writings were accepted by almost all Christians by the middle of the second century" See http://en.wikipedia.org/wiki/Biblical_canon.

328 "Early Christian Persecution." Retrieved from http://www.allaboutfollowingjesus.org/early-christian-persecution-faq.htm.

329 "St. Augustine of Hippo." Retrieved from http://en.wikipedia.org/wiki/St._Augustine_of_Hippo.

330 New International Version Study Bible (2002) footnotes on 2 Peter 3, p. 1943-44.

331 The Catholic cable channel EWTN (Eternal Word Television Network) has a program called *The Journey Home* that promotes the primacy of the Roman Catholic Church above all others churches—calling upon all such "separated brethren" as those who need to "journey home" to the fold of the Roman church in order to be assured of its exclusive claim to sacramental salvation. Also, *The Catholic Verses* by Catholic apologist Dave Armstrong specifically seeks to lend credibility to the Catholic interpretation of Scripture in contradiction to the Protestant perspective. One can sense in the history and rhetoric of Rome that it has never made peace with its

humiliating decline in political or ecclesiastical power. That being said, EWTN is to be commended for many of its programs that are quite helpful for those seeking an accurate portrayal of Roman Catholic faith.

332 History of the Papacy. Retrieved fromt http://en.wikipedia.org/wiki/History_of_the_Papacy.

333 The filioque (lit. meaning "and from the son" in Latin) clause is a change to the Nicene Creed that originally read: "We believe in the Holy Spirit ... who proceeds from the Father", to the amended version, which reads: "We believe in the Holy Spirit ... who proceeds from the Father *and the Son*."

334 The *Summa Theologica* was arguably the "greatest theological statement of the Middle Ages," and yet was originally intended for beginners as a compilation of all of the main theological teachings of the time. The Summa's topics follow a cycle: God, God's creation, Man, Man's purpose, Christ, the Sacraments, and back to God.

335 Aquinas. Retrieved from http://www.ou.edu/cas/psc/bookaquinas.htm.

336 Thomism Philosophy. Retrieved fromt http://en.wikipedia.org/wiki/Thomism.

337 Aquinas. Retrieved from http://www.theuniversityconcourse.com/I,2,2-27-1996/delaPrada.htm.

338 Thomas Aquinas, retrieved from http://en.wikipedia.org/wiki/Thomas_Aquinas.

339 Natural theology is the attempt to derive knowledge of God directly from the study of nature without reference to special revelation. Retrieved from http://www.m-w.com/dictionary/natural%20theology.

340 See St. Thomas Aquinas: The Dumb Ox . Retrieved from http://en.wikisource.org/wiki/St._Thomas_Aquinas:_The_Dumb_Ox/Chapter_III.

341 The Catholic Encyclopedia lists only eight (8) crusades—excluding the 9th crusade by the future Edward I of England in 1271. Retrieved from http://www.newadvent.org/cathen/04543c.htm.

342 "Crusades: An Historical Perspective. Retrieved from http://en.wikipedia.org/wiki/Crusades#Historical_perspective.

343 "Crusades." Retrieved from http://encarta.msn.com/encyclopedia_761561210_1/Crusades.html#S1.

344 New Advent: Catholic Encyclopedia. Retrieved from http://www.newadvent.org/cathen/04543c.htm.

345 "Crusades," Retrieved from http://en.wikipedia.org/wiki/Crusades#_note-9#_note-9.

346 "Crusades" as quoted by British historian Steven Runciman.

347 Roman Catholic conflicts over the Protestant Reformation ended with the Peace of Westphalia in 1648—affirming the sovereign right of European nation-states to determine their own religious orientation whether Roman Catholicism, Lutheranism, or Calvinism. The Latin phrase *cuius regio, eius religio*, the "religion of the ruler was the religion of the ruled" was the principle that expressed the result of religious toleration—at least between Catholics, Lutherans, and Calvinists. Rejecting this principle, Anabaptists were either exterminated or relocated to the New World. Retrieved from http://en.wikipedia.org/wiki/Cuius_regio,_eius_religio.

Addendum 9.

348 Online Catholic Encyclopedia. Retrieved from http://www.newadvent.org/cathen/12700b.htm.

349 "The Protestant Reformation. Retrieved from http://en.wikipedia.org/wiki/The_Protestant_Reformation.

350 Encarta, "Reformation." Retrieved from http://encarta.msn.com/encyclopedia_761562628_3/Reformation.html#s12.

351 "Protestant." Retrieved from http://en.wikipedia.org/wiki/Protestant.

352 Carl Jung once observed that it was the Protestant devaluation of the confessional booth which actually facilitated the emergence of the "secular" psychiatric profession.

353 Luther was actually hesitant to include the book of James into the canon of Scripture because of its perceived "over-emphasis" on works. Retrieved from http://en.wikipedia.org/wiki/Biblical_canon#Reformation_Era.

354 Catholic Encyclopedia article on "Sect and Sects." Retrieved from http://www.newadvent.org/cathen/13674a.htm.

355 Ibid.

356 1 Cor. 10:19.

357 Acts 3:19-21.

358 Matt. 5:9 & James 3:17-18.

359 Ibid.

360 Encarta, "John Calvin." Retrieved from http://encarta.msn.com/encyclopedia_761570916/John_Calvin.html#s1.

361 New Advent, the Catholic Encyclopedia, "Calvin." Retrieved from http://www.newadvent.org/cathen/03195b.htm.

362 Richard Hooker's article on "John Calvin." Retrieved from http://www.wsu.edu/~dee/REFORM/CALVIN.HTM

363 "Protestant work ethic." Retrieved from http://en.wikipedia.org/wiki/Protestant_work_ethic.

364 "John Calvin." Retrieved from http://www.who2.com/johncalvin.html.

365 "John Calvin quote." Retrieved from http://lawandtheology.com/Calvin.html. In a graduate class (in the mid 1990's) at ASU called "The Intellectual Origins of the [U.S.] Constitution," Dr. Richard Wentz (historian and religious studies scholar) made the same observation regarding Calvin's philosophical influence on American governmental structure.

366 John Knox described Geneva under Calvin's influence as "the best school of Christ since the Apostles" Retrieved from http://www.frontline.org.za/articles/thereformation_lectures.htm.

367 Richard Hooker article. Retrieved from http://www.wsu.edu/~dee/REFORM/CALVIN.HTM.

368 Encarta, "Calvinism." Retrieved from http://encarta.msn.com/encyclopedia_761566731/Calvinism.html.

369 John Calvin, *The Institutes* were first written and revised 5 times in Latin and then, under Calvin's oversight were translated 4 times into French. Historians assert that, similar to what the King James Version of the Bible had done for the English language—so too had Calvin's French translations of *The Institutes* helped to "reshape

the French language for Generations to come." Retrieved from http://en.wikipedia.org/wiki/Calvin%27s_institutes.

370 "Apostles Creed." Retrieved from http://www.reformed.org/documents/index.html?mainframe=http://www.reformed.org/documents/apostles_creed.html.

371 The *TULIP*, or the Five (5) points of Calvinism, was actually the product of the Synod of Dort (1618/19) which was responding to criticism of Calvinism from the Armenians who were advocates of free-will; Retrieved from http://en.wikipedia.org/wiki/Synod_of_Dort.

372 "Calvinism Revisited: A Constructive Critique" in which I critically evaluate, among other things, Calvin's idea of "double- predestination…Predestination we call the eternal decree of God, by which He has determined in Himself, what He would have to become of every individual of mankind. For they are not all created with a similar destiny; but eternal life is foreordained for some and eternal death for others. Every man, therefore, being created for one or the other of these ends, we say he is predestinated either to life or to death," (*Institutes*, Book III, Ch. XXI, Sec. 5). Retrieved from ron.woodworth.org under "Article Archives."

373 "John Calvin." Retrieved from http://en.wikipedia.org/wiki/John_Calvin.

374 Ibid.

375 "The Council of Trent" in the Catholic Encyclopedia. Retrieved from http://www.newadvent.org/cathen/1530c.htm. Throughout 18 years, the Council of Trent convened in three phases: 1545-49, 1551-52, and 1562-63.

376 "Council of Trent," Encarta article. Retrieved from http://encarta.msn.com/encyclopedia_761565902_1/Council_of_Trent.html#S1.

377 "Council of Trent, " Wikipedia article. Retrieved from http://en.wikipedia.org/wiki/Council_of_Trent.

378 *Religions of the World*, 9th & 10th Editions, by Hopfe & Woodward, Article on "Christianity," Chapter 12.

379 See *Britannica Concise Encyclopedia*, article on The Council of Trent @ http://www.answers.com/topic/council-of-trent.

380 See *Major World Religions*, (9th & 10th editions) by Hopfe & Woodward, Christianity, Chapter 12 & http://en.wikipedia.org/wiki/Spiritual_Exercises_of_Ignatius_of_Loyola.

381 "Thirty Years War." Retrieved from http://encarta.msn.com/encyclopedia_761572707/Thirty_Years'_War.html.

382 1) See Church of England article @ http://encarta.msn.com/encyclopedia_761578580_1/Church_of_England.html#S1.

383 The 1828 Test and Corporation Acts repeal document from *Parliamentary Debates*, 2nd Series, vol.18, (1828) cols.678, 692-693.

384 3) See article on the Chicago-Lambeth Quadrilateral @ http://en.wikipedia.org/wiki/Chicago-Lambeth_Quadrilateral.

385 Catholic Encyclopedia article on "Puritans" from http://www.newadvent.org/cathen/12581a.htm @ Maitland, op. cit. inf., 590.

386 In *Democracy in America*, Alex de Tocqueville suggests that the Puritanism of the Pilgrims was the foundation for American democracy. He observed the Puritans to be hard-working, egalitarian, and studious. See wikipedia article on Puritan.

Addendum 9.

387 See article on "Methodism" @ http://en.wikipedia.org/wiki/Methodism

388 Charles undoubtedly influenced his brother John by his firm and unbending opposition to any breach with the Church of England into which they had both been ordained as priests.

389 See article on "John Wesley" @ http://en.wikipedia.org/wiki/John_Wesley

390 See *Religious Literacy: What Every American Needs to Know — and Doesn't* by Stephen Prothero, p. 202.

391 Wesley and Whitfield ultimately split over this issue with Whitfield favoring a Calvinistic brand of Methodism while John Wesley chose the Arminianist perspective.

392 Charles Wesley was a prolific writer of such famed hymns as "Or For a Thousand Tongues to Sing," And Can it Be," "Christ the Lord is Risen Today," etc. See http://en.wikipedia.org/wiki/Charles_Wesley.

393 See my book called *For Such a Time as This* (Pleasant Word Books, 2007) Article 39: "A Critique of Modern Theology," where I argue against the liberalism of Methodist theologian Jeffrey Hopper as delineated in his books on *Understanding Modern Theology* I & II (Harper Collins, 2007).

394 See article regarding the controversy over homosexuality within Methodism at http://www.nytimes.com/2012/05/04/us/methodists-wont-change-outlook-on-homosexuality.html?_r=0

395 See *Religious Literacy* by Stephen Prothero. Harper San Francisco, 2007. p. 184.

396 Finney developed what he called the *anxious bench* where people under conviction of the Holy Spirit could sit, in a specially designated area, as they were awaiting personal prayer ministry leading to salvation.

397 Doctrine and Covenants, Section 27 verse 12 @ http://en.wikisource.org/wiki/The_Doctrine_and_Covenants/Covenant_27#12.

398 See the "Syllabus Condemning the Error of the Modernists," 1907 @ http://www.papalencyclicals.net/Pius10/p10lamen.htm.

399 See Article 27: What is an Evangelical in my book *For Such a Time as This* @ www.RonWoodwoth.Org.

400 D.L. Moody is generally considered the Billy Graham of the 19th century.

401 The *Scofield Reference Bible*, by Cyrus I. Scofield (1909), immeasurably helped to popularized John Nelson Darby's dispensational eschatology — which still garners strong support among fundamentalists.

5) See my book, *For Such a Time as This*, Article 39 entitled "A Critical Analysis of Modern Theology."

402 See my book, *For Such a Time as This*, Article 39 entitled "A Critical Analysis of Modern Theology."

403 The *Chicago Statement on Biblical Inerrancy* was signed in 1978 by nearly 300 conservative-fundamental scholars, including James Boice, Norman Geisler, Carl F. H. Henry (founder of *Christianity Today*), John Warwick Montgomery, J. I. Packer, Francis Schaeffer, R. C. Sproul, et al.

404 Unlike Barth's Neo-Orthodoxy, Neo-Protestantism is a Twenty-First Century confluence of three streams: Evangelical-Reformed, Charismatics, and Pentecostals.

405 The conjunction "Evangelical-Reformed" implies here the historic doctrines of the Reformation-Reformed eras vis-à-vis the theology of Martin Luther and John Calvin.

406 A current debate in Reformed circles is the Wayne Grudem argument regarding Continuationism vs. Cessationism—at least in relation to the gift of prophecy.

407 The issue-debate here is over the classic (first wave) Pentecostal doctrine that speaking in tongues is always the "initial evidence" of the Baptism in the Holy Spirit. The "second wave" charismatic renewal (1960's-1980's) was cross-denominational and yet still favorably disposed to tongues as a "primary evidence" of the Baptism in the Holy Spirit. The "third wave" (1980's-present) was/is more evangelical-oriented embracing a post-salvation empowering experience of the Holy Spirit with any number of "biblical evidences"—tongues or otherwise.

408 See the National Association of Evangelicals Statement of Faith at http://www.nae.net/index.cfm?FUSEACTION=nae.statement_of_faith

409 Elsewhere I have described four biblical characteristics of the kingdom of God, namely, (a) providential sovereignty, (b) prophetic nationalism, (c) present spiritual reality, (d) future visible manifestation. See *For Such a Time as This* (Woodworth, 2007) Article 41, "The Kingdom of God", p. 264-266.

410 It may be more accurate to say that 21st Century Neo-Evangelicals are embracing a wider interpretation of Bible prophecy, including historic, preterist, futurist, and idealist perspectives. In this regard, the author has found a text by Steve Greg called *Revelation, Four Views: A Parallel Commentary* to be most helpful. This text was written in 1997 and published by Thomas Nelson Inc.

411 Ibid, p. 261-271.

412 The comparison between OT tribes with the concept of contemporary denominations has been popularized by Dr. Jack Hayford from Church on the Way in Van Nuys, California.

413 See article on "Vatican II & Pope Benedict XVI Recent Communication About Protestants" at http://www.ronwoodworth.org:80/archives-VaticanII.aspx.

414 Word of Grace, Mesa, Arizona.

415 See Article 27, "Church Models" p. 153-154. *For Such a Time as This* (Woodworth, Pleasant Word Pub., 2007)

416 Ralph Winters coined the terms *modality* (local church) and *sodality* (trans-local/apostolic function) referring to "The Two Structures of God's Redemptive Mission." These terms were mentioned in a presentation he made at the All-Asia Mission Consultation in Seoul, Korea in August 1973. Thirty-five years earlier, Watchman Nee used the terms *local* church and *trans-local work* of the apostles to designate the same two concepts in the New Testament, specifically referring to Paul's apostolic ministry. Watchman Nee's findings are printed in *The Normal Christian Church Life*, Colorado: International Students Press, 1938/Chinese & 1969/English.

417 See 1 Cor. 1:10 where Paul describes his apostolic ministry as being that of a "master builder," which is the English word for *architect*.

418 See http://en.wikipedia.org/wiki/The_Protestant_Ethic_and_the_Spirit_of_Capitalism

Addendum 9.

419 See http://herescope.blogspot.com/2007/06/seven-apostolic-spheres.html

420 This would include areas of social injustice and inequities as evangelically defined

421 See Surviving Parental Heartbreak at http://www.ronwoodworth.org/archives-SurviveParenting.aspx

422 See http://www.ronwoodworth.org/homepage-evangelical.aspx

423 See Matthew 9:17

424 For a much broader treatment on NE epistemology see *For Such a Time as This*, Article 46, p. 313.

425 See "Calvinism Revisited: A Constructive Critique" at http://www.ronwoodworth.org/archives-CalvinismRevisited.aspx

426 See "A Hermeneutic of Grace" at http://www.ronwoodworth.org/archives-GraceHermeneutic.aspx .

427 See the First Amendment limestone marker at http://www.bremen.lib.in.us/first_amendment.htm.

428 *A Bridge Too Far*, (1977) is an epic war film originally written by Cornelius Ryan.

429 See Katharina von Bora at http://www.reformationtours.com/site/490868/page/204052.

430 See Mark Twain at http://www.readeasily.com/mark-twain/index.php.

431 See Jefferson's wall of separation letter at http://www.usconstitution.net/jeffwall.html.

432 See Isaac Newton Quotes at http://thinkexist.com/quotation/we_build_too_many_walls_and_not_enough_bridges/220098.html.

433 In their book *Toward Benevolent Neutrality: Church, State, and the Supreme Court*, Flowers & Miller survey all of the Supreme Court cases/decisions regarding the issue of the separation of church and state. Their conclusion is that the relationship between church and state should be one of benevolent neutrality rather than malevolent partiality.

434 See The Holy Quran; 2:244; 4:74; 5:73; 8:38-41; 9:5. See also *Islamic Concept of a Political Order* at http://theamericanmuslim.org/tam.php/features/articles/islamic_concept_of_a_political_order.

435 See *A Christian Critique of World Religions and Atheism* by Ron Woodworth at www.ronwoodworth.org.

436 See The Bible and Government: Biblical Principles and America's Laws at http://www.faithfacts.org/christ-and-the-culture/the-bible-and-government.

437 The term "psychic" is also featured in many variations of *Gnosticism*. See the article on "The Da Vinci Code" by Ron Woodworth. (2009). *For Such a Time as This: Lessons in Discernment for the Thinking Christian*, Winepress Publishing, WA.

438 Article on "Psychics" from Wikipedia @ http://en.wikipedia.org/wiki/Psychic.

439 *The Revell Bible Dictionary* article on "ghost" p. 439.

440 *The Revell Bible Dictionary,* p. 984; *Expository Dictionary of Bible Words*, p. 599, et al

441 Interesting too is the fact that the Greek word for sorcery is *pharmakia* or pharmacy, which is the place of the dispensing of drugs. As a result, illegal drug use (including alcoholic abuse), sexual immorality and cultic music are symptomatic of the presence of the spirits of witchcraft and sorcery. According to John 10:10, satan's objectives are to deceive, enslave, and destroy, which he does through the idolatry of misdirect worship of self and/or other false prophets/prophetesses. See True Discernment at http://truedsicernment.com/2007/07/09/on-the-greek-word-pharmakia.

442 See the "Parable of the Sower" in Luke Chapter 8.

443 See series entitled Biblical Christianity 101 @ www.RonWoodworth.Org.

444 The 19th century evangelist D.L. Moody was the one who popularized the complimentary distinction between the Holy Spirit "within" (for character formation) vs. the Holy Spirit "upon" for powerful service. See also Biblical Christianity 101 Lesson 6: The Person and Power of the Holy Spirit at RonWoodworthMinistries.org.

Index

A

Abbsid Caliphate Empire, 82–83
Abraham, as hero of faith, 298–299
Allah. *See also* Five Pillars of Islam
    Feast of Sacrifice (Id al-Adha), 74
    high god, 74
    names, 87–88
    Qur'an, 78
    submission to, 87
    will of, 73–74
Anti-Christ, 211
Apocrypha, 41
Apostolic and prophetic ministries, 263–264
Apostolic succession, 43
Appearance of design, 171–172
Aquinas, Thomas, 241–242
Arab-Israeli conflict, 85
"Ardi" and bipedalism critiqued, 279–281
Arizona State atheistic-evolutionary debate, 146–147
Aryans, 97–98
Asceticism and critique, 106–107
Atheism and good and evil, 289–290
Atheistic evolution
    debate at Arizona State, 146–147
    misunderstanding of the Bible covenant theology, 142–143
    negative religious stereotyping, 141–142
    scientific overreach, 143–145

versus theistic evolution, 145
Atmosphere translucence, Neo-Creationist Model, 194–195
Atonement, 227
Augustine of Hippo, 238

B
Balfour Declaration, 56
Beginnings of life, Neo-Creationist Model, 198–199
Bhakti Yoga and critique, 109–110
    Brahman and critique, 101
Bible
    definition, 29
    inspiration, 29–30
    interpretation, 30
    Judaism and, 57
    prophesy, 30–31
    scientific contradictions, 30
Birth of the Church at Pentecost, 236
Brahman and critique, 101
Buddhism
    Buddha, 113
    competing sects, 113–114
    enlightenment, 113, 115, 119
    Four Noble Truths and critique, 117–118
    Hindu cultural context and critique, 115
    Mahayanan sect, 114
    Middle Way, 116
    Nirvana and critique, 119–121
    origins, 112–113
    Siddhartha, 112–113
    sin versus lack of enlightenment, 211
    Theravaan sect, 114
    Three Jewels and critique, 116–117

C
Calvin, John, 245–246
Cambrian explosion impasse, 176
Cambrian explosion, Neo-Creationist Model, 199–200
Cell signature, 176–177

Censorship, 84
Chemical evolution, 150–151
Chinese religions—religious thought
    background, 122–123
    Communist takeover of China, 138–139
    Confucianism. *See* Confucianism
    Cultural Revolution, 139–140
    divination and critique, 126–129
    filial piety and ancestor worship and critique, 125–126
    history of, 123–124
    I Ching and critique, 127–129 137–138
    New Culture Movement, 137–138
    polytheism, and critique, 125
    post-Mao, 140
    Taoism and critique, 130–131
    Taoist philosophy and critique, 131–133. *See also* Taoist
philosophy and critique
    Yin and Yang and critique, 129–130
Christian church
    birth of, 33–34
    branches of, 35
    history of, 35
    indwelling of the Holy Spirit, 34
    Judaism and, 68–71
    spiritual successors of apostles, 34–35
Christian criteria, 27–28
    critical thinking and, 27–29. *See also* Critical thinking
    definition, 26
    purpose, 26
Christian fundamentalism, 255–257
Christianity
    anti-Christ, 211
    anxiousness, 216
    Apocrypha, 41
    atonement, 227
    blessings of God, 224–225
    creation, 22, 30, 65, 129–130
    critique of evolution, 170
    diversity versus unity, 40–41

eternal life, 219–220
evil, 222–223
external objections, 43–50. *See also* Christianity, external objections
forgiveness, 116–117
free will, 218–219
gifts, 128–129
grace, 105, 136, 228
Great Schism of, 1054, 37
happiness, 225
Holy Spirit. *See* Holy Spirit
idolatry, 110
immorality, 130, 213–214
internal divisions, 36–37
intransigence between believers, 40
judgment, 104
Kingdom of God, 217, 228
knowledge and truth, 105–106
loving devotion to God, 109–110
meditation, 108, 226–227
occult, 127–128, 303–310
original sin, 222
prayer, 98–99
presence of the Lord, 216
Protestant Reformation, 38–41. *See also* Protestant Reformation
purpose in life, 120–121, 220–221
relationship aspect, xvi, 212
resurrection, 100, 130, 224
Roman Catholic Church, criticisms of, 38
salvation, 41, 46, 69, 105, 115
self-denial, 132–133
standard for truth, xviii
suffering, 118–119
surrender, 213
theocracy versus dual citizenship, 287–289
tongues, 99
transcendence of God, 223
triune God, 101–102
universal truth claims, xv–xvi

Christianity, external objections
    atheism, cannibalism, and sex orgies, 44
    brutality and war, 44–45
    High Criticism, 45–46
    prosperity gospel and clergy sex scandals, 47–50
    science versus religion debate, 46–47

Christian moral response to homosexuality
    compassionate response, 233–235
    destructive consequences of legalization of homosexuality, 232–233
    enlightenment of truth in Jesus, 231–232
    law, purpose of, 230
    principle of evil, 231

Christian persecution by Roman emperors, 237
Church of England and King Henry VIII, 248–250
Common ground, scripture and nature record, 186–187
Communist takeover of China, 138–139
Complexity, Neo-Creationist Model, 193–194

Confucianism
    arts (*Wen*), 137
    benevolent consideration (*Jen*) and critique, 133
    filial piety and reverence (*Hsiao*), 136
    moral wisdom (*Chih*), 136
    origin, 133–134
    proper discharge of political power (*Te*), 137
    righteousness (*Yi*), 136
    superior man (*Chun tzu*) and critique, 134–135
    way things should be done (*Li*) and critique, 135–136

Constantine I and the Edict of Milan, 237–238
Cosmology and cosmic time critiqued, 270–271
Council of Trent, 246–248

Creation-evolution debate
    Charles Darwin, 147
    chemical evolution, 150–151
    common ground, 164–165
    critiques. *See* Creation-evolution debate critiques
    evolution of evolution, 148–152
    Intelligent Design and Scientific Evolution, 156–157
    macroevolution, 150

microevolution, 149, 150
Progressive Creationism and Neo-Darwinism, 160–164
range of opinion, 152–153
Scientific Dissent from Darwinism, 151–152
speciation, 149–150
Theistic Evolution and Atheistic Evolution, 157–160
three great singularities, 166–167
Young-Earth Creationism and Darwinian Evolution, 153–155
Creation-evolution debate critiques
appearance of design, 171–172
Cambrian explosion impasse, 176
cell signature, 176–177
Christianity's critique of evolution, 170
DNA similarity studies, 177–179
evolution's critique of Christian creationism, 167–169
fossil record rethinking, 179–181
macroevolution, fossil record, 174–175
macroevolution, time, 174
origin of life, 172–173
probability problems in protein, 176
soft and hard science distinction, 169
time window for evolution, 173–174
Creation of man, Neo-Creationist Model, 202–203
Critical thinking
Christian elements, 28–29
definition, 27
elements, 27
epistemological perspective, 28
ontological perspective, 28
Critique
critical thinking process, 27–29. *See also* Critical thinking
definition, 26
purpose, 26
Crusades, 242
Cultural Revolution, China, 139–140

D
Darwin, Charles, 147, 148, 150–151, 156, 157, 161, 179
Dating method discrepancies critiqued, 275–276

Dinosaur-to-bird transition critiqued, 273–274
Diversity versus unity, 40–41
Divination and critique, 126–129
DNA similarity studies, 177–179

E
Edwards, Jonathan, 253
Einstein, Albert, xiii–xiv
English Civil War/Puritan Revolution, 250
Enlightenment, 113, 115, 119
Eternal life, 219–220
Evangelicalism, new strain of
    Bible, role in, 29–31. *See also* Bible
    categories of criteria, 28–29
    Christian church, role in, 33–35. *See also* Christian church
    definition, 28
    Jesus Christ, role in, 31–32. *See also* Jesus Christ
    kingdom of God, role in, 32–33. *See also* Kingdom of God
    rise of, 257–258
Evil, 222–223
Evolution-creation debate. *See* Creation-evolution debate
Evolution-creation debate critiques. *See* Creation-evolution debate critiques
Evolution of evolution, 148–152
Evolution, outdated beliefs
    "Ardi" and bipedalism, 279–281
    cosmology and cosmic time, 270–271
    dating method discrepancies, 275–276
    dinosaur-to-bird transition, 273–274
    finches and variability, 283
    fin-to-foot development, 272–273
    "Ida" and early ancestry claim, 277–279
    "Lucy" and direct lineage of modern humans, 276–277
    Neanderthals and DNA relation to humanity, 281–283
    pre-biotic soup conditions, 271–272
Evolution's critique of Christian creationism, 167–169

F
Faith

coming to, 293–294
divine confidence in action, 295
habits of, 300–302
hearing God's word, 297
heroes of faith, 298–300
hopeful certainty, 294–295
justification before God, 296–297
produces proven character, 298
ultimate reality, 296
Feast of Sacrifice (Id al-Adha), 75
Filial piety and ancestor worship and critique, 125–126
Finches and variability critiqued, 283
Finney, Charles G., 254
Fin-to-foot development critiqued, 272–273
First Amendment, 284–285
Five Pillars of Islam
Hajj: The Pilgrimage and critique, 93–94
Salat: Daily Prayers and critique, 88–90
Sawn: Fasting and critique, 91–93
Shahanda: The Islamic Creed and critique, 87–88
Zakat: Almsgiving and critique, 90–91
Forgiveness, 116–117
Fossil record rethinking, 179–181
Four Noble Truths, 117–118, 223
Four Rightly-Guided Caliphs, 81
Free will, 218–219
Frontier cults: Mormons and Jehovah's Witnesses, 254–255

G
Genesis 22, 75
Geologic activity, Neo-Creationist Model, 196–197
Gifts, 128–129
Golden Age of Islam, 53
Gnosticism
asceticism, 107
duality, 100
New Age spirituality, 209
Grace, 105, 136, 228
Great Awakening, 253–254

Great Schism of 1054, 37, 240

H
Hadean period, Neo-Creationist Model, 191–193
Hawking, Stephen, 160, 165, 184
Higher education and cultural engagement, 264–266
Hinduism
    Aryans, 97–98
    asceticism and critique, 106–107
    Bhakti Yoga and critique, 109–110
    Brahman and critique, 101
    divine revelation and critique, 98
    history, 97–98
    Jnanga Yoga and critique, 105–107
    Karma Yoga and critique, 104–105
    karmic consequences, 19, 103, 104
    mantras and critique, 98
    Raja Yoga and critique, 107–108
    reincarnation and critique, 101, 103
    transcendence and critique, 102
    transmitigation of the soul and critique, 101
    Upanishads, 100–101
    Vedas and critique, 99–100
    Vedic literature, 98
Holocaust, 55
Holy Spirit
    baptism with, 31
    empowering of, 259–260
    encounter with, 28,
    fruit, 116
    gift of, 227
    gifts, 129
    indwelling, 34, 69, 227
    obedience to, 316
    outpouring of, 33, 70, 212
    receiving, 316
    renewal, 110, 115
Hydrological cycle, Neo-Creationist Model, 195–196

I

I Ching and critique, 127–129
"Ida" and early ancestry claim critiqued, 277–279
Idolatry, 110
Image of God, Neo-Creationist Model, 202
Immorality, 130, 213–214
India partitioning, 85–86
Intelligent Design and Scientific Evolution, 156–157
Iranian Revolution of 1979, 86
Iraqi wars, 86
Islam
    Abbsid Caliphate Empire, 82–83
    Allah, 74
    Arab-Israeli conflict, 85
    angelic component, 78–79
    background, 73–74
    censorship, 84
    critique of, 88, 89–90, 90–91, 94, 96
    demographics, 74
    divine revelation of, 73
    Feast of Sacrifice (Id al-Adha), 75
    Five Pillars of Islam, 87–94. *See also* Five Pillars of Islam
    Four Rightly-Guided Caliphs, 81
    Genesis 22, 75
    India partitioning, 85–86
Iranian Revolution of 1979
    Iraqi wars, 86
    Jihad, 94–96
    Kaaba Shrine, 74–75
    Muhammad. *See* Muhammad
    9/11 (September 11, 2001), 84, 86
    1920s to present, 83–85
    OPEC, 86
    Ottoman Empire, 83
    pre-Islamic Arab religion, 74–75
    Quran, 77–78
    theology. *See* Five Pillars of Islam
    Umayyad Caliphate-Dynasty, 82
    Wahhabi radicalism, 84

Israel, creation of, 55–56

J
Jesus Christ
    Jewish arguments against the divinity of, 58–59
    Jewish arguments against the Messiahship of, 59–61
    Judaism and, 57–65
    ministry, 31–32
    relational arrangement, 32
    review, 31
Jesus, followers of, tips for
    Bible study, 312–313
    Christian fellowship, 314–315
    obedience to Holy Spirit, 313–314
    prayer, 312
    reasons to believe, 318–319
    receiving Holy Spirit, 316
    sharing faith, 315
    spiritual truths, 311
    water baptism, 316
Jihad
    critique, 95
    definition, 94–95
    separation of church and state, 95–96
    sixth pillar, 95
Jnanga Yoga and critique, 105–107
Judaism
    arguments against divinity of Jesus, 58–59
    arguments against Messiahship of Jesus, 59–61
    Balfour Declaration, 56
    Bible and, 57
    biblical, 51, 52–53
    Christian church and, 68–71
    eschatological meanings and options, 67–68
    Golden Age of Islam, 53
    Holocaust, 55
    Israel, creation of, 55–56
    Jesus and, 57–65
    Kingdom of God and, 65–68

rabbinic, 51, 53–56
Reform movement, 54–55
salvation, 57, 63
Tanakh Messianic texts, 61–65
Zionism, 55–56
Judgment, 104

K
Kaaba Shrine, 74–75
Karma Yoga and critique, 104–105
Karmic consequences, 19, 103, 104
Kingdom-centeredness and Christian unity, 260–261
Kingdom of God
    definition, 32
    Judaism and, 65–68
    nonviolent nature, 33
    parables, role in, 32
    transcendent nature, 33
King James Bible, 250

L
Land animal life, Neo-Creationist Model, 200–201
"Lucy" and direct lineage to modern humans critiqued, 276–277
Luther, Martin, 38, 243, 285–286

M
Macroevolution
    definition, 150
    fossil record, 174–175
    time, 174
Mahayanan sect, 114
Mantras and critique, 98
Mayflower and Massachusetts Bay Colony, 251
Mega-churches, 262–263
Microevolution, 149, 150
Middle-aged universe problem, 183
Middle Way, 116
Monism, 100
Mormonism

angelic component, 78
cult, 254–255
eternal progression, 102

Muhammad
   calendar, 76
   emigration from Mecca, 79–80
   farewell pilgrimage, 81
   marriage, 76–77
   military authority, and campaigns, 80
   polygamy of, 77
   polytheistic background, 75
   prophetic ministry, 77–78
   Quran, 77–78
   rejection of message, 79
   upbringing, 76

N

Nature and scripture versus science and theology, 181–182
Neanderthals and DNA relation to humanity critiqued, 281–283
Neo-Creationism
   common ground, scripture and nature record, 186–187
   faith affirming, 186
   integration, need for, 183–185
   middle-aged universe problem, 183
   nature and scripture versus science and theology, 181–182
   reframing the debate, 181
   science and scientists as valued, 185
   time and timing, 182–183
Neo-Creationist Model
   atmosphere translucence, 194–195
   beginnings of life, 198–199
   Cambrian explosion, 199–200
   complexity, 193–194
   creation of man, 202–203
   definition, 187–188
   geologic activity, 196–197
   Hadean period, 191–193
   hydrological cycle, 195–196
   image of God, 202

land animal life, 200–201
singularity as beginning, 188–191
Neo-Protestantism
apostolic and prophetic ministries, 263–264
flexible structures and mega-churches, 261–263
higher education and cultural engagement, 264–266
history of, 259
Holy Spirit, empowering of, 259–260
Kingdom-centeredness and Christian unity, 260–261
theological balance and hermeneutics of grace, 267–268
world evangelism and strategic church planting, 266–267
New Culture Movement, China, 137–138
New Earth: Awakening to Your Life's Purpose (Tolle)
biographical background, 207–208
introduction, 206–207
major influences, 208–209
New Earth: Awakening to Your Life's Purpose (Tolle), Christian response to
Antichrist, New Age and biblical concepts, 209–211
cure for unhappiness, 223–225
egoic-self and immortality, 212–214
impermanence of form, eternal life, and divine purpose, 219–221
new heaven, new earth, and lordship of Jesus Christ, 227–228
pain-body and presence of the Lord, 214–216
popular psychology and interpreting Jesus, 225–227
problem of evil, 221–223
religion versus spirituality, 211–212
transformation of consciousness, Kingdom of God, and free will, 217–219
New Testament scriptures, development of, 236–237
9/11 (September 11, 2001), 84, 86
Ninety-Five Theses on the Power and Efficacy of Indulgences, 38
Nirvana and critique, 119–121

O

Occult phenomena
demons, 305
ecstasy drug as demonic counterfeit, 307–308
global fascination, 306–307

popularity in media, 303
scriptural prohibition against, 303–305
supernatural dimension of ministry, 310
witch of Endor, 305–306
"Year of the King" (Woodward), 309
Old earth theory, 47
OPEC, 86
Original sin, 222
Origin of life, 172–173
Ottoman Empire, 83

P
Peace of Westphalia, 39
Peter, as hero of faith, 99–300
Pietism, 251–252
Polytheism, and critique, 125
Pre-biotic soup conditions critiqued, 271–272
Presbyterian, Baptist, and Congregational legacy, 252
Probability problems in protein, 176
Progressive Creationism and Neo-Darwinism, 160–164
Protestant Reformation
    Apocrypha, 41
    criticisms of, 39–40, 243
    historic factors, 38, 243
    reactionary theology of, 39
    results of, 39, 243–244
    Roman Catholic Church, criticisms of, 38
Puritanism, 250

Q
Quran, 77–78

R
Raja Yoga and critique, 107–108
Ramadan, 91–93
Reformation. *See* Protestant Reformation
Reincarnation and critique, 101, 103
Relativism, xvi–xvii
Religion

alien manipulation theory of, 22
chronology, 21
definition, 19
demonic impersonation theory of, 24
divine revelation theory of, 23–24
facts and figures, 20–21
history of civilizations, 21
human imagination theory of, 22–23
intelligent manifestation theory of, 24
no origination theory of, 22
theories of origin, 21–22
ultimate reality, 19
Resurrection, 100, 130, 224
Roman Catholic Church
Apocrypha, 41, 57
apostolic succession, 43
criticisms of, 38
criticisms of Protestants, 39
intransigence of, 40
Jewish persecution, 70–71
papacy, 42–43
priests, freedom to marry, critique of, 50
Roman Papacy, rise of, 238–240

S
Sacred-secular dichotomy, 285–286
Salvation, 41, 46, 69, 105, 115
Science versus religion debate, 46–47
Scientific Dissent from Darwinism, 151–152
Second Great Awakening, 254
Secularism
atheism and good and evil, 289–290
Christian theocracy or dual citizenship, 287–289
First Amendment, 284–285
practical steps against, 290–292
sacred-secular dichotomy, 285–286
wall of separation, 286–287
Siddhartha, 112–113
Singularity as beginning, Neo-Creationist Model, 188–191

Soft and hard science distinction, 169
Speciation, 149–150
Statue of Liberty, 84–85
Suffering, 118–119

T
Tanakh Messianic texts, 61–65
Taoism and critique, 130–131
Taoist philosophy and critique
    life is the greatest of all possessions and critique, 131–132
    life is to be lived simply and critique, 132–133
    no action or strain (*Wú wéi*) and critique, 133,
    way of nature (*Dao*) and critique, 131, 132
Theistic Evolution and Atheistic Evolution, 157–160
Theological balance and hermeneutic of grace, 267–268
Theravaan sect, 114
Three great singularities, 166–167
Three Jewels and critique, 116–117
Time window for evolution, 173–174
Transcendence and critique, 102
Transcendent truth-claims
    contradictions, xvii–xviii
    definition, xvii
    infinite duration of, xvii
Transmitigation of the soul and critique, 101
Triune God, 101–102
Twenty-Seven of the Most Important People and Events in Christian History. *See individual people and events*

U
Umayyad Caliphate-Dynasty, 82

V
Vedas and critique, 99–100
Vedic literature, 98

W
Wahhabi radicalism, 84
Wall of separation, 286–287

Wesley, John, and Methodism, 252–253
World evangelism and strategic church planting, 266–267

Y
"Year of the King" (Woodward), 309
Yin and Yang and critique, 129–130
Young-Earth Creationism and Darwinian Evolution, 153–155

Z
Zionism, 55–56

Contact **Dr. Woodworth** at
dr.ron@ronwoodworth.org
or 480.545.7994

and **Stan Reynolds** at
Facebook.com/Reynoldsresources.

CPSIA information can be obtained at www.ICGtesting.com
Printed in the USA
BVOW012033170613

323583BV00002B/3/P